Electrical Principles for Electronics

To Chris, My Son

who is beginning to encounter and see
more and more of life's intricate circuitry.

Electrical Principles for Electronics

THIRD EDITION

Angelo C. Gilli

Texas Southern University, Houston, Texas

Gregg Division
McGraw-Hill Book Company

New York St. Louis Dallas San Francisco Auckland Bogotá Düsseldorf
Johannesburg London **Madrid** Mexico Montreal New Delhi Panama
Paris São Paulo Singapore Sydney Tokyo Toronto

Library of Congress Cataloging in Publication Data

Gilli, Angelo C
  Electrical principles for electronics.

  First-2d ed. published under title: Electrical
principles of electronics.
  Includes index.
  1. Electric engineering. 2. Electronics. I. Title.
TK146.G46 1978   621.3   77-4676
ISBN 0-07-023293-8

Electrical Principles for Electronics, Third Edition

The first and second editions were published under the title
Electrical Principles of Electronics by Angelo C. Gillie.

1234567890 DODO 78321098

The editors for this book were George J. Horesta and Mark Haas, the
designer was Tracy Glasner, the art supervisor was George T. Resch,
and the production supervisor was Regina R. Malone. It was set in
Baskerville by Kingsport Press, Inc.
Printed and bound by R. R. Donnelley & Sons Company.

contents

preface

This book is intended for the first course in a two-year community-junior college program in electrical and/or electronics technology. The material is presented in such a manner that it is suitable for use in both one-semester and two-semester treatments, depending on the intensity and breadth of coverage desired by the instructor. The text can be used in such programs in community junior colleges, university two-year branch campuses, area vocational-technical schools, proprietary schools, adult continuing education centers, military schools, and other associate-degree electrical and electronics technology curricula. After completing the material presented in this work, the student will be ready to proceed to the next course in the program sequence, the basic circuit analysis course.

Students with an appropriate interest in the study of electricity and electronics will find the material presented in such a manner that their interest will be sustained and expanded. Furthermore, the basic teaching concepts so important to learning are carefully incorporated in the design of this book. With this in mind, the subject matter is presented with the following features: (1) First the student is told what is to be learned in this section prior to exposure to the material; (2) this preview is followed by an orderly presentation of the material such that it proceeds from the familiar and simple to the new and more complex; (3) at the end of each section, the student will find appropriate summary-type statements, to review what was covered; (4) problems that provide opportunities for student practice in computations associated with the principles just learned are inserted at the appropriate places in each chapter (with answers readily accessible); (5) questions are included in every chapter so as to assist the student in grasping the meaning of the concepts encountered; (6) illustrations and diagrams are presented whenever deemed necessary as aids to comprehend the material considered.

The provision of over 500 problems (with answers), about 450 questions, and nearly 240 illustrations and diagrams enables the student to successfully use this book in home study as well.

The material presented is considerably different from this author's earlier works, which appeared under the title *Electrical Principles of Electronics*. Major changes have been made in terms of modernizing the subject matter so as to keep pace with changes in technology, reorganizing the overall contents of the book, and reducing the level of presentation. The subject is at the level typically needed in two-year programs such as found in community-junior colleges and area vocational-technical schools.

The book, with a total of 18 chapters, is divided into three parts. Chapters 1 through 4, which make up Part 1, are addressed to the basic concepts essential for mastering the principles of electricity. The text then proceeds to Part 2 (Chaps. 5 through 8) where the fundamentals of resistive circuits are treated. Chapter 8 deals with the principles and use of electrical measuring instruments. The material in Chap. 8 is presented in such a manner that it could be mastered by the student at this point in the course, or, if desired, after completion of Chaps. 11 and 12.

Reactive circuit fundamentals are treated in Part 3, which consists of Chaps. 9 through 18. The principles of magnetism, inductance, and capacitance are introduced in Chaps. 9 through 11. Chapter 11, on the characteristics of capacitance, can be the first chapter treated in Part 3 (i.e., prior to Chap. 9) for those who prefer to study capacitance before magnetism and inductance. Another option is offered to the user of this text with Chap. 12, which examines generators and motors. Chapter 12 is written so that it can be omitted completely, since some users may elect to omit this topic from their studies. On the other hand, the treatment provided is adequately detailed for those who elect to include this subject in their studies.

A special treatment of the sine wave and its relationships to reactance and impedance is provided in Chap. 13. The accumulated knowledge of the student regarding sine wave principles that is acquired in this chapter, in conjunction with information then learned about the characteristics of reactance and impedance, provides the learner with a sound basis for the analysis of sinusoidal circuits that follows. Again, using the important teaching principle of progressing from the simple to the more complex, the text proceeds from treating sinusoidal series circuits to the introduction of basic vector algebra, which is then directly applied to the analysis of sinusoidal parallel circuits. The important characteristics of resonance (both series and parallel) are examined and illustrated in Chap. 17. The last chapter treats the important features of transformers which provide a basis for understanding their use in electrical and electronics circuits.

It is important to note that the use of vector algebra is restricted to those selected places in Chaps. 16 through 18 where its use is deemed necessary for circuit computations and understanding. Whenever practical, more simple mathematical techniques are used. Because of the carefully selected utilization of vector algebra, the student is able to master all material in this work with a background of only one year of high school mathematics and the use of a scientific calculator for work in the limited number of logarithmic and trigonometric computations found in some of the later sections.

While working on this manuscript, the author kept in mind the importance of a broad-based first course in electrical principles. The author believes that this book is sufficiently inclusive to provide a truly comprehensive base upon which many fast-changing applications can be quickly and soundly established. As advances and changes take place in the fields of servicing, computers, radar, telemetering, microwaves, and electronic controls, the fundamentals obtained by the technician from this text can serve as the common bridging element between the old and the new.

The author wishes to express his gratitude to the many students over a period of many years, who, by mirroring their learning, provided him with opportunities to improve his own teaching, as well as to improve the organization and presentation of this material. Also, the author is indebted to the many instructors and reviewers who offered comments, many of which are reflected in the presentation. Another person deserving special appreciation is Charles O. Whitehead, a friend of long standing who helped to provide the environment in a two-year college which was so conducive to the writing of much of this work. Special thanks are extended to the editor, George Horesta, to Mark Haas, the editing supervisor, and the other members of the production team (especially Regina Malone and Tracy Glasner) for their most important efforts and patience. Finally, the writer wishes to offer a word of appreciation to his wife and children for their most cherished support throughout this endeavor.

Angelo C. Gilli

symbols

A	cross-sectional area, area	I_{rms}	root-mean-square current
a	acceleration, transformer turns ratio	I_{sc}	short-circuit current
		i	instantaneous current
C	capacitance	i_{max}	maximum current
D	damping constant	j	j operator, quadrature notation
d	dielectric thickness, pointer deflection		
di	small change in current	K	constant
		k	dielectric constant, coefficient of coupling, current sensitivity
dt	small change in time		
F	force		
f	frequency	kc	critical coefficient of coupling
f_{co}	frequency cutoff		
$f_{co,max}$	upper frequency cutoff	k_{eq}	equivalent coefficient of coupling
$f_{co,min}$	lower frequency cutoff		
f_{mid}	midfrequency	L	length, inductance
f_o	resonant frequency	l	length
f_{op}	primary resonant frequency	L_a	total series-aiding inductance
f_{os}	secondary resonant frequency	L_o	total series-opposing inductance
		M	mutual inductance, meter movement
G	conductance, galvanometer		
		m_o	mass at rest
I	drift intensity (current)	N	ratio of source power to load power, number of mobile electrons, number of coil turns, attenuation ratio
I_{abcd}	current flowing in closed loop $abcd$		
I_{avg}	average current		
I_{max}	maximum current		
$I_{m,max}$	maximum meter-movement current		
		N_e	number of orbital electrons
I_{min}	minimum current		

N_p	number of primary coil turns, number of protons in the nucleus	S	voltmeter sensitivity, speed
N_s	number of secondary coil turns	s	length, distance, secondary coil of a transformer
P	power, permeance	T	torque, transformation ratio
p	primary coil of a transformer, resistivity	t	temperature, time
		t_d	pulse duration
P_{avg}	average power	t_f	pulse fall time
P_i	input power	T_p	time of a period or cycle
P_{max}	maximum power		
P_o	output power	t_r	pulse rise time
Q	charge, coil figure of merit	V	point potential, voltage
Q_c	core charge	v	instantaneous voltage, velocity
Q_e	electron charge		
Q_p	proton charge, transformer primary-circuit Q	v_g	instantaneous generator voltage
		$v_{g,max}$	maximum generator voltage
Q_s	transformer secondary-circuit Q	V_i	rms input voltage
Q_t	total charge	v_i	instantaneous input voltage
$\mathcal{R}$	reluctance	v_{in}	instantaneous induced voltage
R	resistance		
R_{eq}	equivalent resistance	V_{max}	maximum voltage
R_i	input-generator impedance	v_{max}	maximum voltage
		V_{min}	minimum voltage
R_{int}	internal resistance	v_{min}	minimum voltage
R_L	load resistance	V_o	rms output voltage
R_M, R_m	meter-movement resistance	v_o	instantaneous output voltage
R_o	internal resistance of a network, resistance at room temperature, output resistance	V_{rms}	root-mean-square voltage
		V_x	average drift velocity
		W	work, energy

X	reactance	α	temperature co-efficient of resistance, attenuation
X_C	capacitive reactance		
X_L	inductive reactance	B	flux density
X_M	transformer mutual reactance	Δ	increment or small change
X_p	transformer primary-leakage reactance	ϵ	base of natural logarithms
X_s	transformer secondary-leakage reactance	H	magnetizing force
		θ	angle of rotation
		μ	permeability
		π	ratio of circumference to diameter of a circle (3.1416)
Z	impedance		
Z_i	input impedance		
Z_o	load or output impedance	ρ	resistivity
Z_p	transformer reflected primary impedance	Φ	magnetic flux
		ω	angular velocity
Z_s	transformer secondary impedance		

abbreviations

A	ampere	**H**	henry
a	atto, 10^{-18}	**h**	hecto, 10^2
ac	alternating current	**hp**	horsepower
adj	adjacent	**h**	hour
AM	amplitude modulation	**Hz**	hertz
At	ampere-turn		
avg	average	**ID**	inside diameter
		IF	intermediate frequency
Btu	British thermal unit	**in.**	inch
C	centigrade	**J**	joule
c	centi, 10^{-2}		
cemf	counterelectromotive force	**k**	kilo, 10^3
		kg	kilogram
cgs	centimeter-gram-second system	**kHz**	kilohertz
		kpps	kilopulses per second
cm	centimeter	**kW**	kilowatt
Cmil	circular mil	**kΩ**	kilohm
d	deci, 10^{-1}	**lb**	pound
da	deka, 10	**ln**	logarithm to base e
dB	decibel	**log**	logarithm to base 10
dc	direct current		
d.cy.	duty cycle	**M**	mega, 10^6
		m	milli, 10^{-3}
		m	meter
eff	efficiency	**mA**	milliampere
EIA	Electronic Industries Association	**max**	maximum
		min	minute
emf	electromotive force	**m-in.**	milli-inch
		mks	meter-kilogram-second
F	Fahrenheit	**mm**	millimeter
f	femto, 10^{-15}	**mmf**	magnetomotive force
FM	frequency modulation	**ms**	millisecond
ft-lb	foot-pound	**mW**	milliwatt
fps	foot-pound-second system	**MΩ**	megohm
ft	foot		
		n	nano, 10^{-9}
		nF	nanofarad
G	giga, 10^9	**No.**	number
g	gram	**Np**	neper

OD	outside diameter	**T**	tera, 10^{12}
opp	opposite	**tan**$^{-1}$	arctan
		tc	time constant
p	pico, 10^{-12}		
PF	power factor	**V**	volt
pF	picofarad	**VR**	voltage regulation
pps	pulses per second		
PRF	pulse repetition frequency	**W**	watt
PRR	pulse repetition rate	**Wb**	weber
rad	radian	**Δ**	increment or small change
RF	radio frequency	**μ**	micro, 10^{-6}
rms	root mean square	**μA**	microampere
roc	rate of change	**μF**	microfarad
rpm	revolutions per minute	**μs**	microsecond
		μV	microvolt
s	second	**Ω**	ohm
SR	speed regulation		

basic concepts
Part I

introduction

1

The first part of this book presents those basic concepts which you need before actually studying electrical circuits. These concepts are the foundation for later studies in electricity and electrical circuits; therefore it is important to learn them thoroughly.

The first concern is the language of electricity, which is often a blend of terms from physics and mathematics. The language associated with the basic concepts is treated in the first part of this book. After Part 1, any additional terminology needed to understand new concepts is developed in the appropriate place so that you can learn them with the least amount of difficulty.

1-1 THE NATURE OF ENERGY

In this section you will learn about:
* *The definitions of energy, work, and force*
* *The major kinds of energy*
* *The unit in which energy is measured*

No doubt you have heard and used the term *energy* in many conversations with friends and teachers. But have you stopped to think about what energy is? If you are like many people, you may not have bothered to obtain a precise definition of the word. One of the simplest definitions is that *energy is the ability to do work*. And what is work? *Work* is the exertion of a force upon a body with a resulting movement of the body in the direction in which the force acts. *Force* is the physical agent which either causes the speed (velocity) of a body to change or produces a strain in a body. The context within which work is performed determines what kind of energy is used. Several kinds of energy are of interest in the study of electricity and electronics:

1 *Kinetic* energy of motion
2 *Thermal* energy of heat
3 *Radiant* energy of light (and other sources)
4 *Magnetic* energy of a magnetic field

5 *Electric*   energy of charged particles
6 *Potential*   energy because of a body's position

The amount of energy possessed by a body is really the amount of work it is capable of doing. The most common unit of energy in electricity is the *joule*. More will be said about energy and work in Chap. 4.

1-2   THE NATURE OF ELECTRICITY

The most important thing in this section is a definition of electricity.

There is a very close, almost inseparable association between electricity and energy. As an example, consider what takes place when a vocalist is singing into a microphone, which is then amplified and connected to a loudspeaker. Look at Fig. 1-1 for a moment, for it will help you understand the following explanation.

There are five energy conversions associated with Fig. 1-1. First, the girl's voice sets up vibrations in the air surrounding the microphone (therefore the input consists of sound energy). These air vibrations

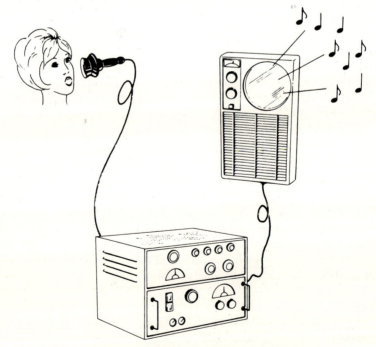

Fig. 1-1   Conveying energy by electricity.

cause the diaphragm of the microphone to move (which is a conversion of sound energy into mechanical energy). The diaphragm movement, in turn, develops a changing voltage (mechanical energy is changed into electrical energy) at the input of the amplifier. The amplifier magnifies the voltage changes. Then these are fed into the speaker input, where they create a movement of the speaker voice coil (the electrical energy is converted back into mechanical energy). The movements of the voice coil create air vibrations which are a reproduction of the original voice (sound energy again).

In reviewing all the above it becomes apparent that the energy conversions which take place in a system like the one displayed in Fig. 1-1 are as follows:

$$\text{Sound energy} \longrightarrow \text{Mechanical energy} \longrightarrow \text{Electrical energy} \longrightarrow \text{Mechanical energy} \longrightarrow \text{Sound energy}$$

Now electricity can be defined:

Electricity is a form of energy resulting from the accumulation or orderly movement of charged particles with associated chemical, magnetic, and radiant effects.

Applying this definition to the example: energy was conveyed from the microphone to the speaker by electricity, and the transfer of energy was accomplished by means of an electric circuit called an *amplifier*. Electricity is used for transferring energy in countless ways, both at home and on the job.

1-3 SCIENTIFIC NOTATION

This section will show you how to:
· Express a number in scientific notation
· Convert a quantity from scientific notation back to the regular number
· Compute with scientific notation

Because many of the quantities used in electricity are very large while others are extremely small, it is necessary to use a technique for expressing them conveniently. This method is called *scientific notation.* You may have heard about it through its other name—*powers of ten.* It is suggested that you practice using scientific notation until it becomes easy for you, because you will need to make such conversions often. This technique, in conjunction with the calculator, is one of your most indispensable tools as an electrical-electronic technician.

Begin with ten and its multiples, which are converted into scientific notation below:

$$10 = 10$$
$$100 = 10^2$$
$$1000 = 10^3$$

Using the same approach for numbers that are smaller yields the following:

$$1 = 10^0$$
$$0.1 = 10^{-1}$$
$$0.01 = 10^{-2}$$

With these examples as a guide, use the same technique for numbers that are more difficult to handle:

$$125 = 1.25(10^2)$$
$$6780 = 6.78(10^3)$$
$$0.0046 = 4.6(10^{-3})$$
$$0.000000000005 = 5(10^{-12})$$

Now the process can be worked the other way around. Notice how the numbers originally expressed in scientific notation below are converted back into ordinary numbers.

$$3.6(10^{-2}) = 0.036$$
$$4.65(10^4) = 46,500$$

It should be stressed again that very large and very small numbers are used commonly in the study of electricity and electronics. For example, resistance values are often in thousands and millions of ohms, and capacitance values are frequently in millionths and millionths of millionths of farads.

PROBLEMS

1-1   Express the following as quantities between 1 and 10 in scientific notation:

a) 300

b) 800,000

c) 0.0009

d) $630(10^3)$

e) $0.0055(10^{-8})$

f) $20,000,000(10^3)$

1-2   Express the following as regular numbers:
   a) $2(10^{-3})$ b) $8.4(10^4)$
   c) $6.77(10^{-8})$ d) $44(10^{10})$
   e) $965(10^{-6})$ f) $7600 \ (10^{12})$

   After you are satisfied with your ability to convert ordinary numbers into scientific notation and vice versa, you are ready to practice computing with scientific notation. The following are the basic rules to guide you in such computations.

Addition with Scientific Notation

Arithmetically add the numbers and carry the power of ten.

Example 1

   Add $2.50(10^3)$ and $6.90(10^3)$.

Solution

   Since each has the same power of ten, then

$$(2.50 + 6.90)10^3 = 9.40(10)^3$$

But what would we do if the numbers to be added had different powers of ten? It is easy. Convert one of them so that both are expressed in the same powers of ten; then proceed with the rule stated above.

Example 2

   Find the sum of $5.4(10)^2$ and $8.6(10)^3$.

Solution

   One of the quantities must be converted so that each is expressed in the same powers of ten. So, convert the first one:

$$5.4(10)^2 = 0.54(10)^3$$

Then find the sum:

$$(0.54 + 8.6)10^3 = 9.14(10)^3$$

Subtraction with Scientific Notation

Arithmetically subtract the numbers and carry the power of ten.

If not all the numbers have the same power of ten, they must be converted until they are all the same.

Example 3

Find the difference between $98(10)^2$ and $16(10)^3$.

Solution

Change $98(10)^2$ to $9.8(10)^3$ and then solve:

$$(16.0 - 9.8)10^3 = 6.2(10)^3$$

Multiplying with Scientific Notation

Multiply the numbers in the usual manner, and find the algebraic sum of the powers of ten.

Example 4

Find the product of $2.5(10)^4$ and $3.0(10)^5$.

Solution

$$2.5 \times 3.0(10)^{4+5} = 7.5(10)^9$$

Dividing with Scientific Notation

Divide the numbers in the conventional way, and find the algebraic difference between the exponents.

Example 5

Find the quotient of $8(10)^{-10}/2(10)^{-4}$.

Solution

$$(8/2)10^{-10+4} = 4(10)^{-6}$$

PROBLEMS

1-3   Find the sums of the following:
  a) $2.5(10)^6 + 3.9(10)^4$
  b) $4.88(10)^{-4} + 7.75(10)^{-3}$
  c) $6.37(10)^{-6} + 4.64(10)^{-5}$
  d) $5.25(10)^{-4} + 8.48(10)^{-3}$

1-4   Find the differences of the following:
   a) $2.65(10)^3 - 1.24(10)^2$
   b) $5.00(10)^4 - 5.00(10)^3$
   c) $4.0(10)^{-5} - 1.8(10)^{-7}$
   d) $8.24(10)^{-12} - 6.84(10)^{-13}$
1-5   Find the products of the following:
   a) $4.00(10)^2 \times 8.00(10)^7$
   b) $8.50(10)^{-7} \times 3.00(10)^{-3}$
   c) $2.50(10)^{-8} \times 4.40(10)^2$
   d) $6.25(10)^4 \times 8.20(10)^7$
1-6   Find the quotients of the following:
   a) $1.50(10)^6/1.20(10)^6$
   b) $8.00(10)^{-10}/4.20(10)^{-5}$
   c) $4.20(10)^{-4}/6.60(10)^7$
   d) $7.93(10)^{-12}/1.82(10)^3$

1-4   UNITS AND PREFIXES

In this section you will learn the basic SI units of measure and the use of prefixes.

   This discussion begins with an idea of what is meant by the term *measurement.* Whenever something is measured, it is being compared to a predetermined standard. For example, the standard unit of length in the International Metric System (SI) is the meter (abbreviated "m"). If the distance between two points is measured as 4.2 m, it is 4.2 times the length of the standard meter. Several basic physical quantities are of great importance in the study of electricity. Five of these are listed in Table 1-1 along with the units they are measured in and the unit abbreviations. SI units are used throughout electricity and electronics, and SI is the measuring system with which you will need to be most familiar.

Table   1-1   Selected Metric Units

Quantity	Unit	Unit Abbreviation
Length	Meter	m
Mass	Kilogram	kg
Force	Newton	N
Time	Second	s
Temperature	Degree Celsius	°C

Many derived units can be obtained from the fundamental ones listed in Table 1-1. Here are several examples:

$$\frac{\text{Length}}{\text{Time}} = \text{speed}$$

$$\frac{\text{Force}}{\text{Mass}} = \text{Acceleration}$$

$$\text{Force} \times \text{length} = \text{work}$$

$$\text{Length} \times \text{width} \times \text{depth} = \text{volume}$$

In addition to the basic units associated with physical quantities, there are others that relate mostly to electricity and electronics. These will be introduced later as they are needed, as will those units derived from them.

Milli and Micro Prefixes

You will find many occasions to express units of measure with special prefixes because of their inconvenient sizes. When a quantity is very small, it is better to express it in thousandths (called *milli*) or millionths (called *micro*) of the unit. The symbol for milli is "m," and the symbol for micro is "μ." Now you will see how these prefixes are used.

Example 1

Convert 0.004 s to milliseconds and 0.000005 s to microseconds.

Solution

$$0.004 \text{ s} = 4(10)^{-3} = 4 \text{ ms}$$

and $\qquad$ $0.000005 \text{ s} = 5(10)^{-6} = 5 \ \mu\text{s}$

Kilo and Mega Prefixes

Two common prefixes for very large quantities in electricity and electronics are *kilo* (thousands, abbreviated as "k") and *mega* (millions, abbreviated as "M"). Here is an illustration of how they are used.

Example 2

Convert 3000 s to kiloseconds and 7,000,000 s to megaseconds.

Solution

$$3000 \text{ s} = 3(10)^3 = 3 \text{ ks}$$

and $\qquad$ $7{,}000{,}000 \text{ s} = 7(10)^6 = 7 \text{ Ms}$

Other Metric Unit Prefixes

In addition to the most common prefixes just described, other decimal multiples and submultiples of metric system units have been established. The complete list is displayed in Table 1-2, so that you can refer to it whenever necessary.

Table 1-2 Metric Unit Prefixes

Multiple	Prefix	Symbol
10^{12}	tera	T
10^9	giga	G
10^6	mega	M
10^3	kilo	k
10^2	hecto	h
10	deka	da
10^{-1}	deci	d
10^{-2}	centi	c
10^{-3}	milli	m
10^{-6}	micro	μ
10^{-9}	nano	n
10^{-12}	pico	p
10^{-15}	femto	f
10^{-18}	atto	a

PROBLEMS

1-7 A unit used in electricity is the ohm. The symbol for ohms is the greek letter omega, Ω.* Express 800,000 ohms as
   a) kilohms
   b) megohms

1-8 Another unit used in electricity is the volt (its symbol is V). Express the following in millivolts.
   a) 0.040 V   b) 0.0062 V
   c) 2.5 V   d) 0.946 V

1-9 Express the following in kilohms.
   a) 1200 Ω b) 680,000 Ω
   c) 4,300,000 Ω d) 2,200,000 Ω

1-10 Express the following in megohms.
   a) 130,000 Ω b) 82,000 Ω
   c) 4,300,000 Ω d) 2,200,000 Ω

---

* Several Greek letters are used as symbols in electricity and electronics. They are included in the list of symbols found in the front of the book.

1-5 ELECTRIC CHARGES

Look for the following ideas in this section:
· How the idea of electric charges originated
· Kinds of electric charges
· How the idea of electrical flow came about
· Things that influence the force acting on charges

Knowledge of what now is called electric charge goes back to the earliest days of recorded history. In ancient Greece (about 600 years B.C.), some learned person stumbled upon a rather interesting happening: when amber was rubbed with animal fur, it attracted objects (such as lint and dust). Since the Greek word for amber was *elektron,* this characteristic of that material was called *electricity.* What happened was that the rubbing of amber *charged,* or electrified, the material. From this came the concept of a charge. It was also found that two pieces of amber, when charged in the manner just described, repelled one another when they were brought sufficiently close together. From this it was found that *like charges repel.*

During this period it was also discovered that rubbing glass with animal fur charged the glass, as indicated by the fact that after the rubbing action, the glass attracted objects such as dust and lint. Later, probably quite by accident, one of these ancient experimenters found that when charged amber and charged glass were brought close enough together, they were attracted to one another. This led to the belief that they contained different kinds of charges, and from it the following law was assumed: *unlike charges attract.*

As the years went on and many other experiments with charging bodies were made, it appeared that only two kinds of charges could be identified. From this the following conclusions were drawn:

1 There are just two kinds of electric charges.
2 Unlike electric charges attract, and like electric charges repel, one another.

The next major breakthrough in electricity was made in 1750 by Benjamin Franklin. He made a series of observations which led him to develop what was called the *fluid theory.* From his many experiments with electricity, he assumed that every body contains an invisible fluid. One that has the normal amount would be neutral, and consequently have no charge. When a body had a smaller than normal amount of this invisible fluid, the body possessed a negative charge. He concluded that a positively charged body was one that had a greater than normal amount of this invisible fluid. This theory held up when tested. One of the experiments consisted of connecting a wire between two opposite charges (they were believed to be opposite because they were attracted to one another). It was found that connecting two opposite charges with a wire resulted in doing away with the force of attraction between them. From this observation Franklin deduced that the excess fluid in the positively charged body flowed through the wire into the negatively charged body to replenish the deficiency of invisible fluid there. When a balance was achieved, the positive body had lost its excess fluid and the negative body had gained the fluid it lacked, making both bodies neutral. In light of what was known in those days, the explanation seemed reasonable and was accepted. From this came the conclusion that *charges flow from positively to negatively charged bodies or regions,* which is the definition of conventional flow. This concept will be examined in more detail later.

Thirty-five years after Franklin proposed the fluid theory, a scientist by the name of Coulomb uncovered a relationship that provided an explanation for the force that acts upon charged bodies. Through carefully prepared and conducted experiments Coulomb found that the force between two charged bodies is directly proportional to the product of the two charges and inversely proportional to the square of the distance between them. This became known as *Coulomb's law,* and it can be expressed as follows:

$$F = \frac{Q_1 Q_2}{Kd^2}$$

where F = force between the charges
   Q_1 = charge on body 1
   Q_2 = charge on body 2
   K = a constant number that depends on the units of measure
   d = distance between bodies 1 and 2

This formula says that the following two relationships exist between two charged bodies:

1 When two charges are drawn closer, the force between them will increase, and vice versa.
2 When one of the two charges is increased, the force between them will also increase, and vice versa.

1-6 ATOMIC STRUCTURE

In this section you will learn about:
* *What elements are*
* *What protons and electrons contribute to the atom's structure*
* *The makeup of the copper atom*

The building blocks of our universe are *elements*. What are they? Elements are substances in their simplest forms, and they cannot be further divided without the use of extraordinary means. There are more than one hundred known elements at this time. Some have been known since ancient times, while others are relatively new discoveries. About ninety of these are found naturally in the crust of the earth, and about 99 percent of the earth's crust is made up of eight elements. These include oxygen (46.6 percent), silicon (27.7 percent), aluminum (8.1 percent), iron (5.0 percent), calcium (3.6 percent), sodium (2.9 percent), potassium (2.6 percent), and magnesium (2.1 percent).

As long ago as 450 B.C., the Greeks developed the idea that all matter was composed of very tiny units, which they called *atoms*. Later, as more was learned about matter and its makeup, the term *atom* was retained to designate the smallest piece of an element that can exist of itself while still retaining the chemical properties of the element. A more precise explanation of the structure of matter was offered many years later, by Dalton in 1802. The Dalton theory was a major breakthrough in understanding the makeup of matter. Dalton claimed:

1   All matter was made up of tiny particles called atoms.
2   Atoms cannot be created or destroyed.
3   Atoms of a given element are unique to that element, and each element has its own particular kind of atom.

Dalton's theory stated, in other words, that an element such as copper has an atom that is different from atoms of other elements. Furthermore, copper atoms are always the same, when they are in their normal state. This provided an important foundation for later work in atomic theory as well as for the study of electricity. In 1895, a number of more specific ideas about the internal structure of the atom appeared. Later, in 1913, Bohr proposed an atomic model that resembled the solar system in its appearance and behavior. This model, with some refinements, is the one used by present-day scientists.

The Bohr model is particularly important in the study of electricity and electronics. Because of this, you are going to learn a bit more about

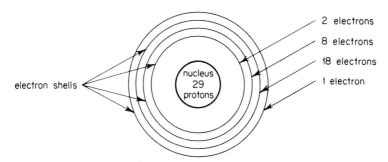

Fig. 1-2   The charges of a copper atom.

atomic structure. Take a minute or two and look over Fig. 1-2, which shows the atomic model for copper. As you go through the following explanation, you might want to go back and look at this illustration again. By the way, if you are wondering why copper was chosen, it is because of its popularity as a conductor in electricity.

The major part of the atom's mass is concentrated at its geometric center, which is called the *nucleus.* The nucleus is occupied by a number of bodies, *protons* and *neutrons* being the most important. The proton has the smallest positive charge used in this study of electricity. The neutron has zero charge, but has a mass about equal to that of the proton. *Electrons* orbit just as the earth and other planets do, but around the nucleus of their own atoms. The number of protons found in the nucleus is always the same as the number of electrons orbiting around the nucleus of that atom when it is undisturbed. This number is unique for each element. Copper, for example, has 29 protons in its nucleus and 29 orbiting electrons. Electrons are very small in mass (about $\frac{1}{1850}$th of a proton), and each has a negative charge equal in quantity to the proton's positive charge. Therefore, a copper atom in its normal condition would have 29 electrons orbiting around its nucleus which contains 29 protons. Since opposite charges cancel (remember Franklin's experiment regarding this), the overall charge of the atom is zero (in this case $-29e + 29p = 0$).

More about Electron Behavior

In a little while, you will study current, and in order to understand what that is all about, the behavior of electrons must be examined more closely. The physical behavior of an electron orbiting around its nucleus is similar to that of the earth orbiting around the sun. The electron is influenced by several major factors:

1   The attraction offered by the positively charged nucleus to the orbiting electrons

2   The force of inertia acting upon the orbiting electrons (The law of inertia states that a body will not change its motion unless it is acted upon by an outside body.)

The interaction of these forces upon the electron results in it orbiting around the nucleus of the atom.

Each electron has its own orbit, and the orbits of electrons are arranged in "shells." In Fig. 1-2, you can see that the first shell has 2 orbiting electrons, while 8 are found in the second shell, 18 in the

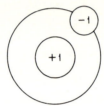

Fig. 1-3   The simplified copper atom.

third, and only 1 in the fourth. The three innermost shells have their maximum number of orbiting electrons, while the fourth shell contains the twenty-ninth orbiting electron of the copper atom (that shell, incidentally, has room for 32 orbiting electrons, but copper uses only one of those allocations). This lone electron is an important one, and it will be examined further, for it holds the secret of what makes copper such a good conductor.

The outer-shell electrons of a material largely determine the electrical qualities of a substance. In the case of copper, it is convenient simply to lump the rest of the copper atom into a body that has a total charge of +1 (since $+29p + -28e = +1p$). So a copper atom can be pictured as having an inside charge of $+1p$, around which revolves an electron having a charge of $-1e$, as shown in Fig. 1-3.

1-7   ELECTRON DISTRIBUTION AND BEHAVIOR IN COPPER

In this section you will learn about:
· The copper lattice structure
· The behavior of free electrons in copper
· How electron current is initiated in copper

Just a while ago it was said that the simplified version of the copper atom could be viewed as having an inside charge of +1 and a single negative electron orbiting around it (the one in the outer shell). But that description is true only in the case of an isolated copper atom, one that is free from other influences. In actuality, copper atoms exist together in tightly packed three-dimensional arrangements called *lattice structures.* A simplified two-dimensional view of this arrangement

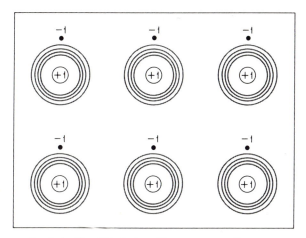

Fig. 1-4   Simplified crystalline structure of copper.

for copper is shown in Fig. 1-4. Take a moment to look it over in preparation for the following discussion.

The inner part of the atom, assigned the overall charge of +1, is locked into its position by the repulsion exerted on it by the other inner atoms surrounding it. It is relatively easy for the outer-shell electron of each of these atoms, because of the relatively great distance from their original nuclei during orbiting, to break away and become associated with other nuclei. The process by which the outer electron migrates from atom to atom goes on naturally, with no unusual external influences exerted on the material. This outer electron is dissociated from any atom while it is enroute from one nuclear influence to another, and it is called a *free* or *mobile* electron during that time.

Because there is one outer electron for each copper atom, the material can have one dissociated electron for each atom in the material. This provides a very generous number of such charges. It has been determined that there are about $1.4(10)^{24}$ free electrons in 1 in^3 of copper. The situation is such that free electrons can be made to drift through the copper by placing an electric field across it. An electric field is created by placing a negative electric charge on one side of the copper material and a positive charge on the other. If this is done so that a complete path is provided, then the mobile electrons move toward the positive charge and away from the negative charge (this agrees with the earlier finding that unlike charges attract and like charges repel—electrons are negative in charge). This is *electron current.* More will be said about this later.

1-8   CONDUCTORS

In this section, you will learn:
• *The meaning of conductivity*
• *The names of some important conductors*

   A material that has a relatively large number of free electrons can be used as a conductor. One of the chief determining factors in deciding whether a material is suitable as an *electric conductor* is the number of free electrons available per unit of volume. Most metals are good conductors, with silver being the best. But, for reasons of cost, silver has not become the most popular conductor. Several metals, and their conductivity as compared to silver, are listed in Table 1-3.

   Conductivity can be considered to be the ease with which free electrons can be made to flow in the material. From the comparative values shown in Table 1-3, you can see that copper is 0.945 as good as silver in this regard, but it has become the most popular metal for use as a conductor because it is less expensive than silver. There is a wide range in the conductivity values of the different metals that are considered good electric conductors. Iron, for example, while only 0.166 as good as silver in terms of conductivity, is considered to be a suitable conductor in some instances. Aluminum, which has a conductivity value about 60 percent that of copper, has become a more popular conductor in recent years because it is more economical.

Table   1-3   Conductivity of Several Metals*

Metal	Conductivity
Silver	1.000
Copper	0.945
Aluminum	0.576
Iron	0.166

* Silver is used as a reference.

1-9 SEMICONDUCTORS

In this section look for:
• The meaning of the term semiconductor
• A description of electron behavior in a semiconductor
• A list of the most popular semiconductors

There are certain metals that have a more limited supply of free electrons that can be utilized in electron current flow. *Semiconductors* are materials that have lower values of conductivity than metals classified as conductors. On the other hand, their conductivity values are higher than those of insulator materials. Since there are fewer free electrons per unit volume in semiconductors, a much smaller number of them will be involved in current flow when an electric field is placed across the material. But those electrons that are available behave in the same way as free electrons do in a conductor—the important difference is the number of free electrons per unit volume that become involved in current flow. There are a number of materials that are classified as semiconductors which are an important ingredient in transistors. Some of the more commonly used semiconductor materials are germanium, silicon, boron, copper oxide, and titanium compounds.

1-10 INSULATORS

Look for the following information in this section:
• An explanation of the makeup of insulators
• A list of common insulator materials and their dielectric strengths

An *insulator* is a material that has very few mobile electrons (actually many fewer than the semiconductor type of material discussed in the preceding section). As a result of this characteristic, an insulator has very low conductivity. Good insulators effectively prevent electron current flow from taking place within them. You should know that just as there are cases where one seeks an easy path for current flow, there are situations in electricity and electronics where it is crucial that electron current flow be prevented. When this is the case, an insulator is utilized.

There is no such thing as a perfect insulator. If a sufficiently large electric field is placed across an insulator, certain of the electrons are drawn out of their normal nuclear orbits and toward the positive charge. Such an action permanently ruptures the material in most cases. It is important to know at what electric field strength this breakdown action—called the *dielectric strength* of the material—will take

Table   1-4   Typical Insulators

Material	Dielectric Strength, V/mm
Air (dry)	$3(10)^3$
Bakelite	$10(10)^3 - 30(10)^3$
Glass	$20(10)^3 - 60(10)^3$
Mica	$50(10)^3 - 220(10)^3$
Porcelain	$5.5(10)^3$
Rubber	$15(10)^3$

place. Knowing this enables the circuit designer to choose an insulator material of sufficient dielectric strength for the anticipated circuit conditions.

To obtain a true comparison of the dielectric strengths of various insulator materials, a fixed thickness of 1 mm is used in stating the values. Table 1-4 gives a list of some typical insulators, with their approximate dielectric strengths.

1-11   THE ELECTRIC CIRCUIT

The electric circuit is the physical apparatus used in conveying electric energy. The actual connection of the various components in the circuit is best illustrated by a drawing called a *circuit diagram,* or *schematic.* Standard graph symbols are used, which will be introduced as they are needed.

QUESTIONS

1-1   What is the definition of energy?
1-2   Name six kinds of energy and describe them.
1-3   What is the definition of electricity?
1-4   What are the advantages of using scientific notation?
1-5   What does the term *measurement* mean?
1-6   What are fundamental units of measurement?
1-7   What are derived units of measurement?
1-8   What are milli prefixes?
1-9   What are micro prefixes?
1-10   How did the term *electricity* originate?
1-11   How many kinds of electric charges are there?
1-12   State the relationship between kinds of electric charges.
1-13   What is conventional current flow?
1-14   State two relationships that are indicated by Coulomb's law.

1-15 What are elements?

1-16 What is the most common element found naturally in the earth's crust?

1-17 What is an atom?

1-18 State Dalton's theory.

1-19 What is the geometric center of the atom called?

1-20 What is a proton?

1-21 What is a neutron?

1-22 What is an electron?

1-23 Describe the copper atom.

1-24 State two major factors that influence electron behavior.

1-25 What is a lattice structure?

1-26 What is a free, or mobile, electron?

1-27 What is conductivity?

1-28 What is electron current?

1-29 What is a semiconductor?

1-30 Name five commonly used semiconductor materials.

1-31 What is the makeup of an insulator?

1-32 What is the dielectric strength of a material?

1-33 Name six common insulators.

1-34 Why is there no perfect insulator?

1-35 What is an electric circuit?

electron current and voltage

2

The three most fundamental properties associated with electricity are current, voltage, and resistance. The kind of current that is most important is electron current, and it is featured throughout this text. In this chapter, you will be introduced to the basic concepts of electron current and voltage. Emphasis is placed on the relationship of energy to the mobile electron, which is central to what goes on in an electric circuit. The major characteristics of a material which enhance the ease with which free electrons are involved in current flow are discussed. Voltage as the force behind current flow is analyzed, along with the common sources of voltage.

2-1 CHARACTERISTICS OF THE SIMPLE ELECTRIC CIRCUIT

In this section you will learn about:
* *Block diagrams*
* *Pictorial diagrams*
* *The general characteristics of a simple electric circuit*

In Sec. 1–11 the electric circuit was defined as the physical apparatus used for conveying electric energy from one point to another. Now the general characteristics of the simple electric circuit can be examined. Take a minute or two to look at Fig. 2-1, which is a *block diagram* of a generalized electric circuit. Such a drawing is called a block diagram because the major components in the circuit are shown as rectangles or blocks.

The source of electric energy is called the *input* of the electric circuit. The possible nature of this source is analyzed in Secs. 2-8 through

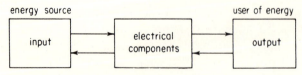

Fig. 2-1 A block diagram of the generalized electric circuit.

2-10. The important thing to remember at this time is that the input delivers the electric energy to the electric components of the circuit. These components in turn feed the energy into the *output* of the circuit. The output of the circuit is a device (several of which are examined later) which uses up the electric energy of the circuit.

When an electric circuit is shown in an illustration such that the components are drawn as they actually appear, such a diagram is called a *pictorial diagram* of the circuit. This approach may be used, for example, when it is felt that the circuit needs to be described to someone

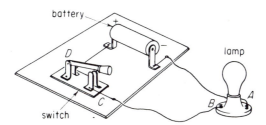

Fig. 2-2   Pictorial diagram.

having no background in electricity (as an example, such diagrams are often provided with the instructions for assembly of certain electric devices that are purchased by hobbyists). A pictorial diagram is shown in Fig. 2-2, which is a simple battery lamp circuit. Look at the figure for a few moments in preparation for the following discussion.

In Fig. 2-2, the source of energy is the battery (what really goes on in a battery will be discussed soon). In many such circuits, the battery is connected to the lamp by copper wires. In this illustration, a manual switch is placed between one side of the lamp and one side of the battery. Thus the circuit can be opened or closed at will. When a circuit is "open," there is no complete path and electric energy cannot flow from the input to the output. A continuous, or "closed," circuit—the condition when electric energy can flow—exists when the switch is closed. Comparing the pictorial diagram with the block diagram of Fig. 2-1, you see that the input is the battery, the electrical components are the wires and manual switch, and the lamp is the output.

Therefore, energy will be conveyed from the input to the output when the manual switch is in its closed position. The starting point can be considered to be the negative terminal of the battery. Trace the entire loop: from the negative terminal of the battery through the wire to side A of the lamp, through the lamp to side B of the lamp, to point C of the switch through the wire, through the switch to point D, from point D through the wire to the positive side of the battery, through the battery to its negative terminal. This is a complete loop (or path) for conveying electric energy.

In the following sections, you will see how a battery serves as a source of energy, and how the wire is able to carry this energy to the output device that uses the energy.

2-2 THE BASIC ELECTRIC CHARGE

In this section you will learn the definition of the coulomb and how it is used to determine amounts of charge.

The nature of electric charge was discussed in several of the sections in Chap. 1. Recall that the charge of a proton was considered to be positive, and that the electron was negative. It was also pointed out that these charges, in addition to being opposite to each other, were also equal in value. The electron and the electric charge it possesses are of major importance in the study of electricity and electronics. Thus they need to be examined further. The negative charge of an electron is very small — so small that it is necessary to use a more practical unit of electric charge.

The basic unit of electric charge in the metric system is the *coulomb* (C). How much electric charge is there in a coulomb? A coulomb is the amount of electric charge held by $6.24(10)^{18}$ electrons. From this definition, a formula for defining a charge in coulombs is

$$Q = \frac{n}{6.24(10)^{18}} \qquad \text{(2-1)}$$

where Q = charge in coulombs, C
n = number of electrons

This relationship can be used to find the amount of charge contained by $20(10)^{18}$ electrons. The quantity of electrons is substituted for n in the defining formula. Then solve:

$$Q = \frac{20(10)^{18}}{6.24(10)^{18}} = 3.21 \text{ C}$$

The use of the coulomb is standard; it is utilized by nearly everyone in the study of electricity and electronics.

2-3 CURRENT AND THE AMPERE

Look for information regarding the following in this section:
· Random motion of electrons
· Electron current
· The battery as an electron pump
· Relationship between coulombs and electron current
· The standard unit of current, the ampere

In the last chapter the behavior of the outer-shell electron in copper was discussed. One of the last observations made at that time was that the electron is the basic charged particle of the medium for transporting electric energy in copper (and other metallic conductors). More detail can be given now on how this is accomplished.

The outer-shell electron in copper is loosely held to its nucleus. This makes it easy for the outer-shell electrons to migrate throughout the lattice structure. When no outside electric field is present, these outer-shell electrons undergo *random motion.* Figure 2-3 illustrates the possible random motion of an electron.

It is important to notice that the net displacement result of random electron motion is zero. The mobile electron zigzags its way around the lattice structure, encountering collisions with the various atoms, but such an electron ends up not really getting anywhere. What the outer-shell electrons need, if they are to move in some specific direction, is the influence of an electric field. A common way of placing an electric field across a material, such as a copper wire, is to connect it to a battery. The battery has two terminals. The negative terminal has a surplus of electrons, and the positive terminal has a shortage of electrons. Figure 2-4 shows this type of connection.

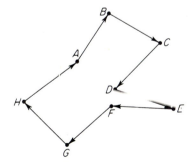

Fig. 2-3   **Random motion of an electron.**

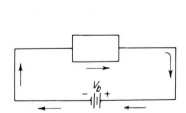

Fig. 2-4   **Displacement of free electrons by the battery** V_b**.**

Remember that copper has the possibility of contributing one free electron per atom, because of the ease with which the outer-shell electron can be pulled away from the influence of its nucleus. Connecting the battery in the way shown in Fig. 2-4 provides the means by which the outer-shell electrons are made to drift toward the positive terminal of the battery. This drift is called *electron current*, or *electron drift*. The

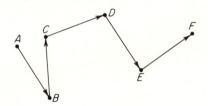

Fig. 2-5   Electron drift.

electrons now have a directional drift imposed on their otherwise random motion. This is shown in Fig. 2-5.

Now look more closely at the way the battery circuit of Fig. 2-4 behaves: The free electrons will be repelled away from the negative battery terminal (since like charges repel) and will be attracted toward the positive terminal of the battery (since unlike charges attract). The result is the flow of electron current. Just what role does the battery play in all this? The battery can be thought of as an electron pump. It injects electrons into the circuit only at the rate at which electrons leave the opposite side of the circuit to enter the positive side of the battery. It is important to realize that *the battery provides the energy to drive the electrons that were already available for this kind of action. The battery is not a source of electrons.* The source of electrons in this example is the copper wire. This works much like a water pump, which serves to propel the water but is not the actual source of water.

The rate at which the free electrons drift is called the *current.* Because electrons have such minute charges, the unit-charge coulomb is used in the fundamental unit of current, which is the ampere (A). We can define it as follows:

One ampere is the current that flows when one coulomb travels past a given point in one second.

From this, the defining equation is:

$$I = \frac{Q}{t}$$

(2-2)

where I = current in amperes, A
Q = quantity of charge in coulombs, C
t = time in seconds, s

The formula can be used to determine the amount of current that exists when a flow of 15 C passes through a particular point of the wire in 3 s. Substituting these values into the defining equation and solving yield

$$I = \frac{15}{3} = 5 \text{ A}$$

Milliamperes and Microamperes

There are many applications of electricity and electronics in which the unit of ampere is very large for the values of current handled in certain circuits. Therefore, the prefixes milli (m) and micro (μ) are in common use. But the basic formula for computing the value of current provides the current magnitude in amperes. Conversions have to be made by you after the computation.

Example

A charge of 0.04 C moves past a given point in 8 s. Express the amount of current in milliamperes (mA) and microamperes (μA).

Solution

$$I = \frac{Q}{t} = \frac{4(10)^{-2}}{8} = 0.5(10)^{-2} \text{ A}$$

which is

$$0.5(10)^{-2}(10)^3 = 5 \text{ mA}$$

and

$$0.5(10)^{-2}(10)^6 = 5000 \text{ } \mu A$$

2-4 CONVENTIONAL CURRENT

This section tells you:
· The origin of the conventional current idea
· The difference between conventional current and electron current
· This text uses electron current throughout

During the time of Benjamin Franklin, it was believed that current was the result of the movement of a fluid. As mentioned in Chap. 1, this gave rise to the fluid theory, first proposed by Franklin. For many years, it was considered to be the correct explanation of current flow. This theory was the major basis for the assumption that current consisted of the directional movement of positive charges through the conductor. Such current flow is called *conventional current.*

Since that time, because of the discovery of electron theory, it was determined that current flow in the usual type of conductor, such as copper, really consists of the flow of electrons, as explained in the preceding section. The important difference between the conventional current and electron current interpretations is the direction of the current flow. Conventional current, since it is viewed as being equivalent to the flow of positive charges, is said to move from the positive to the negative side of the circuit. Electron current flows in the opposite direction — from the negative (because the electrons are repelled) to the positive side of the circuit (to which the mobile electrons are attracted).

There are a number of books dealing with the study of electricity and electronics that use the concept of conventional current in their explanations related to current flow. But, in the interest of using explanations that are in keeping with the way current flow really is, *this text incorporates electron current throughout.*

2-5 POTENTIAL ENERGY AND WORK DONE BY A CHARGED BODY

This section describes:
· Potential energy of a charged body
· Work done by a charged body
· Difference of potential energy of a charged body

Energy was defined in Sec. 1-1 as the ability to do work. That section also listed several types of energy that are important in electricity and electronics. Potential energy was included there, and now the potential energy of electric charges is going to be considered in greater detail. *Potential energy* is the energy possessed by a charged body because of its position in an electric field. Should the charged body be moved such that it loses its potential energy, then it has done *work* on another body. This is an important point that will be clarified with an example.

Look over Fig. 2-6 for a moment. It illustrates a negative charge in an electric field. The charged body is shown to be first at point X, then at

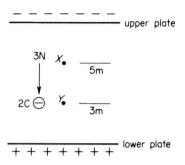

Fig. 2-6 Potential energy of a charge.

point *Y*. The amount of work done by the charged body is equal to its *difference in potential energy* as a result of moving from point *X* to *Y*. That difference in potential energy is the work done by that charged body in moving from *X* to *Y*.

The relationship for computing the amount of potential energy possessed by the charged body is

$$W = fd$$

where W = potential energy in joules (J)
f = force in newtons (N)
d = distance in meters (m)

and d is measured from a reference point of zero potential energy.

In Fig. 2-6, the potential energy of the charge at point *Y* is

$$W = 3 \times 3 = 9 \text{ J}$$

with respect to the lower plate.

Suppose that charge is located at point *X:* now it can exert a downward force of 3 N for a total distance of 8 m (5 m between *X* and *Y*, and 3 m between *Y* and the lower plate) by the time it reaches the lower plate. So the potential energy of the charged body with respect to the lower plate is

$$W = 3 \times 8 = 24 \text{ J}$$

The work done by the charge in moving from *X* to *Y* is equal to the difference in potential energy of the charge between those two points. In this example, the charge is moved through a distance of 5 m when traveling from X to Y, and the difference in potential energy between those two points is

$$W = 3 \times 5 = 15 \text{ J}$$

Therefore, the charged body performed 15 J of work in moving from point X to point Y.

2-6 VOLTAGE AND THE VOLT

In this section look for the meaning of voltage and the volt.

Now that you understand the difference in energy, we can use it in conjunction with the concept of electric charge to define voltage. *Voltage* is the difference in potential energy (which is work done) divided by the charge. Stated in equation form,

$$V = \frac{W}{Q} \qquad\qquad \text{(2-3)}$$

where V = voltage
$\qquad W$ = work or difference in potential energy (joules)
$\qquad Q$ = electrical charge (coulombs)

By using the metric units of joules for difference in potential energy and coulombs for charge, the voltage value can be read as joules of work per coulomb of charge. As an illustration, recall that the charge of 2 C performed 15 J of work in moving from point X to Y (top of p. 27). Therefore,

$$V = \frac{15}{2} = 7.5 \text{ J/C}$$

This answer is read as 7.5 joules per coulomb.

Rather than use the ratio itself when identifying values of voltage, the metric unit of volt (abbreviated V) was devised. *One volt is defined as one joule per coulomb,* or

$$1 \text{ V} = 1 \text{ J/C}$$

When the above is expressed in terms of work, one volt is the voltage that exists between two points when one coulomb can do one joule of work as that charged body moves between the two points.

In the previous illustration, by using the definition of volt you find

$$V = 7.5 \times 1 \text{ J/C} = 7.5 \text{ V}$$

The volt is the unit of measure for voltage used in all electric and electronic circuits, and it is used throughout this text.

2-7 ELECTROMOTIVE FORCE AND VOLTAGE-DROP

In this section look for:
* *the meanings of electromotive force and voltage-drop*
* *the distinction between these two terms*

From the earlier discussions of electron flow it is now clear that free electrons within a conductor are made to drift from one end of the wire to the other end. But the free electrons will undergo this drift action only when an electric pressure, called *electromotive force* (abbreviated "emf"), is applied to the circuit. Take a moment to look over the lamp circuit in Fig. 2-7, which will be used in the following explanation.

There are a number of devices used in electricity and electronics for providing power to a circuit, and they are called sources of electromotive force. Power is the capacity to exert electrical energy at a certain rate. (More will be said about this in Chap. 4.) In Fig. 2-7, the source of electromotive force is a battery (designated as V_b). Notice the symbol used to designate a battery—a series of short and long lines, with the negative side of the battery designated by a short line and the positive terminal noted by the longer line. It was mentioned in a preceding section, remember, that a battery acts like an electron pump, which sets up the drift of mobile electrons in the circuit. In Fig. 2-7, the circuit consists of a lamp (notice the standard symbol used for a lamp), which converts the potential energy of the electrons into heat and light energy. The amount of work done by the electrons in passing through the lamp results in a reduction in their potential energy. The reduction in potential energy of electron charges, because of the work being done (which was a

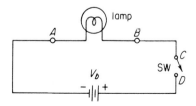

Fig. 2-7   Lamp circuit.

conversion of potential energy into heat energy and light energy in this example), creates a *voltage-drop* (abbreviated "VD") across the lamp. If there is negligible opposition offered to electron drift in the wires leading to and from the lamp, then nearly all the energy used up (or the work done) takes place in the lamp. The amount of energy (in joules per coulomb of charge) used up in the circuit, which is the voltage-drop (VD), is always equal to the amount of energy per coulomb given to the circuit (which is the electromotive force — emf). So,

$$emf = -VD$$

where emf = energy given to the circuit by the energy source
    VD = energy per coulomb of charge used up (work done) in overcoming the opposition to electron flow

If the value of battery V_b in Fig. 2-7 is 3 V, which is the electromotive force of the circuit, then the voltage-drop across the lamp is 3 V if the wiring offers negligible opposition to the current.

Notice the opposite relationship that exists between these two important terms: emf is the *voltage-rise*, which can be viewed as the energy imparted to the free electrons for the development and maintenance of current; the *voltage-drop* of the overall circuit is the energy used by the free electrons while engaged in current flow. Another important fact is that the amount of energy used for electron current flow is always equal to the amount of energy drawn from the energy source (such as the battery V_b in Fig. 2-7).

2-8 THE DRY CELL BATTERY

In this section you will learn about the makeup and action of a dry cell battery.

In several of the preceding sections it was mentioned that a source of electromotive force is necessary in order for an electric circuit to pass energy from one point to another point. You may have been wondering where such sources of energy (emf) can be obtained. There are several types of sources:

1 Chemical
2 Mechanical
3 Thermoelectric
4 Electromagnetic

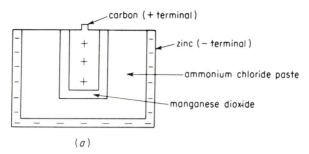

Fig. 2-8   The dry cell battery.

5   Photoelectric
6   Piezoelectric

Batteries (dry and storage types) are chemical sources of electric potential. Look at Fig. 2-8 for a moment. It shows the basic construction of a simple dry cell, which will be discussed next.

In the dry cell battery, a carbon rod is surrounded by manganese dioxide. Around this is an electrolyte in paste form, ammonium chloride. The entire assembly is placed inside a zinc container. When this is done, the carbon and zinc chemicals react with the ammonium chloride in such a way that the carbon rod becomes positive (gives up some of its electrons) and the zinc container becomes negative (picks up the electrons lost by the carbon rod). The difference between the electron concentrations of the carbon and zinc is sufficient to produce an electric potential of just over 1.5 V. Sometimes, a number of these cells are stacked together to form batteries whose electromotive force is a multiple of 1.5 V. A 3-V dry cell battery, for example, is formed by two of these cells stacked together.

Next consider the chemical action that goes on in the dry cell. Hydrogen is formed on the carbon rod as a result of the chemical action. This process, called *polarization,* tends to insulate the rod from the electrolyte. The result is an increase in the internal opposition to electron flow in the cell, which reduces the potential across its external terminals. The manganese dioxide action is slower than the rate at which the hydrogen is deposited; and in order to compensate for this, the cell requires intervals of rest between use.

When the battery is connected to an external circuit, the number of electrons that leave the negative terminal is the same as the number of electrons drawn from the external circuit to the positive terminal (notice the similarity to the action of a pump). At the same time, the same number of electrons moves from the positive terminal through the dry cell solution to the negative terminal. An equal number of electrons drift in the same direction throughout the circuit because of the repelling action that free electrons exert on one another. *The original source of energy (chemical) is converted to electric potential, which furnishes the driving force for the mobile electrons by propelling each of them as they pass through the cell.*

There are several other types of dry cells that offer some advantages over the carbon-zinc variety. The *manganese-alkaline cell,* which generates an emf of 1.5 V, has a longer life than the carbon-zinc variety. The *mercury cell* is a development that has resulted in the construction of very tiny batteries. The carbon-zinc dry cells are relatively large because considerable space is required for housing the depolarization agent within the cell. In the mercury cell, since the positive terminal does not become polarized, it is not necessary to include a depolarization agent. This is the major advantage of the mercury cell — its compactness. The positive electrode is zinc, and the negative electrode is made up of mercuric oxide and graphite. Potassium hydroxide is the electrolyte. The emf generated by the mercury cell is 1.3 V.

2-9 THE SECONDARY BATTERY

In this section you will learn about the makeup and action of the secondary battery.

One of the most commonly used secondary batteries is the wet cell battery. The *lead acid storage cell* is one variety of such a battery. It is called a storage cell because it stores its energy in chemical form and its conversion process is reversible. Look over Fig. 2-9; it will be used in examining the discharge action of the lead acid storage cell.

The electrolyte is sulfuric acid (which has the chemical formula H_2SO_4) diluted with water (H_2O). The positive terminal is made of lead peroxide (PbO_2) built upon a grid of lead and antimony. A grid packed with spongy lead is used for the negative terminal of the battery.

In solution the sulfuric acid develops sulfate ions (SO_4). Ions are atoms that have more or fewer electrons than normal. Therefore a positive ion is an atom that is short one or more electrons, and a negative ion is an atom that has one or more extra electrons. The sulfate ion in this action is positive, so it takes on an electron from each of the two hydrogen atoms found in the molecules of the acid (H_2SO_4). The sulfate ions interact with the lead found in both the positive and negative plates. This results in the formation of lead sulfate, and each battery terminal receives two electrons. This leaves four positive hydrogen ions in the

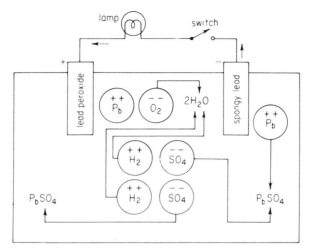

Fig. 2-9   Discharge of the lead acid storage cell.

solution, and they acquire their deficient electrons from the negative oxygen ions. The negative oxygen ions were made available when the lead in the lead peroxide from the positive terminal combined to form lead sulfate.

Here is a summary of the overall chemical action that takes place in the lead acid storage cell when it is discharging. For two molecules of acid:

1 Two free electrons were deposited on the negative terminal.
2 Two free electrons were deposited and four free electrons were taken from the positive terminal.

Therefore the total result is that the positive terminal lost two free electrons.

As the battery is allowed to discharge, both terminals gradually are reduced to lead sulfate by the chemical action just described. At the same time, more water appears and the electrolytic acid begins to disappear. In the external circuit, free electrons flow from the negative terminal through the external circuit into the positive battery terminal. Inside the battery, the overall effect is that the same number of electrons drifts from the positive terminal through the solution onto the negative terminal. Therefore the overall drift of free electrons is the same throughout the external circuit and inside the battery.

The lead acid storage cell is recharged by reversing the chemical action of the battery. Commonly this is done by connecting a dc generator across the terminals such that it pulls electrons out of the positive battery terminal and deposits them on the negative terminal of the battery. This means that the positive terminal of the external dc generator is connected to the positive terminal of the battery. Also, the potential of the dc generator must be sufficiently greater than that of the lead acid cell to permit this action to take place. The lead acid cell produces an emf of 2.0 V. This is the cell used in common automobile batteries.

The *nickel-cadmium cell,* another popular secondary battery, produces an emf of 1.2 V. It is used widely in portable applications, such as cordless electric shavers.

The attempt to design lighter and longer-lasting batteries for spacecraft has sparked interest in the possibility of using batteries for still other purposes. An example of this is the interest in developing battery-powered automobiles (electric cars) because of the air pollution created by the conventional gasoline engine and the anticipated long-range shortage of petroleum. Batteries being developed for spacecraft are a step closer to meeting the power requirements needed for running automobiles. A *sodium-sulfur battery* may have possibilities for running automobiles. Another possibility is the *air battery,* which involves pumping air against zinc (or certain other metals), thus developing a flow of electron current in the zinc.

2-10 OTHER EMF SOURCES

In this section look for the identification of five additional sources of emf.

There are a number of other emf sources in addition to batteries. One of these is the *fuel cell,* in which the chemical action results in the consumption of the fuel, with no damaging effect upon the electrodes. The emf in the fuel cell can be maintained as long as the proper fuel can be fed into the cell. The chemical energy of the fuel is converted by the fuel cell into electric energy.

The most important source of emf is the *dynamo,* or *generator.* The mechanical energy of the dynamo is converted into electromotive force. In some cases, such as the large water power complex located in Niagara Falls, New York, the mechanical energy is obtained from falling water. In many other cases, the dynamo is driven by a heat engine, which in turn derives its energy from coal, oil, diesel fuel, or nuclear energy. In spite of the controversy regarding nuclear power plants, they are becoming an increasingly important source of emf (some estimate that 30 percent or more of electric power will be produced from this source by 1985).

A limited amount of emf can be generated directly from such energy sources as heat, light, and sound. The conversion of heat energy into electric potential is the principle of a *thermocouple.* Two dissimilar metals (such as iron and copper) are joined in a loop so that two junctions are formed. The application of heat to one of the junctions will produce a flow of electrons. As long as one junction is kept at a higher temperature than the other, current will flow.

The *photoelectric* source of energy has found limited use. Solar batteries, used in artificial earth satellites and outer-space missiles, are of this type. This source may become more important as a source of emf as the cost of other fuels increases. When certain materials are exposed to light, enough energy is delivered to the mobile electrons found near the surface of the material to drive them into conduction when an external circuit is connected.

As described in Chap. 1, some microphones convert sound energy into mechanical energy, which in turn is converted into emf. An emf can be generated in this manner by what is called the *piezoelectric* effect.

You should note that in all cases some form of energy is converted into emf. This is used in turn to impose a drift action on the existing free electrons within the external circuit. Under no conditions is the source of electric energy a supply or source of mobile electrons.

2-11 NONMETALLIC CONDUCTORS

In this section you will learn about the conduction of current:
* *by electrolysis*
* *in a vacuum tube*
* *in a gas tube*

Although metallic conductors are in most common use, some nonmetallic conductors are available. Now is the time to look into several of these.

The process of electrolysis is an important source of nonmetallic conduction. Look at Fig. 2-10, which is an illustration of an *electrolytic cell.*

How does current flow in this cell? The steel spoon serves as the positive terminal, and it is called the *cathode.* The current-conducting solution in which the anode and cathode are immersed is the *electrolyte,* which is a silver nitrate solution.

When a source of emf is connected across the anode and cathode in the manner shown in Fig. 2-10, the positive silver ions are drawn to the cathode. Upon contacting the cathode, the silver ion picks up its missing

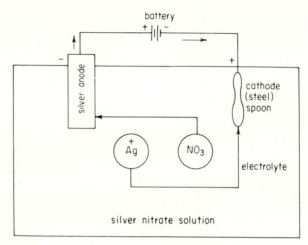

Fig. 2-10   The electrolytic cell.

electron, and this results in pure silver being deposited on the cathode. At the same time the negative nitrate ions are drawn to the anode, where each nitrate ion releases its surplus electron to the anode. This enables each nitrate ion to become chemically active, and it then takes a silver atom from the anode into solution with it. The result is that the electrolyte continues to be the same all the time. It is important to note that no chemical energy is dissipated in the electrolytic cell. The energy required to carry the silver from the anode to the cathode is furnished by the external emf. Also important to note is that two *ion currents* flow in the electrolytic cell of Fig. 2-10: positive silver ions are made to flow to the cathode, and the anode receives negative nitrate ions.

Vacuum tube current is another type of nonmetallic conduction. In this type of current, electrons are made to flow through a space which is under greatly reduced pressure (and therefore called a vacuum tube). When they are heated, certain materials have the property of "boiling off" electrons. These materials are used as the cathode, or filament, of the vacuum tube. The cathode (or filament) is heated to a predetermined temperature range, which causes it to emit free electrons into the surrounding space. These free electrons are then drawn to a positive terminal (called the *anode*, or *plate*) through the near-vacuum space that exists between the cathode and the plate.

A third type of nonmetallic conduction, which is a variation of the vacuum tube type, is the variety of conduction utilized in *gas tubes*. Both the vacuum tube and gas tube kinds of conduction have become less important since the advent of superior solid-state devices such as transistors and control switches.

PROBLEMS

2-1 Express 0.04 A in milliamperes and microamperes.

2-2 Express 3 mA in amperes and microamperes.

2-3 Express 75 μA in amperes and milliamperes.

2-4 Assume that 30 C is moved past a given point in 5 min. Find the value of current. Express it in amperes and milliamperes.

2-5 Assume that 9 C is moved past a given point in 3 min. Find the value of current. Express it in amperes, milliamperes, and microamperes.

2-6 A circuit has a current of 4 A. How long will it take 2 C to pass by a given point?

2-7 A circuit has a current of 6 A. How long will it take 0.75 C to pass by a given point?

2-8 Refer to Fig. 2-7. Assume $V_b = 9$ V. What must be the total voltage-drop of the circuit?

2-9 Refer to Fig. 2-7. Assume that 18 C is moved from point A to B, with the expenditure of 72 J of energy. What is the potential difference between points A and B?

2-10 Refer to Fig. 2-7. Assume 0.2 C is moved from point A to point B with the use of 24 J of energy. What is the potential difference between points A and B?

2-11 Assume that a circuit such as shown in Fig. 2-7 has a current of 1.5 A flowing between points A and B, and 120 J of energy is released in 2 s. What is the potential difference across points A and B?

2-12 Assume that a circuit such as shown in Fig. 2-7 has a current of 25 mA flowing between points A and B, and 200 J of energy is used in 4 s. What is the potential difference across points A and B?

2-13 Find the current passing through point A in Fig. 2-7 if it takes 4 s for 16 C of electrons to pass through it.

2-14 Refer to Fig. 2-7. The current through the lamp is 800 mA. Find the number of coulombs that pass through the lamp in 2 min.

2-15 Refer to Fig. 2-7. Assume that the current passing through the lamp is 500 μA. Find the number of coulombs that pass through the lamp in 5 min.

2-16 Assume that V_b of Fig. 2-7 is the conventional type of dry cell battery shown in Fig. 2-8. Determine the number of coulombs of electrons that would pass from the carbon terminal through the ammonium chloride paste to the zinc terminal in 2 s when the current is:
   a)   50 mA   b)   2 μA

2-17 Repeat Prob. 2-16(a) for the following lengths of time:
   a)   4 ms   b)   1/20 s

2-18 Refer to Fig. 2-9. Assume that the current flowing through the lamp is 1.5 A and the time under consideration is 1 s. Find the number of free electrons:
a) deposited on the negative terminal
b) deposited on the positive terminal
c) taken from the positive terminal

2-19 Refer to Fig. 2-9. Assume the current flowing through the lamp is 400 mA and the time under consideration is 8 s. Find the number of free electrons:
a) deposited on the negative terminal
b) deposited on the positive terminal
c) taken from the positive terminal

2-20 Assume that it takes 30 J of energy to move 10 C of electrons between the positive and negative terminals of a battery. What is the emf of the battery?

2-21 Assume that it takes 24 J of energy to move 2 C of electrons between the positive and negative terminals of a battery. What is the emf of the battery?

2-22 Refer to Fig. 2-7. Assume that 0.2 C flows from the negative terminal of the battery through the lamp into the positive terminal and 12 J of energy is used. What is the voltage-drop across the lamp?

2-23 Assume the voltage-drop of the lamp in Fig. 2-7 is 120 V and 2 C of electrons is moved in 4 s. Find the number of joules required for:
a) the total time
b) 1 s

2-24 A 1.5-V dry cell battery converts 0.6 J of energy while moving electrons from its positive terminal through the electrolyte onto the negative terminal. What quantity of electrons (in coulombs) has been moved?

2-25 Assume that a 1.2-V battery delivers a current of 50 mA. Determine the number of joules of energy expended during:
a) 2 s   b) 1 min

2-26 Assume a battery has an emf of 6 V and delivers a current of 30 mA.
a) How many joules per second are transferred to the circuit from the battery?
b) How long it will take to transfer 36 J of energy?

2-27 Assume the lamp of Fig. 2-7 receives energy at the rate of 45 J/s and has a voltage drop of 3 V. How much current must be flowing through the lamp?

2-28   A battery has an emf of 10 V and is delivering 40 mA of current to a lamp. Find the rate at which chemical energy is being converted.

QUESTIONS

2-1   What is the purpose of the input in an electric circuit?

2-2   What is an open circuit? A closed circuit?

2-3   What is the purpose of the output in an electric circuit?

2-4   What is meant by the circuit's loop?

2-5   What is a coulomb?

2-6   Describe the action of the outer-shell electrons of a copper wire in a circuit like that of Fig. 2-7.

2-7   Explain the random motion of an electron.

2-8   What is electron drift?

2-9   Describe electron-current flow.

2-10   What is the function of a battery in an electric circuit?

2-11   Explain why a battery can be thought of as an electron pump.

2-12   What is the definition of one ampere?

2-13   Explain the difference between electron current and conventional current.

2-14   What type of current flow is used throughout this text? What reason was given?

2-15   Show the interrelationships between ampere, milliampere, and microampere.

2-16   What is the definition of the volt?

2-17   What is the definition of emf?

2-18   What is voltage-drop?

2-19   What is the difference between emf and voltage-drop?

2-20   Explain the relationship between emf and voltage-drop in a circuit.

2-21   What is a positive ion? A negative ion?

2-22   What purpose does the manganese dioxide in the dry cell of Fig. 2-8 serve?

2-23   Describe the process of polarization that takes place in the dry cell battery.

2-24   Explain how the source of energy in the dry cell battery is used to propel current through the lamp in Fig. 2-7.

2-25   What are the advantages of the mercury cell over the carbon-zinc dry cell.

2-26   Describe the overall discharge action of the lead acid storage cell.

2-27   How many lead acid cells are stacked together to form a 12-V automobile battery?

2-28   Describe the charging action of the lead acid storage cell.

2-29   What is a major advantage of the nickel-cadmium cell over the lead acid storage cell?

2-30   How does the fuel cell work?

2-31   Describe how the thermocouple develops an emf.

2-32   How is emf developed by the photoelectric effect?

2-33   Describe how the piezoelectric effect develops an emf.

2-34   What are the anode and cathode terminals of the electrolytic cell?

2-35   Describe how the electrolytic cell works.

2-36   What are the differences between ion current and electron current?

2-37   What is a dynamo?

the nature of
resistance

3

In this chapter the concepts of resistance, conductance, and Ohm's law are explained. Included in the explanations is the part played by several other factors affecting the resistance of materials. Commercial resistors, and the manner in which their values are coded, are given special treatment. Also considered is the effect of temperature on the resistance of materials commonly used in electric and electronic circuits.

3-1 AN EXPLANATION OF RESISTANCE

In this section you will learn about the opposition offered to mobile electrons in copper and other materials used in electric circuits.

Recall that the outer-shell electrons in copper are relatively free to migrate from the outer shell of one copper atom to the outer shell of a neighboring copper atom within the conductor. You learned that if no external electric field is applied, such activity is termed *random motion* and results in no overall direction to the movement of the mobile electrons. When an electric potential is introduced, the random motion changes into an electron drift. The negative terminal of the emf repels the mobile electrons, and the positive side of the emf attracts them, which establishes the direction of the electron drift. This was defined as *electron current.*

Because the explanation remained simple at that time, little detail was given about what the drifting electrons undergo while meandering toward the positive terminal of the applied emf. As the mobile electrons migrate toward the positive side of the emf source, they are accelerated by the forces of attraction (from the positive terminal) and repulsion (from the negative terminal) of the emf. But opposition is also offered to the electron drift. The mobile electrons, while undergoing their drift action, frequently collide with the atoms situated within the structure of the metal. As you would expect, each collision tends to slow down (and in some cases even stop) the drift action of the free electrons. Because of this, they lose much of their *energy of lateral motion* (which is *kinetic* energy) that they had recently acquired from the propelling force of the emf. The "lost" energy is transferred from the electrons to the atoms in the copper structure in the form of *heat.* Therefore, the free electrons must acquire an additional quantity of kinetic energy from the emf source if they are to continue their flow toward the positive terminal of the emf. The process of free electrons alternately acquiring and losing their energy of lateral motion continues throughout the time that the emf is connected to the circuit. It is seen that a portion of the energy obtained from the emf is converted into heat within the copper because of the opposition offered to the mobile electrons by the collisions just described.

Although this explanation was given in terms of a copper conductor, the same experiences are encountered in any material in which electrons are made to drift.

An important characteristic of the opposition to electron drift is that it causes some of the energy derived from the emf source to be converted into heat in the conductor. While this is desirable in certain types of circuits, such as electric heaters, it is generally undesirable in other kinds of electric circuits. Heat energy is dissipated in the surroundings of the circuit and serves no useful purpose in most electric circuits. This is one of the major reasons why copper is used widely in electric circuits — it offers less opposition to the flow of electrons than most other materials. In actual practice, allowances must be made in the design of the circuit to ensure that the circuit will not be damaged by the heat which will develop from the flow of current. Chap. 4 will show ways of dealing with this concern.

Certain materials offer much more opposition to electron flow than others. Resistors are manufactured from materials that present high opposition to electron flow, and they are used in electric circuits to limit current. Both these concerns will be dealt with in the following sections.

3-2 THE DEFINITION OF RESISTANCE

In this section you will learn about:
· *The definition of resistance*
· *The meaning of the term* load
· *How the value of resistance is calculated*

Resistance is the third basic quantity in electricity (the other two are current and voltage). *Resistance* can be defined as the opposition to current flow. The defining formula for resistance is

$$R = \frac{V}{I}$$ (3-1)

where R = resistance in ohms (Ω)
 V = voltage in volts (V)
 I = current in amperes (A)

Now consider several illustrations to see how this important relationship can be used:

Illustration A

The voltage across a load* is 18 V, and the current flowing through it is 2 A. The resistance is

$$R = \frac{V}{I} = \frac{18 \text{ V}}{2 \text{ A}} = 9 \ \Omega$$

Illustration B

A load has 6 V across it when 3 A is flowing through it. The resistance is

$$R = \frac{V}{I} = \frac{6 \text{ V}}{3 \text{ A}} = 2 \ \Omega$$

Illustration C

The load is an electric clothes dryer. It draws 10 A of current, and the voltage across it is 220 V. The resistance of the dryer is

$$R = \frac{V}{I} = \frac{220 \text{ V}}{10 \text{ A}} = 22 \ \Omega$$

Illustration D

A light bulb has 120 V across it when 0.5 A of current is flowing through it. Its resistance at that time is

$$R = \frac{V}{I} = \frac{120 \text{ V}}{0.5 \text{ A}} = 240 \ \Omega$$

---

* A *load* is the name given to any device connected across the energy source (such as a battery). Common loads are light bulbs, electric motors, etc. The current flows through the load, where some of the electric energy is converted into heat.

3-3 OHM'S LAW

In this section you will learn:
* *What Ohm's law is*
* *The graphical representation of Ohm's law*
* *Linear volt-ampere characteristics*
* *Linear resistance*

A mathematical relationship between current, voltage, and resistance was found to exist by George Simon Ohm in 1846. This relationship is one of the most important ones in electricity, and it was named *Ohm's law* in his honor. He found that when the resistance is held constant in a circuit, the voltage and current are directly proportional. This means, for example, that doubling the voltage doubles the current, and halving the voltage halves the current.

Recall that resistance was defined earlier as the opposition to current flow. Recall that resistance can also be defined mathematically as the ratio of the voltage to the current. This is expressed as

$$R = \frac{V}{I}$$

Looking at the formula, you can see that the V/I ratio is constant as long as R does not change its value. You can also see that the converse is true: R will be constant as long as the V/I ratio remains constant, which means V and I are proportional when the resistance is constant.

A Graphical Explanation of Ohm's Law

The proportional relationship between the current and voltage when the resistance is constant can be illustrated graphically. Look at Fig. 3-1, for it will be utilized in the discussion that follows.

Each point on a graph like the one shown in Fig. 3-1 is determined by the value of voltage and the value of current associated with it. Point X, for example, is the condition where $V = 4$ V and $I = 1$ A, and

$$R = \frac{V}{I} = \frac{4}{1} = 4 \ \Omega$$

And point Y is the condition where $V = 8$ V and $I = 2$ A:

$$R = \frac{V}{I} = \frac{8}{2} = 4 \ \Omega$$

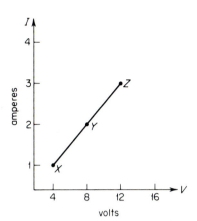

Fig. 3-1   Graphical illustration of Ohm's law.

Point Z is the condition where $V = 12$ V and $I = 3$ A:

$$R = \frac{V}{I} = \frac{12}{3} = 4 \ \Omega$$

Note that the resistance value is the same in each case.

You should observe that the line drawn through the three points is straight. A straight line is also called a *linear* line. This graph, shown in Fig. 3-1, is the *volt-ampere characteristic* of a constant 4-Ω resistance. Since the resistance does not change in value (always 4 Ω in this example), the volt-ampere characteristic is linear. This means that the V/I ratio remains the same for different values of voltage and current when the resistance is fixed.

A resistance whose value remains fixed is a *linear resistance.* Generally one assumes that the resistance in electric circuits is linear, unless special comments are made about it.

3-4   EXPRESSING OHM'S LAW IN THREE WAYS

In this section you will learn about the three ways that Ohm's law can be expressed and used for circuit computations.

Ohm's law was expressed in the preceding section in the following manner:

$$R = \frac{V}{I} \tag{3-1}$$

where R = resistance, Ω
$\quad\quad\quad V$ = voltage, V
$\quad\quad\quad I$ = current, A

As in any mathematical relationship, the factors can be transposed so that the equation can be expressed in terms of any one of the variables. In this way one can solve for resistance as shown in Eq. (3-1), for current by using Eq. (3-2), and for voltage by using Eq. (3-3). In actual practice, one can solve for the third quantity when the remaining two are known.

The Ohm's law relationship for computing the value of current is

$$I = \frac{V}{R} \qquad\qquad\qquad\text{(3-2)}$$

And the Ohm's law relationship for calculating the value of voltage is

$$V = IR \qquad\qquad\qquad\text{(3-3)}$$

With the three equations above, you can calculate the value of the unknown circuit quantity when the other two are known.

Illustration A

A circuit of 2000 Ω has a source emf of 400 V. The circuit current is

$$I = \frac{V}{R} = \frac{400}{2000}$$

$$= 0.2 \text{ A}$$

Illustration B

A circuit has 60 Ω of resistance and a current of 5 A. The circuit voltage is

$$V = IR = 5 \times 60$$
$$= 300 \text{ V}$$

Using Prefix Values When Calculating with Ohm's Law

When Ohm's law is used, the basic units of ohms, volts, and amperes are utilized. If any of these quantities is in one of the other units (such as milliamperes, microamperes, kilohms, megohms, or kilovolts), it must be converted back to the basic units before it can be used in the

Ohm's law equation. For review purposes, the commonly used prefixes are listed here:

$$mA = (10)^{-3} A = milliamperes$$
$$\mu A = (10)^{-6} A = microamperes$$
$$k\Omega = (10)^3 \Omega = kilohms$$
$$M\Omega = (10)^6 \Omega = megohms$$
$$kV = (10)^3 V = kilovolts$$

Illustration C

A circuit with a source emf of 800 V has a current of 20 mA. First the quantity 20 mA must be converted to A, which is 0.020 A. Then it is found that the resistance of the circuit is

$$R = \frac{V}{I} = \frac{800}{0.020}$$
$$= 40,000 \ \Omega$$

This answer can be conveniently expressed as 40 kΩ.

Illustration D

A circuit has 50 kΩ of resistance and a source emf of 25 V. The resistance value must be expressed as 50,000 Ω, or 50(10)^3 Ω. The circuit current is then computed to be

$$I = \frac{V}{R} = \frac{25}{50,000}$$
$$= 0.0005 \ A$$

This can be conveniently expressed as 0.5 mA, or 500 μA.

Illustration E

A circuit has a 25-kΩ resistance and a current of 3 A. If the value of resistance is expressed as 25,000 Ω, or 25(10)^3 Ω, the source emf is found to be

$$V = IR = 3 \times 25,000$$
$$= 75,000 \ V$$

This would be most conveniently expressed as 75 kV.

Because of the importance of Ohm's law, you should practice using its three forms with the various prefixes by completing the following problems.

PROBLEMS

3-1 A circuit with a 120-V emf source draws 0.6 A of current. What is the resistance of the circuit?

3-2 A 50-Ω resistor has a voltage-drop of 10 V. What is the value of current flowing through the resistor?

3-3 A 20-Ω resistor is to pass 4 A of current. Find the value of the required source of emf.

3-4 A circuit with a source emf of 9 V is to have a current value limited to 0.03 A. What circuit resistance is required?

3-5 A 400-Ω resistor has a 40-V voltage-drop. What is the value of current flowing through it?

3-6 A 200-Ω resistor has 50 mA of current passing through it. Find the voltage-drop across the resistor.

3-7 An electric range has a source emf of 120 V and draws 6 A of current. What is its resistance?

3-8 A certain heater element has 10 Ω of resistance and a voltage-drop of 120 V. Find the current flowing through the heater.

3-9 Find the voltage-drop produced by 900 μA of current flowing through a 9-kΩ resistance.

3-10 A resistor voltage-drop is 2.4 V, and its current is 0.2 A. What is the ohmic value of the resistor?

3-11 A circuit with 100-Ω resistance is connected to a 220-V source of emf. What is the value of circuit current?

3-12 A circuit having a total resistance of 300 Ω is to have a current of 0.60 A. Find the value of the required source emf.

3-13 A transistor emitter resistor passes 2 mA of current and has a 1.2-V voltage-drop. What is the ohmic value of the emitter resistor?

3-14 A circuit fuse has 0.02-Ω resistance and a voltage-drop of $5(10)^{-4}$ V. What is the value of the current flowing through the fuse?

3-15 A transistor bias network has a bias resistor of 10 kΩ, and the current passing through it is 50 μA. What is the voltage-drop across the resistor?

3-16 A transistor collector resistor passes 1.6 mA of current, and its voltage-drop is 8 V. Find the ohmic value of the collector resistor.

3-17 A 25-kΩ resistor is connected to a 0.125-V emf source. What is the value of the current flowing through it?

3-18 A transistor amplifier has a collector current of 4 mA passing through a 1.2-kΩ collector load resistor. What is the voltage-drop across this collector load resistor?

3-19 The input signal resistor of a transistor amplifier develops a voltage-drop of $20(10)^{-3}$ V and a current of 5 μA. Find the ohmic value of the input resistance.

3-20 A 2-MΩ resistor is connected to a $500(10)^{-3}$-V source of emf. Find the value of current flowing through it.

3-21 A coil in the collector circuit of a transistor power amplifier has a resistance of 1.5 Ω, and the collector current passing through it is 3 mA. What is the voltage-drop across the coil?

3-22 A certain resistor draws 40 mA of current when connected to a 20-kV emf source. Find the ohmic value of the resistor.

3-23 Assume the operating coil of a certain relay has an energizing current of 2 mA and a resistance of 5 kΩ. What is the required emf that must be applied for energizing the relay?

3-5 FACTORS AFFECTING RESISTANCE OF MATERIALS

In this section you will learn about four factors that affect the resistance of a material.

It was pointed out in an earlier section that opposition to electron flow was caused in large part by collisions of mobile electrons with the atoms in the structure of the material. The number of such encounters and their overall effect upon electron current flow are determined by four factors:

1 Type of material
2 Length of material
3 Cross-sectional area of the material
4 Temperature of the material

The manner in which the resistance of a material is affected by these four factors is examined in the following sections.

3-6 THE RELATIONSHIP BETWEEN RESISTANCE AND RESISTIVITY

In this section, you will learn about:
· Resistivity
· Determination of resistance of a material by its resistivity, length, and cross-sectional area
· Relationships between resistance and conductance

The type of material (copper, aluminum, etc.) determines the number of free electrons available per unit volume. This is known as the *free-electron density* of the material. As stated earlier, copper is one of the choice materials for use as a conductor because it is among the more economical materials with a relatively high level of free-electron density. On the other hand, materials having low free-electron densities are used as insulators. The free-electron density is a major basis for the classification of materials as insulators, semiconductors, and conductors.

Because various materials of given length and cross-sectional area possess different amounts of mobile electrons available for drift at a fixed temperature, some basis of comparison is needed. The basis used is called *resistivity*, or *specific resistance* (and its symbol is ρ, which is the Greek letter rho). The *resistivity* of a material may be defined as the opposition to electron drift per unit length and cross section at a fixed temperature of 20°C. The resistivities of several materials are shown in Table 3-1, which you may use as a reference for several of the problems that follow. Notice that the unit length is the foot, the circular mil* is the unit cross-sectional area, and the reference temperature is 20°C.

Table   3-1

Material	Resistivity ρ, $\Omega/$(cmil)(ft) at 20°C
Copper (annealed)	10.37
Silver	9.9
Aluminum	17.0
Tungsten	33
Manganin	265
Nickel	47
Iron (commercial)	75
Iron (pure)	58
Nichrome I	60
Nichrome II	660

In addition to its resistivity, the resistance of a material increases with the length of that material, as there are a greater total number of collisions between the mobile electrons and atoms in longer lengths of the wire. On the other hand, the resistance is less with larger cross-sectional areas because a greater number of mobile electrons are involved in the drift activity. Temperature also affects the resistance of a

---

* The unit cross-sectional area is the circular mil (cmil). cmil = d^2 where d is the diameter of the wire in thousandths of an inch.

material and this is examined in Section 3-9. The resistance of a material as determined by the above three factors can be calculated from

$$R = \frac{\rho L}{A} \tag{3-4}$$

where R = resistance, Ω
ρ = resistivity, $\Omega/(\text{cmil})(\text{ft})$ at 20°C
L = length, ft
A = circular mil = (diameter in mils)²

Conductance (for which we use the symbol G) can be defined as the ease with which free electrons can be made to flow in a material. You should notice that conductance and resistance have an inverse relationship to one another. Increasing the length of the material and increasing its temperature each results in a corresponding increase in the number of collisions encountered by the mobile electrons, which reduces the conductance. On the other hand, increasing the cross-sectional area of the material permits a greater number of mobile electrons to be available, which results in an increase in its conductance. Therefore we see that conductance varies directly with the cross-sectional area of the material, inversely with its length, and inversely with its resistivity. The relationship between conductance and resistance is

$$G = \frac{1}{R} \tag{3-5}$$

where G = conductance, mhos
R = resistance, Ω

If Eq. (3-4) is substituted for R in Eq. (3-5), with rearranging,

$$G = \frac{1}{\rho L/A} = \frac{A}{\rho L} \tag{3-6}$$

Illustration A

The specific resistance of aluminum is 17. The resistance of a 2000-ft length of aluminum wire with a 51-mil diameter is

$$R = \frac{\rho L}{A} = \frac{17 \times 2000}{(51)^2}$$
$$= 13.07 \ \Omega$$

Illustration B

The conductance of the aluminum wire described in the preceding illustration is

$$G = \frac{1}{R} = \frac{1}{13.07}$$
$$= 0.0765 \text{ mho}$$

And computing the conductance by use of Eq. (3-6) for illustrative purposes, you get

$$G = \frac{A}{\rho L} = \frac{(51)^2}{17 \times 2000}$$
$$= 0.0765 \text{ mho}$$

Therefore it is shown that Eqs. (3-5) and (3-6) are equivalent.

PROBLEMS

3-24   Find the circular mils of wires having the following diameters in inches
    a) 0.064   b) 0.0253
    c) 0.010   d) 0.0063

3-25   Find the resistance of a 4-ft length of copper (annealed) wire 32 mils in diameter.

3-26   Find the resistance of a 2-ft length of manganin wire 64 mils in diameter.

3-27   Find the resistance of a 3-in length of 40-mil-diameter tungsten wire.

3-28   Find the resistance of a 4-ft length of 32-mil-diameter silver wire.

3-29   Find the resistance of an 18-ft length of 25.3-mil-diameter aluminum wire.

3-30   A silver wire has a resistance of 0.05 Ω and is 30 mils in diameter. Find the length of the wire.

3-31   A 20.1-mil iron (pure) wire has a resistance of 1 Ω. Find the length of that wire.

3-32   What is the resistance of 1.2 mi of 25.3-mil-diameter copper wire?

3-33   Find the conductance of the wire considered in Probs.:
    a) 3-25   b) 3-26
    c) 3-27   d) 3-28

3-7 THE AMERICAN WIRE GAGE

In this section you will learn about the gage numbers of commercially available wire and some of the common gage numbers.

It is theoretically possible to manufacture wires ranging in diameter from 1 cmil up to some very large value, in steps of 1 cmil. This is not done in actual practice for pragmatic reasons. Only those sizes used in the various electric and electronics circuits are made available on a commercial basis. Therefore wires are made in certain standard sizes, which are identified by *gage numbers.* The American Wire Gage system (also known as the AWG system) appears to be most widely used, although other systems are used also. Table 3-2 shows the diameter in mils and unit resistance (Ω/1000 ft at 25°C) for several gages of annealed copper wire most commonly found in electric and electronics circuits.

Table 3-2 can be used in calculating the resistance of annealed copper wire of various gage sizes and lengths with the following formula:

$$R = \frac{L}{1000} \times R_{gn} \qquad \text{(3-7)}$$

where L = length of wire, ft
R_{gn} = Resistance of 1000 ft at 25°C of annealed copper wire of that gage (extracted from Table 3-2).

Table   3-2   **Standard Annealed Copper Wire AWG and Resistance**

Gage Number	Diameter, mils	Resistance, Ω/1000 ft at 25°C
4	204.0	0.253
6	162.0	0.403
12	81.0	1.62
14	64.0	2.58
16	51.0	4.09
18	40.0	6.51
20	32.0	10.4
22	25.3	16.5
24	20.1	26.2
26	15.9	41.6
28	12.6	66.2
30	10.0	105.0
32	8.0	167.0
34	0.3	266.0

Table   3-3   Common Gage Numbers

Gage	Use
4	Entrance wire for 100-A service
6	Entrance wire for electric ranges
12	Wiring for common house outlets
20–22	Common hookup wire for radios, television, etc.

The approximate gage numbers of some wires in common application are given in Table 3-3. Note that the smaller gage numbers correspond to the larger cross-sectional areas.

Illustration A

A No. 22 annealed copper wire of 500 ft at 25°C has a resistance of

$$R = \frac{L}{1000} \times R_{gn} = \frac{500}{1000} \times 16.5$$
$$= 8.25 \ \Omega$$

Illustration B

A No. 6 annealed copper wire of 2400 ft at 25°C has a resistance of

$$R = \frac{L}{1000} \times R_{gn} = \frac{2400}{1000} \times 0.403$$
$$= 0.967 \ \Omega$$

Table 3-2 can also be utilized in determining the cross-sectional area of wires where their sizes are given in gage number; then the resistance can be computed from Eq. (3-4).

Illustration C

A No. 22 aluminum wire of 1200-ft length is found from Table 3-2 to have a diameter of 25.3 mils and from Table 3-1 a resistivity of 17. Therefore,

$$R = \frac{\rho L}{A} = \frac{17 \times 1200}{(25.3)^2}$$
$$= 31.87 \ \Omega$$

3-8   RESISTORS AND THE COLOR CODE

In this section you will learn about:
• Three types of resistors

· *The EIA resistor color code*
· *The standard resistor values*

Two kinds of material (carbon composition and metal) are used in the construction of three types of resistors. Consider how the three types of resistors are made.

Carbon Composition Resistors

Carbon (or graphite) granules, bound by a binding material, are usually made into rods. The rods are then cut into short segments, which make up the carbon composition resistor. The specific resistance of carbon and graphite is very high, making it possible to manufacture high-ohmic-value resistors with relatively small amounts of material. Composition resistors are generally less expensive than metal ones, and the commercial values commonly range from 5 Ω to 10 MΩ. The carbon composition type is used to a great extent in low-power work.

Wire-wound Resistors

The metal resistor is customarily wire-wound. The wire is made of an alloy of several elements. It is wound on an insulating frame, which permits the proper length of alloy wire to be used for a given resistance value in the smallest dimension. The entire unit, if designed for high-power work, is sometimes dipped into enamel or porcelain and then baked. Some low-power wire-wound resistors are covered with fiber. The metal type is often used where a high degree of ohmic accuracy is desired (precision resistors) or in those applications where high-power dissipation is encountered. Accuracy within 1 percent or better is achieved with precision resistors. Resistor power ratings up to about 2 W* are obtainable from both the carbon and wire-wound types. The wire-wound variety can be manufactured with power ratings of over 50 W.

Metal-film Resistors

This kind of resistor is manufactured by spraying a relatively thin layer of metal on a glass rod. They are usually highly accurate in ohmic value (precision resistors) and remain stable in value.

---

* W is the symbol for watts, which is discussed in Chap. 4.

The EIA Resistor Color Code

Some resistors have their ohmic value and tolerance coded onto the body of the resistor. A standardized code, called the *EIA resistor color code*, is used in such cases (EIA is the abbreviation for Electronics Industry Association). Table 3-4 lists the values of the code. You should get to know these values since they are commonly used.

Table   3-4   EIA Resistor Color Code

Color	Band 1 (First Significant Figure)	Band 2 (Second Significant Figure)	Band 3 (Multiplier)	Band 4 (Tolerance, percent)
Black	0	0	$\times 10^0$	
Brown	1	1	$\times 10^1$	
Red	2	2	$\times 10^2$	
Orange	3	3	$\times 10^3$	
Yellow	4	4	$\times 10^4$	
Green	5	5	$\times 10^5$	
Blue	6	6	$\times 10^6$	
Purple	7	7	$\times 10^7$	
Gray	8	8	$\times 10^8$	
White	9	9	$\times 10^9$	
None				20
Silver				10
Gold				5

How code colors are placed on the resistor is shown in Fig. 3-2a. Take a moment and familiarize yourself with their placement.

From Fig. 3-2a you should notice that color band 1 is closest to the edge of the resistor, whereas band 4 is located nearest the center. Bands 1 and 2 indicate the two significant figures of the resistor value, band 3 is the multiplier ($\times 10^x$), and band 4 indicates the tolerance in percentage of the color code value. Resistance values of only two significant figures can be stated with the color code. Other resistors, of more precise values, have their values stamped on their bodies. You should notice that a missing fourth band indicates that the resistance value is correct within ±20 percent of the coded value. The electrical symbol

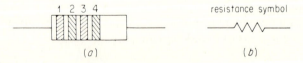

1 2 3 4

resistance symbol

(*a*)   (*b*)

Fig. 3-2 (*a*) **EIA color-coded resistor;** (*b*) **resistance symbol.**

for resistance is shown in Fig. 3-2*b* and it is used in circuit diagrams throughout this book.

Illustration

The color code of a resistor (reading from band 1 through band 4) is yellow, purple, yellow, and silver. Using Table 3-4, you find that band 1 yellow = 4, band 2 purple = 7, band 3 yellow = 10^4, and band 4 silver = 10 percent tolerance, which results in a value of $47(10)^4\ \Omega(\pm10$ percent). This can be stated as 470 kΩ ($\pm$ 10 percent). Therefore, this resistor can be any value between 433 kΩ (470 kΩ − 47 kΩ) and 517 kΩ (470 kΩ + 47 kΩ) and be within its tolerance range.

Standard Resistor Values

Resistors are made available commercially in certain ohmic values, which are displayed in Table 3-5. You should note that the greatest

Table   3-5   Standard Resistor Values

5 Percent Tolerance	10 Percent Tolerance	20 Percent Tolerance
10	10	10
11		
12	12	
13		
15	15	15
16		
18	18	
20		
22	22	22
24		
27	27	
30		
33	33	33
36		
39	39	
43		
47	47	47
51		
56	56	
62		
68	68	68
75		
82	82	
91		

number of values is provided in the 5 percent tolerance range, and the least number of values is in the 20 percent range.

3-9 TEMPERATURE EFFECTS ON RESISTANCE

In this section you will learn about:
* *The temperature coefficient of materials*
* *How to determine resistance values at different temperatures*

Because electric conductors usually undergo relatively small temperature changes during the time they are passing electron current, the change in resistance associated with the rise in temperature is small and can often be ignored. But there are instances when, because of either the type of material or the great rise in temperature encountered, the change in resistance value must be considered. For that reason, the temperature effects on the resistance of materials used in electricity and electronics will be examined next.

The resistance of insulators and semiconductors decreases with increases in their temperature. It is believed that temperature rises in these materials result in an increase in the kinetic energy of the outer-shell orbital electrons; this additional energy enables more of them to break away from their nuclei. Materials that display decreased resistance with increased temperature are said to have *negative temperature coefficients.*

In metals commonly used as conductors (such as copper), temperature increases seem to decrease the kinetic energy of the mobile electrons. Because of the increased number of collisions encountered by these electrons, their mean free paths between collisions are reduced. This makes it more difficult for the electron to remain free of the influence of a nucleus. The result is an increase in resistance. Materials

Table 3-6

Material	Temperature Coefficient (α) at 20°C
Aluminum	$3.9(10^{-3})$
Brass	$2(10^{-3})$
Carbon	$-5(10^{-4})$ to $-3(10^{-3})$
Copper	$3.9(10^{-3})$
Iron	$5(10^{-3})$
Manganin	$6(10^{-6})$
Nickel	$6(10^{-3})$
Tungsten	$5(10^{-3})$

that display increased resistance with rises in temperature are said to have *positive temperature coefficients.*

Now the *temperature coefficient* can be defined as the resistance change of the material per ohm per degree Celsius temperature change. The Greek letter alpha (α) is used to designate this term.

Take a moment to look over Table 3-6, which lists the temperature coefficients of several materials that are important in electricity and electronics.

If the change in temperature of a material is known, its change in resistance can be found from

$$\Delta R^* = R_0\,\alpha\,(t_2 - 20°C) = R_0\alpha\Delta t \qquad \textbf{(3-8)}$$

where ΔR^* = change in resistance
R_0 = resistance at 20°C
α = temperature coefficient
t_2 = the increased temperature in °C
Δt = change in temperature (from 20°C to new temperature)

Now that the change in resistance has been calculated, the new ("hot") resistance is found by adding it to the original resistance,

$$R_h = R_0 + \Delta R \qquad \textbf{(3-9)}$$

where R_h is the "hot" resistance. We can combine those two relationships into one equation. Since $R_h = R_0 + \Delta R$, then

$$R_h = R_0 + R_0\alpha\Delta t$$

and factoring out R_0,

$$R_h = R_0(1 + \Delta t) \qquad \textbf{(3-10)}$$

Illustration

A tungsten filament ($\alpha = 0.005$ from Table 3-6) has a resistance of 3 Ω at 20°C, and after undergoing a temperature increase to 1200°C, its hot resistance is

$$R_h = R_0(1 + \alpha\Delta t) = 3(1 + 0.005 \times 1180)$$
$$= 20.7\ \Omega$$

---

* Notice that the Greek letter delta (Δ) is used to designate "change."

PROBLEMS

Note   Assume the temperature is 25°C in Probs. 3-34 through 3-37.

3-34   Find the resistance of 4000 ft of No. 22 copper wire.

3-35   Find the resistance of 3500 ft of No. 4 copper wire.

3-36   Find the resistance of 2800 ft of No. 34 copper wire.

3-37   Find the resistance of 8000 ft of No. 20 copper wire.

3-38   Find the resistance of a 4-ft length of No. 4 manganin wire.

3-39   Find the resistance of a 20-ft length of No. 12 tungsten wire.

3-40   Find the resistance of a 6-in length of No. 22 silver wire.

3-41   Find the resistance of a 40-ft length of No. 20 aluminum wire.

3-42   A resistor is coded in the following manner: band 1 = brown, band 2 = black, band 3 = black, and band 4 = no color. State the ohmic value and tolerance of the resistor.

3-43   A resistor is coded in the following manner: band 1 = yellow, band 2 = purple, band 3 = orange, and band 4 = gold. State the ohmic value and tolerance of the resistor.

3-44   A resistor is coded in the following manner: band 1 = green, band 2 = blue, band 3 = red, and band 4 = silver. State the ohmic value and tolerance of the resistor.

3-45   A resistor is coded in the following manner: band 1 = brown, band 2 = green, band 3 = yellow, and band 4 = no color. State the ohmic value and tolerance of the resistor.

3-46   A resistor is coded in the following manner: band 1 = orange, band 2 = orange, band 3 = orange, and band 4 = gold. State the ohmic value and tolerance of the resistor.

3-47   An aluminum wire has a resistance of 0.02 Ω at 20°C. Find its resistance at 80°C.

3-48   A tungsten wire has a resistance of 1.5 Ω at 20°C. Find its resistance at 1000°C.

3-49   The resistance of a brass wire is 3 Ω at 20°C, and it is heated to 400°C. What is its hot resistance?

3-50   A nickel wire has a resistance of 0.8 Ω at 20°C. Find its resistance when it is heated to 800°C.

3-51   The resistance of a manganin wire is 5 Ω at 20°C, and it is heated to 1400°C. What is its hot resistance?

3-52   A copper wire has a resistance of 0.05 Ω at 20°C and is heated to 300°C. Find its hot resistance.

3-53   An iron wire has a resistance of 2.4 Ω at 20°C, and it is heated to 500°C. Find its hot resistance.

3-54   Find the resistance of 100 ft of No. 22 copper wire at 60°C.

3-55   To what temperature must a brass conductor be raised so as to increase its resistance from 2 Ω at 20°C to 2.1 Ω?

3-56   A certain carbon resistor whose temperature coefficient is $-5(10)^{-4}$ has a resistance of 47 kΩ at 20°C. What is its resistance at 60°C?

3-57   A circuit element passes 4 A of current when cold and 1.5 A at its maximum operating temperature. The source emf is 12 V. Find:
a) the cold resistance   b) the hot resistance

3-58   A nickel material has a resistance of 0.5 Ω at 20°C and 1.00 Ω at its hottest temperature. What is the hot temperature?

3-59   A circuit element passes 2 A of current when cold and 0.5 A at its maximum operating temperature. The source emf is 10 V. What is the change in resistance?

3-60   The temperature of a tungsten heating element rises from 20°C to 2400°C. Its original resistance is 2 Ω. What is its hot resistance?

QUESTIONS

3-1   What is the definition of resistance?

3-2   What is the relationship between the mobile electrons and resistance?

3-3   How do the mobile electrons acquire kinetic energy?

3-4   What is a resistor?

3-5   What is the definition of conductance?

3-6   What is the relationship between conductance and resistance?

3-7   What are four factors that influence the resistance of a material?

3-8   What is the definition of resistivity?

3-9   What is the unit circular mil?

3-10   What is the relationship between the gage number of a wire and its diameter?

3-11   Express Ohm's law in terms of current.

3-12   Express Ohm's law in terms of voltage.

3-13   Express Ohm's law in terms of resistance.

3-14   What is the unit that can be used when expressing resistance in thousands of ohms?

3-15   What is the unit that can be used in expressing resistance in millions of ohms?

3-16   What is the unit for expressing current in thousandths of an ampere?

3-17   What is the unit for expressing current in millionths of an ampere?

3-18   What is the definition of linear resistance?

3-19   What is a volt-ampere characteristic of a linear resistance?

3-20   What is the x axis in a graph?

3-21   What is the y axis in a graph?

3-22   Where is the origin of a set of axes located in a graph?

3-23   What is the definition of a nonlinear resistance?

3-24   What kind of material has a positive temperature coefficient?

3-25   What kind of material has a negative temperature coefficient?

3-26   How are composition resistors made?

3-27   What types of resistors have their values stamped on their bodies?

3-28   What band denotes the tolerance range of an EIA color-coded resistor?

3-29   How are metal-film resistors made?

3-30   What is the definition of temperature coefficient?

energy and work
4

The basic concepts of energy, work, and power are dealt with in this chapter in preparation for their use in future chapters. The common units and how they are used are studied. A separate section is devoted to examining the power ratings of commercial resistors. If you have learned about energy and work in a previous or concurrent physics course, this chapter may be skipped and you may proceed to Chap. 5.

4-1 ENERGY AND WORK

In this section you will learn about the behavior of a simple electric circuit in terms of energy conversion.

Energy was defined in Chap. 1 as the ability to do work.

Work may be defined as that quantity that an agent does on a body when it exerts a force on it through a distance in the direction of that force.

The symbol for work used in this book is W.

Refer to Fig. 4-1, which is a *schematic* diagram of a simple electric circuit. Reference is made to this circuit in describing how work is performed in an electric circuit.

The circuit in Fig. 4-1 is a single-path electric circuit, called a *series circuit.* The next chapter goes into more detail about the characteristics of such a circuit. The present concern, however, involves the performance of work.

The source of energy in Fig. 4-1 is the battery V_b. Recall from Chap. 2 that a battery is a source of chemical energy, which is converted into a

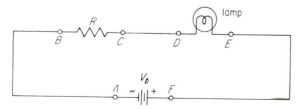

Fig. 4-1 A simple electric circuit.

65

potential difference by the accumulation of extra electrons on one terminal (negative) and a corresponding shortage of electrons on the other terminal (positive). This potential energy (emf) can be used in propelling mobile electrons through the circuit from point A toward point F. The resistor R, as described in Chap. 3, offers an opposition to electron drift, as does the resistance contained within the lamp. Therefore the amount of electron flow that results is that propelled by the emf and limited by the resistance of the circuit. The resistance results from the frequent collisions of mobile electrons within the atoms in the structure of the resistor, wiring, and lamp. Some of the kinetic energy of the free electrons is converted into heat. Under normal circumstances the heat energy is dissipated in the atmosphere surrounding the circuit.

A considerable amount of the energy imparted to the mobile electrons by the battery V_b is transformed into heat within the resistor R, the light bulb, and the wiring. Some of the energy, in this circuit, is also transformed into light energy in the bulb. The work done in the circuit of Fig. 4-1 can be identified as the result of the conversion of some battery energy into kinetic energy and then into:

1   heat energy within the resistor, light bulb, and wiring
2   light energy in the bulb

In summary, then, it is clear that the source of emf serves as the source of energy, and the energy is transformed within the electric circuit. *The result of the process of transforming energy is work.*

4-2 ENERGY AND WORK UNITS

In this section you will learn about:
* *The definition of joule*
* *The relationship between joule and erg*

The most important energy unit is the joule, and it may be defined in the following way:

The joule (J) is considered the basic unit of electric energy or work and is defined as the energy required to move a body one meter against an opposing force of one newton.

A much smaller energy or work unit that is sometimes used in electricity and electronics is the *erg,* and

$$1 \text{ J} = (10)^7 \text{ ergs}$$

4-3   THE EFFICIENCY FORMULA

In this section you will learn about circuit efficiency and how it can be determined.

The law of conservation of energy states that energy cannot be created or destroyed. As was pointed out in a preceding section, when work is performed, there is a transformation of energy from one form into a second form. During the process of transforming energy into the desired form, a certain amount of the input energy is converted into an unusable (and therefore undesirable) form. This is indicated in the brief description of the energy transformation occurring in the electric circuit of Fig. 4-1. The electric energy converted into heat in the resistor R, the wire, and the light bulb is a transformation of energy into an unusable form. The conversion of electric energy into light energy in the bulb is the actual work performance of this circuit (assuming its objective is to light the bulb).

In electric circuits much of the input energy not used in the actual work done by the circuit for its output is converted into circuit heat. This heat is generally dissipated into the surrounding atmosphere. Special precautions must be taken when a substantial amount of heat is developed, and this topic is taken up in the following section.

The ability of a circuit (like any energy-converting device) to convert its input energy into useful output energy can be described in terms of efficiency.

Efficiency is the ratio of useful energy output to the entire energy input.

In equation form,

$$\eta = \frac{W_o}{W_i}$$

where η (eta) = efficiency
W_o = useful output energy
W_i = energy input

Efficiency is generally expressed as a percentage:

$$\eta(\%) = \frac{W_o}{W_i}(100) \qquad \textbf{(4-1)}$$

Illustration

A circuit which has a useful output energy of 4 J for each 20 J of input energy has an efficiency of

$$\eta(\%) = \frac{W_o}{W_i}(100) = \frac{4}{20}(100)$$
$$= 20 \text{ percent}$$

4-4 POWER AND LOAD

In this section you will learn:
- *The definition of the watt*
- *The power equation*
- *More about the concept of load*

As was pointed out several times in previous sections, energy is the ability to do work, and the major energy unit in electricity and electronics is the joule. Also recall that voltage is the ratio of joules divided by coulombs (J/C). The actual amount of joules used will vary with the number of coulombs moved. And the number of coulombs moved per second (C/s) is the current in amperes. Putting all this together, then, you can see that if you consider the number of joules per coulomb that is available, and how many coulombs are moved in one second, you can determine the *rate* at which energy actually is used in that circuit. The relationship can be expressed as

$$\frac{J}{s} = \frac{J}{C} \times \frac{C}{s}$$

where J = joules
  s = seconds
  C = coulombs

The rate of doing work is power (given the symbol P) and is given the unit watt.

Therefore,

$$\frac{J}{s} = P$$

where P = power in watts. Also, $J/C = V$, and C/s = current (in amperes). Therefore, the equation becomes

$$P = VI \qquad \text{(4-2)}$$

where P = power, watts (W)
V = voltage, volts (V)
I = current, amperes (A)

Illustration A

A circuit has a source emf of 150 V and a current of 2 A, and the rate at which energy is used is

$$P = VI = 150 \times 2$$
$$= 300 \text{ W}$$

As was pointed out in earlier sections, the energy used in an electric circuit containing pure resistance is actually transformed from electric energy into heat energy. In some cases (such as toasters, irons, heaters, and clothes dryers), the heat energy is used to perform the intended function of the circuit. In most applications, however, the conversion of electric energy to heat is considered a loss if the heat serves no "useful" function in the circuit. So you can see that the term *energy loss* means that the energy was transformed to a form that serves no useful function in that particular circuit. It is important to realize that energy has not been destroyed, but simply rendered unusable in the particular application.

Also, the following prefixes are used when appropriate:

$$\text{kW} = \text{kilowatts } (10^3 \text{ W})$$
$$\text{mW} = \text{milliwatts } (10^{-3} \text{ W})$$
$$\mu\text{W} = \text{microwatts } (10^{-6} \text{ W})$$

Illustration B

A circuit has a 100-V source emf and 500 Ω of resistance. The current can be found from

$$I = \frac{V}{R} = \frac{100}{500} = 0.2 \text{ A}$$

and the power dissipated in that circuit is

$$P = VI = 100 \times 0.2$$
$$= 20 \text{ W}$$

The above result is expressed thus: energy is transformed from electric energy to heat at the rate of 20 J/s.

Load was discussed in an earlier section. Because load is a very important concept that is often misunderstood, it will be useful to describe it further. Load implies work. The work done in a resistive circuit is the flow of mobile electrons within the circuit. The load of a circuit is actually the current. From this, you can see that *a large load means that the circuit passes a great amount of current* and coincides with low circuit resistance; *a light load coincides with a low value of current* and high circuit resistance.

Illustration C

A source emf of 10 V develops a 2-A load under one set of conditions and a 5-A load under a second set. The first, the lighter load, occurs when

$$R_{L_1} = \frac{V}{I_1} = \frac{10}{2} = 5 \ \Omega$$

And the second, the heavier load, occurs when

$$R_{L_2} = \frac{V}{I_2} = \frac{10}{5} = 2 \ \Omega$$

4-5   THREE METHODS FOR DETERMINING POWER

In this section you will learn about the three ways in which the power dissipation of a circuit can be computed.

Recall that in Sec. 4-4 it was found that the power dissipated in a resistive network is equal to the product of the voltage and current:

$$P = VI \tag{4-3}$$

There are two other ways of determining the power dissipation in a resistive circuit. From Ohm's law you will recall that $V = IR$. Substituting IR for V in the previous power equation yields

$$P = (IR)I = I^2R \tag{4-4}$$

Equation (4-4) makes it possible to calculate the power dissipation of any resistance without knowing its voltage-drop, as long as the ohmic value of the resistance and the magnitude of the current passing through it are known.

A third equation for calculating the power dissipation is available. Making another kind of substitution, V/R for I, in the original power equation yields

$$P = V \times \frac{V}{R} = \frac{V^2}{R} \qquad \textbf{(4-5)}$$

Equation (4–5) can be used to compute the power dissipation of any resistor without the value of current passing through it being known, provided that the voltage-drop and ohmic value of the resistance are known.

The availability of three equations for computing power dissipation permits great flexibility in the analysis of circuits. As long as two of the three Ohm's law factors are known, one of the three relationships provided [Eqs. (4–3), (4–4), and (4–5)] is sufficient to determine the power dissipation.

Illustration A

The power dissipation of a circuit with a source emf of 25 V and 0.4 A of current is

$$P = VI = 25 \times 0.4$$
$$= 10 \text{ W}$$

Illustration B

The power dissipation of a circuit with a current of 3 A and resistance of 47 Ω is

$$P = I^2R = (3)^2 \times 47$$
$$= 423 \text{ W}$$

Illustration C

The power dissipation of a circuit with a 12-V emf and 10-kΩ resistance is

$$P = \frac{V^2}{R} = \frac{(12)^2}{10,000}$$
$$= 0.0144 \text{ W}$$

4-6 POWER DISSIPATION AND RATING OF CIRCUIT COMPONENTS

In this section you will learn about the safety factor used in choosing resistors and other circuit components.

The power dissipated by a resistor, as was pointed out in several preceding sections, is actually a conversion from electric to heat energy. This brings another matter under consideration. As heat is developed in a resistor, it will be distributed in the surrounding atmosphere. If a resistor gives off as much heat as is developed within it by the current, its temperature will remain fairly constant. On the other hand, if the resistor develops heat more rapidly than it is capable of giving off, its temperature will rise. At some high temperature the material of the resistor begins to melt or burn, thereby destroying the component or at least changing its electrical characteristics. It is logical, then, to search for a method by which the heat-handling capabilities of a resistor can be determined. It has been found from general practice that the physical size of the component is a general indication of how much heat it can dissipate safely: a larger surface area indicates a greater ability to conduct heat from within itself to its surroundings.

Resistors are rated by manufacturers in terms of the wattage they can handle safely. In practice, it is suggested that a *safety factor* of at least 100 percent be used. For example, if it is known that a resistor in a given circuit will dissipate 5 W, it is recommended that a 10- to 20-W resistor be used. In this way, if the component should experience momentary surges of current, its rating will not be exceeded. In general, it is recommended that the power rating of a resistor be somewhere between 2 and 4 times the dissipation rating of the resistor. A large amount of circuit failure can be avoided by observing this rule. Particularly in *pure* resistive circuits, no harm will result from use of a higher-wattage resistor. One drawback in using a resistor with a generous safety factor for the conditions in which it is to be used is its cost and physical size, both of which are usually directly proportional to the wattage rating of the component.

Illustration A

A 10-kΩ resistor whose power dissipation is to not exceed 2 W should be limited to a maximum current of $P = I^2R$. Rearranging to solve for I yields

$$I = \left(\frac{P}{R}\right)^{1/2} = \left[\frac{2}{10(10)^3}\right]^{1/2}$$
$$= 14.14 \text{ mA}$$

Also in accordance with the previous discussion on the safety factor, this resistor should have a power-dissipation rating of at least 4 W (which would be a 100 percent safety factor).

Illustration B

The maximum current expected to flow through a 1-kΩ collector load resistor of a transistor amplifier is 8 mA. A 100 percent safety factor is desired. The wattage of the resistor is

$$P = I^2R = (0.008)^2 \times 1000$$
$$= 64 \text{ mW}$$

In order to have a 100 percent safety factor, this resistor should have a power-dissipation rating of $64 \times 2 = 128$ mW. The nearest power-dissipation rating commercially available is the $\frac{1}{4}$-W (250-mW) resistor, which would provide a safety factor of almost 400 percent. Therefore, a 1-kΩ $\frac{1}{4}$-W resistor is recommended.

Also, the safety factors of other components in electric and electronic circuits are considered in the same manner as expressed above.

PROBLEMS

4-1 How many ergs are equivalent to 1.5 J?

4-2 How many joules are equivalent to $3(10)^8$ ergs?

4-3 Find the power rating of a toaster which has a 120-V source and draws 5 A of current.

4-4 The power rating of a certain light bulb is 60 W. It is used with a 120-V source emf. How much current is drawn by this bulb?

4-5 The power rating of another light bulb is 150 W, and it utilizes a 120-V source of emf. How much current is drawn by this bulb?

4-6 Assume that a soldering iron uses a source emf of 120 V and draws 1.2 A of current. What is its power rating?

4-7 The emitter resistor in a certain transistor amplifier has a current of 5 mA, and its voltage-drop is 1.2 V. What is the power dissipation of the emitter resistor?

4-8 A certain resistor has a voltage-drop of 1 V and passes a current of 0.24 A. What is its power dissipation?

4-9 Assuming commercial carbon resistors with power dissipation ratings of $\frac{1}{4}$, $\frac{1}{2}$, 1, and 2 W are available, what rating should be used for the resistor's dissipation of Prob. 4-8 if a power safety factor of at least 100 percent is desired?

4-10   A transistor collector load resistor of 2 kΩ has 4 mA passing through it. What is the power dissipation of the collector load resistor?

4-11   Refer to Prob. 4-7: How many joules of heat energy are produced in the emitter resistor in 1 min?

4-12   How many joules of heat energy are produced in the collector load resistor of Prob. 4-10 in 1 min?

4-13   A 470-Ω resistor is to pass 200 mA of current. What is the power dissipation of the resistor?

4-14   In Prob. 4-13, what is the minimum power dissipation value of the resistor in order to provide a 100 percent safety factor?

4-15   An emitter resistor of 0.25 Ω is to pass 300 mA of current. What is the power dissipation value of the emitter resistor?

4-16   In Prob. 4-15 find the minimum power-dissipation value of the resistor needed to provide a 100 percent safety factor.

4-17   A coil of a transformer has a resistance of 1.2 Ω, and the current passing through that coil is 15 mA. At what rate is heat being dissipated?

4-18   How many joules of electric energy are converted into heat each minute in the coil described in Prob. 4-17?

4-19   A certain motor has a 2-Ω starting resistor and a starting current of 50 A. What is the power dissipation of this resistor?

4-20   In Prob. 4-19, what is the minimum power-dissipation rating for the starting resistor if a 100 percent safety factor is desired?

4-21   How many joules of electric energy are converted into heat energy in the starting resistor of Prob. 4-19 in 1 min?

4-22   What is the maximum current that can be passed through a 10-Ω 10-W resistor without it becoming overheated (assume it begins overheating at its power rating)?

4-23   What is the maximum current allowed through the resistor of Prob. 4-22 if a 100 percent safety factor is desired?

4-24   What is the maximum current that can be passed through a 2-Ω 50-W resistor without it exceeding its power rating?

4-25   What is the maximum current through the resistor of Prob. 4-24 if a 100 percent safety factory is desired?

4-26   What is the maximum emf that can be applied to the resistor in Prob. 4-22 so that it stays within its power rating?

4-27   What is the maximum emf that can be safely applied to the resistor in Prob. 4-24 so that it stays within its power rating?

4-28   Assume the power dissipation of a stove element is 1 kW and its hot resistance is 14 Ω. What is the voltage-drop across the stove element?

4-29 A 3-W bulb has a hot resistance of 75 Ω. What is the voltage-drop across it?

4-30 A 120-V emf source can deliver up to 1.8 kW. What is the minimum resistance value that can be placed across this source of emf?

4-31 A 220-V emf source can deliver up to 4.4 kW. What is the minimum resistance value that can be placed across this emf source?

4-32 Assume that a radio transmitter operates at 50 percent efficiency and has a power output of 100 kW. How much input power is required to operate the transmitter?

4-33 A circuit has an output resistance of 500 Ω and an output voltage of 20 V. What is the circuit load?

QUESTIONS

4-1 What is energy?

4-2 What is work?

4-3 What is the difference between energy and work?

4-4 What is the circuit source of energy called?

4-5 What is a joule of energy?

4-6 Why is it said that heat energy is "lost" in most electric circuits?

4-7 What is the definition of efficiency?

4-8 Efficiency has been expressed as a ratio of power output to power input. Why?

4-9 A certain circuit contains two 1-kΩ resistors. One of these resistors is rated as $\frac{1}{2}$ W, and the other is rated as 2 W. What are the similarities and differences of these two resistors?

4-10 How can power be determined when the current is not known?

4-11 How can the power be determined when the voltage is unknown?

4-12 How can power be determined when the resistance is unknown?

4-13 What is the ratio of joules per coulomb called?

4-14 What is the ratio of coulombs per second called?

4-15 What is the product of the ratios expressed in Questions 4–13 and 4–14 called?

4-16 What does "load" imply?

4-17 What is the load of an electric circuit?

fundamentals of resistive circuits

Part 2

resistive circuits: series and parallel
5

Circuits, in terms of how their components are connected to one another, come in only one of three basic varieties. Two of them (series circuits and parallel circuits) are examined in this chapter, while the third one (series-parallel or combination circuits) is examined in Chap. 6.

In this chapter, the series-circuit principles of current, voltage, and resistance receive early consideration. The series-circuit analysis closes with a treatment of Kirchhoff's series-circuit laws and the basic concepts of power in such circuits.

The last five sections of the chapter are devoted to the analysis of parallel circuits. The parallel-circuit principles of current, voltage, and resistance are presented. This is followed by a treatment of Kirchhoff's parallel-circuit laws and the fundamental power concepts for parallel circuits.

5-1 CURRENT IN A SERIES CIRCUIT

In this section you will learn about:
· The definition of a series circuit
· The series-circuit current law

A *series circuit* is the simplest of the three varieties, and it may be defined as follows:

A series circuit is one in which the mobile electrons have but one path to travel from the negative terminal to the positive terminal of the source emf.

Look at the circuit in Fig. 5-1, which is a series circuit, for it will be used to explain the definition above.

The flow of current in Fig. 5-1 is from the negative side of V_b through each of the resistors that are connected in series with one another and V_b. An examination of this circuit shows that there is only one path for electron flow, which leads to the series-circuit current law:

The current in a series circuit must be the same throughout that circuit.

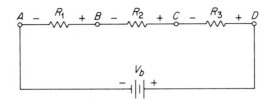

Fig. 5-1   A basic series circuit.

The series-circuit current law, as applied to the circuit of Fig. 5-1, results in the following relationship:

$$I = I_{R_1} = I_{R_2} = I_{R_3}$$

where I = total circuit current
I_{R_1} = current through resistor R_1
I_{R_2} = current through resistor R_2
I_{R_3} = current through resistor R_3

The above relationship holds true for any number of resistors connected in a series circuit;

$$I = I_{R_1} = I_{R_2} = \cdots = I_{R_n} \tag{5-1}$$

where I_{R_n} = current through any resistor R_n in the series circuit

5-2 POTENTIAL AND VOLTAGE-DROPS IN A SERIES CIRCUIT

In this section you will learn about:
· Relationships between voltage-drops and source emf in a series circuit
· The series-circuit voltage law

Recall that the emf is the source of electric energy for a circuit such as shown in Fig. 5-1. Also, the energy provided by V_b will be used by the resistors in the circuit. Common sense indicates that the amount of energy used is limited by the amount of energy available. The energy available is represented by the value of V_b, which is the difference in potential energy per unit charge between the positive and negative terminals, and the energy used is represented by the sum of the voltage-drops. From this originates the series-circuit voltage law:

The sum of the voltage-drops is always equal to the total emf in a series circuit.

In Fig. 5-1,

$$V = V_{R_1} + V_{R_2} + V_{R_3}$$

where V = source emf, V_b
        V_{R_1} = voltage-drop across resistor R_1
        V_{R_2} = voltage-drop across resistor R_2
        V_{R_3} = voltage-drop across resistor R_3

The above relationship can be generalized for any series circuit:

$$V = V_{R_1} + V_{R_2} + \cdots + V_{R_n} \tag{5-2}$$

where V_{R_n} = voltage-drop across resistor R_n in the series circuit

It is interesting to examine the *polarity* of the voltage-drops. Notice, in Fig. 5-1, that the left side of each resistor (R_1, R_2, and R_3) is designated as negative (−) while the right side is positive (+). Recall that the negative side of the source emf is the site of the excess electrons, and it can be viewed as the high potential energy side of the battery (with the positive terminal being its low-energy side). The voltage-drop across a resistor, such as R_1, represents a reduction in the energy made available by the battery. And, as is verified by the series-circuit voltage law [Eq. (5–2)], all the energy will be "used" (that is, converted into heat energy which is then dissipated in the surroundings of the components) by the resistors. In this example, the left side of each resistor is the high-energy side of that component, and its right side is the low-energy side. It is important to see that *the voltage-drop has a polarity opposite to that of the emf.* This point will be elaborated in a later section where Kirchhoff's series-circuit laws are examined.

5-3 RESISTANCE IN A SERIES CIRCUIT

In this section you will learn about:
• The series-circuit resistance law
• Calculating the equivalent resistance of a series circuit

Again the basic series circuit will be utilized in the following discussion. Recall that the total current flows through the entire circuit. This means that each resistance opposes the entire current, which leads to the *series-circuit resistance law:*

The total resistance to current in a series circuit is equal to the sum of resistances in the circuit.

Expressing this mathematically for the circuit in Fig. 5-1 yields

$$R = R_1 + R_2 + R_3$$

where R = total or equivalent resistance of the circuit
R_1 = ohmic value of resistor 1
R_2 = ohmic value of resistor 2
R_3 = ohmic value of resistor 3

Generalizing the above relationship for any series circuit gives

$$R = R_1 + R_2 + \cdots + R_n \qquad \textbf{(5-3)}$$

where R_n = ohmic value of resistor n

5-4 SOME SERIES-CIRCUIT COMPUTATIONS

In this section you will learn how the series-circuit laws for current, voltage, and resistance can be used in conjunction with Ohm's law.

The three series-circuit laws explained in the preceding sections make it possible to utilize Ohm's law in any series resistive circuit. Several illustrations will demonstrate this fact.

Illustration A

The resistors in Fig. 5-1 have the following ohmic values: $R_1 = 20 \ \Omega$, $R_2 = 50 \ \Omega$, and $R_3 = 30 \ \Omega$. When V_b is chosen to be 100 V, then, the equivalent circuit resistance is

$$R = R_1 + R_2 + R_3 = 20 \ \Omega + 50 \ \Omega + 30 \ \Omega$$
$$= 100 \ \Omega$$

Illustration B

If one knows that the equivalent resistance in the preceding illustration is 100 Ω, then the current is

$$I = \frac{V_b}{R} = \frac{100}{100}$$
$$= 1 \ \text{A}$$

and from the series-circuit current law it is clear that

$$I_{R_1} = I_{R_2} = I_{R_3} = 1 \text{ A}$$

Illustration C

With a circuit current of 1 A and resistor values of $R_1 = 20 \ \Omega$, $R_2 = 50 \ \Omega$, and $R_3 = 30 \ \Omega$, the voltage-drop across each can be found in the following way:

$$V_{R_1} = I_{R_1} \times R_1 = 1 \times 20$$
$$= 20 \text{ V}$$
$$V_{R_2} = V_{R_2} \times R_2 = 1 \times 50$$
$$= 50 \text{ V}$$
$$V_{R_3} = V_{R_3} \times R_3 = 1 \times 30$$
$$= 30 \text{ V}$$

In applying the series-circuit voltage law as a check, one finds that the sum of the voltage-drops is

$$V_{R_1} + V_{R_2} + V_{R_3} = 20 + 50 + 30$$
$$= 100 \text{ V}$$

That sum does equal the value of V_b.

5-5 KIRCHHOFF'S SERIES-CIRCUIT LAWS

In this section you will learn about:
• Kirchhoff's voltage law
• Using the voltage law in determining voltages
• Kirchhoff's current law

Recall that it was pointed out earlier that a source emf can be viewed as a voltage-rise (from its positive to negative terminals), and the potentials across resistors are voltage-drops. A statement which indicates the relationship between voltage-rises and voltage-drops is provided by *Kirchhoff's voltage law.* The law states:

The algebraic sum of the voltage-drops and emf in any series loop is equal to zero.

This statement indicates that the energy used (as represented by voltage-drops) is always equal to the energy provided (as represented by the source emf).

Illustration A

Assume that the resistors in the circuit of Fig. 5-1 are $R_1 = 10\ \Omega$, $R_2 = 20\ \Omega$, and $R_3 = 30\ \Omega$. Also assume that $V_b = 120$ V. The circuit current is

$$I = \frac{V_b}{R_1 + R_2 + R_3} = \frac{120}{60}$$
$$= 2\ \text{A}$$

And the voltage-drop across each resistor is

$$V_{R_1} = I \times R_1 = 2 \times 10$$
$$= 20\ \text{V}$$
$$V_{R_2} = I \times R_2 = 2 \times 20$$
$$= 40\ \text{V}$$
$$V_{R_3} = I \times R_3 = 2 \times 30$$
$$= 60\ \text{V}$$

Reviewing the circuit of Fig. 5-1 with regard to the polarities of the voltage-drops shows that they are opposite to the polarity of the source emf (V_b).

The voltage law can be stated as a general equation:

$$V_{R_1} + V_{R_2} + \cdots + V_{R_n} + V_b = 0 \tag{5-4}$$

Illustration B

Using the voltage values calculated in Illustration A, you can now progress around the loop and record the voltages. From the negative terminal of V_b to point A, there is no voltage (assuming that the wire has negligible resistance); point B is +20 V with respect to point A; point C is +40 V with respect to point B; point D is +60 V with respect to point C; point D to the positive terminal of V_b is zero; and point A is −120 V with respect to point D. Now the algebraic addition is

$$V_{R_1} + V_{R_2} + V_{R_3} + V_b = 0$$
$$20 + 40 + 60 \quad 120 - 0$$

It should be noted that while one proceeded through the series loop in a clockwise manner in the above illustration, the counterclockwise direction could have been taken with the same results. You should notice that the loop approach is frequently helpful in determining unknown potentials.

Illustration C

A three-resistor series circuit has an emf of 400 V. $V_{R_1} = 80$ V, and $V_{R_2} = 140$ V. V_{R_3} can be found by rearranging the loop equation and solving for V_{R_3}. The loop equation for the three resistors and V_b is

$$V_{R_1} + V_{R_2} + V_{R_3} + V_b = 0$$

Rearranging gives

$$V_{R_3} = -V_b - V_{R_1} - V_{R_2}$$

Note V_b is an emf and V_{R_1}, V_{R_2}, and V_{R_3} are voltage-drops. If V_b is assigned positive, the voltage-drops will be negative.

$$V_{R_3} = -400 + 80 + 140$$
$$= -180 \text{ V}$$

Kirchhoff's current law is as follows:

The total current entering a junction is equal to the total current leaving that junction.

Note that the series-circuit current law coincides with this statement. The Kirchhoff's current law is of greater value in the analysis of parallel and combination circuits.

5-6 POWER IN A SERIES CIRCUIT

In this section you will learn about power dissipation in series resistors and the overall series circuit.

Recall that the entire circuit current flows through each resistor in a series circuit. Therefore, each resistance opposes the entire current, and the total opposition to the flow of current is equal to the sum of the series resistances. This is the relationship $R = R_1 + \cdots + R_n$ found in Sec. 5-3. Each of the resistors dissipates a fraction of the circuit input power in the form of heat, which can be determined by any one of the following three relationships (depending on which two circuit values are known):

$$P_{R_1} = V_{R_1} \times I = I^2 \times R_1 = \frac{(V_{R_1})^2}{R_1}$$

Expressing this in a general form yields

$$P_{R_n} = V_{R_n} \times I = I^2 \times R_n = \frac{(V_{R_n})^2}{R_n}$$

Note that the above are applications of the three power equations examined in Chap. 4.

The total power dissipation of the circuit is

$$P = P_{R_1} + P_{R_2} + \cdots + P_{R_n} \tag{5-5}$$

where P = total power dissipation in watts

P_{R_n} = power dissipation of the nth resistor

Illustration

A circuit like that in Fig. 5-1 has an emf of 100 V; $R_1 = 50 \, \Omega$, $R_2 = 25 \, \Omega$, and $R_3 = 125 \, \Omega$ (hence $R = 50 + 25 + 125 = 200 \, \Omega$). This results in a circuit current of

$$I = \frac{V}{R} = \frac{100}{200} = 0.5 \text{ A}$$

The power dissipation of each resistor is

$$P_{R_1} = I^2 \times R_1 = (0.5)^2 \times 50$$
$$= 12.5 \text{ W}$$
$$P_{R_2} = I^2 \times R_2 = (0.5)^2 \times 25$$
$$= 6.25 \text{ W}$$
$$P_{R_3} = I^2 \times R_3 = (0.5)^2 \times 125$$
$$= 31.25 \text{ W}$$

The total power dissipation is

$$P = P_{R_1} + P_{R_2} + P_{R_3} = 12.5 + 6.25 + 31.25$$
$$= 50 \text{ W}$$

As a check,

$$P = V_b \times I = 100 \times 0.5$$
$$= 50 \text{ W}$$

PROBLEMS

Draw a fully labeled schematic for each problem.

5-1 $R_1 = 75 \ \Omega$ and $R_2 = 50 \ \Omega$. What is the total resistance when they are connected in series?

5-2 $R_1 = 10 \ \Omega$, $R_2 = 20 \ \Omega$, and $R_3 = 30 \ \Omega$. What is the total resistance if they are connected in series?

5-3 Four resistors are connected in series. $R_1 = 40 \ \Omega$, $R_2 = 60 \ \Omega$, $R_3 = 25 \ \Omega$, and $R_4 = 75 \ \Omega$. Find the total resistance of the circuit.

5-4 What is the total resistance of a series circuit consisting of three resistors — 4.7 kΩ, 3.3 kΩ, and 1 kΩ?

5-5 Refer to Prob. 5-1. Assume the source emf is 25 V. Find the circuit current and voltage-drop across each resistor.

5-6 Find the circuit current and voltage-drop across each resistor in Prob. 5-1 when $V_b = 250$ V.

5-7 Refer to Prob. 5-6. Find the power dissipation of each resistor and total power dissipation of the circuit.

5-8 Refer to Prob. 5-2. Assume the source emf is 6 V. Find the circuit current and voltage-drop across each resistor.

5-9 Find the circuit current and voltage-drop across each resistor in Prob. 5-3 when $V_b = 80$ V.

5-10 Refer to Prob. 5-9. Find the power dissipation of each resistor and total power dissipation of the circuit.

5-11 Refer to Prob. 5-3. Assume the source emf is 50 V. Find the circuit current and voltage-drop across each resistor.

5-12 Refer to Prob. 5-11. Find the power dissipation of each resistor and total power dissipation of the circuit.

5-13 Refer to Prob. 5-4. Assume the source emf is 9 V. Find the circuit current and voltage-drop across each resistor.

5-14 Refer to Prob. 5-13. Find the power dissipation of each resistor and total power dissipation of the circuit.

5-15 Five resistors of equal value are connected in series, and the total resistance is 400 Ω. The circuit current is 1 A. Find:
a) current through each resistor
b) ohmic value of each resistor
c) the source emf
d) the voltage-drop across each resistor

5-16 Six resistors are connected in series, the circuit current is 0.15 A, and the source emf is 120 V. R_1, R_2, and R_3 each have a voltage-drop of 12.5 V; R_4 has a voltage-drop of 25 V; and R_5 has a voltage-drop of 35 V. Find:
a) V_{R_6}
b) R
c) the ohmic value of each resistor

5-17 A motor is in series with a 220-V source. The current drain is 5 A. The wiring between the supply and the motor contains 0.55-Ω resistance. Find:
a) voltage-drop of the wiring
b) voltage-drop of the motor
c) resistance of the motor
d) total circuit resistance

5-18 A 10-V device draws a current of 50 mA. This device is to be operated with a 12-V emf. A resistor is to be connected in series with the device and the emf so as to drop the excess voltage. Find:
1. the series resistance's
   a) voltage-drop
   b) ohmic value
   c) power dissipation
2. the motor's
   d) voltage-drop
   e) ohmic value
   f) power dissipation
3. power dissipation of the entire circuit

5-19 Three resistors are connected in series with a 220-V source. R_1 is 1 kΩ, R_2 passes a current of 22 mA, and R_3 has a voltage-drop of 55 V. Find:
a) R_2 b) R_3
c) V_{R_1} d) V_{R_2}

5-20 Refer to Prob. 5-19. Find:
a) Power dissipation of each resistor
b) Total circuit power dissipation

5-21 Three series resistors are connected to a 100-V source. R_1 and R_2 together drop 75 V, and R_2 and R_3 together drop 75 V. The total series-circuit resistance is 5 kΩ. Find:
a) the resistance of each R
b) the voltage-drop of each R

5-22 Refer to Prob. 5-21. Find:
a) power dissipation of each R
b) total circuit power dissipation

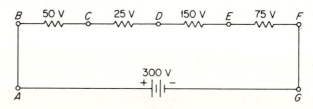

Fig. 5-2

5-23 A 50-Ω resistor is to dissipate heat at the rate of 20 W with a source emf of 120 V. Find:
   a) I
   b) the series resistor

5-24 Four resistors are connected in series. $V_{R_1} = 160$ V $= 0.5V_b$; R of the entire circuit is 2.5 kΩ. Find:
   a) R_1 b) P_{R_1}
   c) I_{R_1} d) P

5-25 The collector load resistance of a transistor is 1.2 kΩ, which is in series with the transistor's resistance. The source emf is 12 V, and the voltage-drop across the transistor is 2 V. Assuming that the transistor, collector load resistance, and source emf are in series, find the collector load resistor's:
   a) voltage-drop
   b) current
   c) power dissipation

5-26 Write the voltage loop equation for the circuit of Fig. 5-2.

5-27 Write the voltage loop equation for the circuit of Fig. 5-3.

Fig. 5-3

QUESTIONS

5-1 What is the definition of a series circuit?
5-2 What is the current relationship in a series circuit?
5-3 What is the voltage relationship in a series circuit?

5-4   What is the resistance relationship in a series circuit?
5-5   What is the power relationship in a series circuit?
5-6   What is Kirchhoff's series-circuit voltage law?
5-7   What is Kirchhoff's current law?
5-8   What is all the energy supplied to a series-resistive circuit converted into?

5-7   CURRENT IN A PARALLEL CIRCUIT

In this section you will learn the definition of a parallel circuit and the distribution of current within it.

This discussion begins by defining a parallel circuit:

A parallel circuit is one in which the current has more than one path in which to flow from the negative side of the source emf to the positive side.

Look over the circuit in Fig. 5-4 for a moment, for it will be used in the following discussion. Now trace the flow of current. Starting from

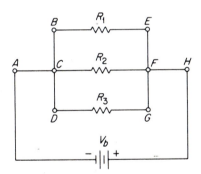

Fig. 5-4   A parallel circuit.

the negative terminal of V_b, current flows through point A and then divides so that a portion of it flows through each of the three resistors (R_1, R_2, and R_3). These branch currents rejoin at point H, and the total current flows back to the positive terminal of the source emf. From this, you can see that *current divides in a parallel circuit, and the sum of the branch currents is equal to the total circuit current.* Stating this in a general equation form yields

$$I = I_1 + I_2 + \cdots + I_n \qquad\qquad (5\text{-}6)$$

5-8 POTENTIAL AND VOLTAGE-DROPS IN A PARALLEL CIRCUIT

In this section you will learn about the relationships of voltage-drops in a parallel circuit.

An examination of the circuit in Fig. 5-4 shows that the left side of each resistor is connected to the same point with regard to the source emf, and the same is true of the right side of each resistor. Therefore *the voltage-drop across parallel branches is the same.* It should be pointed out that this does not mean that the branch currents are equal, since that depends upon the ohmic value of the parallel resistances. Furthermore, it does not mean that the power dissipation is the same for all branches, since this depends upon the value of the branch current as well as on the voltage-drop.

Illustration A

The circuit of Fig. 5-4 has $V_b = 100$ V, $R_1 = 1$ kΩ, $R_2 = 500$ Ω, and $R_3 = 100$ Ω. The current through each branch is

$$I_B = \frac{V_b}{R_1} = \frac{100}{1000} = 0.1 \text{ A}$$
$$I_C = \frac{V_b}{R_2} = \frac{100}{500} = 0.2 \text{ A}$$
$$I_D = \frac{V_b}{R_3} = \frac{100}{100} = 1 \text{ A}$$

And the total current in the circuit is

$$I = I_B + I_C + I_D = 0.1 + 0.2 + 1.0$$
$$= 1.3 \text{ A}$$

Illustration B

From the circuit and current values found in Illustration A, the power dissipation of each branch is

$$P_B = I_B V_b = 0.1 \times 100$$
$$= 10 \text{ W}$$
$$P_C = I_C V_b = 0.2 \times 100$$
$$= 20 \text{ W}$$
$$P_D = I_D V_b = 1 \times 100$$
$$= 100 \text{ W}$$

5-9   RESISTANCE IN A PARALLEL CIRCUIT

In this section you will learn about the relationships between branch resistances and how to calculate the equivalent resistance of a parallel circuit.

The current through each branch of a parallel circuit is determined by two factors: the emf across the branches, and the resistance of each branch. Since the voltage is the same across each branch, as indicated in the preceding section, it is easy to see that the branches having the largest resistance will pass the smallest value of current. By the same token, the smaller branch resistance passes the greatest portion of the circuit current. Therefore, the branch with the smallest resistance will oppose the greatest amount of current. For this reason, the smallest branch resistance has the greatest effect on the total circuit resistance.

It has been found that *the total resistance, also called the equivalent resistance, of a parallel circuit is less than the resistance of any individual branch.* The mathematical relationship is

$$\frac{1}{R} = \frac{1}{R_1} + \frac{1}{R_2} + \cdots + \frac{1}{R_n} \qquad \text{(5-7)}$$

where R = equivalent resistance of the circuit
R_1 = ohmic value of resistor 1
R_2 = ohmic value of resistor 2
R_n = ohmic value of the nth resistor

Illustration A

The circuit of Fig. 5-4 has $R_1 = 100\ \Omega$, $R_2 = 200\ \Omega$, and $R_3 = 50\ \Omega$. The equivalent resistance is

$$\frac{1}{R} = \frac{1}{R_1} + \frac{1}{R_2} + \frac{1}{R_3} = \frac{1}{100} + \frac{1}{200} + \frac{1}{50}$$
$$= 28.57\ \Omega$$

Notice, as indicated in the preceding statement, the equivalent resistance is smaller than the value of any of the branch resistances.

Several Special Cases

There are two special cases that are worth mentioning, because recognizing their existence will simplify circuit calculations. One of these special cases is that condition where there are only two resistances in parallel, when the equivalent resistance is*

$$R = \frac{R_1 R_2}{R_1 + R_2}$$

Another special case is the condition where the branch resistances are the same value, when the equivalent resistance is*

$$R = \frac{R_1}{n}$$

where R_1 = ohmic value of one of the equal branch resistors
      n = number of branches

Illustration B

A parallel circuit has two branches in which $R_1 = 2\ k\Omega$ and $R_2 = 4\ k\Omega$. The equivalent resistance is

$$R = \frac{R_1 R_2}{R_1 + R_2} = \frac{2000 \times 4000}{2000 + 4000}$$
$$= 1333.3\ \Omega$$

Illustration C

A parallel circuit has five branches, each of which has a resistance of $10\ k\Omega$. The equivalent resistance is

$$R = \frac{R_1}{n} = \frac{10,000}{5}$$
$$= 2\ k\Omega$$

5-10   KIRCHHOFF'S LAWS APPLIED TO PARALLEL CIRCUITS

In this section you will learn how Kirchhoff's voltage and current laws are used in the analysis of parallel circuits.

Now apply Kirchhoff's voltage and current laws, which were first discussed in Sec. 5-5, to the circuit illustrated in Fig. 5-4. In this circuit,

* Both special-case equations are derivations from the basic equation (5-7).

the current divides at junction A. The total current I flows into junction A; I_1, I_2, and I_3 flow out of the same junction through the parallel branches. This leads us to our current law:

The sum of the currents flowing out of the junction is equal to the sum of the current flowing into the junction.

In equation form,

$$I = I_1 + I_2 + \cdot \cdot \cdot + I_n \qquad\qquad \textbf{(5-8)}$$

where I = current of total circuit
$\quad I_1$ = current of branch 1
$\quad I_2$ = current of branch 2
$\quad I_n$ = current of branch n

Now examine the same circuit for Kirchhoff's voltage law: V_{R_1} is equal in magnitude and opposite in polarity to V_b; hence the algebraic sum of the emf and voltage-drops in that series loop is zero. The same reasoning applies for the other two series loops in Fig. 5-4. Therefore

$$V_b + V_{R_1} = 0$$
$$V_b + V_{R_2} = 0$$
$$V_b + V_{R_3} = 0$$

The current and voltage laws are frequently of great help in determining voltages and currents in parallel circuits and also in combination circuits (which are treated in the following chapter).

Illustration A

The current in a parallel circuit like that of Fig. 5-4 is 1.20 A. The current of branch 1 is 0.35 A and that of branch 2 is 0.55 A. Using Kirchhoff's current law yields

$$I = I_1 + I_2 + I_3$$

The equation is rearranged in order to solve for the branch 3 current:

$$I_3 = I - I_1 - I_2 - 1.20 - 0.35 - 0.55$$
$$= 0.30 \text{ A}$$

Illustration B

After the current in branch 3 of the circuit in Illustration A is determined, the resistance of that branch, when the source emf is 6 V, is

$$R_3 = \frac{V_b}{I_3} = \frac{6}{0.30}$$
$$= 20 \ \Omega$$

5-11   POWER IN A PARALLEL CIRCUIT

In this section you will learn about the distribution of power in a parallel circuit.

Recall that *energy is dissipated (converted to heat) wherever current flows and resistance is offered to its motion.* Therefore energy is dissipated in each branch of a parallel circuit. The power dissipated in each branch of Fig. 5-4 can be found by using any one of the three power formulas:

$$\text{Branch 1:} \quad P_1 = (I_1)^2 R_1 = \frac{(V_b)^2}{R_1} = V_1 I_1$$

$$\text{Branch 2:} \quad P_2 = (I_2)^2 R_2 = \frac{(V_b)^2}{R_2} = V_2 I_2$$

$$\text{Branch 3:} \quad P_3 = (I_3)^2 R_3 = \frac{(V_b)^2}{R_3} = V_3 I_3$$

The particular formula used is determined by which two of the three factors are most readily obtained from the particular problem.

Another important statement regarding power in parallel circuits is the following:

The total power dissipated in the circuit is equal to the sum of the power dissipated in the branches.

Illustration A

In Fig. 5-4: $R_1 = 2 \ k\Omega$ and $I_1 = 5$ mA; $R_2 = 10 \ k\Omega$ and $I_2 = 1$ mA; $R_3 = 500 \ \Omega$ and $I_3 = 20$ mA; and $V_b = 10$ V. The power dissipation of each branch and of the total circuit is

$$P_1 = (I_1)^2 R_1 = (0.005)^2 \times 2000$$
$$= 50 \text{ mW}$$
$$P_2 = (I_2)^2 R_2 = (0.001)^2 \times 10{,}000$$
$$= 10 \text{ mW}$$
$$P_3 = (I_3)^2 R_3 = (0.020)^2 \times 500$$
$$= 200 \text{ mW}$$

To sum up:

$$P = P_1 + P_2 + P_3 = 50 \text{ mW} + 10 \text{ mW} + 200 \text{ mW}$$
$$= 260 \text{ mW}$$

Another interesting aspect of power in a parallel circuit is to add a parallel load and observe its effect. In the following example it is assumed that the source emf remains fixed at the assigned value.

Illustration B

The source emf of a circuit is 120 V. The circuit resistance is 60 Ω, prior to the addition of two parallel resistances of $R_2 = 20$ Ω and $R_3 = 30$ Ω. Each load (current) can be found by Ohm's law:

$$I_{R_1} = \frac{V_b}{R_1} = \frac{120}{60}$$
$$= 2 \text{ A}$$
$$I_{R_2} = \frac{V_b}{R_2} = \frac{120}{20}$$
$$= 6 \text{ A}$$
$$I_{R_3} = \frac{V_b}{R_3} = \frac{120}{30}$$
$$= 4 \text{ A}$$

The power dissipation of each branch is

$$P_1 = (I_1)^2 R_1 = (2)^2 \times 60$$
$$= 240 \text{ W}$$
$$P_2 = (I_2)^2 R_2 = (6)^2 \times 20$$
$$= 720 \text{ W}$$
$$P_3 = (I_3)^2 R_3 = (4)^2 \times 30$$
$$= 480 \text{ W}$$

The total power dissipation of the circuit is

$$P = P_1 + P_2 + P_3 = 240 \text{ W} + 720 \text{ W} + 480 \text{ W}$$
$$= 1440 \text{ W}$$

Notice that the power drawn from the source (in Illustration B) increased from the original 240 W (with R_1 only) to 1440 W by adding the parallel loads. *The addition of parallel loads did not affect the power dissipation of the original load, but did draw additional power from the source.* That is, the load imposed upon the source emf is increased with the addition of parallel resistance. From this, it can be seen that a *fixed-emf source is actually a variable energy supply to some limit.* Loads beyond the maximum limit create an overload upon the source. Safeguards, such as correctly rated fuses or circuit breakers, must be employed to avoid this condition, since it may damage the source voltage generator.

PROBLEMS

Draw a fully labeled schematic for each problem.

5-28   Three resistors, each equal to 1 kΩ, are connected in parallel. Find the equivalent resistance.

5-29   If $R_1 = 400$ Ω and $R_2 = 800$ Ω are in parallel and the source emf is 100 V, find:
   a)   current through each resistor
   b)   voltage-drop across each resistor
   c)   equivalent resistance
   d)   total circuit current

5-30   Three resistors — $R_1 = 40$ Ω, $R_2 = 75$ Ω, and $R_3 = 130$ Ω — are connected in parallel. The source emf is 25 V. Find:
   a)   voltage-drop across each resistor
   b)   current through each resistor
   c)   total circuit current
   d)   equivalent resistance

5-31   Four resistors — R_1 and R_2 are 400 Ω, $R_3 = 300$ Ω, and $R_4 = 500$ Ω — are connected in parallel. The source emf is 120 V. Find:
   a)   current through each resistor
   b)   total circuit current
   c)   equivalent resistance

5-32   Two resistors are connected in parallel. $V_b = 10$ V, and $R_1 = 4R_2 = 1$ kΩ. Find:
   a) R_2
   b)   branch currents
   c)   equivalent resistance
   d)   total current

5-33   Refer to Prob. 5-32. Assume that R_1 is changed to 600 Ω and R_2 is also changed so that $R_1 = 4R_2$. V_b is increased to 75 V. Find:
   a) R_2
   b)   branch currents
   c)   equivalent resistance
   d)   total current

5-34   Two resistors are connected in parallel. Assume that R_2 is 32 Ω, $R_1 = \frac{1}{4}R_2$, and the circuit current is 800 mA. Find:
  a) R_1
  b) equivalent resistance
  c) source emf
  d) current through each resistor

5-35   Resistors of 35, 14, and 80 Ω are connected in parallel. The total circuit current is 35 mA. Find:
  a) equivalent resistance
  b) source emf
  c) current through each resistor

5-36   Resistors of 6000, 8000, and 3000 Ω are connected in parallel, and 6 mA flows through the 6000-Ω resistor. Find:
  a) source emf
  b) equivalent resistance
  c) total current
  d) current through the other two resistors

5-37 R_1 is twice the value of R_2 and half the value of R_3. The three resistors are in parallel. Equivalent resistance is 400 Ω, and the total current is 50 mA. Find:
  a) source emf
  b) ohmic value of each resistor
  c) current through each resistor

5-38   Refer to Fig. 5-4. Assume that $V_b = 300$ V and $R_1 = 5$ kΩ. Find:
  a) I_{R_1}
  b) P_{R_1}

5-39   In Fig. 5-4, assume that $V_b = 220$ V and each load $= 1.5$ A. Find:
  a) ohmic value of each resistor
  b) power rating of each resistor
  c) power drawn from the source if two of the loads are disconnected
  d) power drawn from the source if three loads equal to the original loads are added in parallel to the original loads
  e) In reference to (d), if the source were fused for 5 A, what effect would the additional loads have?

5-40   A source is rated at 15 A. How many 1.2-A loads can be added without exceeding the rating of the source?

5-41   A source is delivering 8.9 A of current to three loads connected in parallel. Load 1 draws 2.3 A. Find loads 2 and 3, which each draw the same amount of current.

5-42   In Prob. 5-41, assume that a fourth load equal to load 1 is added. The source is fused for 10 A. Would the fuse remain intact? Explain.

5-43 Two loads are connected in parallel to a source of 65 V. The total load is 550 mA. Load 1 is 75 mA. Find:
   a) load 2
   b) resistance of each load
   c) equivalent resistance
   d) power dissipated by each load
   e) total circuit power dissipation

5-44 Two resistors are connected in parallel. The total current is 80 mA, source potential is 90 V, and $R_1 = 1200\ \Omega$. Find:
   a) equivalent resistance
   b) R_2
   c) power dissipated by each resistor
   d) total power dissipation of the circuit

5-45 In Prob. 5-44 if R_1 were removed from the circuit, what would be the total power dissipation?

5-46 A circuit of 110-V potential draws 800 mA of current. With the addition of an unknown load in parallel with the original circuit, the current rises to 1.44 A. Find:
   a) the unknown load
   b) resistance before the addition of the unknown load
   c) resistance after the addition of the unknown load
   d) power dissipation before and after the addition

5-47 In Prob. 5-46, assume that the second load is kept, but the original load of 800 mA is removed and replaced with two loads equal to the one added in Prob. 5-46. Find:
   a) total load
   b) total power dissipation

QUESTIONS

5-9 What is the definition of a parallel circuit?

5-10 What is the relationship between the resistance of two parallel branches and the branch currents?

5-11 What is the relationship between the voltage-drops across the branches of a parallel circuit?

5-12 What is the relationship between the branch resistances and the total resistance of a parallel circuit?

5-13 What is the relationship for finding the total resistance of two parallel resistances?

5-14 What is the relationship for finding the total resistance of several parallel resistors of the same ohmic value?

5-15 What is Kirchhoff's current law for parallel circuits?

5-16   What is the relationship between the power dissipated in the branches and the total power dissipation of the circuit?

5-17   What effect does adding another branch have on the source emf in a parallel circuit?

5-18   What effect does adding additional branches have on the original branches of the parallel circuit?

5-19   What kind of energy supply is a fixed-emf source?

5-20   What technique can be used to guard an emf source from an overload?

series-parallel circuits

6

A series-parallel circuit is also called a combination circuit. *A series-parallel circuit is one in which one or more parallel or series combinations are in series with each other.* Many of these circuits will tend to confuse you unless a systematic approach is utilized. A number of hints will be of great help in many cases. Here are a few:

1   The parallel laws apply to all parallel combinations, and the series-combinations relationships are determined by the series-circuit laws.
2   It is usually advisable to begin with a clear-cut diagram of the circuit to be analyzed.
3   Begin on those components where two of the three Ohm's law factors are known. For example, if the current flowing through a resistor and its ohmic value are known, its voltage-drop can be found readily.
4   Look for the possibilities opened by the solution of one part of the circuit. For example, in the case stated in (3) above, knowing the voltage-drop of the resistor may enable you to find one of the factors for a resistor in series or in parallel with it.
5   As parts of the circuit are solved, it is often useful to simplify the circuit as you progress. For example, three resistors in parallel can be redrawn as one resistor with an ohmic value equal to the equivalent value of the three.
6   Remember that any part of the circuit is either a series or parallel combination, no matter how complicated it may look.

In the following sections, detailed descriptions of resistance, voltage, and current relationships in various combinations are given. The type of approach used is applicable to many combination circuits.

6-1   RESISTANCE IN COMBINATION CIRCUITS

In this section you will learn about determining the equivalent resistance of combination circuits.

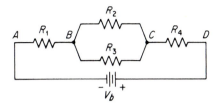

Fig. 6-1 A combination circuit.

Look over the circuit of Fig. 6-1 for a moment, since it will be used in the following analysis. Electron flow will drift from point A toward point D. As you progress, it will be obvious that determining the direction of current flow is frequently a great help in solving a combination circuit. The total current flows through R_1 and divides at junction B, with some of the current passing through R_2 and the remainder through R_3. The two branch currents rejoin at junction C, and the total current passes through R_4. This current analysis makes it possible to determine the series and parallel relationships of the resistors. In this example, R_2 and R_3 are in parallel, and R_1 is in series with R_4.

The total resistance of a series circuit is equal to the sum of the ohmic values, and you can use the special relationship for the two resistors in parallel. The equivalent circuit resistance for Fig. 6-1 can be found from

$$R = R_1 + R_4 + \frac{R_2 R_3}{R_2 + R_3}$$

Illustration

In Fig. 6-1, $R_1 = 30\ \Omega$, $R_2 = 50\ \Omega$, $R_3 = 80\ \Omega$, and $R_4 = 45\ \Omega$; the equivalent resistance is

$$R = R_1 + R_4 + \frac{R_2 R_3}{R_2 + R_3} = 30 + 45 + \frac{50 \times 80}{50 + 80}$$
$$= 105.8\ \Omega$$

6-2 APPLICATIONS OF KIRCHHOFF'S CURRENT LAW TO COMBINATION CIRCUITS

In this section you will learn how the current law can be used in analyzing current in combination circuits.

Recall that the current law states that the current entering a junction is equal to the current leaving the junction. In interpreting this law for Fig. 6-1, it is found that I_{R_1} is equal to $I_{R_2} + I_{R_3}$, which is equal to I_{R_4}. This concept is often useful in determining the current flowing through a particular part of the circuit.

Illustration

If I_{R_1} in Fig. 6-1 is 2 A and I_{R_3} is 1.25 A, the relationship $I_{R_1} = I_{R_2} + I_{R_3}$ can be rearranged, and I_{R_2} can be determined:

$$I_{R_2} = I_{R_1} - I_{R_3} = 2.0 - 1.25$$
$$= 0.75 \text{ A}$$

6-3 POWER IN COMBINATION CIRCUITS

In this section you will learn how the basic power equations can be applied to combination circuits.

The relationship of power dissipation in series and parallel circuits can be applied to the individual portions of the circuit. Refer to Fig. 6-1 again for a moment. The power dissipation by each resistor can be determined by any one of the three power equations, as described and analyzed in Chap. 5. Also, the total power dissipation of the circuit is equal to the sum of the power dissipated by each resistor. That is,

$$P = P_{R_1} + P_{R_2} + P_{R_3} + P_{R_4}$$

Illustration A

In Fig. 6-1, when $I = 600$ mA, $I_{R_2} = 120$ mA and $R_1 = 200 \ \Omega$; then the power dissipated by R_1 is

$$P_{R_1} = (I_{R_1})^2 \times R_1 = (0.600)^2 \times 200$$
$$= 72 \text{ W}$$

Illustration B

In Fig. 6-1, $I = 400$ mA and $I_{R_2} = 150$ mA. Also, $R_1 = 50 \ \Omega$, $R_2 = 100 \ \Omega$, $R_3 = 60 \ \Omega$, and $R_4 = 30 \ \Omega$. Find the power dissipated by each resistor and the total circuit power dissipation.

$$P_{R_1} = (I_{R_1})^2 R_1 = (0.400)^2 \times 50$$
$$= 8 \text{ W}$$
$$P_{R_2} = (I_{R_2})^2 R_2 = (1.150)^2 \times 100$$
$$= 2.25 \text{ W}$$

$$P_{R_3} = (I_{R_3})^2 R_3 = (0.250)^2 \times 60$$
$$= 3.75 \text{ W}$$
$$P_{R_4} = (I_{R_4})^2 R_4 = (0.400)^2 \times 30$$
$$= 4.8 \text{ W}$$
$$P = P_{R_1} + P_{R_2} + P_{R_3} + P_{R_4} = 8 + 2.25 + 3.75 + 4.8$$
$$= 18.8 \text{ W}$$

6-4 EMF AND VOLTAGE-DROPS IN COMBINATION CIRCUITS

In this section you will learn how Kirchhoff's voltage law can be used in analyzing combination circuits.

Refer to Fig. 6-1 for the following discussion. As was stated in several earlier sections, the sum of the voltage-drops in any series loop is equal in value and opposite in polarity to the source emf. V_{R_2} and V_{R_3} are the same voltage-drop, since they are parallel resistors. The parallel combination has a voltage-drop equal to V_{BC}. Considering the resistance between points B and C as one resistance which is equal to the equivalent value of the parallel combination, you can now treat the circuit as one series loop.

Starting from point A and working in a clockwise direction, you get

$$V_{R_1} + V_{BC} + V_{R_4} - V_b = 0$$

Since this has been identified as a series loop, any one of the voltages can be found if the other three are known.

Illustration

Refer to Fig. 6-1. Assume that $V_{R_1} = 45$ V, $V_{R_4} = 64$ V, and $V_b = 180$ V. Find V_{R_2} and V_{R_3}.

These voltage-drops are the same, since the two resistors are in parallel. This voltage-drop can be called V_{BC}. Rearranging Kirchhoff's loop equation allows you to solve:

$$V_{BC} = V_b - V_{R_1} - V_{R_4} = 180 - 45 - 64$$
$$= 71 \text{ V}$$

6-5 SOME TYPICAL COMBINATION CIRCUIT POSSIBILITIES

In this section you will learn about some of the more common approaches to solving combination circuits.

The number of possible series-parallel circuit combinations is almost countless. Several of the more common possibilities will be introduced. Figure 6-2 illustrates a combination circuit often found; look it over for a moment.

The resistors R_1 and R_2 could be devices represented by resistors having unlike current requirements but connected across the same voltage

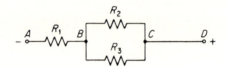

Fig. 6-2   A combination circuit.

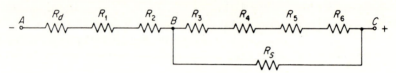

Fig. 6-3   A combination circuit.

source. For example, R_1 could have a current requirement of 0.3 A and the current requirement of R_2 could be 0.15 A. The purpose of R_3 is to bypass the correct amount of circuit current around R_2 so that I_{R_2} will be limited to its required 0.15 A. In this example, the ohmic value of R_3 would be equal to R_2, since I_{R_2} is equal to half the circuit current.

There are cases where the number of series resistances is greater than found in Fig. 6-2, such as the one shown in Fig. 6-3. R_1 to R_6 can represent devices having identical voltage-drops. In this case, R_3 through R_6 do not require as great a current as R_1 and R_2; therefore a portion of the total current is bypassed by the shunting resistor R_s. R_d is commonly called a series-dropping resistor, since its prime function is to drop the excess voltage not used for the devices (the difference between the total source emf and the required voltage for the devices).

Illustration

Assume that each of the six devices drops 6.3 V. The supply potential is 90 V. Devices 1 and 2 draw 0.3 A, while devices 3 through 6 require 0.15 A. Find the ohmic value and power dissipation of R_s and R_d. V_{R_d} must equal the difference between the devices' voltage-drops and the source potential. The total voltage-drop of the devices equals 6×6.3, which is 37.8 V.

$$V_{R_d} = V_b - V_{\text{devices}} = 90 - 37.8$$
$$= 52.2 \text{ V}$$

The total current (0.3 A) flows through R_d, and

$$R_d = \frac{V_{R_d}}{I_{R_d}} = \frac{52.2}{0.300}$$
$$= 174 \ \Omega$$

and

$$P_{R_d} = (I_{R_d})^2 R_d = (0.300)^2 \times 174$$
$$= 15.7 \ \text{W}$$

Next the value of R_s should be considered. The circuit current divides at junction B (considering the current as moving from left to right) in such a way that 0.15 A flows through R_3, R_4, R_5, and R_6, and the remainder of the circuit current flows through R_s. The total current is 0.3 A. I_{R_s} must be equal to the difference between the total current and the current drawn by these four devices. Rearranging the relationship $I = I_{BC} + I_{R_s}$, and knowing that $I_{BC} = 0.15$ A and $I = 0.30$ A, yields

$$I_{R_s} = I - I_{BC} = 0.30 - 0.15$$
$$= 0.15 \ \text{A}$$

Since R_s is in parallel with the four devices, its voltage-drop is the same as the sum of the voltage-drops of the four devices, which is $6.3 \times 4 = 25.2$ V. Knowing V_{R_s} and I_{R_s} yields

$$R_s = \frac{V_{R_s}}{I_{R_s}} = \frac{25.2}{0.15}$$
$$= 168 \ \Omega$$

and

$$P_{R_s} = (I_{R_s})^2 R_s = (0.15)^2 \times 168$$
$$= 3.78 \ \text{W}$$

It is worth repeating, for the purpose of emphasizing its importance, that series and parallel rules are used wherever they apply. In this way, a number of facts are frequently obtainable with a minimum of computation.

Figure 6-4 is another possible combination; study the distribution of its current. Note that the total current flows through R_1. At junction B, the current divides, with a portion of it flowing through R_5 and the remainder flowing through the upper branch. The upper branch cur-

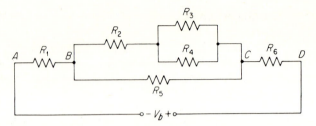

Fig. 6-4   A combination circuit.

rent is further divided after I_{R_2} into I_{R_3} and I_{R_4}. All the branch currents rejoin at junction C, and the total current passes through R_6.

The distribution of voltage can be diagnosed in the same way. Since R_5 is in parallel with the upper branch, then

$$V_{R5} = V_{R2} + V_{R3} = V_{R2} + V_{R4}$$

Therefore

$$V_b = V_{R1} + V_{R5} + V_{R6}$$

The total resistance is obtained by using Ohm's law when the total current and supply potential are known, since $R = V/I$. The total resistance also can be computed the long way if the individual resistances are known. In this case, the relationship is

$$R_{BC} = \frac{[R_2 + R_3R_4/(R_3 + R_4)]R_5}{[R_2 + R_3R_4/(R_3 + R_4)] + R_5}$$

$$R = R_1 + R_{BC} + R_6$$

The problems which follow illustrate several other combination circuit possibilities. The characteristics of voltage, current, and resistance in series and parallel combinations should be memorized. The application of the correct rules to a specific portion of a circuit is important.

PROBLEMS

6-1   Refer to Fig. 6-2. Circuit current = 500 mA, and source potential = 25 V; I_{R_2} = 300 mA; V_{R_1} = 15 V. Find:
   a) I_{R_3}
   b)   ohmic value of each resistance
   c)   power dissipation of each resistor
   d)   total circuit power dissipation

6-2   Refer to Fig. 6-2. Circuit current $= 2$ A; source emf $= 35$ V; $V_{R_1} =$ 5 V; $I_{R_3} = 0.5$ A; and $R_2 = 20$ Ω. Find:
   a) I through R_1, R_2
   b)   voltage-drop across R_2 and R_3
   c)   ohmic value of each resistor
   d)   power dissipation of each resistor

6-3   Refer to Fig. 6-3. R_1 and R_2 each drop 25 V; R_3, R_4, R_5, and R_6 each drop 12.6 V and draw 0.15 A. Total current is 0.5 A; the source potential is 120 V. Find:
   a) R_d
   b) P_{R_d}
   c) R_s
   d) P_{R_s}

6-4   Repeat Prob. 6-3 for the following requirements: R_1 and R_2 each drop 2.8 V; R_3, R_4, R_5, and R_6 each drop 1.4 V. $I_{R_3} = 0.050$ A; total circuit current is 0.150 A. Supply potential is 12 V.

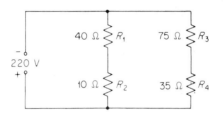

Fig. 6-5   A series-combination circuit.

6-5   Refer to Fig. 6-5. Find:
   a)   current through each resistor
   b)   total current
   c)   voltage-drop across each resistor
   d)   equivalent circuit resistance
   e)   power dissipation of each resistor
   f)   total power dissipation of the circuit

6-6   Refer to the circuit of Fig. 6-5. The values of the resistances are: $R_1 = 20$ Ω; $R_2 = 180$ Ω; $R_3 = 10$ Ω; and $R_4 = 40$ Ω. The source emf is 100 V. Find:
   a)   current through each resistor
   b)   total current
   c)   voltage-drop across each resistor
   d)   equivalent circuit resistance
   e)   power dissipation of each resistor
   f)   total power dissipation of the circuit

6-7   Refer to Fig. 6-4. $R_1 = 10\ \Omega$; $R_6 = \frac{1}{2}R_1$. $V_{R_1} = 20$ V. $R_2 = 40\ \Omega$; $R_3 = R_4 = 60\ \Omega$; and $I_{R_3} = 0.25$ A. Find:
    a)   current through R_1, R_5, and R_6
    b)   total current
    c)   voltage-drop across R_2, R_3, R_5, and R_6
    d) V_b
    e)   ohmic value of R_5 and R_6
    f)   power dissipation of each resistor
    g)   power dissipation of the entire circuit

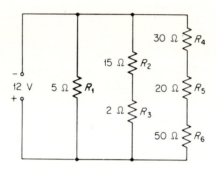

Fig. 6-6   A combination circuit.

6-8   Refer to the circuit of Fig. 6-6. Find:
    a)   equivalent resistance of the circuit
    b)   circuit current
    c)   total circuit power dissipation
6-9   Refer to the circuit of Fig. 6-6. Find:
    a)   current through each resistor
    b)   power dissipation of each resistor
6-10   Refer to Fig. 6-7. Find:
    a)   equivalent resistance
    b)   circuit current
    c)   total circuit power dissipation
6-11   Refer to Fig. 6-7. Find the current through and voltage-drop across each resistor.
6-12   Refer to Prob. 6-11. Find the power dissipation of each resistance
6-13   Refer to Prob. 6-11. Write the voltage equations for the following series loops:
    a) $R_1 - R_3 - R_2 - V_b$
    b) $R_1 - R_4 - R_6 - R_5 - R_2 - V_b$
    c) $R_1 - R_4 - R_7 - R_9 - R_8 - R_5 - R_2 - V_b$

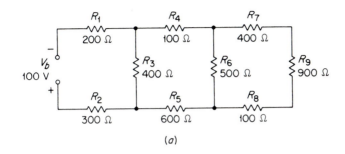

(a)

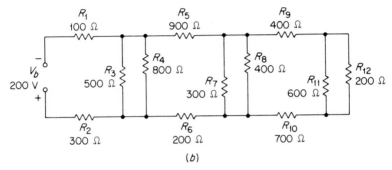

(b)

Fig. 6-7   (a) A combination circuit; (b) a combination circuit.

6-14   Repeat Prob. 6-10 with $V_b = 50$ V.

6-15   Refer to Prob. 6-14. Find the current through and voltage-drop across each resistor.

6-16   Refer to Prob. 6-15. Find the power dissipation of each resistor.

6-17   Write the series loop voltage equations of Prob. 6-13 for Prob. 6-15.

6-18   Refer to the circuit of Fig. 6-8. Find:
   a)   equivalent resistance
   b)   total current
   c)   total power dissipation

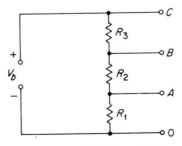

Fig. 6-8   Unloaded voltage divider.

6-19   Refer to the circuit of Fig. 6-8. Find the current through and voltage-drop across each resistor.

6-20   Refer to Prob. 6-19. Find the power dissipation of each resistance.

6-21   Refer to Prob. 6-19. Write the voltage equations for the following series loops:

   a) $R_1 - R_3 - R_2 + V_b$
   b) $R_1 - R_4 - R_2 + V_b$
   c) $R_1 - R_5 - R_7 - R_6 - R_2 + V_b$
   d) $R_1 - R_5 - R_8 - R_6 - R_2 + V_b$

6-22   Repeat Prob. 6-18 with $V_b = 300$ V.

6-23   Refer to Prob. 6-22. Find the current through and voltage-drop across each resistance.

6-24   Refer to Prob. 6-23. Find the power dissipation of each resistance.

6-25   Refer to Prob. 6-23. Write the series loop voltage equations for the loops listed in Prob. 6-21 for Prob. 6-23.

QUESTIONS

6-1   What is the definition of a series-parallel circuit?

6-2   Can you state the six suggested hints for attempting to solve combination circuits?

6-3   How is Kirchhoff's current law applied to combination circuits?

6-4   What is the relationship of the total power dissipation of a combination circuit and the power dissipated by the individual resistors?

6-5   How is Kirchhoff's voltage law applied to combination circuits?

6-6   UNLOADED VOLTAGE DIVIDERS

In this section you will learn how series resistors form the basis for attenuator circuits, which in turn are converted into series-parallel arrangements for loaded voltage-divider purposes.

There are many cases in which it is desirable to have a source emf of several voltages because of the variety of devices in a circuit. One way of obtaining several such voltages is the *voltage divider*. Since the voltage across any one resistor in a series circuit is some fraction of V_b, *any combination of series resistors forms a voltage divider*. If V_o is considered as the voltage across any one or several of the series resistors, then you can see that the output voltage is some value less than V_b. For this reason, any combination of series resistors can also be called an *attenuator* circuit.

Look over Fig. 6-8 for a moment, which is an unloaded voltage-divider circuit. It is to this circuit that reference is made in the analysis that follows. Note that R_1, R_2, and R_3 of Fig. 6-8 are connected in series with the source emf V_b. The current is determined by

$$I = \frac{V_b}{R_1 + R_2 + R_3} = \frac{V_b}{R}$$

and the available output voltages are

$$V_{AO} = V_{R_1} = \frac{R_1}{R} \times V_b$$

$$V_{BO} = V_{R_1} + V_{R_2} = \frac{R_1 + R_2}{R} \times V_b$$

$$V_{CO} = V_{R_1} + V_{R_2} + V_{R_3} = \frac{R_1 + R_2 + R_3}{R} \times V_b = V_b$$

The resistance values are determined by

$$R_1 = \frac{V_{R_1}}{I} = \frac{V_{AO}}{I}$$

$$R_2 = \frac{V_{R_2}}{I} = \frac{V_{BO} - V_{R_1}}{I}$$

$$R_3 = \frac{V_{R_3}}{I} = \frac{V_{CO} - (V_{R_2} + V_{R_1})}{I}$$

Illustration

An unloaded voltage divider is to be designed around $V_b = 12$ V, output voltages of 3 V, 9 V, and 12 V, and a desired current of 30 mA.

Since the 3-V output is across R_1 and the current passing through it is 30 mA,

$$R_1 = \frac{V_{R_1}}{I} = \frac{V_{AO}}{I} = \frac{3}{0.030}$$
$$= 100 \ \Omega$$

The 9-V output is across $R_1 + R_2$. Since $V_{R_1} = 3$ V, then $V_{R_2} = 9 - 3 = 6$ V. And

$$R_2 = \frac{V_{R_2}}{I} = \frac{V_{BO} - V_{R_1}}{I} = \frac{9 - 3}{0.030}$$
$$= 200 \ \Omega$$

The 12-V output is across $R_1 + R_2 + R_3$. Since $V_{R_1} = 3$ V and $V_{R_2} = 6$ V, then

$$R_3 = \frac{V_{R3}}{I} = \frac{V_{CO} - (V_{R_2} + V_{R_1})}{I} = \frac{12 - 9}{0.030}$$
$$= 100 \ \Omega$$

The circuit of Fig. 6-8 was called an unloaded voltage divider because no other components or devices are connected to the voltage taps and no load other than the series current is imposed upon the circuit. This is not a realistic situation, but it was discussed as a means to analyze the voltage-distribution relationships and how the selection of the voltage-divider resistors can be made. Now it is time to turn to the general applications of the voltage divider.

6-7 LOADED VOLTAGE DIVIDERS

In this section you will learn about the overall operation of a loaded voltage divider.

One of the major purposes of a voltage divider is to make a number of voltages available from the same emf source. These potentials are needed for the operation of various electronic devices, including transistors and other solid-state devices.

Look over Fig. 6-9 for a moment. It is the schematic of a loaded voltage divider that will be referred to in the discussion that follows. R_{L_1}, R_{L_2}, and R_{L_3} represent the resistances of the three loads which are connected in the combinations shown. Notice that there are four

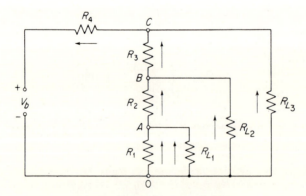

Fig. 6-9 Loaded voltage divider.

currents—the three loads plus the current that flows through the series resistors of the original voltage divider. This fourth current is called the *bleeder* current, since it is the load imposed upon the source emf by the resistances of the unloaded divider arrangement. The bleeder current, which is usually 10 to 25 percent of the total load, serves a useful function in that a path for current will exist through the divider resistors if the loads are opened (disconnected). This improves the voltage regulation of the circuit (which is the extent to which the voltage across the load resistance varies with changes in the load current) and is also a valuable safety feature; this point is discussed later.

You should notice that the circuit of Fig. 6-9 is a series-parallel arrangement. In some cases, the maximum potential desired for use with the various loads is less than the value of the source emf. When this occurs, an additional series resistor, such as R_4 in Fig. 6-9, can be used to drop the excess portion of the source emf. R_4 is often called an *excess-voltage resistor*. R_1, since it passes only the bleeder I, is called the *bleeder resistor*.

Another important point should be made regarding the measurement of voltage. Point O is the reference, or common, point of the circuit. The three voltages available from the voltage taps A, B, and C are measured with point O as their reference point. Therefore the voltage at tap A is measured from point O, and so are the voltages at taps B and C.

6-8 VOLTAGE AND CURRENT DISTRIBUTION IN A LOADED VOLTAGE DIVIDER

In this section you will learn about the voltage and current relationships that will enable you to calculate circuit values in a loaded voltage divider.

From the loaded voltage-divider circuit of Fig. 6-9, the following voltage relationships can be found:

$$V_{R_1} + V_{R_2} + V_{R_3} + V_{R_4} = V_b$$
$$V_{R_{L1}} = V_{R_1}$$
$$V_{R_{L2}} = V_{R_1} + V_{R_2}$$
$$V_{R_{L3}} = V_{R_1} + V_{R_2} + V_{R_3}$$

Now there are a number of interesting facts concerning current relationships. Start at point O. Four currents leave at point O: I_{R_1} (bleeder current), $I_{R_{L1}}$, $I_{R_{L2}}$, and $I_{R_{L3}}$. The bleeder current and load 1 join at point A and together flow through R_2 (I_{R_2} = bleeder I and load 1). Load 2 joins I_{R_2} at point B (I_{R_3} = bleeder I + load 1 + load 2). Load 3 joins I_{R_3} at point C (I_{R_4} = bleeder I + load 1 + load 2 + load 3). This is the total circuit current, and it is equal to the current which enters at point O.

Illustration A

A loaded voltage-divider circuit, like that of Fig. 6-9, has load 1 = 20 mA, load 2 = 30 mA, load 3 = 50 mA, and $I_{bleeder}$ = 10 percent of the full load current. The voltages are $V_b = 14$ V, $V_{AO} = 3$ V, $V_{BO} = 9$ V, and $V_{CO} = 12$ V. Prior to finding the values of the four resistors, determine the total load and bleeder I.

$$\text{Total load} = \text{load 1} + \text{load 2} + \text{load 3} = 0.020 + 0.030 + 0.050$$
$$= 0.100 \text{ A}$$

and since the bleeder $I = 0.10$ full load,

$$\text{Bleeder } I = 0.1 \times 0.100 = 0.010 \text{ A}$$

Now the value of each resistor can be determined, starting with R_1. Thus $V_{R_1} = V_{R_{L1}} = V_{AO} = 3$ V, and I_{R_1} = bleeder $I = 0.010$ A.

$$R_1 = \frac{V_{R_1}}{I_{R_1}} = \frac{3}{0.010}$$
$$= 300 \ \Omega$$

So, $V_{R_2} = V_{BO} - V_{R_1} = 9 - 3 = 6$ V and I_{R_2} = bleeder I + load 1 = 0.010 + 0.020 = 0.030 A.

$$R_2 = \frac{V_{R_2}}{I_{R_2}} = \frac{6}{0.030}$$
$$= 200 \ \Omega$$

The value of V_{R_3} is $V_{CO} - V_{BO} = 12 - 9 = 3$ V and I_{R_3} = bleeder I + load 1 + load 2 = 0.010 + 0.020 + 0.030 = 0.060 A.

$$R_3 = \frac{V_{R_3}}{I_{R_3}} = \frac{3}{0.060}$$
$$= 50 \ \Omega$$

The value of V_{R_4} is $V_b - V_{CO} = 14 - 12 = 2$ V and I_{R_4} = total load + bleeder $I = 0.100 + 0.010 = 0.110$ A.

$$R_4 = \frac{V_{R_4}}{I_{R_4}} = \frac{2}{0.110}$$
$$= 18.2 \ \Omega$$

Also of interest is the resistance and power dissipation associated with each load, as well as the total dissipation of the loads.

Illustration B

From the voltage-divider circuit of Illustration A, one obtains

$$R_{L_1} = \frac{V_{R_{L1}}}{\text{load } 1} = \frac{3}{0.020}$$
$$= 150 \ \Omega$$
$$R_{L_2} = \frac{V_{R_{L2}}}{\text{load } 2} = \frac{9}{0.030}$$
$$= 300 \ \Omega$$
$$R_{L_3} = \frac{V_{R_{L3}}}{\text{load } 3} = \frac{12}{0.050}$$
$$= 240 \ \Omega$$

and

$$P_{R_{L1}} = (\text{load } 1)^2 \times R_{L_1} = (0.020)^2 \times 150$$
$$= 0.060 \text{ W}$$
$$P_{R_{L2}} = (\text{load } 2)^2 \times R_{L_2} = (0.030)^2 \times 300$$
$$= 0.270 \text{ W}$$
$$P_{R_{L3}} = (\text{load } 3)^2 \times R_{L_3} = (0.050)^2 \times 240$$
$$= 0.600 \text{ W}$$

and for the entire load

$$P = P_{R_{L1}} + P_{R_{L2}} + P_{R_{L3}} = 0.060 + 0.270 + 0.600$$
$$= 0.930 \text{ W}$$

6-9 THE EFFECT OF A VARIABLE LOAD ON A SIMPLE LOADED VOLTAGE DIVIDER

In this section you will learn how a variable resistance in parallel with the tap of a voltage divider affects the output voltages.

Up to now, only fixed loads have been considered. *Variable loads* are used often in applications, however. For example, the current drawn by a transistor varies with the change in its resistance. As the resistance of the transistor (or any other device) is made to vary, it in turn causes a change in the current flowing through it. If this arrangement is in series with some other component, the voltage across the transistor will

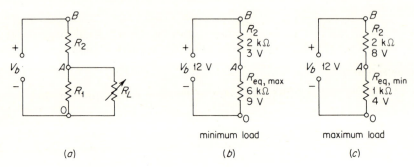

	minimum load	maximum load
(a)	(b)	(c)

Fig. 6-10 **Voltage divider with a variable load.**

also change. Since this is a more realistic situation, it would be well to examine a simplified version of it.

Look over Fig. 6-10 for a moment, which is a voltage divider with a variable load. Notice the symbol for a variable resistance, the original resistance symbol with an arrow through it.

Illustration

Assume that R_L represents the resistance of the load, and let that be the resistance of a transistor. The bleeder current is 1 mA, and the transistor current varies from 0.5 to 3.0 mA. Also assume that the voltage-drop across the transistor is 9 V at minimum current condition, and the source emf = 12 V. Now find the values of R_1 and R_2 under minimum load conditions. Also, the minimum and maximum transistor resistance values $R_{L,\min}$ and $R_{L,\max}$, and the change in the distribution of the voltage as the circuit changes from minimum load to maximum load condition will be determined.

Minimum Load Condition Calculations

Now, $R_1 = 9$ V at the minimum load condition, and the bleeder I flows through it:

$$R_1 = \frac{V_{R_1}}{I_{\text{bleeder}}} = \frac{9}{0.001}$$
$$= 9000 \ \Omega$$

$R_2 = 3$ V at this time, and the current flowing through it is the sum of the bleeder I and the minimum load I:

$$R_2 = \frac{V_b - V_{R_1}}{I_{\text{bleeder}} + I_{RL,\text{min}}} = \frac{3}{0.001 + 0.0005}$$
$$= 2000 \ \Omega$$

The transistor's maximum resistance, $R_{L,\text{max}}$, can be determined. Its voltage-drop is the same as V_{R_1}, and the current passing through it at that condition is 0.0005 A:

$$R_{L,\text{max}} = \frac{V_{RL,\text{max}}}{I_{RL,\text{min}}} = \frac{9}{0.0005}$$
$$= 18 \ \text{k}\Omega$$

The equivalent value of the transistor's maximum resistance and R_1 is

$$R_{\text{eq,max}} = \frac{R_1 \times R_{L,\text{max}}}{R_1 + R_{L,\text{max}}} = \frac{9000 \times 18,000}{9000 + 18,000}$$
$$= 6000 \ \Omega$$

Maximum Load Condition Calculations

In calculating the resistance of the transistor at the time it is passing its maximum current, several factors need to be considered. First, when the transistor current increases to 3 mA, the total resistance of the voltage-divider network is reduced (as shown in Fig. 6-10c). Since $V_b/I = R$, and the new $I = I_{\text{bleeder}} + I_{RL,\text{max}}$, which is $0.001 + 0.003 = 0.004$ A, the new resistance of the voltage-divider network is

$$R = \frac{12}{0.004} = 3000 \ \Omega$$

But, R_1 and R_2 are fixed in value (9000 Ω and 2000 Ω respectively); therefore the change in circuit R is caused by the change in R_L. The total circuit $R = R_{\text{eq,min}} + R_2$, and rearranging gives

$$R_{\text{eq,min}} = R - R_2 = 3000 - 2000$$
$$= 1000 \ \Omega$$

Using a rearranged version of $1/R_{\text{eq,min}} = 1/R_1 + 1/R_{L,\text{min}}$ yields

$$\frac{1}{R_{L,\min}} = \frac{1}{R_{eq,\min}} - \frac{1}{R_1} = \frac{1}{1000} - \frac{1}{9000}$$
$$R_{L,\min} = 1125\ \Omega$$

This is the minimum transistor resistance.

At maximum load condition V_{R_2} is determined by the ratio of R_2 to the total resistance of the voltage-divider network, which is

$$V_{R_2} = \frac{R_2}{R_{eq,\min} + R_2} \times V_b = \frac{2000}{3000} \times 12$$
$$= 8\ \text{V}$$

and the voltage across the load is equal to V_{R_1}:

$$V_{R_1} = V_b - V_{R_2} = 12 - 8$$
$$= 4\ \text{V}$$

You can see from the above calculations that the introduction of a variable load complicates the analysis of the voltage-divider circuit with its associated loads. If one is aware of the changes brought on by the varying load, these problems can be reasoned out with a fair degree of accuracy.

PROBLEMS

6-26 Refer to Fig. 6-8. $V_b = 220$ V. The following voltage taps are desired: 90, 150, and 220 V. Bleeder I is 30 mA. Find:
   a) resistance values
   b) power dissipation of each resistance
   c) total circuit power dissipation

6-27 Repeat Prob. 6-26 for the following requirements: $V_b = 500$ V; voltage taps are 120, 440, and 500 V; bleeder $I = 12$ mA. Find:
   a) resistance values
   b) power dissipation of each resistor
   c) total circuit power dissipation

6-28 Refer to Fig. 6-9. $V_b = 440$ V; bleeder $I = 14$ mA; load 1 = 10 mA; load 2 = 34 mA; load 3 = 70 mA. Voltage taps are 60, 200, and 360 V. Find:
   a) voltage-divider resistance values
   b) power dissipation of each voltage-divider resistance
   c) power dissipation of all voltage-divider resistances

6-29 Refer to Prob. 6-28. Find:
    a) resistance associated with each load
    b) power dissipation associated with each load
    c) total load power dissipation

6-30 Refer to Fig. 6-9. $V_b = 24$ V; bleeder $I = 1$ mA; load 1 $= 4$ mA; load 2 $= 7$ mA; load 3 $= 3$ mA. Voltage taps are 3, 9, and 21 V. Find:
    a) voltage-divider resistance values
    b) power dissipation of each voltage-divider resistance
    c) total power dissipation of voltage-divider resistances

6-31 Refer to Prob. 6-30. Find:
    a) resistance associated with each load
    b) power dissipation associated with each load
    c) total load power dissipation

6-32 Refer to Fig. 6-9. Voltage taps are 3, 9, and 12 V. $V_{R_4} = 3$ V. Find V_b.

6-33 Refer to Prob. 6-32. Load 1 $= 6$ mA; load 2 $= 4$ mA; load 3 $= 20$ mA. Bleeder $I = 10$ percent of the total load current. Find:
    a) bleeder I
    b) voltage-divider resistance values
    c) power dissipation of each voltage-divider resistance
    d) total power dissipation of voltage-divider resistances

6-34 Refer to Prob. 6-33. Find:
    a) resistance associated with each load
    b) power dissipation of each load
    c) total load power dissipation

6-35 A voltage divider has the following requirements: voltage taps are 3, 6, and 10 V; the overvoltage resistor drops 2 V; load 1 $= 8$ mA; load 2 $= 8$ mA; load 3 $= 4$ mA; bleeder $I = 10$ percent of the total load. After drawing the schematic, find:
    a) voltage-divider resistances
    b) power dissipation of each voltage-divider resistance
    c) total power dissipation of the voltage-divider resistances

6-36 Refer to Prob. 6-35. Find:
    a) resistance associated with each load
    b) power dissipation associated with each load
    c) total load power dissipation

6-37 Design a voltage divider to supply 5 mA at 3 V and 4 mA at 6 V from a 6-V source of emf. Assume bleeder $I = 1$ mA.

6-38 Design a voltage divider to supply 10 mA at 6 V and 8 mA at 9 V from a 9-V source of emf. Assume bleeder $I = 2$ mA.

6-39   A voltage divider has the following loads: 4 mA at 3 V, 7 mA at 8V, and 5 mA at 10 V; bleeder $I = 2$ mA; $V_b = 12$ V. Find:
   a)   voltage-divider resistance values
   b)   power dissipation of each voltage-divider resistance
   c)   total power dissipation of voltage-divider resistances

6-40   Refer to Prob. 6-39. Find:
   a)   resistance associated with each load
   b)   power dissipation associated with each load
   c)   total load power dissipation

QUESTIONS

6-6   What is a voltage divider?

6-7   What is an unloaded voltage divider?

6-8   Why can a voltage divider also be called a voltage attenuator?

6-9   What is a loaded voltage divider?

6-10   What is the current and voltage distribution of a two-tap loaded voltage divider?

analysis techniques for resistive networks 7

This chapter begins with a description of the voltage generator and its internal resistance. The relationship between the internal resistance of the generator and circuit efficiency is analyzed, as is the maximum-power-transfer theorem. Then six methods that can be helpful in the analysis of more complex circuits are discussed. Those networks having more than one source of emf and/or current can be examined by use of a number of special analysis techniques. Those considered to be most useful are studied here. Included in this group are the superposition theorem, Thévenin's theorem, and Norton's theorem. The final technique examined is that dealing with the analysis of delta-wye circuits, with particular attention being given to the conversion of one to the other.

7-1 A THEORETICAL CONSTANT-VOLTAGE GENERATOR

In this section you will learn about the characteristics of the ideal, or "perfect," voltage generator.

Up to now, the source of energy for the circuit has been referred to as the source emf. Now the characteristics of the source emf in the ideal condition can be studied further. Another name for source emf is a constant-voltage generator. The next task is to point out that the generator, which serves as the source of electric energy for the circuit, is not a true source of energy but converts some other form of energy into electric energy (as in the case of dry cells and secondary cells in an earlier chapter). It should also be pointed out that the generator can be one of two general types: constant-voltage and constant-current.

The constant-voltage generator will be discussed first, because it is the most frequently used. If there existed a "perfect" constant-voltage generator, it would display the following properties:

1 The output voltage is independent of the externally connected resistance.

2   The internal resistance of the generator is zero ohms.
3   The load (output current) is inversely proportional to the value of the load resistance. For example, doubling the load resistance value reduces the load by 50 percent.
4   The power delivered to the output is inversely proportional to the load resistance.

It should be pointed out that these are the properties of the perfect constant-voltage generator, which does not exist. But these criteria will serve as a point of comparison with a practical constant-voltage generator.

7-2 A PRACTICAL CONSTANT-VOLTAGE GENERATOR

In this section you will learn about the differences between the perfect and practical constant-voltage generators.

Since the conditions of the perfect constant-voltage generator have been specified, consider what a practical generator should embody. The generator is a converter of energy, not a true source of energy. Furthermore, only a limited amount of energy can be converted by the generator; this means that it can furnish only a limited amount of power.
Within these limitations the characteristics of a good practical constant-voltage generator can be stated thus:

1   The output voltage will be very nearly fixed for light loads.
2   The internal resistance of the generator should be a fixed, low value.
3   The maximum output power of the generator is obtained when the output resistance is equal to the internal resistance of the generator.

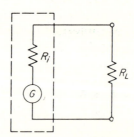

Fig. 7-1   **An imperfect generator in series with R_L.**

The internal resistance of the generator must be considered in many practical cases. When the circuit is drawn, the internal resistance can be shown in series with a constant-voltage, zero-ohm generator. Both components can be enclosed with a dotted line to indicate that they are physically inseparable, as shown in Fig. 7-1.

7-3 THE EFFECT OF THE INTERNAL RESISTANCE OF THE GENERATOR ON AN EXTERNAL SERIES CIRCUIT

In this section you will learn:
· How the internal resistance of the generator affects the output voltage
· How to determine the internal resistance of a generator

In order to show the effect of the internal resistance of the generator on the output voltage of a series circuit, examine two situations: (1) where the internal resistance of the generator is large as compared to R_L, (2) where it is small as compared to R_L. Refer to Fig. 7-1 for both illustrations.

Illustration A

$V_g = 100$ V, $R_L = 10\ \Omega$, and $R_i = 100\ \Omega$. Determine: I, V_{R_L}, and V_{R_i}.

The circuit current is determined by the value of the generator voltage V_g divided by the total resistance of the circuit, which is $R_L + R_i$:

$$I = \frac{V_g}{R_L + R_i} = \frac{100}{110}$$
$$= 0.909 \text{ A}$$

and the voltage across the load resistor R_L is

$$V_{R_L} = I_{R_L} \times R_L = 0.909 \times 10$$
$$= 9.09 \text{ V}$$

The voltage-drop across the internal resistance of the generator is determined by the product of the circuit current, which is also I_{R_i}, and the internal resistance,

$$V_{R_i} = I_{R_i} \times R_i = 0.909 \times 100$$
$$= 90.9 \text{ V}$$

The internal resistance of the generator, being large in comparison with R_L, dropped the greater portion of the generator voltage. From this, you can see that it is most desirable to utilize a voltage generator whose internal resistance is much smaller than the load resistor. The following illustration shows this.

Illustration B

Assume that the generator used in Illustration A is connected with $R_L = 1000 \ \Omega$. Again determine: I, V_{R_L}, and V_{R_i}.

Calculating the new current value yields

$$I = \frac{V_g}{R_L + R_i} = \frac{100}{1100}$$
$$= 0.0909 \ \text{A}$$

and the voltage-drop of the load resistor is

$$V_{R_L} = I_{R_L} \times R_L = 0.0909 \times 1000$$
$$= 90.9 \ \text{V}$$

The voltage-drop across the generator's internal R is

$$V_{R_i} = I_{R_i} \times R_i = 0.0909 \times 100$$
$$= 9.09 \ \text{V}$$

In the second illustration, a greater portion of the generator voltage was dropped across R_L, because R_L is greater than R_i. The ratio of V_{R_L}/V_g approaches 1 when R_L becomes many times greater than R_i. Therefore, if the maximum value of output voltage is desired, a generator should be selected whose internal resistance is much smaller than the value of R_L.

Determining the Voltage Generator's Internal Resistance R_i

Because the internal resistance of a voltage generator is important, one should consider a practical way in which it can be determined. The following list details a procedure for determining the internal resistance of a voltage generator.

1   Measure the open-circuit potential (no external circuit connected) of the generator with a good voltmeter.
2   Connect a large potentiometer (1 MΩ will do in most cases) across the terminals with the generator voltage and potentiometer at their maximum settings.

3   Place the voltmeter probes across the potentiometer.
4   Vary the potentiometer until the voltage across it is equal to 50 percent of the open-circuit voltage obtained in step 1.
5   Remove the potentiometer from the circuit. The resistance setting at this time, which can be measured with an ohmmeter, is equal to R_i of the generator.

Since the internal resistance of the generator and the potentiometer are in series, they must drop the entire generator potential. A good voltmeter has such a high resistance that it is many times greater than the ohmic value of R_i in most voltage supplies. For most practical purposes, it may be assumed that V_{R_i} for this condition is negligible (zero volts). Therefore the entire generator potential is dropped across the voltmeter resistance. The placement of a variable resistance (potentiometer) across the output terminals makes it possible to alter the external resistance until it is equal to R_i. At that time, only half the generator potential is available across the terminals, since the remaining half is dropped across the internal resistance of the generator. This is a rapid and practical method of determining the internal resistance of many generators.

The extent to which the internal resistance of the generator affects the output current and voltage is determined by the ratio of R_i to R_L. When R_i is small compared to R_L, its effect on the external circuit becomes less important. This is the reason why a generator may be good in one circuit but prove unsatisfactory in another with less external resistance.

7-4 CIRCUIT EFFICIENCY

In this section you will learn about the relationship of load resistance and circuit resistance to circuit efficiency.

Circuit efficiency was defined in an earlier chapter as the ratio of the power delivered to the load to the power developed by the source. Expressing this ratio as a percent gives

$$\eta = \frac{P_{R_L}}{P_i} \times 100$$

where η = circuit efficiency in percent
P_{R_L} = power delivered to the load
P_i = power developed by the source

Recall that one of the three power equations is the I^2R relationship. Using it in place of P_{R_L} and P_i in the equation above yields

$$\eta = \frac{I^2 R_L}{I^2 R} \times 100$$

where I = circuit load
   R_L = resistance of the load
   R = total resistance of the circuit

and the equation reduces to

$$\eta = \frac{R_L}{R} \times 100 \tag{7-1}$$

Illustration A

Assume the circuit of Fig. 7-1 has $V_g = 250$ V, $R_i = 10\ \Omega$, and $R_L = 30\ \Omega$. The circuit efficiency needs to be found. Since in Fig. 7-1 the total resistance is the sum of R_i and R_L, then

$$\eta = \frac{R_L}{R} \times 100 = \frac{R_L}{R_i + R_L} \times 100$$
$$= \frac{30}{30 + 10} \times 100$$
$$= 75 \text{ percent}$$

In order to show the relationship of the value of R_L to that of R_i in circuit efficiency, replace the original R_L with a larger value.

Illustration B

Replace the original R_L with a 240-Ω R_L. The circuit efficiency is

$$\eta = \frac{R_L}{R_i + R_L} \times 100 = \frac{240}{10 + 240} \times 100$$
$$= 96 \text{ percent}$$

Therefore, you can see that the circuit efficiency is directly proportional to the R_L/R ratio.

7-5 MAXIMUM-POWER-TRANSFER THEOREM

In this section you will learn about two relationships: the power transfer to the load and the R_L/R ratio, and power transfer and circuit efficiency.

Of particular interest is the condition at which the maximum amount of power is delivered to the load. The maximum-power-transfer theorem alludes to this relationship:

The greatest amount of power is transferred to the resistive load R_L of a circuit when R_L is equal to 50 percent of the total circuit resistance.

In equation form it is stated as

$$PT_{max} = PT \qquad \text{when} \qquad \frac{R_L}{R} = 0.5 \qquad \textbf{(7-2)}$$

Illustration

Consider the circuit of Fig. 7-2. Assume that $R_i = 100\ \Omega$. Also let R_L be set at five successive values: 10, 50, 100, 500, and 1000 Ω. $V_g = 100$ V. Calculate P_{R_L} and the circuit efficiency for each setting of R_L.

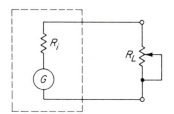

Fig. 7-2   Variable R_L in series with an imperfect generator.

The circuit current for each setting is determined by

$$I = \frac{V_g}{R_i + R_L}$$

and the power transfer to the load is

$$P_{R_L} = I^2 R_L$$

and circuit efficiency is

$$\eta = \frac{R_L}{R_i + R_L} \times 100$$

Using these equations, one can find the values of I, P_{R_L}, and circuit efficiency when $R_L = 10 \ \Omega$:

$$I = \frac{V_g}{R_i + R_L} = \frac{100}{100 + 10}$$
$$= 0.91 \ \text{A}$$

and

$$P_{R_L} = I^2 R_L = (0.91)^2 \times 10$$
$$= 8.28 \ \text{W}$$

and

$$\eta = \frac{R_L}{R_i + R_L} \times 100 = \frac{10}{100 + 10} \times 100$$
$$= 9.1 \ \text{percent}$$

Since values for several settings of R_L are to be found, Table 7-1 is developed. The procedure just described is repeated for each setting of R_L, and these values are placed in Table 7-1. They can be computed by the reader in the same manner.

Note that P_{R_L} is maximum when $R_L / R_i = 1$. This verifies the statement made by the maximum-power-transfer theorem, and it is of considerable importance in electric circuits. Also of interest is the fact that the

Table   7-1

R_L (Ω)	P_{R_L} (W)*	Circuit Efficiency* (percent)
10	8.28	9.1
50	22.45	33.3
100	25	50
500	14.45	83.3
1000	8.10	90.9

* These values are based on computations in which the current is rounded to the nearest hundredth ampere and circuit efficiency to the nearest tenth of a percent.

circuit efficiency is 50 percent at the condition where maximum power transfer occurs.

PROBLEMS

7-1 A generator with an internal resistance of 4 kΩ has an open circuit potential of 50 V. When R_L is connected, $V_o = 40$ V. Find:
   a) V_{R_i}
   b) circuit current
   c) external resistance R_L
7-2 Refer to Prob. 7-1. That generator is connected to an R_L such that $V_{R_L} = 25$ V. Find:
   a) V_{R_i}
   b) circuit current
   c) R_L
7-3 Refer to Prob. 7-1. That generator is connected to an R_L such that its $V_{R_L} = 10$ V. Find:
   a) V_{R_i}
   b) circuit current
   c) R_L
7-4 Refer to Prob. 7-1. Calculate:
   a) P_{R_L}
   b) circuit efficiency
7-5 Refer to Prob. 7-2. Calculate:
   a) P_{R_L}
   b) circuit efficiency
7-6 Refer to Prob. 7-3. Calculate:
   a) P_{R_L}
   b) circuit efficiency
7-7 Refer to Fig. 7-1. $R_i = 10$ kΩ, $V_g = 100$ V, and $V_{R_L} = 75$ V. Find:
   a) V_{R_i} b) I c) R_L
7-8 Refer to Prob. 7-7. Find:
   a) P_{R_L}
   b) circuit efficiency
7-9 Refer to Prob. 7-7.
   a) At what value of R_L will maximum power transfer occur?
   b) What is P_{R_L} at this condition?
7-10 Refer to Fig. 7-1. Assume an additional resistance R_x is placed in series with the generator and R_L. $V_g = 12$ V, $R_i = 50$ Ω, circuit $I = 0.010$ A, and $V_{R_L} = 10$ V. Find:
   a) R_L b) V_{R_i} c) V_{R_x} d) R_x

7-11 The open-circuit potential of a generator (infinite ohms between its external terminals) is 100 V. The external potential decreases to 80 V when $R_L = 400\ \Omega$ is connected across the output terminals. Find:
  a) R_i
  b) I
  c) P_{R_L}
  d) circuit efficiency

7-12 In a circuit like that of Fig. 7-1, the generator operates at 50 percent efficiency. At that condition $I = 0.7$ A and $V_{R_L} = 24$ V. Find:
  a) R_L b) R_i c) P_{R_L} d) V_g

7-13 Repeat Prob. 7-12. The load is 45 mA, and the external potential at 50 percent efficiency is 3 V.

7-14 The open-circuit voltage of a generator is 12 V. An unknown resistor is connected across the terminals, causing the output potential to decrease to 1 V. Find the value of that resistance when the internal resistance of the generator is 1 ohm.

7-15 Repeat Prob. 7-14 for $R_i = 5$ kΩ.

7-16 The internal resistance of a 90-V generator is 1.5 kΩ. A potentiometer of 0 to 3 kΩ is connected across the terminals. The potentiometer is varied in steps of 500 Ω from zero to maximum. Find the following for each step:
  a) current   b) P_{R_L} c) circuit efficiency

7-17 What R_L is needed to achieve 95 percent circuit efficiency with the generator of Prob. 7-16?

7-18 A 30-V generator has an internal resistance of 50 Ω. The potentiometer across the output terminals is varied in steps of 20 Ω from 0 to 100 Ω. Find the following for each step:
  a) current   b) P_{R_L} c) circuit efficiency

7-19 What R_L is needed to achieve 95 percent circuit efficiency with the generator of Prob. 7-18?

7-20 In Prob. 7-18 find the minimum power rating of the potentiometer.

QUESTIONS

7-1 What are three major characteristics of the theoretical constant-voltage generator?

7-2 Why is a generator not a true source of energy?

7-3 What are three major characteristics of a good practical constant-voltage generator?

7-4 What effect does the internal resistance of a generator have on an external series circuit?

7-5 Does the internal resistance of the generator have the greatest effect on the external circuit when R_i is many times smaller or many times larger than R_L?

7-6 What is the procedure for determining the internal resistance of a generator?

7-7 Why can the voltage reading obtained from a good voltmeter be considered an accurate reading of a generator's open-circuit voltage?

7-8 What is circuit efficiency?

7-9 What is the maximum-power-transfer theorem?

7-10 Why does maximum power transfer occur when circuit efficiency is 50 percent?

7-11 What is the relationship between circuit efficiency and maximum power transfer?

7-12 In the circuit of Fig. 7-2, when is P_{R_L} at its maximum value?

7-6 THE VOLTAGE-DIVIDER TECHNIQUE

The voltage-divider technique is a useful tool for solving certain series-circuit problems. Look at Fig. 7-3 for a moment, for it will be used in the following analysis.

Assume that V_{R_1} of Fig. 7-3 is to be determined. What relationship is needed to find that value of voltage? According to Ohm's law for a series circuit,

$$V_{R_1} = I \times R_1$$

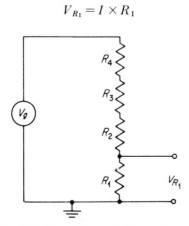

Fig. 7-3 The voltage-divider technique.

and

$$I = \frac{V_g}{R_1 + R_2 + \cdots + R_n} = \frac{V_g}{R}$$

Now, substituting back into the original equation for V_{R_1} yields

$$V_{R_1} = \frac{V_g R_1}{R}$$

Examination of the preceding relationships demonstrates that the specific equation can be made into a general equation for use in any series network. This general equation can be expressed as

$$V_{R_n} = \frac{V_g R_n}{R} \tag{7-3}$$

where R_n = particular resistor whose voltage-drop is to be found
$\quad\quad R$ = sum of the series-circuit resistances
$\quad\quad V_g$ = generator voltage

Illustration

A circuit like that shown in Fig. 7-3 has $V_g = 12$ V, $R_1 = 400$ Ω, and $R = 2$ kΩ. Using the general equation gives

$$V_{R_1} = \frac{V_g R_1}{R} = \frac{12 \times 400}{2000}$$
$$= 2.4 \text{ V}$$

7-7 THE CURRENT-DIVIDER TECHNIQUE

In this section you will learn about a special technique for determining a branch current in a two-branch parallel circuit.

When parallel circuits limited to two branches are analyzed, the current-divider technique can have considerable timesaving value. Look over the circuit of Fig. 7-4 for a moment, in preparation for the following discussion.

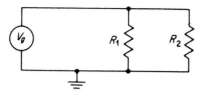

Fig. 7-4   The current-divider technique.

Now an approach must be chosen to find I_{R_1} in Fig. 7-4. According to Ohm's law,

$$I_{R_1} = \frac{V_g}{R_1}$$

and

$$V_g = I \times R$$

and

$$R = \frac{R_1 \times R_2}{R_1 + R_2}$$

Substituting this value back into the equation for V_g yields

$$V_g = \frac{I \times R_1 \times R_2}{R_1 + R_2}$$

Then substituting this back into the original equation gives

$$I_{R_1} = \frac{I \times R_1 \times R_2}{R_1(R_1 + R_2)}$$

Simplify:

$$I_{R_1} = \frac{I \times R_2}{R_1 + R_2}$$

Examination of the preceding relationship indicates that the specific equation can be made into a general equation for use in any two-branch parallel circuit. This general equation can be expressed as

$$I_{R_X} = \frac{I \times R_Y}{R_X + R_Y} \tag{7-4}$$

where I_{R_X} = current in branch X
$\qquad R_X$ = resistance of branch X
$\qquad R_Y$ = resistance of branch Y

Illustration

A two-branch parallel circuit such as that shown in Fig. 7-4 has a total current of 12 mA; $R_1 = 400\ \Omega$, and $R_2 = 2000\ \Omega$. Using the current-divider equation gives

$$I_{R_1} = \frac{I \times R_2}{R_1 + R_2} = \frac{0.012 \times 2000}{400 + 2000}$$
$$= 0.010\ \text{A}$$

Note   As indicated at the beginning of this section, this technique is of timesaving value only when the parallel circuit consists of two branches. When more than two branches are involved, use of the conventional Ohm's law approach is suggested.

7-8   THE SUPERPOSITION THEOREM

In this section you will learn:
· The definition of the superposition theorem
· How it is used in finding a branch current in a two-generator circuit
· How it can be used in other multigenerator circuits

The superposition theorem is an invaluable technique for the analysis of some complex networks that have more than one generator. The theorem can be stated in terms of voltage or in terms of current. Here the theorem is stated in terms of current:

The current flow through any branch of a network which has several generators is the algebraic sum of the component currents of a branch that would result if each generator were connected alone into the circuit with the other generators replaced by their respective internal resistances.

The steps for utilizing the superposition theorem to work out a complex network of two generators are as follows:

1   Remove one of the generators, replacing it with its internal resistance.
2   Determine the branch current desired for this circuit, which can be called "test circuit 1."

3   Place the first generator back into the circuit. Remove the second generator and replace it with its internal resistance.
4   Repeat step 2 for test circuit 2.
5   Determine the algebraic sum of the test circuit 1 and test circuit 1 currents. This is the composite value of that branch current being sought.

Before the superposition theorem is illustrated, it is necessary to consider the definitions of current and voltage generators.

An "ideal," or perfect, current generator is a source of current that has an infinite value of resistance.

Recall from Secs. 7-1 and 7-2 that an ideal voltage generator was defined as a source of voltage that has zero-ohm internal resistance.
Look over the circuit of Fig. 7-5, which is the network to be used in the following illustration.

Illustration

Determine the composite value of I_{R_L} in the circuit of Fig. 7-5 by using the superposition theorem. Note that the network has two generators; therefore, two test circuits are to be evaluated in order to determine composite I_{R_L}.

1   *Test 1.* Remove I_g from the circuit and replace it with its resistance value. It is assumed that I_g is a perfect generator and is therefore replaced with an open circuit (infinite resistance). The test circuit is shown in Fig. 7-6. Examination of Fig. 7-6 reveals that it is a series-parallel arrangement, which can be redrawn as shown in Fig. 7-7 for clarity.

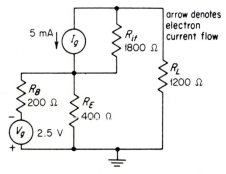

Fig. 7-5   **Circuit for superposition theorem problem.**

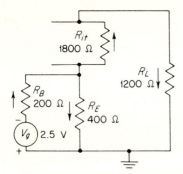

Fig. 7-6   Superposition test circuit 1 (I_g removed).

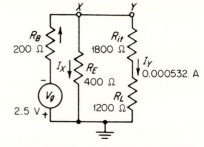

Fig. 7-7   Test circuit 1 simplified.

First the total circuit resistance must be found:

$$R = R_B + \frac{R_E(R_{it} + R_L)}{R_E + R_{it} + R_L} = 200 + \frac{400(1800 + 1200)}{400 + 1800 + 1200}$$
$$= 553 \ \Omega$$

And the total current is

$$I = \frac{V_g}{R} = \frac{2.5}{553}$$
$$= 0.00452 \ \text{A}$$

The current through branch Y, which is I_{R_L} (test 1) can be found by utilizing the current-divider technique analyzed in Sec. 7-7. Note that $R_X = R_E = 400 \ \Omega$, and $R_Y = R_{it} + R_L = 3000 \ \Omega$.

$$I_Y = \frac{I \times R_X}{R_X + R_Y} = \frac{0.00452 \times 400}{400 + 3000}$$
$$= 0.000532 \ \text{A}$$

It should be carefully noted that the direction of I_{R_L} (test 1) is *downward*, as shown in Fig. 7-7.

2   *Test 2.* I_g is returned to the network. Now V_g is removed and replaced with a short circuit. The test circuit is shown in Fig. 7-8.
    Since the object is to find I_{R_L} (test 2) in this step, the circuit can be reduced to that of Fig. 7-9. Note that

$$R_Y = \frac{R_B R_E}{R_B + R_E} + R_L = \frac{200 \times 400}{200 + 400} + 1200$$
$$= 1333 \ \Omega$$

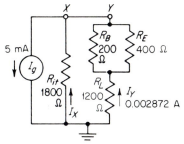

Fig. 7-8   Test circuit 2 (V_g removed).

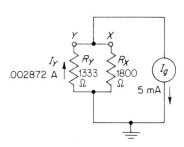

Fig. 7-9   Test circuit 2 simplified.

and

$$R_X = R_{it} = 1800 \ \Omega$$

Again the current-divider technique can be used to find I_{R_L}, which is I_Y:

$$I_Y = \frac{I \times R_X}{R_X + R_Y} = \frac{0.005 \times 1800}{1800 + 1333}$$
$$= 0.002872 \ \text{A}$$

Note that the direction of I_{R_L} (test 2) is *upward,* as shown in Fig. 7-9.

3 *Composite Analysis.* The composite value of I_{R_L} is equal to the difference of the two test currents, since they were flowing in opposite directions. The direction of the composite current is that of the larger test current.

$$\begin{aligned} I_{R_L(\text{composite})} &= I_{R_L} \ (\text{test 2}) - I_{R_L} \ (\text{test 1}) \\ &= 0.002872 \ (\text{up}) - 0.000532 \ (\text{down}) \\ &= 0.0023 \ \text{A (up)} \end{aligned}$$

The preceding illustration analyzed a complex network which had two generators. In many cases, however, the circuit may have three or more generators. In such instances, all but one of the generators must be removed each time, as is explained in the following procedure for working out such circuits with the superposition theorem.

1 Remove all the generators from the circuit except one (G_1), and replace each with its internal resistance. Compute the desired branch current for this test.

2 Repeat step 1, with all generators removed except G_2.

3 Repeat step 1, with all generators removed except G_3.
4 Repeat step 1 until every generator has been in the circuit by itself.
5 Determine the composite of the branch currents found in the preceding test circuits, carefully observing the direction of each test current.

7-9 THÉVENIN'S THEOREM

In this section you will learn about the definition of Thévenin's theorem and how it can be used in finding the load current of a complex circuit.

Another technique used in the solution of certain complex networks is Thévenin's theorem. It can be stated as follows:

The load current of a complex network is equal to the open-circuit voltage of the network divided by the resistance looking into the open circuit (after all generators have been replaced by their respective internal resistances) plus the value of the load resistance.

The theorem can be stated in equation form as

$$I_{R_L} = \frac{V_{gt}}{R_{gt} + R_L} \tag{7-5}$$

where V_{gt} = open-circuit voltage of the network = Thévenin generator voltage
R_{gt} = resistance seen from the open terminals = Thévenin generator resistance
R_L = load resistance

A complex network can be converted into a Thévenin equivalent circuit as follows:

1 Remove the load resistance from the network, leaving those terminals open.
2 Calculate or measure the voltage across the open-circuit terminals. This is the Thévenin generator voltage V_{gt}. The method of calculation is shown in the following illustration. If the circuit is actually present, V_{gt} can be measured with any good-quality voltmeter in low- to medium-resistance networks.
3 Remove all generators and replace them with their respective internal resistances. Calculate the resistance as seen from the open

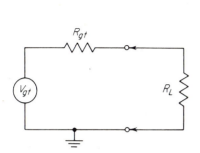

Fig. 7-10   Thévenin theorem equivalent circuit.

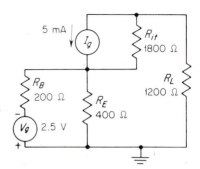

Fig. 7-11   Circuit for Thévenin theorem analysis.

terminals, which is the Thévenin generator resistance R_{gt}. How this can be done is shown in the illustration below.

4   Reconnect the load resistance R_L into the Thévenin equivalent circuit, as shown in Fig. 7-10.

5   Any required calculations or measurements can now be made.

Look over the circuit in Fig. 7-11 for a moment, for it will be used in the analysis that follows.

Illustration

Find the I_{R_L} of Fig. 7-11 by Thévenin's theorem in accordance with the procedure just described.

1   *Remove* R_L. Calculate V_{gt}. With R_L removed, the circuit can be redrawn as shown in Fig. 7-12. In Fig. 7-12, note that I_g current passes

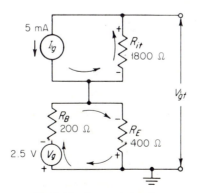

Fig. 7-12   Determining V_{gt}.

only through R_{it}, and the V_g current is restricted to $R_B + R_E$. A further inspection of Fig. 7-12 shows that the open-circuit voltage V_{gt} is obtainable from the relationship

$$V_{gt} = V_{Rit} + V_{R_E}$$

where $V_{Rit} = I_g \times R_{it} = 0.005 \times 1800$
$$= 9 \text{ V}$$

And V_{R_E} can be found by utilizing the voltage-divider method:

$$V_{R_E} = \frac{R_E V_g}{R_E + R_B} = \frac{400 \times 2.5}{600}$$
$$= 1.67 \text{ V}$$

Note the polarities of V_{Rit} and V_{R_E} Since they are opposite,

$$V_{gt} = V_{R_E} + V_{Rit} = -1.67 + 9$$
$$= 7.33 \text{ V}$$

2 *Remove all generators and replace them with their respective internal resistances.* Assume that the internal resistance of V_g is zero ohms and that of I_g is infinite ohms. This reduces the circuit to that shown in Fig. 7-13.

3 *Calculate the Thévenin generator resistance R_{gt}.* Looking into the circuit of Fig. 7-13, you see a simple series-parallel arrangement, which is redrawn in Fig. 7-14. Now compute R_{gt}:

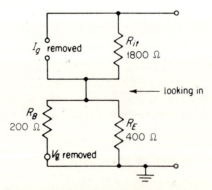

Fig. 7-13 Looking into the network (with I_g and V_g removed) to determine R_{gt}.

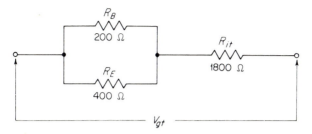

Fig. 7-14   Circuit of Fig. 7-13 redrawn.

$$R_{gt} = R_{it} + \frac{R_B \times R_E}{R_B + R_E} = 1800 + \frac{200 \times 400}{600}$$
$$= 1933 \ \Omega$$

4   *Reconnect the load resistance into the Thévenin equivalent circuit.* This is shown in Fig. 7-15.

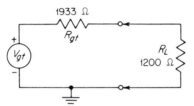

Fig. 7-15   Thévenin equivalent circuit with R_L reconnected.

5   *Calculate I_{R_L}.*

$$I_{R_L} = \frac{V_{gt}}{R_{gt} + R_L} = \frac{7.33}{1933 + 1200}$$
$$= 0.0023 \ A$$

Note   The circuit used in this illustration is the same network analyzed in the example for the superposition theorem. In both cases I_{R_L} was the parameter being sought; the same value should be obtained in each instance, and it is seen that 0.0023 A was found to be the value of I_{R_L} in both examples.

7-10   NORTON'S THEOREM

In this section you will learn about the definition of Norton's theorem and how it can be used in determining the load current in complex circuits.

To begin, Norton's theorem can be stated thus:

The load current of a complex network is equal to the load current of the Norton equivalent generator connected to R_L.

This equivalent network consists of a constant-current generator I_{gn}, which is equal to the short-circuit current of the original network. The resistance of the equivalent network is the resistance seen by looking into the original network from the open-circuit terminals of R_L with all generators removed (but replaced by their internal resistances).

The following procedure can be followed to utilize Norton's theorem for determining the load current I_{R_L} of a complex circuit.

1 Remove R_L and replace it with a short circuit. Compute the current through the short circuit. This is the value of the current I_{gn} in the Norton equivalent generator. *Note:* If the complex network has several generators, the superposition theorem or Thévenin's theorem may be used to find the current through the short circuit. In those cases where the complex circuit contains a constant-voltage generator and a constant-current generator, it is sometimes most convenient to compute the short-circuit current by Thévenin's theorem.

2 Remove the short circuit, to create an open circuit at the terminals of R_L. Remove all generators and replace them with their respective resistances.

3 Compute the resistance looking into the circuit via the open-circuit terminals of R_L, which can be called R_{gn}. This is identical to the method used in computing R_{gt} by the Thévenin theorem method. Therefore,

$$R_{gn} = R_{gt}$$

4 Connect the original R_L across the equivalent Norton generator. Compute I_{R_L}, which is equal to I_{R_L} of the original complex network. Figure 7-16 illustrates the Norton equivalent generator with R_L connected.

Look over the circuit of Fig. 7-17 for a moment; it is used in the following illustration.

Illustration

Find I_{R_L} of Fig. 7-17 by Norton's theorem in accordance with the procedure described above.

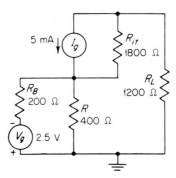

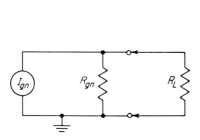

Fig. 7-16 Norton equivalent generator with R_L connected.

Fig. 7-17 Circuit for Norton's theorem analysis.

1 *Remove R_L and replace it with a short circuit (see Fig. 7-18).* Note that Fig. 7-18 (with the shorted R_L represented by the point SC) is still a complex circuit. Thévenin's theorem can be used to find I_{SC}. This approach is suggested because the original circuit has both a constant-voltage generator and a constant-current generator. According to Thévenin's theorem,

$$I_{SC} = \frac{V_{gt}}{R_{gt} + R_L}$$

Since it is I_{SC} instead of I_{R_L}, that is being sought, this means that $R_L = 0\ \Omega$. Therefore

$$I_{SC} = \frac{V_{gt}}{R_{gt}}$$

To find V_{gt}, point SC must be opened, as shown in Fig. 7-19. Inspection of Fig. 7-19 reveals that

$$V_{gt} = V_{R_E} + V_{R_{it}}$$

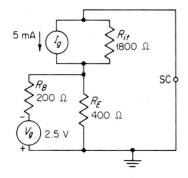
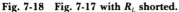

Fig. 7-18   Fig. 7-17 with R_L shorted.

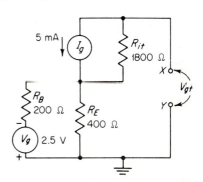

Fig. 7-19   Circuit for determining V_{gt}.

where, using the voltage-divider technique,

$$V_{R_E} = \frac{V_g R_E}{R_E + R_B} = \frac{2.5 \times 400}{600}$$
$$= -1.67 \text{ V}$$

and

$$V_{R_{it}} = I_g \times R_{it} = 0.005 \times 1800$$
$$= 9 \text{ V}$$

Therefore

$$V_{gt} = -1.67 + 9 = 7.33 \text{ V}$$

Now, looking into the network from the open terminals (with V_g replaced with a short circuit and I_g replaced with an open circuit), you see Fig. 7-20.
Solving for R_{gt} gives

$$R_{gt} = R_{it} + \frac{R_B \times R_E}{R_B + R_E} = 1800 + \frac{200 \times 400}{600}$$
$$= 1933 \text{ }\Omega$$

And I_{SC} of Fig. 7-18 can be found now by use of the Thévenin equivalent circuit of Fig. 7-21. Find I_{SC}:

$$I_{SC} = \frac{V_{gt}}{R_{gt}} = \frac{7.33}{1933}$$
$$= 0.0038 \text{ A}$$

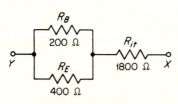

Fig. 7-20 R_{gt} **circuit.**

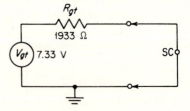

Fig. 7-21 Thévenin equivalent circuit for determining I_{sc}.

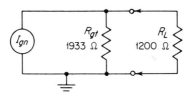

Fig. 7-22   Norton equivalent circuit with
R_L **connected.**

This is I_{gn} of the Norton equivalent generator.

2 *Remove the short circuit of Fig. 7-18.* Replace all generators with their respective resistances. This was already done as a part of step 1, and it results in the circuit of Fig. 7-20. That is,

$$R_{gn} = R_{gt} = R_{it} + \frac{R_B \times R_E}{R_B + R_E} = 1933 \ \Omega$$

3 *Connect the original R_L (1200 Ω in Fig. 7-17) to the Norton equivalent generator,* as shown in Fig. 7-22. Using the current-divider technique yields

$$I_{R_L} = \frac{I \times R_{gn}}{R_{gn} + R_L} = \frac{0.0038 \times 1933}{3133}$$
$$= 0.0023 \ A$$

Note   The circuit used here is the same one used for the superposition theorem and Thévenin theorem problems illustrated in the two preceding sections. It should be noticed that the same I_{R_L} value was found in all three examples.

7-11   DELTA-WYE CIRCUITS

In this section you will learn about converting delta circuits to wye circuits and vice versa.

Refer to Fig. 7-23, which shows both types of networks. It is sometimes convenient to transform one of these two kinds of network into the other. Consider the transformation equations needed.

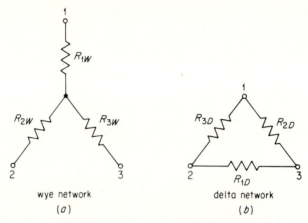

Fig. 7-23   Delta and wye networks.

The Delta-Wye Transformation Equations

Using the notation of Fig. 7-23, you obtain

$$R_{1W} = \frac{R_{2D}R_{3D}}{R_{1D} + R_{2D} + R_{3D}}$$

$$R_{2W} = \frac{R_{1D}R_{3D}}{R_{1D} + R_{2D} + R_{3D}}$$

$$R_{3W} = \frac{R_{1D}R_{2D}}{R_{1D} + R_{2D} + R_{3D}}$$

Note that the subscript W is used to denote a resistor in the wye circuit and D to denote a resistor in the delta circuit.

The Wye-Delta Transformation Equations

$$R_{1D} = \frac{R_{1W}R_{2W} + R_{2W}R_{3W} + R_{1W}R_{3W}}{R_{1W}}$$

$$R_{2D} = \frac{R_{1W}R_{2W} + R_{2W}R_{3W} + R_{1W}R_{3W}}{R_{2W}}$$

$$R_{3D} = \frac{R_{1W}R_{2W} + R_{2W}R_{3W} + R_{1W}R_{3W}}{R_{3W}}$$

The two transformations (delta to wye and wye to delta) can be very useful in the analysis of certain bridge circuits. Look over the bridge

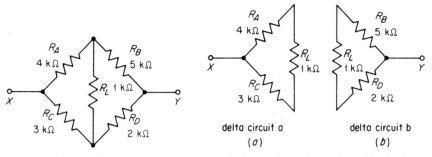

Fig. 7-24   Bridge circuit.   Fig. 7-25   Delta circuit from Fig. 7-24.

circuit in Fig. 7-24 for a moment, for it is used in the following illustration.

Illustration

Find the total resistance seen across terminals X and Y in the bridge circuit of Fig. 7-24. Note that the bridge circuit can be viewed as two delta circuits, as shown in Fig. 7-25. The bridge circuit can be readily converted into a series-parallel circuit (thereby permitting the use of the routine equations for resistance) by transforming one of the delta circuits into a wye network.

Now convert the delta circuit of Fig. 7-25b into its equivalent wye circuit. Using Fig. 7-23b and the delta-wye transformation equations, you get

$$R_{1W} = \frac{R_L R_B}{R_L + R_D + R_B} = \frac{2000 \times 5000}{1000 + 2000 + 5000}$$
$$= 1250 \ \Omega$$

and

$$R_{2W} = \frac{R_L R_B}{R_L + R_D + R_B} = \frac{1000 \times 5000}{8000}$$
$$= 625 \ \Omega$$

and

$$R_{3W} = \frac{R_L R_D}{R_L + R_D + R_B} = \frac{1000 \times 2000}{8000}$$
$$= 250 \ \Omega$$

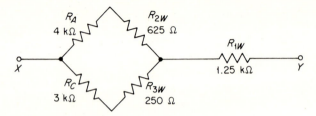

Fig. 7-26 The converted bridge circuit.

The converted circuit is as shown in Fig. 7-26. Note that R_A and R_C of the original bridge circuit remain.

The resistance of the circuit is

$$R_{XY} = R_{1W} + \frac{(R_A + R_{2W})(R_C + R_{3W})}{(R_A + R_{2W}) + (R_C + R_{3W})}$$

$$= 1250 + \frac{(4000 + 625)(3000 + 250)}{4000 + 625 + 3000 + 250}$$

$$= 3159 \ \Omega$$

It can be seen that the process illustrated above can be reversed by starting with a circuit like that of Fig. 7-26 (which contains a wye circuit). With wye-delta transformation equations, such a circuit could be converted into an equivalent bridge circuit.

PROBLEMS

Note Refer to Fig. 7-3 for Probs. 7-21 through 7-25.

7-21 $R_1 = 100 \ \Omega$; $R_2 = 50 \ \Omega$; $R_3 = 300 \ \Omega$; $R_4 = 250 \ \Omega$; $V_g = 12$ V. Find:
  a) V_{R_1} b) V_{R_2}
  c) V_{R_3} d) V_{R_4}

7-22 $R_1 = 470 \ \Omega$; $R_2 = 330 \ \Omega$; $R_3 = 1200 \ \Omega$; $R_4 = 1000 \ \Omega$; $V_g = 20$ V. Find:
  a) V_{R_1} b) V_{R_2}
  c) V_{R_3} d) V_{R_4}

7-23 $R = 2500 \ \Omega$; $R_2 = 400 \ \Omega$; $V_g = 9$ V. Find V_{R_2}.

7-24 $V_{R_3} = 4$ V; $R = 1.4$ kΩ; $R_3 = 300 \ \Omega$. Find V_g.

7-25 $R = 3000 \ \Omega$; $V_{R_4} = 3.2$ V; $V_g = 9$ V. Find R_4.

Note Refer to Fig. 7-4 for Probs. 7-26 through 7-30.

7-26 $R_1 = 3300 \ \Omega$; $R_2 = 4700 \ \Omega$; $I = 10$ mA. Find:
  a) I_1 b) I_2

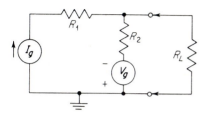

Fig. 7-27   A two-generator circuit.

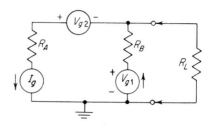

Fig. 7-28   A three-generator circuit.

7-27 $R_1 = 1200\ \Omega$; $I = 15$ mA; $R_2 = 470\ \Omega$. Find:
   a) I_1 b) I_2

7-28 $R_1 = 2200\ \Omega$; $I = 5$ mA; $I_2 = 2.1$ mA. Find R_2.

7-29 $R_2 = 330\ \Omega$; $I = 12$ mA; $I_1 = 7$ mA. Find R_1.

7-30 $R_1 = 470\ \Omega$; $R_2 = 1000\ \Omega$; $I_2 = 4$ mA. Find I.

Note   Refer to Fig. 7-27 for Probs. 7-31 and 7-32.

7-31   Assume: $I_g = 6$ mA; $V_g = 1.5$ V; $R_1 = 400\ \Omega$; $R_2 = 300\ \Omega$; and $R_L = 800\ \Omega$. Find I_{R_L} by use of the superposition theorem.

7-32   Assume all the parameters are as given in Prob. 7-31 except $R_L = 1200\ \Omega$. Find I_{R_L} by use of the superposition theorem.

Note   Refer to Fig. 7-28 for Probs. 7-33 and 7-34.

7-33 $I_g = 6$ mA; $V_{g_1} = 8$ V; $V_{g_2} = 4$ V; $R_A = 220\ \Omega$; $R_B = 470\ \Omega$; and $R_L = 1000\ \Omega$. Find I_{R_L} by use of the superposition theorem.

7-34 $I_g = 2$ mA; $V_{g_1} = 3.4$ V; $V_{g_2} = 1.4$ V; $R_A = 500\ \Omega$; $R_B = 300\ \Omega$; $R_L = 470\ \Omega$. Find I_{R_L} by use of the superposition theorem.

Note   Refer to the circuit of Fig. 7-5 for Probs. 7-35 and 7-36.

7-35   Assume the following parameters: $I_g = 10$ mA; $V_g = 2$ V; $R_B = 300\ \Omega$; $R_E = 100\ \Omega$; $R_{it} = 1000\ \Omega$; $R_L = 750\ \Omega$. Find I_{R_L} by:
   a)   the superposition theorem ·
   b)   Thévenin's theorem
   c)   Norton's theorem

7-36   Assume that the circuit of Prob. 7-35 has I_g reversed, and V_g is also reversed. All other components are the same. Find I_{R_L} by:
   a)   the superposition theorem
   b)   Thévenin's theorem
   c)   Norton's theorem

7-37   Refer to the wye network of Fig. 7-23a. $R_{1W} - 1000\ \Omega$; $R_{2W} - 1200\ \Omega$; and $R_{3W} = 2000\ \Omega$. Find:
   a) R_{1D} b) R_{2D} c) R_{3D}

7-38   Refer to the network of Fig. 7-23a. $R_{1W} = 4700\ \Omega$; $R_{2W} = 6000\ \Omega$; $R_{3W} = 3300\ \Omega$. Find:
   a) R_{1D} b) R_{2D} c) R_{3D}

7-39   Refer to the delta network of Fig. 7-23b. $R_{1D} = 200 \; \Omega$; $R_{2D} = 100$ Ω; $R_{3D} = 300 \; \Omega$. Find:
  a) R_{1W} b) R_{2W} c) R_{3W}

7-40   Refer to the delta network of Fig. 7-24b. $R_{1D} = 4000 \; \Omega$; $R_{2D} = 1000 \; \Omega$; $R_{3D} = 2000 \; \Omega$. Find:
  a) R_{1W} b) R_{2W} c) R_{3W}

QUESTIONS

7-13   How can the voltage-divider technique be used to find the voltage-drop of one of three series resistors?

7-14   How can the current-divider technique be used in finding one of two branch currents?

7-15   What are the five steps utilized in the superposition theorem?

7-16   What is the definition of a current generator?

7-17   What are the steps for converting a complex network into a Thévenin equivalent circuit?

7-18   What are the steps for determining the load current of a complex circuit by use of Norton's theorem?

7-19   What is a wye network?

7-20   What is a delta network?

electrical measuring instruments
8

8-1 PURPOSES OF MEASURING INSTRUMENTS

The purpose of measuring instruments, as used in this text, is to measure the magnitude of current, voltage, and resistance. Current is measured by ammeters, voltage by voltmeters, and resistance by ohmmeters. The passage of current through a conductor can produce any of three effects: thermal, chemical, or magnetic. The amplitude of the current can be determined by the magnitude of any one of these effects, depending upon the measuring instrument. Although the magnetic-effect type of meter is in most common use, the thermal- and chemical-effect techniques have a number of industrial applications and are therefore considered in this chapter.

8-2 CURRENT MEASUREMENT BY THE HEATING EFFECT

In this section you will learn about the hot-wire ammeter and the bolometer.

Look at Fig. 8-1 for a moment, which is a representation of a hot-wire ammeter, in preparation for discussing how it works.

Current in the hot-wire ammeter of Fig. 8-1 is made to flow through the wire, which becomes heated and expands in proportion to the current squared. As the wire expands, its tension becomes less, causing

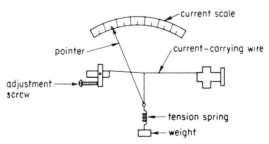

Fig. 8-1   The hot-wire ammeter.

it to sag from the weight of the pointer, tension spring, and weight. As it sags, the pointer moves in a clockwise direction, as can be seen from the diagram. The scale is so calibrated that the magnitude of the current can be read under the setting of the pointer. The scale may or may not be linear, depending upon the mechanical linkage between the wire and pointer. This type of apparatus has been found unsatisfactory and has been replaced by thermo instruments (a combination of a heating element and a magnetic movement), discussed in Sec. 8-11.

The *bolometer* is an instrument which can be used to measure current by its heating effect, which is indicated by a change in resistance. Since the temperature of the bolometer is a function of the current magnitude, it can be used as a current indicator.

8-3 CURRENT MEASUREMENT BY THE CHEMICAL EFFECT

In this section you will learn that the legal ampere is based upon current flow in a chemical solution.

A positive ion is an atom which lacks one or more electrons because of an ionization process; a negative ion has gained one or more electrons in an ionization process. Ionization, which is one of the chief chemical effects of electric current, may be described as the process of adding or removing electrons from the atoms of chemical solutions that are conductors of current. These liquid conductors are called *electrolytes*.

Electric current can be defined as the flow of charged particles. Current flow in an electrolytic solution may consist of ions passing through the solution, resulting in the deposit of a substance upon a plate immersed in the solution. The rate at which the material is deposited is a function of the current passing through the chemical solution. The legal ampere is defined by a chemical effect of current.

The steady unidirectional current passing through a silver nitrate solution for 1 s depositing 0.00111800 g of silver is defined as the legal ampere.

Measuring current by its chemical effect is very accurate, but it is a slow, cumbersome process. The chemical effect of current is utilized in the dry cell, storage (wet) cell, and various types of electroplating processes.

8-4 CURRENT MEASUREMENT BY THE MAGNETIC EFFECT

In this section you will learn that the interaction of two magnetic fields is the basis for an important way of measuring current.

A basic law of magnetism, which will be discussed further later, is that like poles of two magnetic fields oppose each other and unlike poles attract. This law is one of the basic principles used for measuring current by its magnetic effect. One magnetic field, or flux, is stationary, and is usually a permanent magnet. The second flux field is that developed by the current to be measured. The two fields are placed so that an opposing action develops. The opposing force developed must be a function of the current passing through the wire, since the intensity of the permanent-magnet field is fixed. This opposing action, by the proper physical setup, can be made to develop a rotational movement of the electromagnet, which has the meter pointer attached to it. By the proper calibration of a scale, the pointer can be made to read the correct magnitude of the current flowing through the electromagnet. More details will be given in a later section.

8-5 TORQUE AND ITS DEVELOPMENT BY THE MAGNETIC EFFECT OF CURRENT

In this section you will learn about torque and its relationship to magnetic meter movements.

Torque, or moment of force, is the effectiveness of a force in setting a body into *rotation;* it is measured by the product of the force and the perpendicular distance from the axis of rotation to the line of action of the force. The force between two magnetic fields is in a given direction; therefore it can be classified as a torque. This torque is a direct function of: (1) magnetic flux of the permanent magnet and (2) current intensity in the electromagnet. That is,

$$T \propto \Phi I_{em}$$

where T = torque
Φ = magnetic flux of the permanent magnet
I_{em} = current in the electromagnet

The torque is a function of either factor if the other is held constant. In magnetic meter movements, the magnetic flux of the permanent magnet is constant. The strength of the flux developed by the electromagnet hinges directly on the magnitude of the current; therefore the developed torque varies directly with the magnitude of the current passing through the electromagnet.

8-6 THE D'ARSONVAL GALVANOMETER

*In this section you will learn how the D'Arsonval galvanometer is con-
structed and how it operates.*

Figure 8-2*a* illustrates the general principles behind the D'Arsonval
galvanometer. A coil (labeled *L*) is mounted on a carefully designed
soft-iron core (labeled *C*). The core is designed so that a radial flux field
is developed within the air gap between the permanent magnetic poles
and the core. A small metallic ribbon is used to suspend the coil and
core between the poles of the permanent magnet. With no current
passing through the coil, the only flux field is that developed by the
permanent magnet, which is fixed. At that time, the position of the coil
is as shown in Fig. 8-2*b*.

Passing a current through the coil develops a flux field around the
core and coil. If this current is made to flow in the proper direction,
the electromagnetic flux field will be such that its north pole faces the
north pole of the permanent magnet. Therefore a force of repulsion
is developed. In an attempt to move its north pole away from the north
pole of the permanent magnet, the core and coil will rotate as indicated
by the arrow in Fig. 8-2*b*. This is a torque which the electromagnetic
flux field developed, and it must be proportional to the magnitude of
the current passing through the coil. There is a second factor involved.
The metallic ribbon undergoes a twisting action when the core rotates,
developing a countertorque. The countertorque of the ribbon is directly
proportional to the amount of twisting. There will be a point where the
torque produced by the ribbon is equal and opposite to the torque
created by the electromagnetic flux. At this point, the core stops its
rotating action. It can be seen that the angle of rotation is directly
proportional to the magnitude of the current passing through the coil.

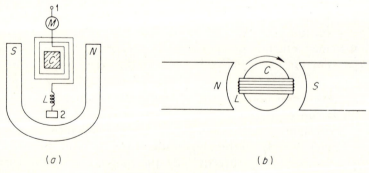

(*a*)   (*b*)

Fig. 8-2   D'Arsonval movement.

The mirror, labeled M in Fig. 8-2a, is used to determine the amount of rotation of the coil by reflecting light on a scale or by reproducing a scale image. As the reader may sense, this instrument is very delicate and must be constructed with a high degree of skill. Section 8-7 discusses a more practical meter movement, based on the same general principles.

8-7 THE PORTABLE METER MOVEMENT

In this section you will learn about the portable, magnetic, meter movement and how it works.

Figure 8-3a illustrates the portable type of meter movement, while Fig. 8-3b shows an actual commercial type. The principle of a fixed magnetic field interacting with a variable electromagnetic field is also incorporated in this type of movement. The soft-iron core, which has a cylindrical shape, is mounted on bearings so that it has ease of movement with a minimum of friction. When current is passed through the coil, the terminals of which are labeled A and B in the diagram, the electromagnetic field is established. An opposing action is set up between the flux fields, causing the soft-iron core to rotate in a clockwise direction, carrying the coil and the attached pointer with it. The scale is so calibrated that the magnitude of the current can be read directly.

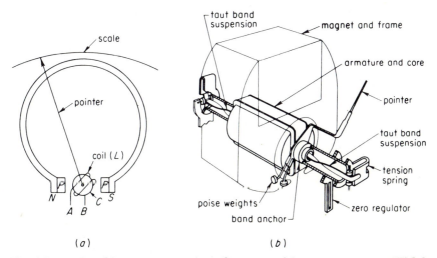

(a)   (b)

Fig. 8-3 (a) Portable meter movement; (b) commercial meter movement (*Hickok Instruments*).

The use of balance weights and springs reduces some of the mechanical problems of the movement. In this way, a restoring torque is present when the current is interrupted, thereby providing a force to bring the pointer back to the rest position. The soft-iron pole pieces (labeled P) in Fig. 8-3a concentrate the flux lines from pole to pole of the permanent magnet.

The movement described in this section is widely utilized in the multimeters and voltmeters frequently used in electrical and electronic work. This is the movement used in the analysis of ammeters, voltmeters, and ohmmeters in the following sections.

8-8   THE NEED FOR DAMPING

In this section you will learn that the meter pointer tends to oscillate above and below its true reading unless provisions for damping are made.

Figure 8-4a illustrates the behavior of the pointer when it is allowed complete freedom of movement. The pointer will not stop at precisely the point where it should (point A) because its own inertia tends to continue the existing motion. When it does come to rest (at point B), it will then move back too far (point C), and so on, until finally it is brought to rest at the correct point (A). This vibratory, or oscillatory, action makes it difficult to obtain the correct scale reading, and it is desirable to eliminate it.

The reduction of the oscillating motion is called *damping*. A properly damped meter movement minimizes the vibratory motion, as shown in Fig. 8-4b. A number of meters wind the coil on an aluminum frame. Current is induced in the frame, which effectively produces an opposing force, which results in damping. Meters can be designed in such a skillful manner that the vibratory motion of the pointer is hardly noticeable.

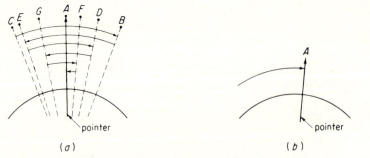

(a)   (b)

Fig. 8-4   Pointer action: (*a*) without damping; (*b*) with damping.

8-9 CURRENT SENSITIVITY

In this section you will learn about current sensitivity and its relationship to the amount of current required to energize a magnetic meter movement.

The amount of deflection produced by a given magnitude of current may be used to indicate the sensitivity of a meter. A very sensitive meter requires a very small current to produce a given pointer deflection. The ratio of the meter current to the pointer deflection created by that current is termed the *current sensitivity* of the meter, and it can be expressed as

$$k = \frac{I}{d} \qquad \text{(8-1)}$$

where k = current sensitivity of meter, μA/mm
I = meter current, μA
d = pointer deflection, mm

Note that a very sensitive meter is one in which full-scale deflection of the pointer is obtained by use of a relatively small energizing current through the moving coil.

8-10 VOLTAGE SENSITIVITY

In this section you will learn about voltage sensitivity and its relationship to the amount of voltage required to energize a magnetic meter movement.

Given a distance for a standard pointer deflection, a certain amount of current is required to produce this deflection. The same problem can be analyzed in terms of the potential which must be applied across the terminals of the coil to produce the same standard deflection. Since a very sensitive meter requires only a small current to obtain full-scale deflection, the potential necessary to drive the energizing current through the moving coil is likewise small. This potential is equal to the product of the required energizing moving-coil current per millimeter and the resistance of the moving coil (Ohm's law). In equation form,

$$V \text{ sensitivity} = kR_m \qquad \text{(8-2)}$$

where V sensitivity = microvolts per millimeter of deflection
k = current sensitivity, μA/mm of deflection
R_m = meter-movement resistance, Ω

8-11 THERMO INSTRUMENTS

*In this section you will learn how a thermo instrument operates and how
it measures current.*

Thermo instruments measure the heating effect of current by use of the
magnetic meter movement discussed in the preceding sections.

Refer to Fig. 8-5 for the following discussion. The circuit current
flows from x to y as illustrated. Point 1 is a junction made by two dissimilar metals. One of the metals is connected between points 1 and 2
and the second metal between points 1 and 3. The current flowing from
x to y generates heat at the junction labeled point 1. Since this is a
junction made by dissimilar metals, a potential is developed at the
junction which is directly proportional to the temperature difference
between the hot and cold ends.

It is important that the temperature difference between the hot and
cold ends (points 1 and 2 and points 1 and 3) be solely the result of the
current flowing from x to y. Therefore points 2 and 3 must be kept at
the same temperature as points A and B. Thermal contact is made between points 3 and A and points 2 and B, as shown in Fig. 8-5, but they
are electrically insulated. In this way, the effect of surrounding temperature changes is minimized between the junction and the ends of the
dissimilar metals, and the temperature difference is more nearly the
result of heat produced by the previously mentioned current.

The junction potential drives current through the moving coil of
the galvanometer, causing a deflection which can be read on the scale.
In this way, the heating effect of any current made to flow between
points x and y can be measured with considerable accuracy. This type
of meter is especially useful in measuring nonsinusoidal currents.

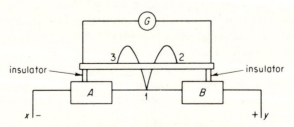

Fig. 8-5   Thermo measuring instrument.

PROBLEMS

8-1   A meter movement undergoes a 6-mm deflection when passing 75 μA of current. Find its current sensitivity.

8-2   The meter of Prob. 8-1 has a resistance of 32 Ω. Find its voltage sensitivity.

8-3   A galvanometer undergoes a 15-cm full-scale deflection. Maximum meter current is 50 μA. Find its current sensitivity.

8-4   The meter of Prob. 8-3 has 12 Ω of resistance. Find its voltage sensitivity.

8-5   A galvanometer undergoes a full-scale deflection of 15 cm with 150 μA of current. The meter resistance is 40 Ω. Find the following:

   a)   current sensitivity   b)   voltage sensitivity

8-12   COMMON TYPES OF MEASURING INSTRUMENTS

The ammeter, voltmeter, and ohmmeter are frequently necessary for the analysis of various electric and electronic circuits. These instruments consist of a magnetic meter movement (as used here) in conjunction with a circuit. The circuitry associated with each type of measuring instrument is studied individually, and then a composite measuring instrument, called the *multimeter*, is examined. A study of the circuitry behind these instruments leads to an understanding of the advantages and limitations of each type.

8-13   DESIGN OF A ONE-SCALE AMMETER

In this section you will learn about how an ammeter operates and how to design a one-scale ammeter.

The maximum current allowed through a meter movement hinges on the amount of current required to develop the torque necessary to bring the pointer to its maximum position. In the type of magnetic meter movement discussed, the current must be made to flow in a predetermined direction if the opposing action between the two magnetic fields is to be developed. The point at which the current enters the ammeter circuit is here called the *negative probe;* the *positive probe* is the terminal by which the current leaves.

At first thought, it seems impossible to measure current the magnitude of which exceeds the maximum rating of the meter movement.

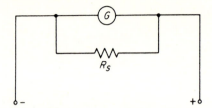

Fig. 8-6 A one-scale ammeter.

In reviewing a basic Ohm's law principle, however, it will be recalled that current can be divided by provision of a parallel path.

In Fig. 8-6, the parallel combination consists of two branches: through the galvanometer and also through the shunt resistor R_S. Let us state a hypothetical problem and see how it can be solved.

Illustration

An ammeter with a 10-mA scale is to be constructed. Available is a meter movement which registers a full deflection when 1 mA is passing through it. The internal resistance of the galvanometer is 30 Ω.

It is obvious that this movement cannot pass 10 mA without being damaged. However, it is possible, by placing the correct value of resistance in parallel with the movement, to have a total circuit current of 10 mA at the time the movement is passing 1 mA and registering a full deflection.

Since the circuit of Fig. 8-6 is a two-branch parallel circuit, you know that the total current is equal to the sum of the two branch currents $(I = I_M + I_{R_S})$, and

$$I_{R_S} = I - I_M = 0.010 - 0.001$$
$$= 0.009 \text{ A}$$

The current-divider equation, when rearranged and adapted to this case, can be used for finding the value of the shunt resistance R_S:

$$I_{R_S} = \frac{I \times R_M}{R_S + R_M}$$

Rearranging to solve for R_S gives

$$R_S = \frac{R_M(I - I_{R_S})}{I_{R_S}}$$

where R_M = resistance of the meter movement
$\quad\quad R_S$ = resistance of the shunt
$\quad\quad\; I$ = total current
$\quad\quad I_{R_S}$ = current through the shunt resistance

Now, by substituting the known values, the shunt resistance is

$$R_S = \frac{R_M(I - I_{R_S})}{I_{R_S}} = \frac{30(0.010 - 0.009)}{0.009}$$
$$= 3.33 \ \Omega$$

8-14 A MULTISCALE AMMETER

In this section you will learn how to design three kinds of multiscale ammeters.

Parallel-Shunt Ammeter

Look over the three-scale ammeter shown in Fig. 8-7. This is called the parallel-shunt type of ammeter.

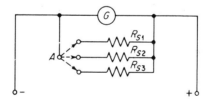

Fig. 8-7 A multiscale ammeter (parallel shunt).

Switching from one range to another is done manually at the control labeled *A*. In this circuit, a new shunt resistance is placed in parallel with the movement for each current range. Using the same approach shown in the preceding section, calculate the shunt resistances for a hypothetical three-range ammeter.

Illustration

A three-range parallel-shunt ammeter like that shown in Fig. 8-7 is to be designed. The meter-movement current is 1 mA; resistance of the meter movement is 30 Ω. The three scales are 5, 50, and 100 mA. Calculate the value of the three shunts.

Shunt 1   Since for range 1 $I = 5$ mA, $I_{R_{S1}} = 4$ mA, and

$$R_{S_1} = \frac{R_M(I_1 - I_{R_{S1}})}{I_{R_{S1}}} = \frac{30(0.005 - 0.004)}{0.004}$$
$$= 7.5 \ \Omega$$

Shunt 2   For range 2 $I = 50$ mA, $R_{S_2} = 49$ mA, and

$$R_{S_2} = \frac{R_M(I_2 - I_{R_{S2}})}{I_{R_{S2}}} = \frac{30(0.050 - 0.049)}{0.049}$$
$$= 0.612 \ \Omega$$

Shunt 3   The total current for range 3 is 100 mA, $I_{R_{S3}} = 99$ mA, and

$$R_{S_3} = \frac{R_M(I_3 - I_{R_{S3}})}{I_{R_{S3}}} = \frac{30(0.100 - 0.099)}{0.099}$$
$$= 0.303 \ \Omega$$

Notice the decrease in the ohmic value of the shunt resistance at the higher current values. This must be so, since they are required to pass more current while the current and resistance of the meter movement are fixed. The design of an ammeter, utilizing these techniques, is a relatively simple process.

Series-Shunt Ammeters

Many ammeters, although incorporating the principles mentioned in this section, are designed in a different manner. Figure 8-8a illustrates the second technique for an ammeter whose movement, and scales are the same as in the preceding problem.

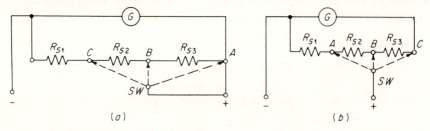

Fig. 8-8   Other multiscale ammeters: (*a*) series shunt; (*b*) Ayrton shunt.

As previously calculated, 7.5 Ω is needed in parallel with this meter movement for the 5-mA range; i.e.,

$$R_{S_1} + R_{S_2} + R_{S_3} = 7.5 \ \Omega$$

The range switch would be in position A for the 5-mA range.

On the 50-mA range, it was found that 0.612 Ω must be placed in parallel with the meter movement. The range switch would be placed in position B. Therefore,

$$R_{S_1} + R_{S_2} = 0.612 \ \Omega$$

and

$$R_{S_1} + R_{S_2} + R_{S_3} = 7.5 \ \Omega$$

Solving for R_{S_3},

$$R_{S_3} = 7.5 \ \Omega - (R_{S_1} + R_{S_2}) = 7.5 - 0.612 = 6.888 \ \Omega$$

Now proceed to the 100-mA range, where the shunt resistance was found to be 0.303 Ω. The range switch would be in position C for this range. Since R_{S_1} is the only resistance in parallel with the movement in this range, it must be equal to 0.303 Ω. The ohmic value of R_{S_2} now can be readily calculated.

$$R_{S_1} + R_{S_2} = 0.612 \ \Omega$$

Substituting and transposing,

$$R_{S_2} = 0.612 - 0.303 = 0.309 \ \Omega$$

In looking back upon the manner in which the shunt values were calculated, it can be seen that calculating the shunt for the highest range as a first step is a convenient approach. The design of ammeters where the shunts are in series with one another is very common.

Ayrton-Shunt Ammeter

Figure 8-8b illustrates the Ayrton-shunt ammeter, a third variation of ammeter design. When the switch is in position A, R_{S_1} serves as the shunt resistance, while R_{S_2} and R_{S_3} are in series with the movement. At position

B, R_{S_1} and R_{S_2} are in series and thereby make up the composite shunt resistance in this setting, while R_{S_3} is in series with the meter movement. In position C, no resistance is in series with the meter movement, and the shunt resistance is made up of R_{S_1}, R_{S_2}, and R_{S_3} in series. This type of ammeter has a special advantage in that R_{S_1} need not be an extremely small value because of the additional resistance (R_{S_1} and R_{S_2}) in series with the movement for the high-current scale (position A). The same advantage extends to any of the successively lower ranges in which the same type of problem is encountered. In some cases, an additional resistance is placed in the circuit so that it is always in series with the movement. The disadvantage of this type of ammeter is that it is best used in high-resistance circuits.

8-15   THE EFFECT OF AN AMMETER UPON THE CIRCUIT

In this section you will learn how and to what extent the resistance of an ammeter disturbs the circuit in which it is inserted.

Sections 8-13 and 8-14 indicate that an ammeter possesses a certain amount of internal resistance. In order to measure current, the ammeter must be placed in series with the circuit. The resistance of the ammeter is therefore inserted into the circuit. The effect of this resistance on the circuit is determined by several factors, including (1) the circuit resistance and (2) the ammeter resistance.

First consider the relationship of the circuit resistance and how the ammeter affects the circuit. Refer to Fig. 8-9 for the following discussion. Figure 8-9a illustrates a case in which the internal resistance of the ammeter is equal to the circuit resistance. Prior to insertion of the ammeter, the circuit current is

$$I = \frac{V}{R} = \frac{100}{10} = 10 \text{ A}$$

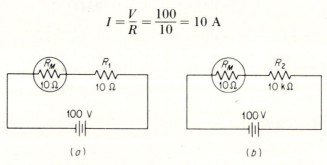

(a)   (b)

Fig. 8-9   The effect of an ammeter upon (a) low- and (b) high-resistance circuits.

With the ammeter placed in the circuit, the resistance is increased to 20 Ω, and the current becomes

$$I = \frac{100}{20} = 5 \text{ A}$$

It can be seen that the insertion of the ammeter disturbed the true circuit conditions to the point where the ammeter reading is highly misleading. Note that this does not imply that the ammeter is inaccurate. The ammeter will read the current which flows through it. A reading of the exact current value which flows in the original circuit is not obtainable. The solution to this problem, which is a compromise, is to use a low-internal-resistance ammeter. In this way, the circuit disturbance created is minimized. For example, assume that a 1-Ω ammeter is used to measure the current of the circuit shown in Fig. 8-9a.

$$I = \frac{V}{R} = \frac{100}{1 + 10} = \frac{100}{11} = 9.1 \text{ A}$$

The percentage of disturbance can be determined by

$$\% \text{ disturbance} = \frac{I \text{ difference (with and without ammeter)}}{I \text{ without ammeter in circuit}} \times 100$$

(8-3)

In the original example,

$$\% \text{ disturbance} = \frac{10 - 5}{10} \times 100 = \frac{5}{10} \times 100 = 50\% \text{ disturbance}$$

and in the second example,

$$\% \text{ disturbance} = \frac{10 - 9.1}{10} \times 100 = \frac{0.9 \times 100}{10} = 9\% \text{ disturbance}$$

From the comparison above, it can readily be seen that a low-resistance ammeter produces a smaller disturbance upon the circuit. The percentage of disturbance is zero only for the theoretically perfect ammeter, which has an internal resistance of 0 Ω. Such an ammeter does not exist, of course.

Consider the high-resistance circuit of Fig. 8-9b. The current without the ammeter in the circuit is

$$I = \frac{V}{R} = \frac{100}{10,000} = 0.01 \text{ A}$$

The current with the ammeter in the circuit is

$$I = \frac{100}{10,000 + 10} = \frac{100}{10,010} = 0.0099 + \text{ A}$$

Percentage of disturbance is

$$\frac{0.01 - 0.0099}{0.01} \times 100 = \frac{0.0001}{0.01} \times 100 = 1\% \text{ disturbance}$$

From these calculations you can see that an ammeter creates a much smaller disturbance on a high-resistance circuit. With many high-resistance circuits, the disturbance is sufficiently small to be considered negligible. The following statements, by way of conclusion, can be made:

1   Any ammeter disturbs the circuit to some extent.
2   Low-resistance ammeters create less disturbance than high-resistance ammeters.
3   An ammeter creates the greatest disturbance in low-resistance circuits and proportionately less disturbance for higher-resistance circuits.

You should be cognizant of these facts when using the instrument. The ammeter is a highly useful measuring device, but it is important that its limitations be duly considered so as to avoid misleading conclusions.

PROBLEMS

8-6   A multiscale ammeter has the following scales: 0.1, 1, 15, and 50 mA. A 50-μA movement, with 30 Ω of resistance, is used. Calculate the values of the four shunt resistors for:
  a)   the parallel-shunt ammeter
  b)   the series-shunt ammeter

8-7   Using the same movement as in Prob. 8-6, calculate the shunt resistances for the ranges 5 mA, 20 mA, 100 mA, and 1 A, for:
a)   the parallel-shunt ammeter
b)   the series-shunt ammeter

8-8   A multiscale ammeter has the same scales as in Prob. 8-6. A 20-μA movement with 45 Ω of resistance is used. Calculate the values of the shunt resistors for:
a)   the parallel-shunt ammeter
b)   the series-shunt ammeter

8-9   Using the movement of Prob. 8-8 and the scales of Prob. 8-7, calculate the shunt resistors for the:
a)   parallel-shunt ammeter
b)   series-shunt ammeter

8-10   A multiscale ammeter with a 500-μA 50-Ω resistance meter movement has the following ranges: 1, 25, 50, 100, and 500 mA, and 1 and 10 A. Calculate the ohmic value of each shunt resistor for a parallel-shunt ammeter.

8-11   A circuit has 100 Ω of resistance and a source voltage of 300 V. An ammeter reads 2.75 A. Assuming the ammeter is accurate, determine the internal resistance of the ammeter and the percentage of disturbance it creates when introduced to the circuit.

8-12   A circuit has 10 A, with a source emf of 50 V. When the ammeter is put into the circuit, the current decreases to 6 A. Find:
a)   circuit resistance prior to insertion of the ammeter
b)   circuit resistance with the ammeter in the circuit
c)   internal resistance of the ammeter
d)   percentage of disturbance created by the ammeter

QUESTIONS

8-1   Explain how an ammeter measures current.
8-2   Where does the energy needed by the ammeter come from?
8-3   Why must an ammeter be placed into the circuit whose current is to be measured?
8-4   When an ammeter is being used, what does the circuit "see" it as? Explain.
8-5   Explain the relationship between current sensitivity and what the circuit "sees" when that ammeter is being used.
8-6   What is voltage sensitivity?
8-7   Explain the relationship between voltage sensitivity and current sensitivity.
8-8   What is the purpose of the shunt resistor in an ammeter?

8-9 Explain why the value of the shunt resistor is changed with each range.

8-10 When will the ammeter create the greatest circuit disturbance — on its highest or lowest current scale? Explain.

8-11 When will the ammeter create the greatest circuit disturbance — in a high-R or a low-R circuit? Explain.

8-12 Explain the difference between the parallel-shunt and the series-shunt ammeters.

8-13 How are the shunts arranged for the several ranges in the Ayrton-shunt ammeter?

8-16 DESIGN OF A ONE-SCALE VOLTMETER

In this section you will learn how a voltmeter functions and how to design a one-scale voltmeter.

In this study of parallel circuits it was found that the voltage across the branches in a parallel combination is the same for each branch. This basic principle, coupled with the magnetic-meter movement, is the basis for the common voltmeter. The makeup of a simple one-scale voltmeter will be studied first. Refer to the circuit of Fig. 8-10 for the following discussion. Assume R_1 and R_2 of the circuit are equal in ohmic value, which means that each resistor will drop one-half of the supply voltage, namely, 25 V each. Also assume that the voltmeter has a 25-V scale. The voltmeter should register a full deflection under the stated conditions. Obviously, the application of 25 V across the meter movement will produce a prohibitive flow of current, possibly resulting in the destruction of the movement. Using 1 mA as the maximum allowable current permitted to flow through the movement leads to this question: How much resistance must be placed in series with the meter movement in order to limit the current to 1 mA when 25 V is felt across the probes? The answer is found in simple Ohm's law relationships.

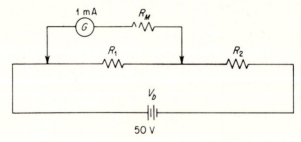

Fig. 8-10 A simple one-scale voltmeter.

$$R_M = \frac{V \text{ of range}}{I_{M,\text{max}}} \qquad \text{(8-4)}$$

where R_M = resistance required in series with meter movement
V = maximum voltage desired for particular range
$I_{M,\text{max}}$ = maximum current permitted through movement

In this example, the range is 25 V, and maximum meter current is 1 mA. The value of resistance required (this series resistance is frequently called the *multiplier*) can be calculated easily:

$$R_M = \frac{25}{0.001} = 25{,}000 \ \Omega$$

Assuming that the resistance of the movement is negligible, you can see that the multiplier-resistance vaiue is 25 kΩ.

In voltmeters the current is limited through the meter movement by means of series resistors, whereas in an ammeter the current is bypassed around the movement by means of shunts. In a short time, you will see that the voltmeter affects the circuit in a different manner than the ammeter.

8-17   A MULTISCALE VOLTMETER

In this section you will learn how a multiscale voltmeter functions and how to design a multiscale voltmeter.

Using the approach discussed in the preceding section, you can readily calculate the ohmic value of each multiplier of the voltmeter illustrated in Fig. 8-11. Remember that each scale must contain sufficient

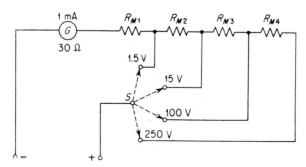

Fig. 8-11   A multiscale voltmeter.

resistance in series with the movement to limit the current through the movement to its maximum value.

Illustration

In the illustration, the maximum meter-movement current is 1 mA. Compute the required multiplier-resistance values needed with voltage scales of 1.5, 15, 100, and 250 V.

Range 1 (1.5 V): maximum meter current is 1 mA. The series resistance required to limit the current to this value is

$$R_{M_1} = \frac{V_{range}}{I_{M,max}} = \frac{1.5}{0.001} = 1500 \ \Omega$$

Since the resistance of the meter movement (30 Ω) is only a small fraction of the required resistance, it may be assumed to be negligible for computation convenience. The first multiplier (R_{M_1}) must be equal to 1.5 kΩ.

Range 2 (15 V): the required series resistance is

$$R = \frac{V_{range}}{I_{M,max}} = \frac{15}{0.001} = 15,000 \ \Omega$$

But R_{M_1} is 1500 Ω; therefore, R_{M_2} must be equal to the difference between 15 and 1.5 kΩ.

R_{M_2} = required series resistance − total of preceding multiplier resistance
    = $15,000 - 1500 = 13,500 \ \Omega$

The same approach can be used to calculate the two remaining multipliers.

Range 3 (100 V):

$$R = \frac{V_{range}}{I_{M,max}} = \frac{100}{0.001} = 100,000 \ \Omega$$

Subtracting the total resistance from the preceding multiplier-resistance total yields

$$R_{M_3} = 100,000 - 15,000 = 85,000 \ \Omega$$

In words, a total of 100 kΩ is required as the resistance in series with the meter movement to limit the current to 1 mA. Since R_{M_1} and R_{M_2} possess a total of 15 kΩ, then R_{M_3} must be equal to the difference between 100 and 15 kΩ.

Range 4 (250 V):

$$R = \frac{V_{\text{range}}}{I_{M,\text{max}}} = \frac{250}{0.001} = 250,000 \ \Omega$$

and

$$R_{M_4} = 250,000 - 100,000 = 150,000 \ \Omega$$

As can be seen, the calculation of multiplier resistors requires the use of Ohm's law, since their purpose is to limit the current to a certain maximum value with a specified potential. Notice how multipliers are added to the series arrangement at the higher ranges by the switch SW in Fig. 8-11. This points out that the voltmeter shown contains more resistance at the higher than at the lower ranges. Many modern voltmeters circumvent this problem with special circuit designs which place the minimum resistance at a high value.

8-18 THE EFFECT OF A VOLTMETER UPON THE CIRCUIT AND VOLTMETER SENSITIVITY

In this section you will learn how the voltmeter appears as a resistance in parallel with the component whose voltage is being measured and how the voltmeter sensitivity is used as a measure to determine the degree of disturbance a voltmeter introduces in the circuit to which it is applied.

As was mentioned in an earlier section, the voltmeter is placed in parallel with the component whose voltage is to be measured. The circuit will see the voltmeter as a resistance in parallel with that component. Consider the circuit of Fig. 8-12a. With the 100-V scale of the volt-

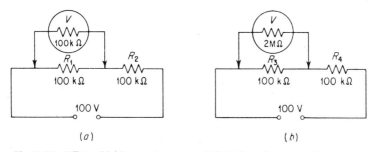

Fig. 8-12 Effect of (a) low-resistance and (b) high-resistance voltmeter on a circuit.

meter calculated in the preceding section, the voltmeter appears as a 100-kΩ resistance in parallel with R_1. Before placing the voltmeter in the circuit, one can determine by Ohm's law that V_{R_1} is 50 V. Placing the 100 kΩ of the voltmeter in parallel with R_1 reduces the resistance in that part of the circuit.

$$\text{Equivalent } R = \frac{R_1 R_V}{R_1 + R_V} = \frac{1(10)^5 \times 1(10)^5}{2(10)^5} = 50{,}000 \ \Omega$$

where R_V is the resistance of the voltmeter. The equivalent resistance for that portion of the circuit has been reduced by placing the voltmeter in the circuit. Before insertion of the voltmeter, R_1 was the only resistance in this part of the circuit, and it made up 50 percent of the circuit resistance. The total resistance of this parallel network, by insertion of the voltmeter, was decreased from 200 to 150 kΩ. In the discussion on series circuits and voltage dividers, it was found that the voltage-drop across a resistor in a series circuit may be determined in the following manner:

$$V_{R_1} = \frac{R_1}{R} V_b$$

Applying this to the circuit in Fig. 8-12a, R_1 would consist of the equivalent resistance of the original R_1 and the voltmeter resistance.

$$V_{R_1} = \frac{50{,}000}{150{,}000} \times 100 = 33.3 \text{ V}$$

Therefore the voltmeter will read 33.3 V as the *IR*-drop across R_1. You might conclude that the voltmeter is rendering an inaccurate reading; this is not necessarily the case. Placing the voltmeter in the circuit altered the circuit resistance distribution, which in turn changed the distribution of the voltage-drops. By affecting the circuit to this extent, the voltmeter used in the illustration falls short of rendering a true reading of V_{R_1} in the original circuit. It becomes obvious then that validity of readings from this voltmeter is limited to circuits containing low resistance.

The solution to this problem lies in the use of a voltmeter that contains a greater amount of resistance. Assume a voltmeter which possessed 2 million Ω of resistance on the 100-V scale. Compute the change in circuit resistance and voltage distribution created by this voltmeter (Fig. 8-12b illustrates this condition).

$$\text{Equivalent } R = \frac{R_3 R_V}{R_3 + R_V} = \frac{1(10)^5 \times 2(10)^6}{2.1(10)^6} = 95,238 \ \Omega$$

$$\text{Circuit } R_{\text{total}} = 95,238 \ \Omega + 100,000 \ \Omega = 195,238 \ \Omega$$

$$V_{R_3} = \frac{95,238}{195,238} \times 100 = 48.8 \ V$$

The second voltmeter, used in the circuit of Fig. 8-12b, created a smaller disturbance upon the original circuit. Therefore the reading obtained from the voltmeter is considerably closer to the actual voltage-drop of R_3 prior to insertion of the voltmeter.

The resistance of the voltmeter has much to do with the *reliability* of its readings, particularly in high-resistance circuits. The maximum allowable movement current dictates the value of series resistance for any particular voltmeter range. A meter movement whose maximum current is 1 mA requires a smaller value of series resistance than a movement with a maximum current of 100 μA. Therefore a voltmeter incorporating a meter movement whose maximum current is lower (such as 100 μA instead of 1 mA) introduces a larger value of resistance in parallel with the component to be measured. Recall the parallel-resistance relationship: a larger parallel resistance (the voltmeter) places the equivalent resistance of the circuit component and voltmeter closer to the original resistance value of the circuit component alone. The higher the resistance of the voltmeter, the less *disturbing* its effect upon the circuit. A convenient method for describing the amount of resistance possessed by a voltmeter is the ratio of the number of ohms per volt of the range, which is called the *voltmeter sensitivity*. In equation form,

$$S = \frac{R_{\text{range}}}{V_{\text{range}}} \qquad \text{(8-5)}$$

where S is the voltmeter sensitivity in ohms per volt. Since R/V is the reciprocal of V/R and $V/R = I$, $R/V = 1/I$, and

$$S = \frac{R_{\text{range}}}{V_{\text{range}}} = \frac{1}{I_{M,\text{max}}} \qquad \text{(8-5a)}$$

In an earlier example, it was found that 100 kΩ of series resistance is required for the 100-V range if the voltmeter has a 1-mA meter movement. Determine the required series resistance for the 100-V range of a voltmeter which utilizes a 50-μA movement.

$$R = \frac{V_{\text{range}}}{I_{M,\text{max}}} = \frac{100}{50(10)^{-6}} = 2(10)^6 \ \Omega$$

and the sensitivity of this voltmeter is

$$S = \frac{R_{range}}{V_{range}} = \frac{2(10)^6}{100} = 20(10)^3 \ \Omega/V$$

It will be recalled that this is the voltmeter used in the circuit of Fig. 8-12b. Notice that this voltmeter, in placing 2 million Ω across the component whose voltage is to be measured, produced a smaller disturbance effect upon the circuit, which leads to this important conclusion: *a higher-sensitivity voltmeter creates a smaller disturbance effect upon the circuit than would be created by a lower-sensitivity voltmeter under the same circuit conditions.* The preceding analysis of the circuits in Fig. 8-12a and b verifies this statement.

In the majority of common electronic circuits, voltmeters possessing sensitivity values of 20 kΩ/V will perform satisfactorily. Voltmeters whose sensitivity exceeds this may be used in those circuits containing resistance running into megohms. Many of the modern voltmeters are designed so that the resistance of the lowest ranges is set at a rather high minimum so as to reduce greatly the disturbing effect.

PROBLEMS

8-13 Calculate the multipliers required for a voltmeter using a 0.5-mA movement and the following scales: 1.5, 5, 50, and 150 V.

8-14 Find the sensitivity of the voltmeter in Prob. 8-13.

8-15 Compute the sensitivity of a voltmeter which has 500 kΩ on a 75-V range.

8-16 Calculate the sensitivity of voltmeters using the following meter movements:
a) 75 μA   b) 5 mA   c) 200 μA
d) 350 μA   e) 250 μA

8-17 Using the movement of Prob. 8-16(a), calculate the multipliers for the following voltage ranges:
a) 1.5 V   b) 5 V   c) 15 V
d) 50 V   e) 150 V

8-18 Calculate the multipliers for a voltmeter using the movement of Prob. 8-16(c) and the ranges of Prob. 8-17.

8-19 Calculate the multipliers for a voltmeter using the movement of Prob. 8-16(b) and the ranges of Prob. 8-17.

8-20 Calculate the multipliers for a voltmeter using the movement of Prob. 8-16(d) and the ranges of Prob. 8-17.

8-21   Calculate the multipliers for a voltmeter using the movement of Prob. 8-16(e) and the ranges of Prob. 8-17.

8-22   Find the equivalent resistance resulting from the placement of the voltmeter of Prob. 8-13 on its 1.5-V scale across each of the following resistances:
a)   3000 Ω   b)   50 kΩ   c)   2 MΩ

8-23   Repeat Prob. 8-22 with the voltmeter switched to its 150-V scale.

8-24   Find the equivalent resistance resulting from the placement of the voltmeter of Prob. 8-17 on its 1.5-V scale across each of the resistances listed in Prob. 8-22.

8-25   Repeat Prob. 8-24 with the voltmeter switched to its 150-V scale.

QUESTIONS

8-14   Explain how a voltmeter measures voltage.

8-15   What is the purpose of the *multiplier* resistor in the voltmeter?

8-16   Why is the voltmeter placed in parallel with the component whose voltage is being measured?

8-17   Where does the voltmeter obtain the energy it needs for operation?

8-18   What does the circuit see when a voltmeter is placed across a resistor? Explain.

8-19   What is the relationship between voltmeter sensitivity and circuit disturbance?

8-20   When will a voltmeter create the most circuit disturbance – when using its lowest or highest range? Explain.

8-21   When will a voltmeter create the most circuit disturbance – in a high-R or low-R circuit? Explain.

8-19   DESIGN OF A ONE-SCALE OHMMETER

In this section you will learn how two basic kinds of ohmmeters operate and how to design the series-type one-scale ohmmeter.

The Series Ohmmeter

As shown in Fig. 8-13, there are two basic ohmmeter types, the *series* and the *shunt*. Consider the series type first. Assume that V_b is 6 V, the maximum meter-movement current is 1 mA, and its resistance is 30 Ω.

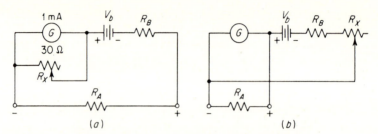

Fig. 8-13   Ohmmeters: (*a*) series type; (*b*) shunt type.

When the two probes are shorted, the movement should register full deflection. By Ohm's law,

$$R_i = \frac{V_b}{I_{M,\text{max}}} = \frac{6}{0.001} = 6000 \ \Omega$$

That is, the internal resistance of the meter must be 6 kΩ when V_b is 6 V. A fraction of this resistance is fixed (R_B), and the remaining portion is obtained from the variable shunt resistance R_X. The reason for obtaining a part of the internal resistance from a variable resistor is to compensate for the battery as it weakens with age. R_X, in most ohmmeters, can be varied from the front panel of the meter and is generally labeled *Ohms adjust.* By increasing the ohmic value of R_X, more of the total current is passed through the movement. Eventually, the battery voltage will become so low that the pointer cannot be brought back to 0 Ω, since the total current will be less than required by the movement for full deflection. When this occurs, the battery must be replaced.

The manner in which the resistance can be calculated for the one-scale series ohmmeter is worthy of consideration (refer to Fig. 8-13*a*). Assume that the battery potential is 6 V, full-scale movement current is 1 mA, and the resistance of the movement is 30 Ω. It is often most convenient, in designing such an ohmmeter, to specify the value of a resistor R_A between the prods which will render a midpoint reading on the scale. Assume that R_A is 4000 Ω to obtain a midpoint reading; i.e., the movement current is 0.5 mA. Since placing R_A between the prods decreased the current to 50 percent of its original value, R_A must be equal to the internal resistance of the meter, which is determined by

$$R_i = R_B + \frac{R_X R_M}{R_X + R_M}$$

where R_i = total internal resistance of meter
$\quad\quad R_X$ = shunt resistance
$\quad\quad R_M$ = movement resistance
$\quad\quad R_B$ = resistance in series with movement

If you desire the movement to be at half-scale deflection when R_A is 4000 Ω, then the internal resistance of the meter must also be 4000 Ω. Knowing the battery potential (6 V) and R_M (30 Ω), you can design the ohmmeter. By shorting the prods, the following values can be determined:

$$I = \frac{V_b}{R} = \frac{6}{4000} = 0.0015 \text{ A}$$

and

$$I_{RX} = I - I_{M,\max} = 0.0015 - 0.001 = 0.0005 \text{ A}$$

Now compute R_X.

$$\frac{R_X}{R_M} = \frac{I_{R_M}}{I_{R_X}}$$

Rearranging yields

$$R_X = R_M \frac{I_{R_M}}{I_{R_X}}$$

and

$$R_X = 30 \times \frac{1}{0.5} = 60 \ \Omega$$

The equivalent resistance of R_X and R_M is

$$\frac{60 \times 30}{60 + 30} = 20 \ \Omega$$

R_B is equal to the difference between this value and the total internal resistance:

$$R_B = 4000 - 20 = 3980 \ \Omega$$

In the series type of ohmmeter, maximum current flows through the movement when the resistance between the prods is 0 Ω. Therefore, the full-scale deflection is labeled 0 Ω on the face of the meter. This adjustment should be made before the ohmmeter is used. When the prods are opened, no current flows, and there is no meter deflection. Most ohmmeters have a second adjustment on the face of the panel, which adjusts the springs of the movement so that the pointer can be made to read exactly zero (infinite Ω) when the prods are opened. This adjustment also should be made before the ohmmeter is used, to ensure the most accurate readings possible. When the resistance between the prods is much less (1 percent) or greater (100 times) than the internal resistance of the meter, it becomes difficult to read the meter deflection correctly. For this reason, a good ohmmeter contains more than one scale; this fact is examined in the following section.

The Shunt Ohmmeter

The other basic type of ohmmeter, called the shunt ohmmeter, often is used for the measurement of small resistances. The unknown resistance, when connected between the prods, acts as a shunt to the movement (see Fig. 8-13b). When the probes are held apart, the shunt has infinite resistance, and the movement is adjusted for full-scale deflection and labeled infinite Ω on the face of the meter. When the probes are shorted, all the battery current will flow through the shorted shunt, leaving none to flow through the movement. There will be no deflection; this is labeled 0 Ω on the face of the meter. This is the reason why some ohmmeters have 0 Ω on the left side of the meter face, while others use the right side. (In the series type, zero resistance is present when meter current is maximum; there is zero resistance present at the zero meter-current condition of the shunt type.)

Placing a resistance between the probes adds resistance to the shunt, increasing the meter-movement current and reducing the shunt current. A larger deflection is seen, and it is calibrated to read the ohmic value of the shunt resistance. As in the series type, when the resistance between the prods is equal to the internal resistance of the ohmmeter, the meter reading is at half scale. Since this can be a small value of resistance in this type of ohmmeter, it can be used to measure the values of low resistances.

8-20 A MULTISCALE OHMMETER

In this section you will learn about designing a simple multiscale ohmmeter.

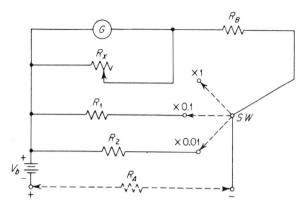

Fig. 8-14   Multiscale ohmmeter (shunted series).

When the unknown resistance R_A is 1 percent of the internal resistance, or 100 times greater than it, a reliable reading is difficult to obtain. One method to overcome this problem is to provide a shunt arrangement, as shown in Fig. 8-14. Examine the manner in which this arrangement can be designed.

Example

The one-scale series-type ohmmeter of Sec. 8-19 is to be used as the basis for a multiscale ohmmeter. Find the ohmic value of the shunts to be used for a 0.1 and 0.01 range.

Solution

Let us select the first shunt, R_1, so that it is equal to one-ninth of the original R_i ($\frac{1}{9}$ of 4000 = 444 Ω). Hence the new total internal resistance will be (444 × 4000)/(444 + 4000) = 400 Ω. That is, the addition of R_1 reduced the internal resistance of the meter on the 0.1 range to 10 percent of its value on the 1.0 range. With R_1 at 444 Ω, 90 percent of the battery current will flow through it, and 10 percent will flow through the original 1.0-range circuit. Since the resistance presented to the battery has been reduced to 10 percent, the battery current is 10 times greater; the current through the movement is the same.

It will be recalled that a half-scale reading was obtained by making R_A equal to 4000 Ω in the original problem of Sec. 8-19. This was due to the fact that R_A and R_i were equal, and a half-scale reading was obtained. With the addition of R_1, the internal resistance is reduced to 10 percent. Therefore an R_A of 400 Ω will render a half-scale reading with this condition. As shown in Fig. 8-14, this is called the $\times 0.1$ range of the ohmmeter. In using the same type of analysis, the correct R_2 value (about one-ninth of the internal resistance of the 0.1 range) is found to be about 44 Ω. Ranges below this may draw too much current from the dry cell; this imposes a limitation on how low a range can be designed.

The voltage used in some ohmmeters is made available by a special power supply in which the potential can be changed with different ranges. In ohmmeters of this type, wide ranges of resistance can be measured. The value of R_B is also changed with range-switching along with the change in potential in this type of ohmmeter.

8-21 NONLINEARITY OF THE OHMMETER SCALES

The scale readings for the ammeter and voltmeter can be made linear, but this is not the case with the ohmmeter, because the current is varied by changes in resistance. The low values of resistance can be read on a given scale much more easily than the higher values. Beyond the half-scale deflection, large changes in resistance produce corresponding smaller deflections of the pointer. This leads to an increased probability of inaccurate readings and is one of the main reasons for having multirange ohmmeters.

Whenever possible, it is recommended that the range be so selected that a reading is obtained somewhere near the middle of the scale. Furthermore, it is suggested that the face of the meter be read from a direct view and not from a side angle, since a side view introduces a parallax error in reading the scale.

8-22 THE MULTIMETER

The multimeter is a combination ammeter, voltmeter, and ohmmeter in one compact unit. Many multimeters are portable, with the necessary source potential for the ohmmeter available from batteries. The advantage of the multimeter over the separate meters for each type of measurement is decidedly great, since a simple switching action and prod change enables the operator to use any one of the meter sections at will. Caution should be exercised to ensure the use of the correct prods in the right manner (voltmeter prods in parallel with the voltage to be measured, ammeter in series, ohmmeter across the resistance to be measured, with the circuit broken).

8-23 THE WATTMETER

In this section you will learn how the basic wattmeter functions as a combined voltmeter and ammeter with output readings calibrated in watts.

It will be recalled that power can be determined by the product of the potential and current. An instrument designed to measure power is called the *wattmeter;* it must have provisions to measure the effect of both the current and potential at the same time. At first glance this may seem a difficult problem, since current is measured by placing the ammeter in series with the circuit element, while its potential is measured by placing the voltmeter in parallel with the component under investigation.

Figure 8-15 illustrates the fundamental wattmeter. Electromagnets, which are magnets developed by electric current, are described in Chap. 9. The permanent magnet of the basic portable meter movement of Fig. 8-3 is replaced with a second electromagnet, which consists of L_1 and L_2 (the symbol for electromagnets). This meter movement is called an *electrodynamometer.* L_1 and L_2 are fixed in positions on each side of the moving coil L_3. L_1 and L_2 are connected in series, and their unconnected ends are brought out to terminals A and B in Fig. 8-15. The circuit which is to be measured is broken, and terminals A and B are connected in series with the circuit. L_1 and L_2 are called the *current coils,* since they are energized by the circuit current. The effect of the circuit current upon the movement is obtained by this technique. The voltage of the circuit is made to affect the meter movement in the

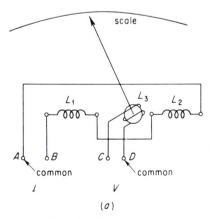

Fig. 8-15   The wattmeter.

manner described for the basic voltmeter. Terminals C and D are connected in parallel with the component whose power is to be measured. The voltage across the component will determine the potential across L_3, thereby enabling current to flow through L_3. This energizes the moving electromagnet L_3, called the *potential coil*. The interaction of the energized current coils and potential coil results in a pointer deflection which can be calibrated to read power in watts. The common terminal of each electromagnet must be observed; otherwise, the pointer will deflect to the left instead of to the right.

8-24 THE WHEATSTONE BRIDGE

In this section you will learn how a Wheatstone bridge can be used to measure resistance.

Figure 8-16 illustrates the Wheatstone bridge, which can be used to measure an unknown resistance R_X. Note the use of two switches. The galvanometer connected between B and $SW1$ reads zero at mid-scale, thereby enabling it to indicate current flow in either direction. The first step in using the Wheatstone bridge is to close $SW2$ (but keep $SW1$ open) so as to permit electron flow as indicated by the arrows. Notice that, with $SW1$ open, R_X and R_3 are in parallel with R_1 and R_2, which means that

$$V_{R_X} + V_{R_3} = V_{R_1} + V_{R_2}$$

When $SW1$ is closed for a brief instant, electrons may flow from point C through the galvanometer through R_3 or from point B through the galvanometer through R_2, depending upon the path of least resistance. If R_1 is varied until $V_{R_1} = V_{R_X}$, then $V_{R_2} = V_{R_3}$, and the potential across the galvanometer (with $SW1$ closed) is zero and no current flows through

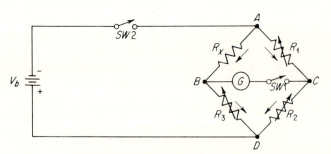

Fig. 8-16 The Wheatstone bridge.

it. Step 2 in the use of the Wheatstone bridge utilizes this principle: two of the three resistors (R_1, R_2, and R_3) are varied, and $SW1$ is momentarily closed until the galvanometer deflection is zero. When this condition is achieved, the bridge is balanced, and V_{BC} is zero. When the bridge is balanced, the following conditions exist:

$$V_{R_X} = V_{R_1} \quad \text{and} \quad V_{R_3} = V_{R_2}$$

Since $V_{R_X} + V_{R_3} = V_{R_1} + V_{R_2}$,

$$\frac{V_{R_X}}{V_{R_3}} = \frac{V_{R_1}}{V_{R_2}}$$

When the bridge is balanced, R_X and R_3 are in series, and R_1 and R_2 are in series; therefore the resistances possess the same ratio as their voltage-drops.

$$\frac{R_X}{R_3} = \frac{R_1}{R_2}$$

Solving for R_X,

$$R_X = \frac{R_1}{R_2} R_3$$

The ratio arm of the bridge is R_1/R_2. A rotary switching arrangement is used commonly in commercial bridges to adjust the ratio arm with a relatively wide range of ratios available. A decade box, the resistance of which can be varied in small ohmic steps up to as high as 10 kΩ, is often used as R_3 of the commercial bridge. Highest accuracy is obtained by selecting a ratio-arm setting which permits the use of the largest R_3.

The Wheatstone bridge is an effective resistance-measurement technique for values down to several ohms. The measurement of even smaller resistances can be achieved most accurately by use of the Kelvin bridge, a modification of the Wheatstone bridge. Resistances as low as 10^{-6} Ω have been measured within 5 percent accuracy by use of a Kelvin bridge.

The Wheatstone bridge may also be used in the strain gage, which consists of several folds of wire. Stretching or compressing this wire results in a change in the resistance of the strain gage (stretching the wire reduces its cross-sectional area, which increases its resistance; compressing the wire produces the opposite effect). The strain gage may be used as R_2 of the bridge shown in Fig. 8-16. In this way, any change in the mechanical properties of the material to which it is attached results in unbalancing the bridge. This technique is used by engineers and metallurgists in the study of the mechanical properties of a material under various conditions of stress and strain.

PROBLEMS

8-26   Refer to the circuit of Fig. 8-13a. Maximum meter-movement current is 50 μA; meter-movement $R = 25\ \Omega$; $V_b = 3$ V. The meter registers a half-scale deflection when 2 kΩ of resistance is placed between the prods. Find:
a) R_i
b) I when the prods are shorted
c) I_{R_X} when the prods are shorted
d) R_X
e) R_B

8-27   With the same meter movement and battery potential of Prob. 8-26, it is desired that the meter register a half-scale deflection when a 3-kΩ resistance is placed between the prods. Find:
a) R_i
b) I when the prods are shorted
c) I_{R_X} when the prods are shorted
d) R_X
e) R_B

8-28   Repeat Prob. 8-26 with a battery potential of 6 V.

8-29   Repeat Prob. 8-26 with a battery potential of 6 V and a 1-mA 30-Ω meter movement.

8-30   Refer to Prob. 8-26. Because of aging, the battery potential decreased to 2.9 V. In order to obtain the full deflection of the pointer with the prods shorted, R_X can be adjusted to compensate for the change in battery potential. Find:
a) current when the prods are shorted
b) I_{R_X}
c) R_X

8-31   Repeat Prob. 8-30 for the ohmmeter of Prob. 8-29, where the battery potential decreases to 5.7 V.

8-32   Refer to Fig. 8-14. A multiscale ohmmeter is to be designed; a 1-mA 30-Ω movement is available, and a half-scale deflection is desired on the highest range when 5000 Ω is connected be-

tween the prods. A 6-V dry cell will be the source of potential. Find:
a) R_i on range × 1
b) I when the prods are shorted on range × 1
c) I_{R_X}
d) R_X
e) R_B
f) R_1
g) R_2

8-33 Repeat Prob. 8-32 with a 50-μA 24-Ω movement where a half-scale deflection is desired when a 10,000-Ω resistance is connected between the prods. Battery potential is 3 V.

8-34 Repeat Prob. 8-33 with a half-scale deflection when 6000 Ω of resistance is connected between the prods.

8-35 Repeat Prob. 8-32 with a 200-μA scale and a 27-Ω movement.

QUESTIONS

8-22 Where does the ohmmeter obtain its energy to operate?
8-23 When an ohmmeter is used in a circuit, in what condition should the circuit be placed? Explain.
8-24 Explain how the ohmmeter measures resistance.
8-25 What are the differences between the *series* and the *shunt* ohmmeters?
8-26 What is the relationship in an ohmmeter between R_i of the meter and its full-scale deflection?
8-27 What is the purpose of R_X in an ohmmeter? Explain how it accomplishes its function.
8-28 What is the relationship in an ohmmeter between R_X and R_B?
8-29 Why is the shunt ohmmeter best for measurement of small resistances?
8-30 What is the relationship between the shunt R's in the shunted series-type ohmmeter?
8-31 Why are the ohmmeter scales nonlinear?
8-32 What is a multimeter?
8-33 How does the wattmeter work?
8-34 Explain how the Wheatstone bridge measures resistance.
8-35 How can the Wheatstone bridge be used in a strain gage?

fundamentals of reactive circuits

Part 3

magnetism and electromagnetism
9

The principles of magnetism are closely related to many electronic devices, since one source of magnetic energy is electron drift. Many of these relationships are developed in the chapters that follow. The prime purpose of this chapter is to describe and analyze the fundamental principles of magnetism and electromagnetism, which provide the groundwork for integrating magnetic and electric properties.

9-1 ELECTRON MAGNETISM

In this section you will learn about three kinds of materials and the relationship of electron spins to magnetic materials.

An electron in motion, since it has an electric charge, generates its own magnetic field, which consists of magnetic lines of force. There are two general types of magnetic behavior, which are determined by the type of motion which creates the greatest effect: (1) diamagnetic and (2) paramagnetic.

As was pointed out in Chap. 1, any electron attracted by a nucleus will exhibit two kinds of motion. First, the electron revolves around the core of the atom in a spherical orbit. The second kind of motion, which plays an important part in magnetic behavior, is that of the electron spinning on its own axis. These two motions are illustrated in Fig. 9-1.

Diamagnetic materials are those which are repelled by an external

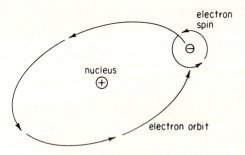

Fig. 9-1 Electron motions.

magnetic field. If an atom of a diamagnetic material is placed in an external magnetic field, the atom is repelled. It is more difficult to establish magnetic lines of force (flux) within these materials than in free space. Diamagnetic materials include antimony, bismuth, copper, gold, sodium chloride, and mercury. It should be pointed out that the diamagnetic characteristics are so slight that often they can be neglected and may be referred to as nonmagnetic substances. Section 9-6 deals with this subject.

Paramagnetic materials are those which display a slight attraction to an external magnetic field, having a magnetic permeability greater than unity. In these materials, the introduction of an external magnetic field may tend to align more electron spins in one direction than in the opposite direction. The atom will possess magnetic properties, but the distance between the atoms may be so great that the similar magnetic fields of adjacent atoms cannot create an additive effect. If the atoms are close together, the directions of electron spin may be opposed. If either of these conditions exists to a substantial extent, the material is only slightly (if at all) attracted to the external magnetic field. Aluminum, copper sulfate, and many metallic salts fall within this category. As with diamagnetic materials, the effect is so small in most cases that frequently it is neglected, and they may be classified as nonmagnetic substances. Section 9-6 also deals with this topic.

A third group, called *ferromagnetic substances,* includes materials which are strongly attracted by external magnetic fields. This is the most important of the three groups and warrants a more detailed analysis.

In a nonmagnetic material, the number of *electron spins* in one direction (clockwise, for example) is equal to the number of electron spins in the opposite direction (counterclockwise). Certain materials, when exposed to an external magnetic field, will experience a decrease in the number of electron spins in one direction, while the electron spins in the opposite direction will increase by the same number (see Table 9-1). The imbalance of electron spins is developed in the second-outermost shell of the atom. When this occurs, the atom possesses magnetic qualities. Iron is one of the most common magnetic materials; there-

Table 9-1

Iron	Clockwise Spins	Counter-clockwise Spins
Nonmagnetized	13	13
Magnetized	11	15

fore, the effect of an external magnetic field upon its electron spins will be examined.

The fact that the electron spins in an individual atom are unbalanced will not itself produce significant magnetic properties within the material. The neighboring atoms must undergo the same kind of change in electron spins and must be located close enough to one another for an additive effect to occur. When the distance between the atoms is too great, there is no additive effect. When the distance between atoms is less, the additive effect is more pronounced. There is a *critical atomic distance*, at which the electron-spin discrepancies are canceled and the material displays nonmagnetic properties.

When the atoms are relatively close, but not at the critical distance described, the electron spins of neighboring atoms become additive. The additive effect, rather than occurring throughout the entire material, takes place within a small portion, which is called a *domain.*

Ferromagnetic substances have many domains. When the material is unmagnetized, the magnetization forces of all the domains display no overall directional characteristics. The introduction of a small external magnetic field expands the size of those domains whose magnetic forces are nearly the same in the direction of the external field. As these domains become larger, the rest of the domains become correspondingly smaller. Increasing the external field further causes more domains to become aligned with the enlarged domains. This occurs because the increase in the external magnetic field alters the electron spins within the atoms in the previously unaffected domains. These domains become larger with further increases of the external magnetic field, thus reducing further the number and size of the domains not under the influence of the external field. At a certain external field strength, all the domains are aligned, and the material is magnetically saturated.

9-2 CHARACTERISTICS OF FERROMAGNETIC MATERIALS

In this section you will learn how to identify a magnetic field with a compass and its shape by use of iron filings.

Magnetic fields are easily detected by use of a compass. A compass is itself a magnet which is mounted in such a way that it is relatively free to rotate if acted upon by an outside force. It is found that one end of the compass needle will point to one end of a bar magnet if the bar magnet is moved close enough. This is illustrated in Fig. 9-2. If the bar magnet is moved around the compass (say in a clockwise direction),

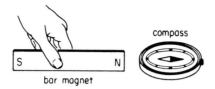

Fig. 9-2   Detecting a magnetic field.

the compass needle will move in the same direction. It is said that magnetic lines of force exist in the area surrounding a magnet, and this is why the bar magnet is able to move the compass needle without actually coming in contact with it. The area around a magnet in which the forces of the magnetic lines can be detected is called the *magnetic field.*

The simple experiment illustrated in Fig. 9-2 merely detected the presence of a magnetic field, whereas the pattern of a magnetic field can be shown by use of some iron filings. This can be done in the following manner:

1   Place the magnet under a sheet of paper.
2   Carefully sprinkle iron filings on the paper and observe the pattern that is formed.

It will be noted that a pattern similar to that shown in Fig. 9-3 will result.

Notice that there is a tendency for the filings to be more heavily concentrated near and about the two ends of the bar magnet. These two ends are called *poles* and are the regions in which the magnetic lines of force are said to be concentrated. The next section examines the characteristics of these lines.

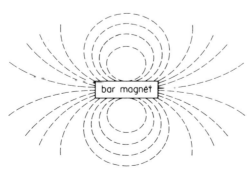

Fig. 9-3   Iron-filing pattern of a bar-magnet field.

9-3 CHARACTERISTICS OF MAGNETIC LINES OF FORCE

In this section you will learn about the major characteristics of magnetic lines of force.

The major characteristics of magnetic lines of force are best described by the following seven statements:

1 Magnetic lines of force are said to possess direction.
2 Magnetic lines of force are always closed loops.
3 Magnetic lines of force tend to be as short as possible, which develops tension along their length.
4 Like magnetic poles repel, and unlike magnetic poles attract one another.
5 Magnetic lines of force repel one another.
6 Every magnetic line of force must form its own completed loop and will not intersect any other magnetic line of force.
7 There is a tendency for magnetic fields to establish themselves in such a way that the greatest number of lines of force is set up.

Several of the preceding statements should be expanded. Let us consider Fig. 9-4, in which the direction of the magnetic field is indicated by the arrows. It is seen that the magnetic lines of force leave the magnet at the north pole and enter the magnet at the south pole. Also notice, in accordance with the second statement, that every magnetic line is a closed loop. The fact that these lines are curved indicates that they are taking the shortest possible path from pole to pole in the external field.

Figure 9-5 is an illustration of the fact that like magnetic poles repel. This repulsion results in a distortion of the normal shape of the magnetic field. In Fig. 9-6, the effect of placing two magnets with opposite poles adjacent to each other is shown. It is seen that the effect is additive in that the overall magnetic field is increased in size and is not altered in shape.

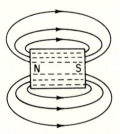

Fig. 9-4   Magnetic field.

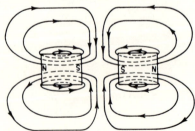

Fig. 9-5   Like poles repel.

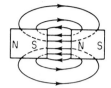

Fig. 9-6   Unlike poles attract.

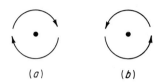

(a)   (b)

Fig. 9-7   Flux development due to current. (a) *I* approaching reader; (b) *I* leaving reader.

Figures 9-5 and 9-6 both show the effect of statements 5 and 6. Notice that every line is a completely closed loop, and in no case do lines of force (flux) intersect one another. In Fig. 9-5, the magnetic fields are distorted so that the magnetic lines of force do not intersect.

The tension developed along the length of the magnetic lines can be seen in the effects of a very simple experiment. Place two bar magnets near each other, first in the manner shown in Fig. 9-5 and then as illustrated in Fig. 9-6. It will be seen that when two like poles are brought near each other, the two magnets (if they are of sufficient strength) move away from each other. Likewise, placing the two magnets together such that the north pole of one magnet faces the south pole of the other magnet will result in a force of attraction. If the magnets are of sufficient strength and the distance between them is not too great, they will be physically drawn to each other.

9-4   DEVELOPMENT OF FLUX BY ELECTRON CURRENT

In this section you will learn about developing magnetic lines of force by use of electron flow, coils and electromagnets, and determining the direction of a magnetic field.

The fundamental concept of current as electron drift has been analyzed in earlier chapters. This chapter has revealed some of the fundamental characteristics of magnetism. The next logical point to consider is the means by which magnetic lines of force can be developed.

Electrons are negative particles, which, when liberated from their nucleus, can be made to drift in a specified direction. As pointed out earlier, any motion of an electron has magnetic energy associated with it. When mobile electrons are made to drift in a conductor, the magnetic fields of the electrons are such that they aid one another, resulting in a flux field outside the wire.

Figure 9-7 illustrates the relationship between the direction of the current flow and that of the developed flux field. Assume that the dot

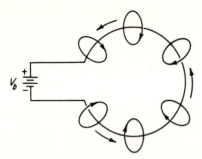

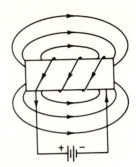

Fig. 9-8 Flux field in a wire loop.

Fig. 9-9 Magnetic field of a current-carrying coil.

is a cross-sectional view of the conductor. If the electron drift is toward the reader, the flux field is clockwise; the field is counterclockwise when the current flows away from the reader. In a common straight conductor, the density of the flux field in most cases is so small that it may be considered negligible. In order to have a flux field sufficiently dense to be useful, a number of factors must be taken into consideration.

When a current-carrying wire is formed into a loop, all the magnetic lines (called flux) pass through the center of the loop. Also of importance is the fact that all the flux lines are in the same direction. This is shown in Fig. 9-8.

Now consider forming the current-carrying wire into a series of loops, which is called a *coil*, or *solenoid*. Note that the current in each turn is actually moving in the same overall direction within the circumference of the solenoid. Therefore, the entire coil functions like a single loop but has a greatly concentrated magnetic field, which has the characteristic of the magnetic field of Fig. 9-4. The magnetic field of the coil is depicted in Fig. 9-9, and the solenoid is called an *electromagnet*.

The direction of the magnetic lines of force around a coil can be determined by use of the *left-hand rule*. Refer to Fig. 9-10, which illus-

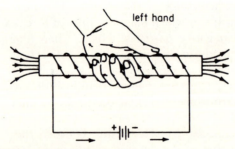

left hand

Fig. 9-10 Determining direction of a magnetic field by use of the left-hand rule.

trates how the coil should be held while applying the rule. The left-hand rule is as follows:

1   Hold the coil in the left hand such that the fingers follow the direction of electron current flow around the circumference of the coil.
2   The thumb will point in the direction of the magnetic flux within the center of the coil.

9-5 MAGNETIC UNITS

There are a number of terms and units commonly used in the analysis of magnetism and magnetic circuits. Several of the most significant ones are treated in this section.

The term *magnetic flux* or *flux* is simply another name for *magnetic lines* or *magnetic lines of force*. A *magnetic circuit* is the path taken by the magnetic flux. Section 9-9 deals with magnetic circuits in greater detail.

An important concept to be mentioned here only briefly is *electromagnetic induction*. It will be shown in Chap. 10 that when flux is made to cut across a conductor (or vice versa), an emf is established within that conductor that will cause current to flow if the circuit is closed. This is called electromagnetic induction, and it is one of the underlying principles behind the operation of certain electromagnetic devices, such as the transformer.

The SI unit of magnetic flux is called the *weber*, which is defined as follows:

A flux Φ that builds up from zero at such a rate that it will induce an emf of one volt in the coil at the end of one second will have a value of one weber.

The abbreviation for the weber is Wb.

Recall that an emf in an electric circuit is the force that develops current flow. The force that establishes magnetic lines of force is called the *magnetomotive force* (*mmf*). The mmf is directly created by electric current, since the development of magnetic flux is the result of current flow in a wire or coil. The magnitude of the flux is directly proportional to the number of turns in the coil and the magnitude of the current. Therefore, the SI unit of the mmf is the *ampere-turn*, abbreviated At. In equation form,

$$mmf = NI \qquad \qquad \textbf{(9-1)}$$

where mmf = magnetomotive force, At
N = number of wire turns in coil
I = current through the coil, A

The *reluctance* of a magnetic circuit is analogous to electric-circuit resistance. The script letter $\mathscr{R}$ is the letter symbol for reluctance.

Reluctance can be defined as the constant proportionality between the magnetomotive force and the magnetic flux, or the ampere-turns per weber.

In equation form,

$$\mathscr{R} = \frac{\text{mmf}}{\Phi} \qquad \text{(9-2)}$$

where $\mathscr{R}$ = reluctance
  mmf = magnetomotive force, At
  Φ = flux, Wb

The *permeance* of a magnetic circuit is analogous to electric-circuit conductance and may be defined as the ability of a magnetic circuit to permit the establishment of flux. The script letter $\mathscr{P}$ is the letter symbol used to designate permeance. In equation form:

$$\mathscr{P} = \frac{1}{\mathscr{R}} \qquad \text{(9-3)}$$

Permeability is defined as the permeance per unit length and cross-sectional area and can be considered as an indication of the ability of a material to permit the establishment of flux. The Greek letter μ (mu) is the letter symbol used to designate permeability. In equation form,

$$\mu = \mathscr{P}\frac{l}{A} = \frac{l}{\mathscr{R}A} \qquad \text{(9-4)}$$

where μ = permeability, mks units
  l = length of the magnetic circuit, m
  A = cross-sectional area, m^2
  $\mathscr{P}$ = permeance
  $\mathscr{R}$ = reluctance, At/Wb

Flux density may be defined as the flux per unit cross-sectional area. In equation form,

$$B = \frac{\Phi}{A} \qquad \text{(9-5)}$$

where B (beta) = flux density, Wb/m²
     Φ = total flux, Wb
     A = cross-sectional area of magnetic circuit, m²

The amount of magnetomotive force per unit length of a magnetic circuit can be called the *magnetizing force*. It can also be called the *mmf gradient*, or *magnetic intensity*, and is designated by the Greek letter H (eta). In equation form:

$$H = \frac{mmf}{l} \qquad \text{(9-6)}$$

where   H = magnetizing force, At/m
       mmf = magnetomotive force, At
         l = magnetic circuit length, m

It can be shown that the permeability of a magnetic circuit can be determined from the following relationship:

$$\mu = \frac{B}{H} \qquad \text{(9-7)}$$

where μ = permeability
       B = flux density, Wb/m²
       H = magnetizing force, At/m

9-6 INDUCED VOLTAGE AND THE METHOD BY WHICH IT IS PRODUCED

In this section you will learn how magnetic lines cutting across a conductor develop an induced voltage.

One of the fundamental laws of physics states that for every action there is an equal and opposite reaction. How can this be applied to certain electric circuits? Flux lines are developed around a conductor when current is made to flow through it. These magnetic lines originate within the center of the conductor and expand outward as the electron drift is imposed. The flux cuts the conductor at right angles as the lines expand, before finally arriving outside the wire. In cutting the conductor, the flux acts upon the mobile electrons in such a way as to oppose their change in motion. This opposition to the change in mobile-electron motion is called *self-induced voltage*.

The self-induced voltage is the reaction which sets in when the flux lines, which were produced by the change in current, cut the conductor. When the flux lines are expanding outward, the cutting is from inside to outside the wire; this occurs when the current is increasing. The original action was the attempt to increase the current, and the reaction is to oppose the increase (change). That is, the reaction is the establishment of an emf which is counter to the change in the source emf. This results in a delay in the time it takes the current to undergo the complete change dictated by the change in source voltage. It should be clearly understood that the induced emf opposes the *change* in current and not the current as such.

There is no self-induced voltage where a fixed magnitude of current has been flowing for some time. The time it takes the induced emf to settle down after a change is considered in the next chapter. If the steady-state current is made to decrease, a number of the expanded flux lines will collapse and return within the conductor. Under this condition, flux lines are cutting from *outside to inside* the conductor. Notice that this is opposite to the original cutting action; but also notice that the change in current is opposite to the original change (it is now decreasing instead of increasing). The cutting of the collapsing flux lines develops an induced emf which opposes the decrease in current magnitude, thereby causing the current to decrease more slowly than is dictated by the source-voltage change. It can be seen that the induced voltage opposes the change in current in both cases.

9-7   COIL CHARACTERISTICS WHICH INFLUENCE FLUX DENSITY

In this section you will learn four general characteristics which affect the flux density:
* *The magnitude of the current I flowing through the coil*
* *The number N of coil turns*
* *The type of core material*
* *Core size and shape*

The density of the flux field is directly proportional to the current magnitude and the number of coil turns. The use of magnetic materials for the core of the inductor results in a stronger field than would be possible with an air core. A larger cross section of a magnetic core, with all other conditions fixed, results in more flux lines, since this allows more space for the development of additional flux. Increasing the length of the core and coil lengthens the magnetic-circuit path, thereby increasing the difficulty of flux development. This reduces the flux density.

Magnetic flux Φ represents the number of flux lines. From the preceding statements, the following proportion for magnetic-core coils can be deduced:

$$\Phi \propto \frac{NIA}{l} \quad \text{or} \quad \Phi \propto \frac{\text{At}(A)}{l}$$

where Φ = number of flux lines
     N = coil turns
     I = coil current
     A = cross-sectional area of core
     l = length of coil
    At = ampere-turns

9-8 MAGNETIZATION CURVE OF AN AIR-CORE INDUCTOR

In this section you will learn about the magnetization curve of an air-core inductor, the definition of inductance, and the relationship between an air core's magnetization curve and its inductance.

In order to describe adequately the behavior of a magnetic circuit, a means of illustrating the relationship of magnetomotive force and flux is required. The use of flux density (flux lines per square unit) and ampere-turns per unit length is satisfactory, as the relationship can be depicted without being influenced by the size of the specific coil in question. The flux density is denoted by B, and the ampere-turns per unit length are designated by the letter H. It is logical to call the relationship by these symbols, namely, the BH curve.

An air-core coil has no magnetic material in which the flux can pass; i.e., the permeability of the circuit is essentially unity for all conditions. Since the turns of the coil are fixed, it can be seen that varying the current will result in the same kind of change in H. Since the permeability of the circuit is always unity, the reluctance is fixed for all values of current. With a fixed reluctance, it can be seen that the flux density (lines per square inch) will vary directly in a linear fashion with the changes in

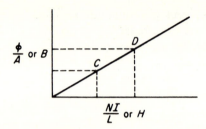

Fig. 9-11   Magnetization curve of an air-core inductor.

coil current. As shown by Fig. 9-11, the BH characteristic of an air-core coil is linear. The *slope* of the characteristic, which is the B/H ratio, is the permeability of the coil. The inductance is the property of an electromagnetic component to produce a voltage as to oppose a change in current. This property is the ratio of the induced voltage to the rate of change of current which produces a change in the flux. Then the inductance is that property which, for N turns, produces an incremental change in flux caused by an incremental change in current. That is,

$$L = N\frac{\Delta\phi}{\Delta I},$$

which is related to only the BH curves. For a fixed area, length, and coil turns N, the inductance of an air-core coil can be determined from the magnetization curve since, for air, ϕ is directly proportional to I. Thus:

$$L = N\frac{\phi}{I} = N\frac{BA}{Hl/N} = \frac{N^2A}{l} \times \frac{B}{H}$$

and

$$\frac{B}{H} = \frac{L}{N^2} \times \frac{l}{A}$$

The above represents the mathematical relationship between the BH curve and the inductance for an air-core coil.

A BH characteristic denotes more inductance when the characteristic is more vertical and less inductance when it is more horizontal. Furthermore, if a given change in ampere-turns per unit length produces the same change in flux density throughout the range of operation, the characteristic will be a straight line, denoting a fixed inductance. This statement is very important:

The inductance of an air-core coil is constant for all values of current.

9-9 MAGNETIZATION CURVE OF A MAGNETIC CORE

In this section you will learn about the relationship between the magnetization curve of a magnetic core and changes in its inductance with changes in flux density.

Figure 9-12 is the BH characteristic of a magnetic material. At point 0, where there is no flux in the material, the establishment of magnetic lines is easily accomplished, since there is ample space for their development. That is, the permeability is high, and the reluctance is low. As

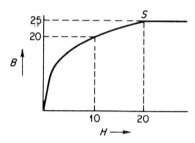

Fig. 9-12   BH curve of a magnetic material.

more flux is developed in the material, it becomes increasingly difficult to add more lines of force, since the BH curve becomes more horizontal, which denotes a decrease in inductance. For example, increasing H from 0 to 10 increases B from 0 to 20, whereas increasing H from 10 to 20 increases B only from 20 to 25. This indicates that the development of flux becomes more difficult as the flux density of the material increases. That is, the permeability decreases and the reluctance increases as the flux density increases. H is increased until point S is reached, where no additional flux can be established within the material. This is the point at which all domains are aligned, and the core is said to be *magnetically saturated.* Increasing the magnetizing force H beyond this value fails to develop additional flux; in addition, the core would develop heat.

It can be seen that the material begins to behave more like a nonmagnetic material beyond the saturation point. Using such a material for the core of an inductor has a pronounced effect upon the coil. It is sufficient to say, at this point, that the magnetic-core material displays nonlinear inductive qualities, which are an inverse function of H. The material is most inductive at minimum H and least inductive at the maximum H value. H is usually varied by means of the current, which develops the flux.

9-10 MAGNETIZATION CURVE OF A MAGNETIC-CORE INDUCTOR

In this section you will learn about the relationship between the magnetization curve of a magnetic-core inductor and the change in its inductance with changes in flux density.

The characteristic of an inductor with a magnetic core is illustrated in Fig. 9-13. As pointed out previously, a change in the slope of the BH characteristic indicates a change in the inductance of the component.

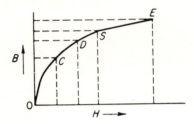

Fig. 9-13   BH curve of a magnetic-core inductor.

First consider the characteristic between points 0 and C. This is the region where the core has only a few flux lines within it. Therefore a relatively small change in H results in a correspondingly large change in B, since the opposition to the development of new flux is smallest in this region. Since the flux lines are so easily developed between points 0 and C, it is the region where the greatest self-induced emf is developed for a given change in coil current (which is incorporated in H). Therefore it can be seen that this region of Fig. 9-13 is the high-inductance portion of the BH characteristic.

The slope of the characteristic between points C and D becomes less vertical. The flux lines in the core material are becoming more crowded, resulting in a reduced permeability and increased reluctance. A given increase in coil current will result in a smaller increase of flux lines in this region than would have been the case in the 0-to-D region. Fewer developed flux lines for a given change result in a smaller induced emf. The opposition to current changes in the C-to-D region is less, and the inductance has decreased.

The same kind of action continues, with the inductance decreasing, up to point S. At and beyond point S, the core no longer contributes inductance to the coil. Further increases of current develop additional flux lines, not from the core contribution but from the effect of the coil itself (the inductance of which is constant). From points S to E, the inductance of the coil is the total inductance of the component.

From the analysis made of the coil and core individually, the behavior of the combination is seen to be as follows: with little or no flux, the total inductance is equal to that contributed by the core and coil. The coil inductance remains constant for the entire range of the characteristic (0 to E). The core inductance varies from its maximum value at point 0 to zero at point S. Therefore the overall inductance of the circuit decreases in a nonlinear fashion with rises in H up to point S. At point S, the inductance is at its minimum value, equal to that of the coil alone, and it remains constant at this value for the remainder of the characteristic (S to E).

9-11   MAGNETIC LOSSES

In this section you will learn about magnetic losses resulting from hysteresis and eddy currents.

Several types of losses which can occur in magnetic circuits are analyzed in this section. First consider the *hysteresis loss*. Figure 9-14

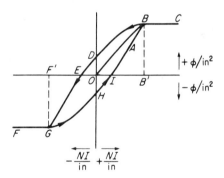

Fig. 9-14   **Hysteresis loop of an iron core.**

illustrates a typical hysteresis loop of an iron core. Examine this curve in order to describe the behavior of the iron core. The ampere-turns per inch of length are plotted on the *x* axis. To reveal the effects of current reversal, positive ampere-turns per inch are plotted on the positive *x* axis, and negative ampere-turns per inch are shown on the negative *x* axis. The flux density per square inch is plotted on the *y* axis. The ampere-turns per unit length are denoted by the letter H and the flux density by B. In equation form,

$$B = \frac{\Phi}{A}$$

and

$$H = \frac{NI}{l} = \frac{At}{l}$$

where At = ampere-turns
    B = flux density
    Φ = flux lines
    A = unit area
    H = At/unit length
    N = turns of excitation (primary) coil
    I = excitation current
    l = core length

Begin the analysis with the core completely unmagnetized, which is the condition at point O. The development of positive current results in a positive ampere-turn value. As the current is increased, the flux density undergoes corresponding increases up to point B. At point B, which is the saturation point, no additional flux lines can be added within the core. The saturation current is shown as B' on the curve. Further increases in the current create heat in the core but no significant increase in the flux density, resulting in the BC portion of the curve being parallel to the x axis. As was pointed out earlier, the slope of the curve indicates the core inductance. Between points B and C, the core has little or no inductance, because of its inability to develop additional flux while in this region.

After point B has been reached, assume that the current is decreased. Because of the core retentivity, its flux density will not decrease in exactly the same manner in which it was first developed. When the current is zero, the core still possesses flux lines, to the extent indicated by the length of OD. In higher-retentivity cores, point D would be farther away from point O on the y axis, while those cores possessing lower retentivity would show point D closer to point O. In order to clear the core entirely of the remaining flux field, a negative current of magnitude OE must be made to flow through the magnetizing coil. In this region, the lower values of negative current attempt to set up a magnetic force opposite to that force already residing in the core, thereby resulting in the cancellation of the remaining positive flux. Increasing the negative current beyond this value results in the creation of a negative flux field in a direct fashion until the saturation point F is achieved. Like the positive saturation point B, this is the condition where the core possesses its densest flux field. Any additional increases in the magnitude of the negative current fail to increase the flux density, and the core is least inductive when in the saturation region.

Reducing the current from magnitude F' reduces the negative flux density, but not as rapidly as it was developed, again because of core retentivity. At zero-current condition, some flux still is present, as indicated by OH in the characteristic. Note that $OD = OH$, since the characteristics of retentivity are bidirectional. A positive current of magnitude OI is required to clear the core completely of the negative flux field. Further increases in the positive current result in the development of a positive flux field again. At point A, the hysteresis, or magnetization, loop is completed, and the action is repetitive thereafter.

The hysteresis loop of a particular core depends directly upon the type of iron used and the manner in which it is prepared. The retentivity values can be made extremely low or substantially great, as determined by the intended application. The saturation points (B and F) also are determined largely by the core construction and size.

The fact that the magnetic domains in a ferromagnetic material tend not to return to their earlier orientation unless forced to do so is the cause of hysteresis. Inasmuch as there is an opposition to the magnetization, energy is drawn from the source emf and transferred as heat to the molecules of the ferromagnetic material. Therefore, hysteresis can be defined as a loss. Furthermore, the hysteresis loss increases as the frequency of the coil's alternating current is increased. Also, the greater the retentivity (which is the tendency to retain the flux field after the energizing current has been turned off), the greater the hysteresis loss. Since an amount of flux left in the material after removal of the energizing current is an indication of the amount of retentivity, the size of the area within the hysteresis loop of the material (within points $IBEG$ in Fig. 9-14) can be used as a practical indicator of hysteresis loss.

Another important magnetic-circuit loss is that associated with *eddy currents*. If the core of a coil were made of a solid magnetic material, the expanding and collapsing flux lines would induce voltages within the core itself that would drive small core currents, called eddy currents. The eddy currents travel at right angles to the length of the coil; i.e., they flow through the cross section of the core. This is illustrated in Fig. 9-15.

The use of laminations increases the cross-sectional resistance of the

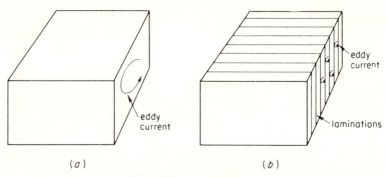

(a)   *(b)*

Fig. 9-15   Laminated core.

core to such an extent that the development of eddy currents becomes very difficult, since the laminations are glued to one another by a non-conducting material. You may ask why the eddy currents are undesirable. The answer is found by examining the behavior of a perfect inductor with no losses. Energy is drawn from the circuit source and stored in the magnetic field when it expands. When the flux collapses, all the stored energy should be returned to the coil, if the electromagnet is to be perfect. On the other hand, if the flux developed an induced voltage in the core, resulting in an induced current, a certain quantity of energy which was drawn from the flux would be used to drive this induced core current (eddy current). Heat would be developed, which means that the energy is not returned to the flux. This is an energy loss and serves no useful function for the coil; therefore it should be reduced as much as possible. The introduction of a laminated core reduces the possibility of developing eddy current, thereby eliminating a means by which energy can be lost within the circuit. The laminated core is often used for coils which are subjected to relatively heavy current.

Another answer to the eddy-current problem has been found by using a powdered-iron core. Small particles of specially prepared iron are joined by a gluelike material which is a poor conductor, thereby increasing the cross-sectional resistance. Powdered-iron-core coils are frequently used in circuits associated with frequencies above 20 kHz.

The powdered-iron core also has found use in the permeability-tuned coil. The inductance is varied by threaded cores, which can be partially removed by unscrewing them. As the core is partially removed, it is replaced with air, which increases the reluctance and decreases the permeability of the magnetic circuit. As was pointed out in a preceding section, reducing the permeability decreases the inductance of the coil. The opposite effect is achieved by screwing in the core slug. In this way, the coil has an inductance that can be varied by the adjustable core. The permeability-tuned coil is used widely in applications where frequencies are above 20 kHz and the current demands are low to medium.

9-12 MAGNETIC SHIELDING

In this section you will learn about the purpose of magnetic shielding.

Recall that there is no material which is an insulator for magnetic lines of force. However, there is a method by which flux can be kept out of a specific area (see Fig. 9-16). The distortion or reshaping of the

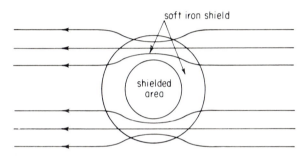

Fig. 9-16   Magnetic shielding.

magnetic field so as to keep the flux out of a specific area in the manner shown in Fig. 9-16 is called *shielding* and is a popular technique in electricity and electronics.

9-13 PERMANENT AND TEMPORARY MAGNETS

In this section you will learn about the differences and similarities of permanent and temporary magnets.

Another factor worthy of consideration is the length of time that the material remains magnetized after the external flux field has been removed. Materials which remain magnetized for long periods of time possess high *retentivity,* which is a characteristic of permanent magnets. On the other hand, materials that quickly lose their magnetization upon removal of the external flux field possess low retentivity and are used for temporary magnets. Generally speaking, high-retentivity materials require a stronger external field to magnetize them to the same degree as low-retentivity materials.

Permanent and temporary magnets are used frequently in electric and electronic circuitry. The permanent magnet has the advantage of always being magnetized, but its disadvantages are as follows: (1) it weakens with aging; (2) it is often large and cumbersome; (3) a magnetic field exists even when not needed. The temporary magnet, which is more commonly used, has the following advantages: (1) the magnetic field dies out to a great extent upon removal of the force which developed the field, and so it is a magnet only when desired; (2) it can be designed more readily in many shapes and sizes to fit the particular application.

PROBLEMS

9-1 Refer to Fig. 9-17a. Draw the flux lines around the wire and indicate their direction.

9-2 Repeat Prob. 9-1 for Fig. 9-17b.

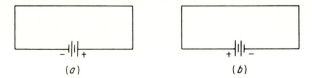

(a)   (b)

Fig. 9-17 Diagrams for Probs. 9-1 and 9-2.

9-3 Refer to Fig. 9-18a. Indicate the polarity of V_b and the direction of electron current.

9-4 Repeat Prob. 9-3 for Fig. 9-18b.

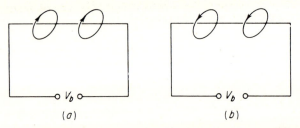

(a)   (b)

Fig. 9-18 Diagrams for Probs. 9-3 and 9-4.

9-5 Refer to Fig. 9-19a. Draw the flux field about this coil and indicate its direction.

9-6 Repeat Prob. 9-5 for Fig. 9-19b.

9-7 Refer to Fig. 9-20a. Draw the flux field about this coil and indicate the direction of electron current.

9-8 Repeat Prob. 9-7 for Fig. 9-20b.

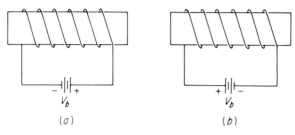

Fig. 9-19 Diagrams for Probs. 9-5 and 9-6.

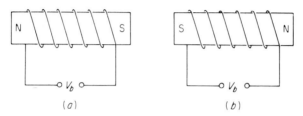

Fig. 9-20 Diagrams for Probs. 9-7 and 9-8.

QUESTIONS

9-1   What is reluctance?

9-2   What is permeability?

9-3   What is the relationship between reluctance and permeability?

9-4   What is the permeability of air?

9-5   How is it possible to determine the direction of current in a wire by use of a compass? Use drawings to illustrate.

9-6   Why is the flux density in the center of a coil that has current passing through it greater than that found around a straight wire passing the same amount of current?

9-7   What is mmf?

9-8   What is magnetizing force?

9-9   What is the difference between mmf and magnetizing force?

9-10   What is retentivity?

9-11   What is hysteresis?

9-12   Refer to the hysteresis loop of Fig. 9-14. What is the relationship between the distance found between points E and I and the retentivity of the iron core?

9-13   What is leakage flux, and what is its cause?

9-14   What is fringing, and what is its cause?

characteristics of inductance

10

10-1 PRINCIPLES OF ELECTROMAGNETIC INDUCTION

In this section you will learn how:
· Voltage is induced in a conductor
· The polarity of the induced voltage is determined
· Voltage can be induced in a coil by a change in its current
· Voltage can be induced in one coil by another

It was pointed out in Chap. 9 that an emf can be developed in a conductor by moving the conductor through the flux lines or by moving the lines of force through the conductor. This concept of electromagnetic induction is illustrated with the help of Fig. 10-1.

In Fig. 10-1 a galvanometer is connected in series with a conductor. A galvanometer is a device which measures magnitude of the current and indicates its direction. (Galvanometers were analyzed in Chap. 8.) Note that the conductor is placed in such a position that it lies within the flux field of the magnet. When the conductor is moved upward, the conductor cuts the flux field in an upward direction, and the pointer of the galvanometer moves to one side. When the conductor completes its movement through the flux field, the galvanometer pointer returns to its zero setting in the center of the galvanometer face. Since current

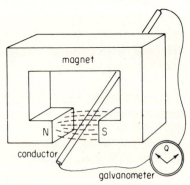

Fig. 10-1 Electromagnetic induction.

210

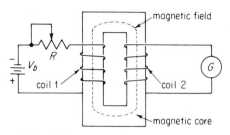

Fig. 10-2   Mutual electromagnetic induction.

flowed during the time the conductor was cutting across the flux, it is reasonable to assume that an emf was present in the conductor. This emf is developed as a result of the cutting action between the conductor and the magnetic lines of force and is called an *induced electromotive force*, or *induced emf.*

It is of interest to note that the polarity of the induced emf is determined by the direction of cutting between the conductor and flux. In Fig. 10-1, moving the conductor through the flux in a downward direction results in a current flow opposite in direction to that found when the conductor is moved upward.

In Fig. 10-1, it was shown how an induced emf is generated. This process is called *electromagnetic induction*. The process of electromagnetic induction can be developed by moving the magnetic lines of force and keeping both the magnetic circuit and the conductor stationary. This is the underlying principle of the transformer.

In Fig. 10-2 two coils wound on a magnetic core are electrically insulated from each other and the core. A voltage V_b is applied to coil 1, causing current to flow through it. The magnitude of the current through coil 1 is made to vary by changing the resistance (R) value in series with V_b.

Assume R is reduced in ohmic value. This causes an increase in coil 1 current and a corresponding increase in the magnetic lines of force in the core. These same magnetic lines of force also pass through coil 2, since it is wound on the same core. As the new flux lines develop, they cut across coil 2, and the galvanometer indicates a flow of current. Now increase R in series with coil 1. The current in coil 1 decreases, and a number of the existing flux lines collapse. During the period of collapse these flux lines cut coil 2 in the opposite direction. An induced emf is generated in coil 2, and the galvanometer indicates a current flowing in the opposite direction. It is important to note that the current flow occurs only during the time when the flux lines are either building up or collapsing (which is during the time R is being varied). The development of an induced emf in coil 2 by changing the current in coil 1 is called *mutual induction.*

Mutual Induction: Faraday's Law

Also of significance is that the magnitude of the coil 2 induced emf is increased if the coil 1 current is changed more rapidly. This relationship is called *Faraday's law* and can be stated in the following manner:

The magnitude of the induced emf is directly proportional to the rate of change of the energizing current.

10-2   LENZ' LAW

In this section you will learn about transformer primary and secondary coils, how each coil has its own induced voltage, and how these induced voltages influence one another.

Recall from Sec. 10-1 that the polarity of the induced emf is determined by the direction of the flux cutting. In Fig. 10-1 it was determined by the direction in which the conductor cuts across the flux field, and in Fig. 10-2 the polarity of the induced emf in coil 2 was determined by the direction in which the flux lines cut across coil 2. The induced emf is a reaction, and it is logical to assume that it is equal and opposite to an original action. Lenz' law is based on this principle and can be stated in the following manner:

The polarity of the induced emf is such that its resulting current will develop a flux which will oppose any change in the original flux.

How can Lenz' law be applied to a mutual-induction type of circuit (Fig. 10-3)? The coil connected to V_b is called the *primary,* and the coil connected to the load resistance R_L is called the *secondary.* The placement of two coils in such a way that the flux of one coil can reach the other coil results in a device called a *transformer.* Therefore, Figs. 10-2 and 10-3 are transformers.

In Fig. 10-3*a* assume the switch *SW* has just been closed, and a surge of current flows through the primary coil in the direction indicated by the arrows. As the current rises from zero to some value, the flux field around the primary rises. The expanding primary flux cuts the secondary coil and produces an induced emf in the secondary. Since the secondary coil is connected to a load resistor R_L, the mutually induced emf in the secondary causes current to flow. This secondary current will

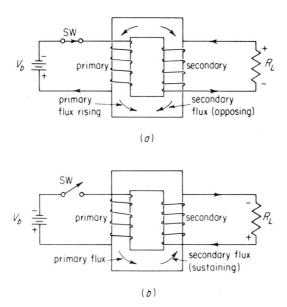

Fig. 10-3   Polarity of induced emf: (*a*) rising primary
flux; (*b*) collapsing primary flux.

produce its own flux and, according to Lenz' law, should oppose the
expanding primary flux.

In order to investigate whether this is true, use the left-hand rule to
determine the direction of the primary flux. The primary coil is held
in the left hand such that the fingers follow the direction that is opposite
to the direction of electron-current flow around the circumference of
the coil (see Fig. 9-10). The thumb will point in the direction of the
magnetic flux within the center of that coil. Therefore, it is found that
the primary flux has a counterclockwise direction. Now to apply the
same left-hand rule to the secondary coil, the secondary flux has a
clockwise direction. Hence, it is seen that Lenz' law holds for the case
of the rising primary flux.

Now consider Lenz' law for the case where the primary flux is collapsing, as shown in Fig. 10-3*b*. The switch *SW* is opened, the primary
current decreases to zero, and the primary flux collapses. While undergoing this collapsing action, the primary flux cuts across the secondary.
Since this flux cuts the secondary in a direction opposite to that found
in the first case, the induced secondary emf is opposite in polarity to the
original secondary induced emf. This secondary emf generates a current, which in turn develops its own flux. The secondary flux, according
to Lenz' law, should be of such a polarity as to oppose the change in the

primary current. Recall that in this case the primary current was decreasing. Therefore, the secondary flux should be of such a polarity that it should *oppose the decrease*, which means it will attempt to *sustain* the primary current. If this is true, then the primary and secondary flux fields should be in the same direction at this time. Check this out with the left-hand rule. The collapsing primary flux is in the same direction as determined in the first case, which is counterclockwise. The secondary current is now opposite in direction to that found in the first case. Applying the left-hand rule shows that the secondary flux is also counterclockwise, and Lenz' law again holds true.

10-3 PRINCIPLES OF SELF-INDUCTION AND SELF-INDUCTANCE

In this section you will learn how a coil develops an induced voltage within itself and the relationship of this action to the coil's inductance.

In Sec. 10-1 it was pointed out how the moving flux field of one coil induced an emf in a second coil called mutual induction. Now the effect of the expanding and contracting flux field on the coil in which the flux originates will be examined.

Figure 10-4*a* to *c* shows the symbols used to designate three of the more common types of inductors. The *air-core* type of coil is most frequently used in circuits where frequencies above the audio range are involved. The *iron-core* type is used widely in audio (below 20 kHz) circuits. The iron core is usually made of laminated sheets or of powdered iron so as to minimize eddy-current losses in the core.

Consider the operation of the circuit in Fig. 10-5 when the switch *SW*

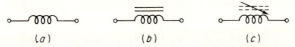

(a)   (b)   (c)

Fig. 10-4   General types of inductors: (*a*) air core; (*b*) iron core; (*c*) permeability-tuned.

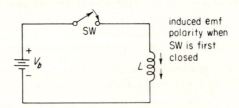

Fig. 10-5   Principle of self-induction.

is first closed. Upon closing *SW*, a surge of current flows through the coil *L*. This rising current develops an expanding flux field, which cuts the turns of the coil as they expand outward. The flux cutting across the coil induces an emf in the coil. Lenz' law applies here, and therefore the polarity of the induced emf should be such as to oppose the rise in the current. Hence, the induced emf is opposite in polarity to V_b, as shown by the arrows adjacent to *L*. Since the emf is induced in the same circuit, this action is called *self-induction*. The self-induced emf is also called a *counter-emf* (cemf).

It can be seen that a cemf of the opposite polarity will be developed when the coil current is made to decrease to zero. Also important to recognize is that the inductive circuit of Fig. 10-5 has the characteristic of opposing any changes in its own current, which is called *self-inductance*. Self-inductance is most commonly called *inductance* and can be defined as follows:

Inductance is the ability of a component to develop an induced emf.

The intensity of the magnetic flux and the rate at which the flux cuts the turns are factors which determine the magnitude of the induced emf. The unit of inductance is the henry. It is defined as follows

A component which develops a cemf of one volt when the current is changing at the rate of one ampere per second has an inductance of one henry.

$$v_{in} = L\frac{\Delta i}{\Delta t} = L\frac{di}{dt} \qquad \textbf{(10-1)}$$

where v_{in} = instantaneous induced voltage
$\quad\quad L$ = inductance, H
$\quad \Delta i/\Delta t$ = roc *i* at the instant = di/dt (roc = rate of change)

By using the preceding equation, the following relationship to find *L* can be established:

$$L = \frac{v_{in}}{\text{roc } i} \qquad \textbf{(10-1a)}$$

The preceding relationship reveals several significant features of induced voltage. A larger inductance value indicates that the coil is capable of developing a stronger flux field, thereby creating a greater amount of flux-cutting action. Furthermore, for the flux lines to cut the coil, the current must be undergoing a change (increase or decrease in magnitude). A faster change in current results in a greater magnitude of cemf.

10-4 FACTORS DETERMINING INDUCTANCE

In this section you will learn how several factors affect the inductance of a coil.

Every conductor possesses some inductance, in that flux develops in the center of the conductor, expands outward, and cuts across the wire as the current increases. Therefore, a small amount of cemf is induced in the conductor which opposes the *change* in the current. A cemf of the opposite polarity is induced in the conductor when the current is decreased. In this instance, since the cemf is to oppose the current change, it will be of such a polarity that it will try to sustain the decreasing current. Also it will be recalled from earlier discussions that the flux field associated with a straight-wire conductor is very small. Therefore, the inductance of a straight wire is sufficiently small to be neglected at all but the higher frequencies.

It has been determined that winding the conductor into loops and thereby constructing a coil results in a component that has a greater inductance. The value of inductance of a coil (also called a *choke* in the literature) can be found from this relationship:

$$L = \frac{N^2}{\mathcal{R}}$$

where N = number of coil turns
    $\mathcal{R}$ = reluctance of magnetic circuit upon which the coil is wound

Since the reluctance appears in the denominator of the equation, it is clear that reducing the reluctance of the magnetic circuit results in a larger value of inductance. Hence, the use of a ferromagnetic core for the inductor would greatly increase the inductance of that coil. Notice that N, the number of coil turns, appears as a squared quantity in this relationship. This indicates that the inductance can be greatly increased by adding more turns to the coil.

It will be recalled from Chap. 9 that

$$\mathcal{R} = \frac{l}{\mu A}$$

Substituting this quantity for $\mathcal{R}$ in the preceding equation results in

$$L = \frac{N^2}{l/\mu A}$$

Expressing this in a more convenient manner,

$$L = \frac{N^2 \mu A}{l} \qquad\qquad \textbf{(10-2)}$$

where L = inductance, H
  μ = permeability of magnetic circuit, mks units, H/m
  N = number of coil turns
  A = magnetic-circuit cross-sectional area, m^2
  l = magnetic-circuit length, m

In English units, the preceding equation becomes

$$L = \frac{N^2 \mu A}{10^8 l} \qquad\qquad \textbf{(10-2a)}$$

where μ = magnetic-circuit permeability, English units = B/H
  A = in^2
  l = in

The factor 10^8 appears here because 1 Wb (mks) is equal to 10^8 lines of force.
   A note of caution with reference to the two inductance equations should be added here. These equations are applicable with reasonable accuracy only when considering inductors whose leakage flux is small enough to be considered insignificant. Therefore, the use of these equations is recommended only for toroids and iron-core inductors. Special formulas (not presented in this text) must be used for determining the inductance of coils having a greater leakage flux.

Example

   An iron-core coil has the following parameters: N = 1000 turns; A = 0.4 in^2; l (average path length) = 12 in; μ = 1500 English units. Find the inductance of the coil.

Solution

Using the equation for English units and substituting values yield

$$L = \frac{(1000)^2(1500)(0.4)}{12(10)^8} = 0.5 \text{ H}$$

10-5 SERIES INDUCTANCE

In this section you will learn how to calculate the total inductance of several inductors connected in series.

The placement of two inductances in series in such a way that the flux of each coil does not touch any other coil is equivalent to adding inductance to the circuit. The cutting action of the flux field associated with each coil develops an induced voltage. The change in the current must be the same for each coil, since it is a series circuit. Each induced voltage opposes the change in current; therefore the induced voltages are additive. The total induced voltage present at any instant is equal to the sum of the individual induced emf. Since the induced voltage of each coil is directly proportional to the inductance of each coil, the total inductance is equal to the sum of the individual inductances. That is,

$$L = L_1 + L_2 + L_3 + \cdots + L_n \qquad \text{(10-3)}$$

where L = total inductance in henrys (H)
$\quad L_1$ = inductance of coil 1, etc.
$\quad L_n$ = inductance of coil n

10-6 PARALLEL INDUCTANCE

In this section you will learn how to calculate the total inductance of several inductors connected in parallel.

Next consider the effect of placing several inductors in parallel in such a way that the magnetic field of each coil does not affect any other inductor. It should be recalled that inductance is the property of a component to oppose a change in current. In any parallel circuit, the current is made to divide among the various branches. No branch will pass the total circuit current. Although the total current may change from 0 to

10 A, for example, none of the branch currents shows the total amount of change. Each branch current will change from 0 to some fraction of 10 A (current divides in a parallel circuit). Since the change in current is less in each branch, the induced voltage developed by each branch inductance must be less. The net effect is the development of less induced voltage, since the emf's do not add in a parallel circuit. This indicates a reduction of inductance by the placement of coils in parallel. The total inductance can be determined by the relationship

$$\frac{1}{L} = \frac{1}{L_1} + \frac{1}{L_2} + \cdots + \frac{1}{L_n} \qquad \text{(10-4)}$$

where L = total inductance in henrys, H
$\quad L_1$ = inductance of coil 1, etc.
$\quad L_n$ = inductance of coil n

10-7 DEVELOPMENT OF CURRENT IN A PURE INDUCTIVE CIRCUIT

In this section you will learn about the relationship between roc i and inductance.

Recall that the voltage relationship in a series circuit is that the total voltage-drop(s) is always equal to the applied emf. It was found, when studying series resistive circuits, that the current flowing through the resistance produced the voltage-drop. In the case of resistive circuits, the current instantaneously increased to its full Ohm's law value when the switch was closed, i.e.,

$$I = \frac{V}{R}$$

Now consider the case of a pure inductive circuit, as shown in Fig. 10-5. There can be no IR-drop in this circuit (since there is no resistance). Therefore, there must appear a voltage across the inductor that is equal and opposite to the applied emf. Since V_b in Fig. 10-5 is shown as a constant voltage value, the voltage across the coil must also be constant, equal in magnitude and opposite in polarity to V_b. In equation form,

$$-V_L = V_b$$

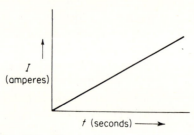

Fig. 10-6 Rise in *i* in a pure inductive circuit.

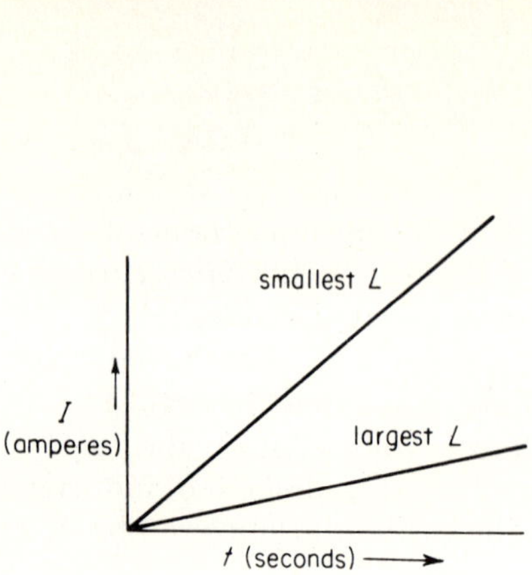

Fig. 10-7 Roc *i* as a function of *L* value.

And the current that will flow in this pure inductive circuit can be found from

$$I = \frac{V_b}{L} t \qquad\qquad \textbf{(10-5)}$$

where V_b = applied emf, V
$\quad\;\; L$ = coil inductance, H
$\quad\;\; t$ = time after closing switch, s

Since V_b and L are constant, it is seen that the circuit current will increase in a linear manner as time goes on after the switch is closed. This is shown in Fig. 10-6.

The *slope* of this graph represents roc *i* (rate of change of the current), since it is the ratio of

$$\frac{\text{Change in current}}{\text{Change in time}} = \frac{\Delta i}{\Delta t}$$

With large values of L, a smaller roc *i* would generate the required emf. And a larger roc *i* would be needed to develop the required cemf for small L values. The relationship between L values and roc *i* is depicted in Fig. 10-7.

10-8 THE EFFECT OF RESISTANCE AND INDUCTANCE ON INDUCED VOLTAGE

In this section you will learn how the circuit resistance as well as inductance help to determine the value of induced voltage developed in the inductor.

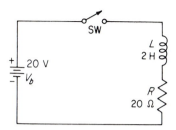

Fig. 10-8   Series-*RL* circuit.

Figure 10-8 illustrates a 2-H inductance in series with a 20-Ω resistance. Assume that the inductance has only a negligible value of resistance within its windings. Notice the switch *SW*, which makes it possible to open or close the circuit at will.

Upon closing the switch, the circuit current changes from zero to its full value in amperes, which is determined by

$$I_{max} = \frac{V_b}{R} = \frac{20}{20} = 1 \text{ A}$$

At the instant the current changes (zero time after the switch is closed), flux lines begin cutting the coil from within the windings. This flux cutting (from in to out) develops an induced voltage within the inductor which opposes the rise in current. The induced voltage, as stated in an earlier section, is determined by the following:

$$v_{in} = L \frac{di}{dt}$$

where v_{in} = instantaneous induced voltage
$\quad\quad L$ = inductance of coil, H
$\quad di/dt$ = change of current at that instant

As can be seen from this relationship, the magnitude of the instantaneous induced voltage hinges on roc i (di/dt). The roc i is obviously greatest immediately after the switch is closed (i tends to rise from zero to its full Ohm's law value). It can be seen that the induced voltage is greatest at the instant the switch is closed (zero time). Since the induced voltage is a cemf, it is in opposition to the supply voltage, and the instantaneous current is determined by

$$i = \frac{V_b - v_{in}}{R} \quad\quad\quad\quad\quad \textbf{(10-6)}$$

where i = instantaneous current
 V_b = supply voltage
 v_{in} = instantaneous induced voltage
 R = circuit resistance

Assume that the instantaneous induced voltage at zero time is 19 V; the instantaneous current can be readily calculated.

$$i = \frac{20 - 19}{20} = \frac{1}{20} = 0.05 \text{ A}$$

At the next instant the current makes a smaller change (from 0.05 to 1 A instead of the original 0 to 1 A). In other words, roc i is less; this results in a reduced value of instantaneous induced voltage. Assume that the induced voltage decreased to 18 V.

$$i = \frac{20 - 18}{20} = \frac{2}{20} = 0.1 \text{ A}$$

At the next instant, roc i becomes still less, resulting in a further decrease of induced voltage. This action continues until the instantaneous current arrives at the full Ohm's law value, at which time the induced voltage is zero, since the current is no longer changing (roc i is zero).

The inverse relationship between the induced voltage and the circuit current should be remembered. The induced voltage acts in such a way that it delays the buildup of the current to its full value. Whatever affects the magnitude of the induced voltage will also affect the time of current buildup. Increasing the circuit resistance reduces the initial change in current (from 0 to 0.5 A if a 40-Ω resistance is used in Fig. 10-8, instead of from 0 to 1 A with a 20-Ω resistance). If the current makes a smaller change because of greater resistance, the beginning roc i is not affected (with V_b and L fixed). The maximum current value is smaller. Since the initial roc i is not affected and the maximum current is smaller, the full Ohm's law current value will be reached in less time.

Figure 10-9a illustrates the relationship between the duration of the induced voltage and time with two values of circuit resistances (high and low). As previously stated, the induced voltage is maximum at zero time and gradually decays to zero (in an exponential manner). Figure 10-9b depicts the relationship between circuit resistance and current. With a low resistance, the Ohm's law current is greater, and more time is required for the current to reach that value. With a higher resistance, the induced voltage (see Fig. 10-9a) takes less time to decay to zero, and

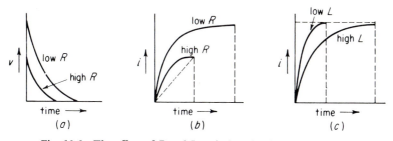

Fig. 10-9   The effect of R and L on induced voltage and current.

the current arrives at its full value (since it is less than that with a smaller resistance) in less time. The relationships shown by Fig. 10-9a and b are in a coil of fixed inductance and fixed supply voltage. In Fig. 10-9c the circuit resistance and supply voltage are fixed, but the inductance is changed. A low inductance indicates that the coil will produce relatively small induced voltages, and the current will take less time to arrive at its full value. A larger inductance produces a greater induced voltage, resulting in a reduced development of current; the buildup to the full Ohm's law value requires more time.

Now the statements above can be combined and several conclusions can be drawn about the effect of resistance and inductance on the induced voltage and current development:

1   A change in resistance, with a fixed V_b and L, results in no change in the beginning roc i but does change the time it takes for the current to reach its full Ohm's law value in an inverse fashion.
2   An increase in L, with V_b and R fixed, results in a decrease in the beginning roc i, with a corresponding increase in the time it takes for the current to reach its full Ohm's law value.

10-9   THE RELATIONSHIP BETWEEN CURRENT AND TIME IN A SERIES-RL CIRCUIT

In this section you will learn about the instantaneous values of current as a function of time.

If i is varied in a linear fashion, as shown by the dotted line in Fig. 10-9b, simple interpolation would obtain any instantaneous value. For example, at half the total time indicated, i would have reached half its full Ohm's law value. It is obvious, however, that the current at half time is greater than the linear value. Furthermore, the slope of the curve indicates a nonlinear function. The function is related to a mathematical constant, called epsilon (Greek letter ϵ, whose numerical value is 2.71828).

The preceding section stressed the effect of resistance and inductance upon the beginning roc i and upon the time of current buildup. Figure 10-9 illustrates these relationships. It is frequently necessary to know how much time elapses between zero time and the time when the current builds up to a certain value. The instantaneous rising current can be determined by

$$i = \frac{V_b}{R} (1 - \epsilon^{-Rt/L}) \qquad \text{(10-7)}$$

where i = instantaneous current, A
V_b = circuit supply voltage, V
R = circuit resistance, Ω
ϵ = base of the natural logarithm = 2.72
t = time when current is to be determined, s
L = inductance of coil, H

Note ϵ^{-x} values can be found directly from the exponential table in the Appendix.

Example

A 10-H inductance and a 10-Ω resistance are connected across a 100-V supply. Find i at the end of 1.7 s after closing the circuit (which is connected as shown in Fig. 10-8).

Solution

Substituting the known values into the current equation yields

$$i = \frac{100}{10} (1 - \epsilon^{10 \times 1.7/10}) = 10(1 - \epsilon^{-1.7})$$

From the exponential table in the Appendix,

$$\epsilon^{-1.7} = 0.183$$

and substituting back into the equation and solving for i,

$$i = 10(1 - 0.183) = 10(0.817) = 8.17 \text{ A}$$

10-10   THE SERIES-*RL* TIME CONSTANT

*In this section you will learn how circuit resistance and inductance affect
current increases.*

The current in a series-*RL* circuit is zero at the instant the circuit is
closed and exponentially builds up to a maximum value as the induced
voltage exponentially decays to zero. A rather simple relationship can
be conveniently used to examine the magnitude of the instantaneous
current at certain times. The circuit current will build up from zero
to 63.2 percent of its full Ohm's law value in L/R s after the circuit is
closed. This is defined as the *time constant* (tc) of the *RL* circuit. In
equation form,

$$tc = \frac{L}{R} \qquad\qquad (10\text{-}8)$$

where tc = time constant, s
$\quad L$ = inductance, H
$\quad R$ = resistance, Ω

In the second tc, the current will rise from 63.2 percent of maximum
to (63.2 percent plus 63.2 percent of the remaining 36.8 percent,
which equals 63.2 percent plus 23.2 percent) about 86.4 of the maximum current (where $I_{max} = V_b/R$).

During the third tc the current increases from 86.4 to 95 percent,
since 63.2 percent of the difference between the current at the beginning of the interval and maximum current is added to the instantaneous
current flowing at the start of the interval. Figure 10-10*a* illustrates
the growth of current, and Fig. 10-10*b* depicts the decay of induced emf.

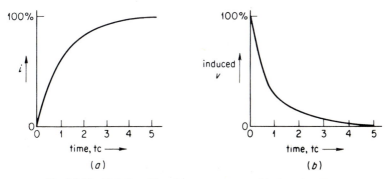

Fig. 10-10   Relationship of tc to current and induced voltage.

Table   10-1

tc	i, %	v_{in}, %
0	0	100
1	63.2	36.8
2	86.4	13.6
3	95	5
4	98.2	1.8
5	99.3	0.7

Table 10-1 lists the changes of induced voltage and current in relation to the time constant. For all practical purposes, the instantaneous current is at its maximum value at the end of 5 tc (at which time the induced voltage is zero).

Table 10-1 illustrates several important facts about the behavior of the current and induced voltage. When the circuit (which has a constant-amplitude supply voltage) is closed, the following events occur:

1   The current, in any one tc, increases by 63.2 percent of the difference between the current at the beginning of the tc and the Ohm's law maximum.

2   The induced voltage, in any one tc, decreases by 63.2 percent of the difference between the induced voltage at the beginning of the tc and the supply voltage.

3   The greatest roc i and roc v induced occur during the first tc.

4   The smallest roc i and roc v induced occur during the fifth tc.

5   The time of the first 5 tc may be called the *transient period* of the circuit.

6   After the passing of 5 tc, s the circuit is said to be *settled down*.

The ease with which the tc principle can be utilized is illustrated as follows.

Example

An inductance of 2.5 H and a resistance of 100 Ω are connected in series with a supply potential of 50 V. Find: (*a*) the magnitude of the current at the end of the second tc after the switch is closed; (*b*) the time after closing the switch when this current will flow.

Solution

(*a*) $I_{max} = \dfrac{V_b}{R} = \dfrac{50}{100} = 0.5$ A

At the end of the second tc the circuit current equals 86.4 percent of maximum (see Table 10-1).

i after the second tc $= 0.865 \times 0.5 = 0.432$ A

(b) $\text{tc} = \dfrac{L}{R} = \dfrac{2.5}{100} = 0.025$ s

The end of the second tc is 2×0.025 after the switch is closed. Hence 2 tc $= 0.050$ s.

10-11 DISCHARGE TC CONSIDERATIONS

In this section you will learn how circuit resistance and inductance affect current decreases.

It is important to note that the discharge LR tc is determined in the same manner as was described for the charging conditions. Recall that

$$\text{tc} = \frac{L}{R}$$

The value of the instantaneous decaying current can be found from

$$i_{\text{decay}} = I_o \epsilon^{-x}$$

(10-9)

where $I_o =$ initial current when switch is opened
$\epsilon = 2.718$
$x = Rt/L$
$t =$ time after onset of discharge time at which i is to be found, s
$R =$ total discharge circuit resistance, Ω
$L =$ inductor value, H

The application of this relationship is illustrated in the following examples.

Example 1

Refer to the circuit of Fig. 10-11. Find: (a) charging tc, (b) charging transient time, (c) discharging tc, and (d) discharging transient time.

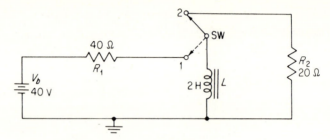

Fig. 10-11   Circuit for Example 1 and 2.

Solution

(*a*)   Find the charging tc:

$$\text{Charging tc} = \frac{L}{R_{\text{charging circuit}}} = \frac{L}{R_1}$$

Substituting values and solving yield

$$\text{tc} = \tfrac{2}{40} = 0.05 \text{ s}$$

(*b*)   Find the charging transient time:

Charging transient time $= 5$ charging tc $= 5 \times 0.05 = 0.25$ s

(*c*)   Find the discharging tc:

$$\text{Discharging tc} = \frac{L}{R_{\text{discharging}}} = \frac{L}{R_2}$$

Substituting values and solving give

$$\text{tc} = \tfrac{2}{20} = 0.10 \text{ s}$$

(*d*)   Find the discharging transient period:

Discharge transient period $= 5$ discharge tc $= 5 \times 0.10 = 0.50$ s

Example 2

Refer to Fig. 10-11. Assume that the switch was in position 1 for 0.08 s and then changed over to position 2. Find the discharge current that will be flowing 0.06 s after the switch is placed in position 2.

Solution

1   First determine the magnitude of coil current that was flowing at the instant the switch position was changed. Since this is a charging action,

$$i = \frac{V_b}{R}(1 - \epsilon^{-Rt/L})$$

where $R = R_1 = 40 \; \Omega$
  $V_b = 40 \; \text{V}$
  $t = 0.08 \; \text{s}$
  $L = 2 \; \text{H}$

Substituting values,

$$i = \tfrac{40}{40}(1 - \epsilon^{-(40 \times 0.08)/2)}) = 1(1 - \epsilon^{-1.6})$$

And from the exponential table in the Appendix,

$$\epsilon^{-1.6} = 0.202$$

Now solving,

$$i = 1(1 - 0.202) = 0.798 \; \text{A}$$

and this is the coil current at the onset of the coil discharge.

2   Now determine the discharge current that will flow 0.06 s after the switch is placed in position 2. Recall that the equation for determining instantaneous values of the coil discharge current is

$$i_{\text{decay}} = I_0 \epsilon^{-Rt/L}$$

where $I_0 = 0.798 \; \text{A}$
  $R = R_2 = 20 \; \Omega$
  $t = 0.06 \; \text{s}$
  $L = 2 \; \text{H}$

Substituting values gives

$$i_{\text{decay}} = 0.798 \epsilon^{-(20 \times 0.06/2)} = 0.798 \epsilon^{-0.6}$$

and from the exponential table in the Appendix,

$$\epsilon^{-0.6} = 0.549$$

Now solving,

$$i_{decay} = 0.798 \times 0.549 = 0.438 \text{ A}$$

10-12 MUTUAL INDUCTANCE, SERIES-AIDING

In this section you will learn how the total inductance of two coils in series can be greater than the sum of their individual values.

Up to this point what has been primarily considered is self-inductance. That is, the current changes produce a moving flux, which induces voltage in the coil, which passes the changing current. Recall that two or more coils can be so placed that the moving-flux field of coil 1 can cut the second coil, thereby establishing an induced emf in the second coil. The circuit is said to possess mutual inductance.

The unit of mutual inductance is the same as for self-inductance, the henry. Two coils can be series-connected in such a manner that the flux field of coil 1 is in the same direction as the flux field of coil 2. This condition is known as *mutual inductance, series-aiding.* The total induced voltage in the circuit is equal to the sum of the self-induced voltage of each coil and the mutually induced voltage of each coil; i.e., the total induced voltage is equal to the sum of the four induced voltages.

Assuming that all the flux lines of coil 1 cut coil 2 and vice versa, the mutual inductance M can be calculated from the following equation:

$$M = \sqrt{L_1 L_2} \qquad\qquad (10\text{-}10)$$

where M, L_1, and L_2 are in henrys. The total inductance of a series-aiding circuit is determined by the total effect of each coil upon itself and upon the other coil.

$$L_a = L_1 + L_2 + 2M \qquad\qquad (10\text{-}11)$$

where L_a = total series-aiding inductance, H
L_1, L_2 = inductance of each coil, H
M = mutual inductance, H

When two coils are connected in such a way that the flux field of coil 1 cuts coil 2 and vice versa, the two coils are said to be *magnetically coupled.*

10-13 MUTUAL INDUCTANCE, SERIES-OPPOSING

In this section you will learn how the total inductance of two coils in series can be less than the sum of their individual values.

Two coils can also be series-connected in such a way that the flux of coil 1 opposes the flux of coil 2. This can be done simply by reversing the connections of either coil, and it is known as *series-opposing*. The four induced voltages are such that the two self-induced voltages are "bucked" by the two mutually induced voltages. Therefore the total induced voltage is less than the sum of the self-induced emf by the amount of the mutual induced emf of the circuit. That is, the mutual inductance acts to reduce the effective inductance of the two series coils. The total inductance, for series-opposing, can be found by the following relationship:

$$L_o = L_1 + L_2 - 2M \tag{10-12}$$

where L_o = the total series-opposing inductance in henrys
$\quad L_1, L_2$ = inductance of each coil, H
$\quad M$ = mutual inductance, H

10-14 COEFFICIENT OF COUPLING AND MAGNETIC COUPLING

In this section you will learn about the coefficient of coupling and how it affects mutual inductance.

Up to this point in our discussion, it was arbitrarily assumed that all the flux lines from each coil cut the other coil, which is not the case in a great many applications. The term *coefficient of coupling*, k, is used to designate the ratio of the flux lines originating from one coil that cut a second coil to the total number of flux lines developed about the first coil. In equation form,

$$k = \frac{\text{number of flux lines linked to coil 2 from coil 1}}{\text{total number of flux lines developed about coil 1}} \tag{10-13}$$

There are many occasions when two or more coils are electrically insulated from each other, with their property of mutual inductance retained. Two or more coils in such an arrangement are said to be magnetically coupled, which is one of the basic principles of trans-former action. The greatest effect of mutual inductance is achieved at the time when all the flux from one coil cuts the second coil, and vice versa. In other words, the effect of mutual inductance is greatest when the coefficient of coupling is equal to unity.

The mutual-inductance equation of Sec. 10-12 is true when the coefficient of coupling is equal to unity. The mutual inductance is reduced when the coefficient of coupling is less than 1, as shown in the relationship

$$M = k \sqrt{L_1 L_2} \qquad \text{(10-14)}$$

where k is the coefficient of coupling (as a decimal) and M, L_1, and L_2 are in henrys.

The relationship above can be used to determine the coefficient of coupling if the mutual inductance and the inductance of each coil are known. Transposing gives

$$k = \frac{M}{\sqrt{L_1 L_2}}$$

Very often, the mutual inductance and the coefficient of coupling are both unknown. The mutual inductance of two coils can be determined by examining their effect on each other when connected series-aiding and then series-opposing. The difference of the two effects divided by 4 is equal to the mutual inductance.

$$M = \frac{L_a - L_o}{4} \qquad \text{(10-15)}$$

Example

The primary coil of a transformer is equal to 0.2 H, and the secondary is equal to 0.05 H. The series-aiding inductance is equal to 0.4 H; series-opposing inductance, 0.10 H. Find: (a) mutual inductance; (b) coefficient of coupling.

Solution

(a) $M = \dfrac{L_a - L_o}{4} = \dfrac{0.4 - 0.1}{4} = 0.075 \text{ H}$

(b) $k = \dfrac{M}{\sqrt{L_1 L_2}} = \dfrac{0.075}{(0.2 \times 0.05)^{1/2}} = 0.75$

When $k = 0.75$, it means that 75 percent of the flux from each coil cuts the other coil.

PROBLEMS

10-1   A coil has the following parameters: roc $i = 100$ mA/s; $v_{in} = 20$ mV. Find the inductance.

10-2   Repeat Prob. 10-1 with roc $i = 75$ mA/s and $v_{in} = 25$ mV.

10-3   A 5-H inductor undergoes a current change from 4 A to 2 A in 50 ms. Find the value of cemf.

10-4   A 10-H inductor has a cemf value of 5 V. How long will it take the current to increase from 0 to 3 A?

10-5   A magnetic core coil has the following parameters: $N = 500$ turns; $A = 0.5$ in²; $l = 3$ in; $u = 1200$ English units. Find the inductance (assume that the amount of leakage flux is negligible).

10-6   A magnetic core coil has the following parameters: $A = 0.6$ in²; $l = 2$ in; $L = 50$ mH; $u = 1000$ English units. Find N.

10-7   A magnetic core coil has the following parameters: $A = 0.12$ in²; $l = 3$ in; $L = 100$ mH; $u = 1400$ English units. Find N.

10-8   Refer to the circuit of Fig. 10-8. $L = 0.5$ H; $R = 100$ Ω; $V_b = 100$ V. Find the instantaneous current for:
   a)   0 s   b)   0.0025 s   c)   0.005 s
   d)   0.0075 s   e)   0.010 s   f)   0.015 s
   g)   0.020 s   h)   0.025 s

10-9   Using the values of current found in Prob. 10-8, calculate the voltage-drop across R for the same times.

10-10   Assume the circuit of Fig. 10-8 has the following parameters: $L = 4$ H; $R = 20$ Ω; $V_b = 10$ V. Find:
   a)   1 tc
   b)   5 tc
   c)   current after 5 tc
   d)   current at 0.08 s after closing the switch

10-11   Assume the circuit of Fig. 10-8 has the following parameters: $L = 1.5$ H; $V_b = 75$ V; R is varied from 2 to 10 Ω in 2-Ω increments. Find:
   a)   tc for each R value
   b)   maximum current for each R
   c)   transient time for each R
   d) i at 1.5 s after closing the switch for each R

10-12   Assume the inductance in Fig. 10-8 is 10 H. Find the resistance in order to have the following time constants:
   a)   1 s   b)   5 s   c)   16 s
   d)   50 ms   e)   26 μs

10-13   Assume the inductance in Fig. 10-8 is 100 mH and it takes the current 2 s to reach its maximum value. Find circuit R.

10-14 Assume the circuit of Fig. 10-11 has the following parameters: $V_b = 20$ V; $R_1 = 50$ Ω; $R_2 = 100$ Ω; $L = 5$ H. Find:
a) charging tc
b) charging transient time
c) discharging tc
d) discharging transient time

10-15 Assume the circuit of Fig. 10-11 has the parameters stated in Prob. 10-14. The switch was in position 1 for 0.12 s and then changed over to position 2. Find the discharge current that would be flowing 0.18 s after the switch is placed in position 2.

10-16 Assume the circuit of Fig. 10-11 has the following parameters: $V_b = 50$ V; $R_1 = 10$ Ω; $R_2 = 8$ Ω; $L = 4$ H. Find:
a) charging tc
b) charging transient time
c) discharging tc
d) discharging transient time

10-17 Assume the circuit of Fig. 10-11 has the parameters stated in Prob. 10-16. The switch was in position 1 for 1 s and then changed over to position 2. Find the discharge current that will be flowing 1.8 s after the switch is placed in position 2.

10-18 Two inductors, 0.8 and 1.3 H respectively, are connected such that they are series-aiding. Assume the coefficient of coupling is unity. Calculate the mutual inductance.

10-19 Find the following for the two inductors mentioned in Prob. 10-18:
a) total series-aiding inductance
b) total series-opposing inductance

10-20 A 2-H and a 5-H coil are connected in series. $k = 0.65$. Find M.

10-21 Refer to Prob. 10-20. Calculate:
a) total series-aiding inductance
b) total series-opposing inductance

10-22 Find the mutual inductance between the two coils in Prob. 10-18 if the coefficient of coupling is 0.25.

10-23 The primary and secondary coils of a transformer are both equal to 0.15 H. $k = 0.40$. Find:
a) mutual inductance
b) total series-aiding inductance
c) total series-opposing inductance

QUESTIONS

10-1 What is an induced emf?
10-2 What is electromagnetic induction?

10-3   What determines the polarity of the induced emf?

10-4   What is mutual induction?

10-5   What is Faraday's law?

10-6   What is Lenz' law?

10-7   In Fig. 10-3, what is the relationship between the primary and secondary coils?

10-8   When does the induced emf oppose the current?

10-9   When does the induced emf attempt to sustain the current?

10-10   What does the induced emf always oppose?

10-11   What is self-induction?

10-12   What is a cemf?

10-13   What is self-inductance?

10-14   What is the relationship between roc i and L?

10-15   What is the relationship between v_{in} and L?

10-16   What is the relationship between the number of coil turns and inductance?

10-17   What is the relationship between the reluctance of the magnetic circuit upon which the coil is wound and inductance?

10-18   What is the series relationship for total inductance?

10-19   What is the parallel relationship for total inductance?

10-20   What is the relationship of V_b to the value of I in a pure inductive circuit?

10-21   What is the relationship of L to the value of I in a pure inductive circuit?

10-22   What is the relationship of time to the value of I in a pure inductive circuit?

10-23   Refer to Fig. 10-7. Why does a smaller roc i generate the required emf in the larger value of L?

10-24   Refer to Fig. 10-8. Why is the current value zero at the instant the switch is closed?

10-25   In Fig. 10-8, what is the time required for the current to reach its full Ohm's law value called?

10-26   What effect does a higher value of R in a series-RL circuit have on the induced voltage?

10-27   What effect does a higher value of R in a series-RL circuit have on the current?

10-28   What effect does a higher value of L in a series-RL circuit have on the current?

10-29   What is the series-RL tc?

10-30   What is the relationship between current and time in a series-RL charging circuit?

10-31   What is the relationship between induced emf and time in a series-RL discharging circuit?

10-32   What is the relationship between current and time in a series-RL discharging circuit?

10-33   What is the relationship between induced emf and time in a series-RL discharging circuit?

10-34   What determines the tc of the series-RL charging circuit?

10-35   What determines the tc of the series-RL discharging circuit?

10-36   What is mutual inductance, series-aiding?

10-37   What determines the total inductance of a mutual-inductance series-aiding circuit?

10-38   What is mutual inductance, series-opposing?

10-39   What is the coefficient of coupling between two coils?

10 40   What does $k = 1.0$ between two coils indicate?

characteristics of capacitance

11

Capacitance is the third basic circuit component to be considered up to this point in the text. It will be analyzed in terms of its properties as well as its behavior in the basic circuit connections of series and parallel.

11-1 ELECTRICAL ASPECTS OF A CAPACITOR

In this section you will learn about:
* *How capacitors are used*
* *How capacitance behaves electrically*
* *The dielectric constant*
* *The unit of capacitance, the farad*

A capacitor can be used for a number of purposes. (1) It may serve as a charge-storage center. In this case it stores a charge and releases it at predetermined times. (2) A capacitor may be used to block unidirectional current. After the initial charging action, no current will flow, resulting in a blocking action imposed by the capacitor. (3) Capacitors also serve useful functions in various filter circuits.

Basically, a capacitor is formed when two conducting materials (called plates) separated by an insulator (called the dielectric) are facing each other. Examine the capacitor illustrated in Fig. 11-1.

Notice the polarity of the supply potential in Fig. 11-1. Prior to the closing of the switch, plates *A* and *B* of the capacitor are neutral in

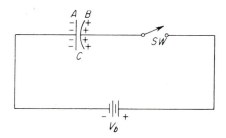

Fig. 11-1 Pure capacitive circuit.

237

charge, and the potential between plates A and B is zero. When the switch is closed, electrons move from the negative terminal of the supply to plate A and from plate B toward the positive terminal of V_b.

Plate A has mobile electrons stored within it at this time, and plate B has an equal number of electrons removed from it. A question which arises at this point is: How does this action come about? It should be recalled that like charges repel. At the time the switch is closed, the supply emf imposes a drift action upon the mobile electrons. The electrons arriving at plate A exert a repelling effect on the same number of electrons on plate B through the dielectric, thereby forcing them to drift toward the positive terminal of V_b. As the action of electron storage on plate A and electron displacement from plate B progresses, energy from the source is stored within the dielectric in electrostatic form. As the source drives more electrons onto plate A, they are repelled by those electrons already stored on plate A. A difference of potential is developed across the capacitor as a direct function of the discrepancy between the electrons on plates A and B. Since the plate receiving the electrons repels the oncoming electrons, a difference of potential, which is opposite in polarity to the supply voltage, is developed. Notice that the polarity of plate A (Fig. 11-1) is negative with respect to plate B and is nearest to the negative terminal of V_b. Since the high side $(-)$ of the capacitor potential is nearest to the high side of V_b, it is a cemf. Eventually the cemf becomes equal to V_b, the capacitor is said to be charged, and electron current ceases. The cemf is the equal and opposite reaction to V_b. Since the repelling effect of the cemf is equal to the propelling effect of V_b, a condition of equilibrium is achieved when the capacitor is charged. It should be pointed out that the work done by V_b is equal to the work capable of being done by the charged capacitor (assuming that the circuit is perfect, with no losses). In effect, the capacitor stores the energy drawn from the supply voltage. Later sections reveal possible actions of a charged capacitor.

The dielectric field of the stored electrons exists in the insulator material between plates A and B. If the distance between the plates is reduced (dielectric thickness is reduced), the effect of the stored plate A electrons upon those at plate B is more pronounced. This is verified by Coulomb's law, which states that the force between two charges is directly proportional to the product of the charges and inversely proportional to the square of the distance between them. Coulomb's law also implies that a greater number of charges results in a larger force exerted between them. If the area of plates A and B is made larger, more electrons can be stored, establishing a stronger force.

The type of dielectric material determines the ease with which the electrons on plate A can exert an effect on the plate B electrons (estab-

Table   11-1

Material	Dielectric Constant k
Air	1.00054
Aluminum oxide	10
Glass	4.2
Mica	7.5
Paper	4
Polyester	3
Polystyrene	2.6
Porcelain	6.2
Tantalum oxide	11
Vacuum	1

lish dielectric flux). The dielectric constant k of a material denotes this effect and can be defined as the ratio

$$k = \frac{\text{capacitance with material as dielectric}}{\text{capacitance with vacuum as dielectric}}$$

A vacuum is arbitrarily given a dielectric constant k of 1. A dielectric material which is four times more effective than a vacuum in establishing dielectric flux between the plates has a dielectric constant of 4 ($k = 4$). Several typical dielectric materials, with their dielectric constants, are listed in Table 11-1. It can be seen that three physical factors determine the ability of a capacitor to store a charge: (1) plate area, (2) dielectric thickness, and (3) dielectric constant. The capacitance is directly proportional to the plate area and dielectric constant and inversely proportional to the dielectric thickness.

$$C \propto \frac{Ak}{d}$$

where A = plate area
k = dielectric constant
d = dielectric thickness

The unit of capacitance is the farad.

A capacitor having one volt across its plates when it stores one coulomb of charge possesses a capacitance of one farad.

This may be reexpressed in a second manner.

A capacitance has a capacity of one farad if the voltage across its plates rises at the rate of one volt per second when one ampere is flowing through it.

The farad is too large a unit for the great majority of electronic circuits; microfarad (μF) and picofarad (pF) are used more frequently.

In equation form, capacitance is equal to the ratio of the charge it contains to the potential difference across it:

$$C = \frac{Q}{V} \qquad\qquad \textbf{(11-1)}$$

where C = capacitance, F
$\quad$ Q = charge, C
$\quad$ V = volts across capacitor

In describing the action of the capacitor in Fig. 11-1 when the switch was closed, it was found that the least opposition to the charging action occurred at the instant the switch was closed. Furthermore, it was seen that the force of opposition developed by the cemf gradually became equal to the force developed by the supply potential, and current stopped. This implies that a greater current flow existed at zero time and that it gradually decayed to zero. The voltage across the capacitor v_C increases from zero to the magnitude of the supply potential at a rate determined by the ratio of current to capacitance. In equation form,

$$\text{roc } v_C = \frac{i}{C} \qquad\qquad \textbf{(11-2)}$$

where roc v_C = rate of change of capacitor voltage
$\quad$ i = current, A
$\quad$ C = capacitance, F

Transposing the equation makes it possible to solve for i and/or C:

$$i = \text{roc } v_C \times C \qquad\qquad \textbf{(11-2a)}$$
$$C = \frac{i}{\text{roc } v_C} \qquad\qquad \textbf{(11-2b)}$$

Examination of the preceding equations leads to a better understanding of capacitive action. There is a redistribution of charges in a capacitor when a voltage is applied to its plates. These charges are redistributed by a current in the circuit external to the capacitor. The amount of redistribution in a capacitor at a particular instant is equal to the product of the rate of change of the voltage and the size of the capacitor. A greater amount indicates a larger coulombs-per-second ratio. If more

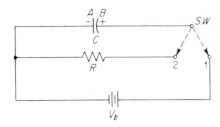

Fig. 11-2   Capacitive circuit with separate charging and discharging paths.

coulombs are moved per second, the capacitor voltage will charge at a faster rate. With a larger capacitor, the number of coulombs per second will be greater, thereby resulting in a faster change in capacitor voltage.

It can be seen that the three factors (i, C, and roc v_C) are closely related and mutually dependent upon one another. Refer to Fig. 11-2. Soon after the switch is placed in position 1, the capacitor is charged (V_C is equal to V_b). All action in the circuit stops, and the current is zero. Now move the switch to position 2, which places R across the capacitor terminals and removes V_b from the circuit. V_C will drive current from plate A (negative) toward plate B (positive) via the external circuit. Electrons leave plate A, making it less negative, and other electrons enter plate B, making it less positive. This action continues until both plates are neutral in charge. At this time the capacitor is fully discharged, and current ceases, since the capacitor potential has decayed to zero. The energy stored in the dielectric field while the switch was in position 1 is returned to the circuit and dissipated by R in this discharge action.

11-2 TYPES OF COMMERCIAL CAPACITORS

In this section you will learn about the important types of commercial capacitors: air, mica, paper, glass, electrolytics, plastic-film, and ceramic.

Air Capacitors

The air capacitor is a variable capacitor with air as its dielectric. The capacitance, which can range from 1 to 500 pF for this variety, is varied by changing its plate area. This is the type of capacitor used in selecting stations on radios. Turning the shaft of the unit in one direction increases the plate area by meshing a set of parallel connected plates in with another set of parallel plates. This increases the overall plate area of the capacitor, resulting in an increase in its capacitance.

Trimmers and Padders

There are several types of semivariable capacitors in use, commonly called *trimmers* or *padders*. A trimmer consists of two conductor plates separated by an insulator material, usually mica. A screw is mounted such that tightening the screw compresses the two plates more tightly against the mica, thereby reducing the dielectric thickness and increasing the capacitance. Loosening the screw reduces the pressure against the dielectric, increasing its thickness and reducing the capacitance. Trimmers are frequently 10 pF or less in value. They are used in parallel with another capacitor. If the capacitance of a unit is to be made slightly larger, as with a tuning capacitor such as the air variety just described, the trimmer is placed in parallel with it. The final adjustment of the trimmer is made with the trimmer actually in the circuit. The same semivariable unit is frequently used in series with another capacitor, so as to reduce the overall capacitance; the unit is then called a padder. As with the trimmer, the final adjustment is made with the padder actually in the circuit. Trimmers and padders are called semivariable because they are adjusted prior to circuit operation and then left alone.

Mica Capacitors

Mica capacitors are in common use because of their small size, high working voltages, low losses, and economy. Physically, they consist of alternate layers of aluminum foil and sheets of mica. Tinfoil has sometimes been used in place of the aluminum foil. The entire unit is generally encased in Bakelite or other insulating material, as a seal against moisture.

Mica capacitors can also be made by stacking or paralleling layers of silver heat-bonded to the mica. These silvered-mica sheets are free of air gaps, and the capacitor is considered to be more reliable than the mica-foil variety just described. The mica-type capacitors are available in sizes as small as 10 pF and as large as 10,000 pF.

Paper Capacitors

Paper capacitors are in common use chiefly because of their low cost and small size. The plates are often made of tinfoil or some similar conducting material. Several layers of relatively thin paper, specially treated, make up the dielectric. The plate material and dielectric are cut into long, narrow strips and then rolled into a compact unit. The entire unit usually is encapsulated and enclosed in a container, which is sealed against moisture by wax or pitch. The paper capacitors generally display higher leakage losses than their mica counterparts and have a shorter life. They range from 500 pF to 1 μF.

Glass Capacitors

This variety is made of sheets of glass for the dielectric and sheets of aluminum foil for the plates. They are more costly than the mica type, but are more resistant to moisture. They are commercially available in values from around 5 pF to 10,000 pF.

Electrolytic Capacitors

Electrolytic capacitors can be subdivided into two classes: wet and dry. A borax solution is often used as the electrolyte in this type of capacitor. Aluminum foil is brought into contact with the borax solution, resulting in a chemical action that produces a deposit of a thin film of aluminum oxide on the aluminum foil. The aluminum oxide film is the dielectric of the capacitor. The borax electrolyte is the negative plate, and the aluminum foil is the positive terminal. The borax is in liquid form in the wet type and in paste form in the dry type.

One of the unusual features of the electrolytic capacitor is that it has polarity, which must be observed. The leakage current, which is the current that flows through the dielectric, is an important consideration. Electron flow from the negative terminal through the dielectric to the positive terminal is kept at relatively low values because of the resistance to this leakage flow. The resistance to electron flow from the positive terminal through the oxide film to the negative plate is relatively low, resulting in high values of leakage current in this direction; this develops heat in the circuit. This heat in turn causes a change in the molecular structure of the borax solution, which further decreases the resistance. If a reverse leakage current of sufficient magnitude is allowed to flow for a substantial length of time, the oxide-film structure will be disrupted, and the capacitor will be damaged. The flow of a small reverse leakage current (electron flow from the positive plate through the dielectric to the negative plate) for a short period of time may not damage the unit permanently, since a return to normal conditions with flow of a small forward leakage current (from the negative plate through the dielectric to the positive plate) will restore the oxide film to its original condition.

The thickness of the aluminum oxide film, along with its area, is a contributing factor in the determination of the capacitance value of the unit. The breakdown voltage (the potential at which the dielectric breaks down) is also determined by the thickness of the oxide film (a thinner film results in a lower breakdown voltage). Relatively large values of capacitance are obtainable (over 100 μF) in electrolytic units.

The dry type is most popular because of economy in packaging compared with the wet type. The aluminum foil and borax solution are separated by an absorbent material to prevent them from actually touching and to keep the electrolyte in its proper position. The unit is encapsulated in a cardboard or metal container. Several units are often enclosed in one container.

As was pointed out before, single electrolytic capacitors can be used in unidirectional-current circuits only. Because of the large values of capacitance obtainable from electrolytic capacitors, it is sometimes desirable to use them in bidirectional-current circuits. Connecting two units back to back makes it possible to utilize them in such circuits. For example, a back-to-back connection of two 10-μF units joins the positive terminals to each other. The negative terminal of C_1 is joined to one side of the circuit, and the negative terminal of C_2 is connected to the second side of the circuit. When current flows in a given direction (positive), C_1 is effectively shorted, since its leakage resistance to current flow in this direction is low; C_2 functions in its normal manner. Because the forward leakage current of C_2 is small, the reverse leakage current of C_1 is restricted to this value, and the unit is not damaged. C_2 appears as the only capacitance in the circuit during the time current flows in this direction. When current flow is in the opposite direction (negative), C_2 is effectively shorted and C_1 functions in its normal manner, thereby preventing damage to C_2. C_2 is the only capacitance in the circuit during the time current flows in this reverse direction. Thus, if a 10-μF capacitance is required in a bidirectional circuit, two electrolytic capacitors (each 10 μF) in a back-to-back connection can be utilized. This is a valuable feature of the electrolytic capacitors, since they are obtainable in higher values than the other types. A typical application of the back-to-back application is in conjunction with bidirectional-current motor starters.

Tantalum Capacitors

This is a new type of electrolytic capacitor which uses tantalum instead of aluminum. The advantages of the tantalum capacitor include (1) larger values of capacitance for smaller physical size, (2) less leakage current, and (3) longer shelf life. Their major disadvantage is lower voltage ratings. They are used commonly in transistor circuits.

Plastic-Film Capacitors

The plastics, polyester and polystyrene, serve very well as dielectrics in capacitors. Sheets of metal foil are used as capacitor plates, and sheets of the plastic serve as the dielectric. An important limitation of the plastic dielectrics is their sensitivity to temperature. Values from 0.001 to 10 μF are available in the polyester-film type and from 5 pF to 0.5 μF in the polystyrene-film variety.

Ceramic Capacitors

Ceramics includes a variety of materials which cover a wide range of dielectric properties. Capacitors having ceramic dielectrics are commercially available in sizes from 10 pF to 1 μF.

Table 11-2 lists the types of capacitors described in this section and the capacitance range of each variety.

Table 11-2

Capacitor Type	Range	
	Minimum	Maximum
Air	1 pF	500 pF
Ceramic	10 pF	1 μF
Electrolytic	1 μF	10,000 μF
Glass	1 pF	10,000 pF
Mica	1 pF	10,000 pF
Paper	500 pF	1 μF
Polyester	0.001 μF	10 μF
Polystyrene	5 pF	0.5 μF

11-3   SERIES CAPACITANCE

In this section you will learn how to calculate the total capacitance of several capacitors connected in series.

In Fig. 11-3, C_1 and C_2 are connected in series. When the switch is closed, plate A charges and plate B discharges. The electrons which leave plate B move toward plate C; the same number of electrons leave plate D to drift toward the positive terminal of V_b. The placement of C_1 and C_2 in series did not affect the plate area for storage, but it effectively increased the dielectric thickness, resulting in a total capacitance which is smaller than either one alone. The total capacitance can be found by

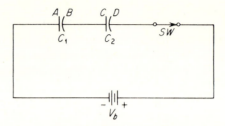

Fig. 11-3   Series capacitors.

$$\frac{1}{C} = \frac{1}{C_1} + \frac{1}{C_2} + \cdots + \frac{1}{C_n}$$ (11-3)

and

$$C = \frac{Q}{V}$$ (11-4)

where C = total capacitance, F
Q = total charge, C
V = supply potential, V
C_1 = capacitance of C_1, etc.

The charge developed by each capacitor is the same and is equal to the charge obtained from the source.

$$Q = Q_1 = Q_2 = \cdots = Q_n$$ (11-5)

Each capacitor develops a potential. Being a series circuit, the capacitor voltages must equal the supply voltage.

$$V = V_{C_1} + V_{C_2} + \cdots + V_{C_n}$$ (11-6)

Since the charge of each series capacitor is the same and equal to the charge supplied by the source potential, the voltage across each capacitor can be readily computed.

Example

Three capacitors, of values given in Fig. 11-4, are connected in series with a supply potential of 100 V. Find: (*a*) the total charge; (*b*) voltage across each capacitor.

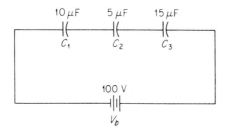

Fig. 11-4   Three capacitors in series.

Solution

First determine the total capacitance:

$$\frac{1}{C} = \frac{1}{C_1} + \frac{1}{C_2} + \frac{1}{C_3} + \cdots$$

Substituting values,

$$\frac{1}{C} = \frac{1}{10(10)^{-6}} + \frac{1}{5(10)^{-6}} + \frac{1}{15(10)^{-6}} = 366{,}667$$
$$C = 2.73(10)^{-6} \text{ F} = 2.73 \ \mu\text{F}$$

Since the total capacitance and the total voltage are known, the total charge can be determined:

$$V = \frac{Q}{C}$$

and transposing,

$$Q = VC$$

Substituting,

$$Q = 100 \times 2.73(10)^{-6} = 273(10)^{-6} \text{ C}$$

Since the charge of each C is the same as Q total and the value of each capacitor is known, the voltage across each C can be calculated.

$$V_{C_1} = \frac{Q_1}{C_1} = \frac{273(10)^{-6}}{10(10)^{-6}} = 27.3 \text{ V}$$
$$V_{C_2} = \frac{Q_2}{C_2} = \frac{273(10)^{-6}}{5(10)^{-6}} = 54.6 \text{ V}$$
$$V_{C_3} = \frac{Q_3}{C_3} = \frac{273(10)^{-6}}{15(10)^{-6}} = 18.2 \text{ V}$$

Notice that the three voltages add up to the supply potential, which is always a series-circuit requirement. An important relationship between the size of a series capacitor and the voltage across it is that the ratio of any two series capacitances is inversely proportional to the voltage across them. In the above,

$$\frac{C_1}{C_2} = \frac{V_{C_2}}{V_{C_1}}$$

and using the values above gives

$$\frac{10(10)^{-6}}{5(10)^{-6}} = \frac{54.6}{27.3}$$

11-4 PARALLEL CAPACITANCE

In this section you will learn how to calculate the total capacitance of several capacitors connected in parallel.

Like the series arrangement discussed in Sec. 11-3, a value of equivalent capacitance can be obtained by connecting in parallel. Refer to Fig. 11-5 for the following discussion. Assume that C_1 is 10 μF, C_2 is 20 μF, and V_b is 100 V. At the instant the switch is closed, plates A and C take on negative charges. C_1 and C_2, being in parallel, develop the same cemf, which is 100 V in our example. The amount of charge developed by 100 V is directly proportional to the size of the capacitors, since

$$Q = VC$$

Since C_2 is twice the size of C_1 and their voltages are equal, the charge of C_2 will be twice that of C_1. The actual charge developed by each capacitor can be found easily.

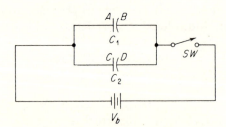

Fig. 11-5 Two capacitors in parallel.

$$Q_1 = V_{C_1}C_1 \qquad Q_2 = V_{C_2}C_2$$

Substituting values,

$$Q_1 = 100 \times 10(10)^{-6} = 0.001 \text{ C}$$
$$Q_2 = 100 \times 20(10)^{-6} = 0.002 \text{ C}$$

The supply potential furnished the charge of each capacitor; hence, the total charge contained by parallel capacitors is equal to the sum of the individual charges.

$$Q = Q_1 + Q_2$$

Substituting values,

$$Q = 0.001 + 0.002 = 0.003 \text{ C}$$

The charge stored by the individual capacitors is directly proportional to the size of each capacitor connected in parallel. This increases the total capacitance of the circuit. The equivalent capacitance of parallel-connected capacitors is equal to the sum of the individual capacitors. In equation form,

$$C = C_1 + C_2 + \cdots + C_n \tag{11-7}$$

Example

Three capacitors are connected in parallel with a source potential of 400 V. C_1 is 8 μF, C_2 is 20 μF, and C_3 is 12 μF. Find: (a) equivalent capacitance; (b) charge of each capacitor; (c) total charge.

Solution

(a) The equivalent capacitance is

$$C = C_1 + C_2 + C_3 = 8 + 20 + 12 = 40 \ \mu\text{F}$$

(b) The charge of each capacitor can be found, since each value is known and the voltage across each one is the same.

$$Q_1 = V_{C_1} \times C_1 = 400 \times 8(10)^{-6} = 0.0032 \text{ C}$$
$$Q_2 = V_{C_2} \times C_2 = 400 \times 20(10)^{-6} = 0.0080 \text{ C}$$
$$Q_3 = V_{C_3} \times C_3 = 400 \times 12(10)^{-6} = 0.0048 \text{ C}$$

(*c*)   The total charge is

$$Q = Q_1 + Q_2 + Q_3$$
$$= 0.0032 + 0.0080 + 0.0048 = 0.0160 \text{ C}$$

Note that C_2 is equal to one-half the total capacitance and that the charge of C_2 is one-half of the total charge. The ratio of a capacitor value to the total capacitance is equal to the ratio of the capacitor charge to the total charge. In equation form,

$$\frac{C_1}{C} = \frac{Q_1}{Q}$$

PROBLEMS

11-1   The following capacitors are connected in series: $C_1 = 5 \ \mu\text{F}$, $C_2 = 3 \ \mu\text{F}$, $C_3 = 9 \ \mu\text{F}$. Source potential is 200 V. Find:
a)   equivalent capacitance
b)   voltage across each capacitor
c)   total charge

11-2   Repeat Prob. 11-1 with the following capacitor values: $C_1 = 0.05 \ \mu\text{F}$, $C_2 = 0.02 \ \mu\text{F}$, $C_3 = 0.08 \ \mu\text{F}$.

11-3   A circuit with two capacitors in series has a total capacitance of $10 \ \mu\text{F}$. Find:
a) C_2 if $C_1 = 18 \ \mu\text{F}$
b) C_2 if $C_1 = 40 \ \mu\text{F}$
c) C_2 if $C_1 = 25 \ \mu\text{F}$

11-4   In Prob. 11-3, if the supply potential is 50 V, find:
a)   total charge for conditions (a) to (c)
b)   voltage distribution for (a)
c)   voltage distribution for (b)
d)   voltage distribution for (c)

11-5   Three capacitors are in series. V_{C_1} is one-half of V_{C_2}. The sum of these two voltages is equal to 75 percent of the source potential. Find C_2 and C_3 if C_1 is $5 \ \mu\text{F}$.

11-6   Four capacitors are connected in parallel. $C_1 = 0.005 \ \mu\text{F}$; $C_2 = 0.02 \ \mu\text{F}$; $C_3 = 0.03 \ \mu\text{F}$; $C_4 = 0.05 \ \mu\text{F}$. Source potential is 250 V. Find:
a)   equivalent capacitance
b)   charge for each capacitor
c)   total charge

11-7 In Prob. 11-6, find the charge of each capacitor and the total charge for a source potential of 14 V.

11-8 A parallel circuit is to possess an equivalent capacitance of 20 μF. C_1 is to be four times the size of C_2. Find:
   a) C_1
   b) C_2

11-9 In Prob. 11-8, if the source potential is 90 V, find:
   a) charge of each capacitor
   b) total charge

11-10 Repeat Prob. 11-9 for a source potential of 40 V.

QUESTIONS

11-1 How does a capacitor develop a cemf?

11-2 What is the dielectric constant of a material?

11-3 Why is the value of a capacitor directly proportional to its plate area?

11-4 Why is the value of a capacitor inversely proportional to its dielectric constant?

11-5 What is the relationship between the units of farad, microfarad, and picofarad? ~/2

11-6 What is the difference between a trimmer and a padder?

11-7 What variety of commercial capacitor provides the largest values of capacitance?

11-8 What are three purposes for which capacitors can be used?

11-9 Why is the total capacitance in a series circuit less than the value of the smallest capacitor in that circuit?

11-10 What are the voltage relationships in a series-C circuit?

11-11 What are the charge relationships in a series-C circuit?

11-12 Why is the total capacitance in a parallel-C circuit equal to the sum of the capacitance in that circuit?

11-13 What are the charge relationships in a parallel-C circuit?

11-14 What are the voltage relationships in a parallel-C circuit?

11-5 SERIES-*RC* RELATIONSHIPS (TIME, CURRENT, *R*, AND *C*)

In this section you will learn how circuit resistance and capacitance affect current changes.

A capacitor is rarely used as the only component in a circuit. One common combination is a resistor in series with a capacitor (called a series-*RC*

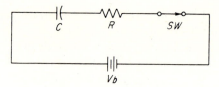

Fig. 11-6   Series-*RC* circuit.

circuit). Refer to Fig. 11-6. At the instant the switch is closed, the capacitor begins to charge in a direction determined by the polarity of V_b. Since the capacitor offers no opposition at the instant the switch is closed, it appears as a short circuit. In a series-*RC* circuit, the current at this time would be infinite if there were no resistance in the circuit. The current at zero time, which is the maximum current, is limited by the magnitude of resistance in series with the capacitor. In equation form,

$$I_{\max} = I_{0 \text{ time}} = \frac{V_b}{R} \tag{11-8}$$

where $I_{\max}$ = maximum current, A
    V_b = source potential, V
    R = series-circuit resistance, Ω

The current immediately begins to decrease, gradually decaying to zero in an exponential fashion. Figure 11-7 illustrates the manner in which the circuit current decays.

The relationship of time, resistance, and capacitance to the magnitude of the current at any instant (called an *instantaneous-current value*)

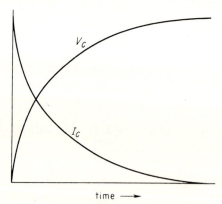

Fig. 11-7 V_C and I_C of a charging series-*RC* circuit.

is of particular interest. The instantaneous current can be determined from the following relationship:

$$i = I_{max} \epsilon^{-t/(RC)} \qquad\qquad \textbf{(11-9)}$$

where i = instantaneous current, A
   I_{max} = maximum current, A (zero-time current)
   ϵ = base of the natural logarithm, 2.72
   t = time, s
   R = resistance, Ω
   C = capacitance, F

Example

A 10-μF capacitor is in series with a 5-kΩ resistor. V_b is 500 V. Find the current at (*a*) zero time and (*b*) 25 ms.

Solution

(*a*)   Current at zero time:

$$I_{max} = \frac{V_b}{R} = \frac{500}{5000} = 0.1 \text{ A}$$

(*b*)   Current at 25 ms:

$$i = I_{max} \epsilon^{-t/(RC)} = 1 \times 10^{-1} \times 2.72^{-(0.025)/[5000 \times 10(10)-6]}$$
$$i = 1 \times 10^{-1} \times \epsilon^{-0.5}$$

and from the exponential table in the Appendix,

$$\epsilon^{-0.5} = 0.607$$

Substituting back into the equation and solving,

$$i = 0.1 \times 0.607 = 0.0607 \text{ A}$$

The instantaneous-current equation enables us to calculate any point on the current-charge curve of Fig. 11-7.
   The value of current at any specific instant hinges on four factors:

1   Supply potential
2   Time elapsed
3   Circuit resistance
4   Circuit capacitance

The relationship of time to current magnitude is important. The rate of current change (roc i) is not fixed, as indicated by the fact that the i_C-time relationship of Fig. 11-7 is represented by a curved line. The slope of this line is most vertical at the instant that the switch is closed, which means that roc i is greatest at that time. At the end of the time displayed on the graph, the line is closest to the horizontal, and roc i is smallest. With a fixed supply potential, resistance, and capacitance, roc i varies inversely with time. The development of current, and its decay to zero with a decreasing roc, is called the *transient time* of the circuit. In the series-RC circuit with a fixed supply potential, the capacitor appears as an open circuit after the transient period. At this time the capacitor is charged and will remain so until a change in the circuit is made.

The relationship of R and C on the charging current deserves separate consideration as well. The magnitude of the zero-time current is an inverse function of the circuit resistance (larger R reduces the zero-time current, and vice versa). Since the initial current is smaller, the time for charging the capacitor is increased, because the rate at which electrons are stored on the charging plate is reduced. The value of C has no effect on the magnitude of the initial current, since it appears as a short circuit at zero time, but it does affect the charging time. With all other factors constant, a larger capacitor has the ability to store a greater charge, which causes the decaying charging current to flow for a longer time.

11-6 THE RC TIME CONSTANT

In this section you will learn about the relationship of voltage and current values to the time constant in a series RC circuit.

The RC tc may be defined in a number of ways, each of which states one of the characteristics which take place in the time interval. Following are several descriptions of the tc in terms of the circuit current:

1   The time it takes the current to decay from maximum to 36.8 percent of maximum
2   The time it takes the current to decrease from its value at the beginning of the interval in question to 36.8 percent of that value
3   An interval in which the current decreases by 63.2 percent of its value at the beginning of the interval

The tc may also be described in terms of voltage. At zero time, the current is maximum, the capacitor acts as a short circuit, and the entire supply potential is dropped across the circuit resistance. The current begins to decay exponentially, as must the voltage-drop across the resistance. Assuming that the supply potential remains constant, the capacitor must have a voltage-drop equal to the arithmetic difference between the source voltage and V_R. This is where the cemf of the capacitor comes into the picture. Soon after zero time, the capacitor cemf begins to develop in an exponential manner (illustrated as V_C in Fig. 11-7). The cemf builds up as the charge is accumulated by the capacitor, causing the current to decay in the same way. Since the cemf is opposite in polarity to the source potential, it may be treated as a voltage-drop in analyzing the voltage distribution of the circuit. The cemf increases exponentially, and V_R must decrease in the same exponential manner, since the sum of the two must always be equal to the fixed source potential.

$$V_b = \text{cemf} + V_R \qquad \text{or} \qquad V_b = V_C + V_R \text{ at any time}$$

Refer to Fig. 11-8 for the following discussion. Examine the distribution of voltage at the end of the first tc. It was stated before that the current at the end of the first tc is 36.8 percent of maximum. In using simple Ohm's law relationships, it becomes apparent that V_R must have decreased from a value equal to the source potential to 36.8 percent of V_b. This is shown as point A in Fig. 11-8. Recall the reason why the current decayed to 36.8 percent of maximum: the cemf built up from zero to 63.2 percent of V_b at the end of the first tc (shown as point B in Fig. 11-8). Next construct a vertical line from point D on the x axis (which represents 1 tc) through points A and B. Extending this vertical line until it intercepts the V_b line gives point C. The magnitude of any

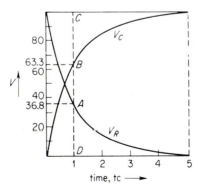

Fig. 11-8   Voltage relationship in a charging series-*RC* circuit.

of the three voltages at the end of 1 tc is indicated by the length of the vertical line from that voltage curve to point D.

V_R is designated by the length of line AD, V_C by BD, and the fixed V_b by CD. It can be seen that adding line AD to the top of line BD equals line CD. This shows graphically that the sum of V_R and V_C is equal to V_b. This can be done at any tc value or any other time and will always be true, proving that the sum of the voltage-drop across the resistor and the cemf will be equal to the supply potential at each and every instant.

Fortunately, there is a simple way in which the tc of any series-RC circuit can be determined:

$$tc - RC \qquad\qquad (11\text{-}10)$$

where tc = time for current to decay from maximum to 36.8 percent of maximum

R = series-circuit resistance, Ω

C = capacitance, F

Example

A series-RC circuit consists of a 10-μF capacitor, 5-kΩ resistance, and a supply potential of 5000 V. Find: (a) current at zero time and at the end of each tc for 5 tc; (b) V_C at zero time and at the end of each tc for 5 tc; (c) V_R at zero time and at the end of each tc for 5 tc.

Solution

(a)   The current at zero time:

$$I_{o\ \text{time}} = I_{\max} = \frac{V_b}{R} = \frac{5000}{5000} = 1\ \text{A}$$

Current at the end of 1 tc: the current decreased to 36.8 percent of the current flowing at the beginning of the tc.

$$I_{1\text{tc}} = 0.368 I_{\max} = 0.368 \times 1\ \text{A} = 0.368\ \text{A}$$

The current at the end of the second tc is 36.8 percent of the current flowing at the beginning of the second tc, which is the current flowing at the end of the first tc.

$$I_{2\text{tc}} = 0.368 I_{1\text{tc}} = 0.368 \times 0.368 = 0.135\ \text{A}$$

which is 13.5 percent of I_{max}. The current at the end of the third tc is equal to 36.8 percent of the current at the end of the second tc.

$$I_{3tc} = 0.368\,I_{2tc} = 0.368 \times 0.135 = 0.0497 \text{ A}$$

which is 4.97 percent of I_{max}.

$$I_{4tc} = 0.368\,I_{3tc} = 0.368 \times 0.0497 = 0.0183 \text{ A}$$

which is 1.83 percent of I_{max}.

$$I_{5tc} = 0.368\,I_{4tc} = 0.368 \times 0.0183 = 0.0067 \text{ A}$$

which is 0.67 percent of I_{max}.

(*b*) Knowing the current at the end of each tc provides an easy method for computing V_R and V_C; therefore one can work on parts (*b*) and (*c*) at the same time. (Small computational discrepancies will be noted because of rounding.)

$$V_{R,0 \text{ time}} = V_b = 5000 \text{ V}$$

and

$$V_{C,0 \text{ time}} = 0 \text{ V}$$

since C appears as a short circuit.

$$V_{R,1tc} = 0.368 V_b$$

since the current flowing through the fixed resistor decreased to 36.8 percent of I_{max}.

$$V_{R,1tc} = 0.368 \times 5000 = 1840 \text{ V}$$

and

$$V_{C,1tc} = V_b - V_{R,1tc} = 5000 - 1840 = 3160 = 63.2\% \times V_b$$

At the end of the second tc, the current again decreases by 63.2 percent to 13.5 percent of I_{max}.

$$V_{R,2tc} = 0.135 V_b = 0.135 \times 5000 = 675 \text{ V}$$

and

$$V_{C,2tc} = V_b - V_{R,2tc} = 5000 - 675 = 4325 \text{ V} = 0.865 V_b$$

At the end of the third tc, the current decreased to 4.97 percent of I_{max}:

$$V_{R,3tc} = 0.0497 V_b = 0.0497 \times 5000 = 249 \text{ V}$$

and

$$V_{C,3tc} = V_b - V_{R,3tc} = 5000 - 249 = 4751 \text{ V} = 0.953 V_b$$
$$V_{R,4tc} = 0.0183 V_b = 0.0183 \times 5000 = 92 \text{ V}$$

and

$$V_{C,4tc} = V_b - V_{R,4tc} = 5000 - 92 = 4908 \text{ V} = 0.9817 V_b$$
$$V_{R,5tc} = 0.0067 V_b = 0.0067 \times 5000 = 34 \text{ V}$$

and

$$V_{C,5tc} = V_b - V_{R,5tc} = 5000 - 34 = 4966 \text{ V} = 99.33\% \ V_b$$

Table 11-3 lists the most significant values calculated in the preceding example.

The relationships depicted in Table 11-3 are of great importance. First, it should be noted that, for all practical purposes, the capacitor is fully charged at the end of the fifth tc. This is considered the full charging time of a capacitor (5 tc). The horizontal addition of V_R and V_C will always have a sum of 100 percent. It is recommended that the student draw a charging curve for I_C and V_C, using the percentage values listed in Table 11-3.

Table 11-3   Five-tc Values of Current and Voltage

tc	V_b %	I, % of I_{max}	V_R, % of V_b	V_C, % of V_b
0	100	100	100	0
1	100	36.8	36.8	63.2
2	100	13.5	13.5	86.5
3	100	4.97	4.97	95.03
4	100	1.83	1.83	98.17
5	100	0.67	0.67	99.33

11-7 CHARGING AND DISCHARGING CURRENT AND VOLTAGE

In this section you will learn the relationship between charging and discharging currents and voltages.

The relationship of circuit current and voltages in a discharging *RC* circuit warrants special attention. Discharging is that action by which the capacitor returns its stored energy to the circuit. Figure 11-9 illustrates a circuit where charging takes place in position 1; placing the switch in position 2 enables the capacitor to discharge through another resistance.

Refer to Fig. 11-9 for the circuit and waveforms for the following discussion. In position 1, *C* will charge by way of R_1.

$$\mathrm{tc}_{charge} = R_1 C$$

and

$$\text{Full charging time (transient period)} = 5 \text{ tc}$$
$$= 5 \ R_1 C \text{ s}$$

Once the transient period has elapsed, current flow ceases, and the circuit has settled down. At this time V_C equals V_b.

Throw the switch from position 1, with the capacitor fully charged, into position 2. The source potential is out of the circuit with the switch in position 2, and V_C acts as a source voltage; but V_C, as the capacitor discharges through R_2, decays to zero during $5 \ R_2 C$ s. V_{R_2} must be equal and opposite in polarity to V_C at every instant. When V_C becomes zero, the capacitor is discharged, and all circuit action ceases until the switch is thrown back into position 1 (at which time the capaci-

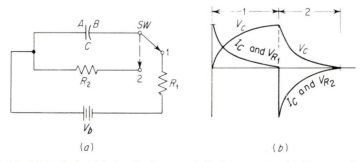

(a)

(b)

Fig. 11-9   Series-*RC* circuit, charge and discharge action. (*a*) **Charge and discharge circuit;** (*b*) **waveforms.**

tor again charges). It can be seen from the waveforms of Fig. 11-9*b* that the direction of the discharging current is opposite to that of the charging current.

11-8 THE EFFECT OF *R* AND *C* ON WAVEFORMS

In this section you will learn how changes in R *and* C *affect current wave-forms.*

The effect of a variable resistor and variable capacitor upon the wave-forms warrants special consideration.

Refer to Fig. 11-10 for the following discussion. Now examine the effect of a variable resistance on the current of Fig. 11-10*c*. Figure 11-10*a* depicts the relationship between circuit resistance and I_C. Curve *A* has the highest zero-time current, indicating the lowest circuit resistance (the resistor is in position 1). When the resistor is in position 2, the zero-time current is one-half of the initial current in position 1, since the resistance is doubled. Also notice that the transient time is doubled from *y* to 2*y* s. The same trend is apparent when the resistance is three times the original value (position 3 in the circuit). The initial current is reduced to 33 percent of the position 1 value, since the resistance is tripled and the source potential is fixed. The transient time (which is usually considered to be 5 tc) is three times as long as the original (from *y* to 3*y* s).

Figure 11-10*b* illustrates the effect of a variable capacitor and fixed resistance on the current waveform. Curve *D* represents the waveform for the smallest capacitor value, when the transient time is smallest. Increasing the capacitance increases the transient time but has no effect on the magnitude of the initial current. As was pointed out earlier, the

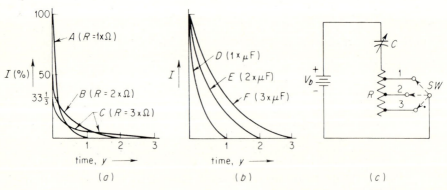

Fig. 11-10   The effects of *R* and *C* on waveforms: (*a*) variable *R*, fixed *C*; (*b*) variable *C*, fixed *R*; (*c*) circuit.

initial current is determined only by the circuit resistance and source potential, since the capacitor appears as a short circuit at the instant the circuit is closed.

From the discussion in the preceding two paragraphs, it can be seen that the waveforms can be altered by changing the value of R and/or C.

11-9 ANALYSIS OF A SERIES-PARALLEL-*RC* CIRCUIT

*In this section you will analyze a series-parallel-*RC* circuit using the Thévenin theorem.*

A series-parallel-*RC* circuit is a rather common type of circuit and is worthy of special analysis. The time constant of this circuit can be determined by use of the Thévenin theorem technique that was analyzed in Chap. 8. Refer to Fig. 11-11 for the following discussion.

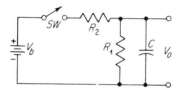

Fig. 11-11 The series-parallel-*RC* circuit.

Upon closing the circuit switch, C appears as a short circuit. Therefore, the output is shorted, and this effectively removes R_1 from the circuit at that instant. Since V_o is taken across C, then $V_o = 0$ V at this time. R_2 is the only resistance effectively in the circuit at this time (assuming that the internal resistance of V_b is negligible); then

$$V_{R_2} = V_g \qquad \text{at zero time}$$

where V_g is the voltage of the Thévenin circuit generator, and is equal to V_b. This is shown as point O in the V_{R_2} waveform of Fig. 11-12.

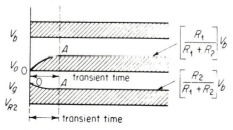

Fig. 11-12 Waveforms for the series-parallel-*RC* circuit.

The maximum current, which flows at zero time, is limited by the value of R_2; that is,

$$i_{0 \text{ time}} = \frac{V_g}{R_2} = \frac{V_b}{R_2}$$

Immediately after zero time, the capacitor begins to charge. The circuit resistance through which the capacitor charges is that resistance seen from the capacitor terminals when C is removed. Therefore, the circuit resistance R is found by

$$R = \frac{R_1 R_2}{R_1 + R_2}$$

Since the equivalent circuit resistance has been determined, the tc of the circuit is now obtainable from

$$\text{tc} = RC = \frac{R_1 R_2}{R_1 + R_2} C \qquad \text{(11-11)}$$

and since the circuit transient time is equal to 5 tc,

$$\text{Transient time} = 5RC$$

This equation determines the length of line OA in Fig. 11-12. It should be noted how the value of V_o is determined after the completion of the transient time. Recall that the capacitor appears as an open circuit after the transient time has passed; therefore, the circuit appears as a series resistive network. Since V_o is across R_1, then

$$V_o \text{ (after 5 tc)} = \frac{R_1}{R_1 + R_2} V_b$$

PROBLEMS

11-11   A 5-μF C is in series with a 1-kΩ resistance, and $V_b = 500$ V. Find the current at:
    a) zero time   b) 1 tc   c) 2 tc
    d) 3 tc   e) 4 tc   f) 5 tc

11-12   Repeat Prob. 11-11 for a circuit in which $R = 250$ Ω.

11-13   In the circuit of Prob. 11-11, find V_R and V_C for the times indicated.

11-14 A 20-μF C, 500-Ω R, and 250-V supply are in series. Find the current at:

a) zero time   b) 0.005 s   c) 0.010 s
d) 0.020 s   e) 0.030 s   f) 0.035 s
g) 0.040 s   h) 0.050 s

11-15 In the circuit of Prob. 11-14, find V_R and V_C for the indicated times.

11-16 In Prob. 11-14, C is changed to 30 μF. Find the current at the indicated times.

11-17 Find V_R and V_C for the circuit and indicated times of Prob. 11-16.

11-18 Refer to the circuit of Fig. 11-10. $C = 0.04$ μF; R in position 1 = 500 Ω, R in position 2 = 2 kΩ, R in position 3 = 5 kΩ. $V_b =$ 250 V. Find:

a) tc in each position of R
b) total transient time for each R position
c) zero-time current for each R position

11-19 In the circuit of Prob. 11-18, find I at the end of each tc in position:

a) 1   b) 2   c) 3

11-20 In the circuit of Prob. 11-18, find V_R and V_C for each tc in position:

a) 1   b) 2   c) 3

11-21 Refer to Fig. 11-11. $V_b = 400$ V; $R_1 = 1$ kΩ; $R_2 = 200$ Ω; $C = 20$ μF. Find:

a) tc
b) transient time
c) zero-time current
d) current after transient time

11-22 In Prob. 11-21, calculate V_o after transient time.

11-23 Repeat Prob. 11-21 for the following component values: $V_b =$ 1000 V, $R_1 = 100$ Ω, $R_2 = 400$ Ω.

11-24 Using the values of Prob. 11-23, find V_o after transient time.

QUESTIONS

11-15 Why does the maximum current flow at zero time in a series-RC circuit?

11-16 How long after the introduction of a supply potential does it take the current in a series-RC circuit to decay to zero?

11-17 What is the RC time constant?

11-18 What effect does the resistance in a series-RC circuit have on the time constant?

11-19   What effect does the resistance in a series-RC circuit have on the initial circuit current?

11-20   What effect does the capacitance in a series-RC circuit have on the time constant?

11-21   What effect does the capacitance in a series-RC circuit have on the initial circuit current?

11-22   What effect does the supply potential in a series-RC circuit have on the time constant?

11-23   What effect does the supply potential in a series-RC circuit have on the initial circuit current?

11-24   What is the transient time of a series-RC circuit?

11-25   What does V_b "see" after completion of the transient time in a series-RC circuit?

11-26   When is V_R greatest in a series-RC circuit?

11-27   When is V_C greatest in a series-RC circuit?

11-28   What is the relationship between V_C and I in a series-RC circuit?

11-29   What is the relationship between V_C and time in a series-RC circuit?

11-30   Why is V_R minimum when V_C is maximum in a series-RC circuit?

fundamentals of generators and motors

12

Many people in the field of electric and electronic technology believe that the technician should have a broad understanding of generator and motor operation. This chapter is designed to accommodate that belief by providing the technician with some broad background information about generators and motors. The material is presented as a brief survey of these devices. Those who elect not to include the study of generators and motors may skip this chapter and go on to Chap. 13 with no loss in continuity.

12-1 THE DC GENERATOR

In this section you will learn about how the induced voltage is developed in a dc generator, commutation action, and the role of the armature and the field coil.

Recall that in the analysis of induced voltage in Chap. 10 it was found that an induced voltage is developed when:

1 A conductor cuts across a flux field.
2 A flux field cuts across the conductor.

In the case of the dc generator, the conductor is moved through the magnetic field, and an induced emf is developed by this action. The value of the induced emf can be found from the following relationship:

$$v_{in} = N \text{ roc } \Phi \tag{12-1}$$

where v_{in} = volts
N = number of coil turns in conductor
roc $\Phi = \Delta\Phi/\Delta t$ = rate of change of flux cutting

Now consider how the rate of change of the flux cutting can take place.

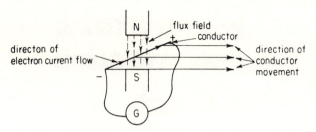

Fig. 12-1 Developing an induced emf in a conductor.

Assume a magnet is set up as shown in Fig. 12-1, the poles being oriented with the north pole on top and the south pole on the bottom. The direction of the flux lines (shown by the arrows) is from the north pole to the south pole. Now assume that a conductor series-connected with a galvanometer is moved through the flux field of the magnet from the left to the right. When the conductor is to the left of the field and is being moved toward the right, there will be no flux cutting, since the conductor is still outside the field. Hence, there is zero induced voltage, and this is point A in Fig. 12-2. As the conductor moves to the right, it begins to enter the flux field, and there is some cutting action. This results in the generation of an induced emf, which drives a current in the direction determined by the left-hand rule.

The induced emf generated will increase as the conductor moves toward the center of the flux field. Maximum flux cutting occurs at the center of the field; therefore, the maximum induced emf is developed at that time. This is depicted as point C in Fig. 12.2. As the conductor continues its movement from the center of the flux field toward the right, the amount of flux cutting begins to decrease, and so does the magnitude of the induced emf. This is shown as point D. Eventually, the conductor moves out of the flux field completely, thereby bringing the cutting action to a stop, and the magnitude of the induced voltage becomes zero (see point E in Fig. 12-2). Notice the shape of the induced emf waveform.

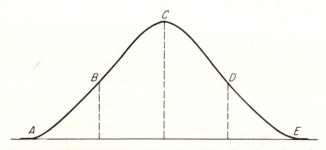

Fig. 12-2 Magnitude of an induced emf as a function of roc ϕ.

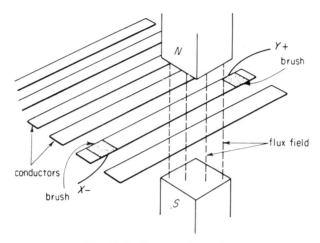

Fig. 12-3   Commutation action.

Commutation

Now consider a technique in which the induced voltage can be developed in a large number of conductors that are mounted on a circular object. A belt of conductors is mounted in such a way that they circulate through the flux field of the magnet (Fig. 12-3). Each conductor is separate from all the others, and they are electrically insulated from each other. Two brushes, labeled *x* and *y* in Fig. 12-3, are mounted in the center of the flux field. The brushes are graphite connectors which are spring-mounted so as to brush against the spinning rings of the rotor. Connected between the brushes and the rotating loop are stationary external leads. The brushes make contact with each conductor when it passes through the center of the flux field. Since the induced voltage across the brushes occurs only at the instant each conductor is passing through the center of the flux field, the brush emf is always at the maximum induced value. As the induced voltage begins to decrease, the conductor breaks its contact with the brushes, and the next conductor establishes contact with them. Connections from each brush are brought to the output of the generator, and the voltage developed across the brushes becomes the output voltage. The generator output voltage will have a waveform like that shown in Fig. 12-4.

Fig. 12-4   Dc generator output voltage.

Examination of the dc generator output waveform shows that the output voltage has a *ripple* content. This ripple content has a trapezoidal appearance in well-designed dc generators, and the ripple content of the brush voltage is minimized.

Commutation is the name given to the action in which the brushes make and break successive contacts with the conductors. A number of practical problems are associated with commutation. The distance between neighboring conductors is critical. If the spacing exceeds the brush width, there will be instances during which the brush voltage will drop to zero. This situation is to be avoided. Therefore, the width of the brush should exceed the width of the spacing between two adjacent conductors, such that the brushes will be in contact with two conductors at any one instant. The brush contact must be limited to two conductors, however, since secondary effects developed within the machine create short-circuit currents. The overlapping brush results in a limited amount of arcing at the point of contact between the brush and each conductor upon contact.

It should be noted that moving the circular belt of conductors between the magnetic poles in the opposite direction results in the same action except that the output-voltage polarity is reversed.

The Armature or Rotor

An armature is a drum upon which the insulated conductors are placed. The diametrically opposite conductors are series-connected, which reduces the required number of brushes from four to two. Figure 12-5*a* shows how the conductors can be mounted on an armature. The manner in which the diametrically opposite conductors can be con-

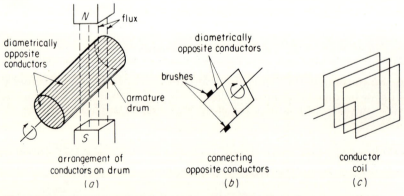

Fig. 12-5 **Armature connections.** (*a*) **Arrangement of conductors on the drum;** (*b*) **connection of opposite conductors;** (*c*) **conductor coil.**

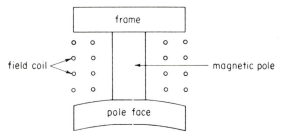

Fig. 12-6   Placement of the pole face.

nected is depicted in *b*. Up to this point the single armature coil was considered as being made up of one turn of wire, as shown in Fig. 12-5*b*. However, more than one turn of wire is generally used so as to permit the development of the desired induced emf at the generator output. Recall that

$$v_{in} = N \text{ roc } \phi = \frac{N^2}{R} \text{ roc } i$$

where *N* is the number of coil turns. Therefore, for a given roc *i*, a larger magnitude of induced voltage can be developed by using more turns in each conductor coil. This is shown in Fig. 12-5*c*. These coil turns are insulated from one another. The number of turns used is determined by the desired output voltage of the generator. For example, if each conductor of the coil in Fig. 12-5*c* developed 2 V, then the generator output voltage would be equal to the product of 2 V times the number of *coil sides*, that is, 2 × 6, or 12 V, in this case.

The magnetic poles shown in the preceding illustrations are electromagnets in most generators. The *field coil* of the electromagnet is designed to develop the required flux field at the magnetic poles. The magnetic pole is joined to a pole face, as shown in Fig. 12-6. The purpose of the pole face is to create a flux field of reasonably uniform density over a relatively large part of the armature surface. This permits the generator output voltage to have a smaller ripple content.

12-2 OPERATION OF THE SEPARATELY EXCITED DC GENERATOR

In this section you will learn how the output voltage is developed in a separately excited dc generator.

Consider the operation of a separately excited dc generator (Fig. 12-7). The field winding current is I_L and is obtained from the external

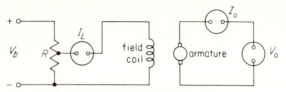

Fig. 12-7   Separately excited generator.

voltage source V_b. This field current develops the flux that is to be at the magnetic poles. Therefore, changing the magnitude of the field current is a method of controlling the flux. Use of the potentiometer R in the generator of Fig. 12-7 to control the flux permits the relatively smooth change in I_L from some predetermined maximum value down to zero.

Notice that the armature is shown adjacent to the field coil, since it will rotate the conductors through the magnetic field. Not shown in Fig. 12-7 is the device that will rotate the armature. It is called a *prime mover* and may be one of many kinds of machine. An automobile engine is a common example of a prime mover.

Since the value of the generated induced voltage is directly proportional to the value of roc Φ, it is desirable to keep the armature rotating at a constant speed S. This is not possible under certain conditions and presents special design problems not discussed here. Roc Φ is the rate of change at which the flux is cut by the conductor being rotated by the armature. The fundamental equation for the dc generator is

$$V_o = K\Phi S \tag{12-2}$$

where V_o = generated emf between brushes
$\quad\quad S$ = armature speed, rpm
$\quad\quad \Phi$ = pole flux

It will be recalled from Chap. 9 that the BH curve of a magnetic material is nonlinear. Therefore, the magnetic curve used for the analysis of the dc generator depicts a relationship between the flux and the field current in place of the traditional BH curve.

The armature speed S is held constant, and V_o then becomes proportional to Φ. Therefore, the dc-generator saturation curve, as shown in Fig. 12-8, is a plot of the field current I_L versus the output voltage (V_o). It should be noted that readings of V_o, S, and I_L are easily obtainable when testing a dc generator. Changes in the rotation speed of the armature create a change in the saturation curve, as shown by the curves for three speeds in Fig. 12-8.

A residual emf, developed by the residual magnetism of the field coil

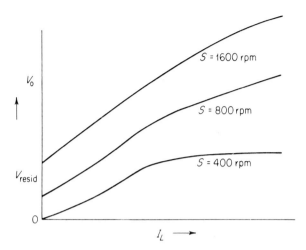

Fig. 12-8   Saturation curve of a dc generator.

from the last time it was used, is present when the field current is zero. This residual emf causes the generator to have a small output voltage at the time it is off. Examination of the curves shows that changes in the field current produce corresponding changes in the output voltage up to the knee of the curve. Once the field-current value is great enough to be to the right of the knee of the curve, the generator saturates, and V_o tends to remain fairly constant for relatively large changes in the field current.

12-3   OPERATION OF THE SELF-EXCITED DC GENERATOR

In this section you will learn about the self-excited dc generator operation, causes for generator failure, factors that affect voltage regulation, and the compound generator.

Figure 12-9 is the circuit for the self-excited dc generator, which is the most common type. This generator supplies its own field current. The total resistance R of the field circuit is

$$R = R_{\text{field coil}} + R_1 \qquad\qquad \textbf{(12-3)}$$

where $R_{\text{field coil}}$ = resistance of field coil
R_1 = resistance of *field rheostat*
R = total resistance of the field circuit

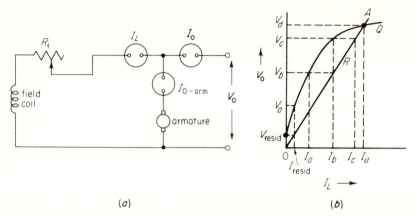

(a)   (b)

Fig. 12-9   A self-excited dc generator: (a) circuit; (b) saturation curve.

Recall from the treatment of linear resistance in Chap. 3 that its VI characteristic will be a straight line (line OA in Fig. 12-9 b).

The residual voltage V_{resid} drives a residual current I_{resid} in the field circuit. The presence of I_{resid} causes the generator voltage to change to the value V_a (see Fig. 12-9 b). This increased value of generator voltage in turn causes the current to increase to I_a. The larger value of field current results in a further rise in V_o to value V_b. It can be seen that this sequence of events will continue until the generator becomes stabilized at the operating point Q.

It is important to notice that the entire process relies on the presence of a residual voltage in the generator. There are times when the generator will not have this residual voltage. In such an event, a battery can be briefly connected across the field terminals. This action should produce a sufficient flux field to leave some residual magnetism in the poles. The introduction of a battery for this purpose is a process called *flashing*.

Another cause for the inability of a generator to build up to its operating point is the possibility of the residual flux generating an armature emf of the wrong polarity. If this happens, the field current that develops will produce a flux that will oppose the residual flux, and the output voltage drops to zero instead of building up to its operating-point value. The remedy for this situation is to reverse the field-coil connections or reverse the connections to the armature.

A third possible cause of a generator's failing to build up to its normal operating-point potential is having a field-circuit resistance that is too large. The field-circuit resistance must be sufficiently small to permit its characteristic to intersect the saturation curve to the right of the knee.

It is important to note that the resistance of the armature decreases with larger values of armature current. The armature resistance consists of the following components:

$$R_{arm} = R_{winding} + R_{brushes} + R_{contact} \qquad \text{(12-4)}$$

where R_{arm} = total armature resistance
$R_{winding}$ = resistance of copper winding
$R_{brushes}$ = resistance of carbon brushes
$R_{contact}$ = resistance of contact between carbon brush and surface

The values of R_{brush} and $R_{contact}$ actually become smaller with increases in armature current, thereby producing an overall decrease in R_{arm} with larger values of I_{arm}. Since R_{arm} decreases with increases of I_{arm}, it is said to have a *negative resistance* characteristic.

Voltage Regulation

The output voltage V_o of the generator is equal to

$$V_o = V_{arm} - I_{arm} R_{arm} \qquad \text{(12-5)}$$

where V_o = generator output terminal voltage
V_{arm} = emf produced
I_{arm} = armature current
R_{arm} = armature resistance

In a self-excited generator, both the load current and the field current must be furnished by the armature; therefore,

$$I_{arm} = I_L + I_o$$

where I_L = field current
I_o = output load current

The output voltage of the generator is highest when it is unloaded, i.e., when there is no call for an output current. As the output current is increased, the output voltage will decrease by the increased $I_{arm} R_{arm}$-drop. This is analogous to the voltage-drop across the internal resistance of the generator that was analyzed in Sec. 8-3.

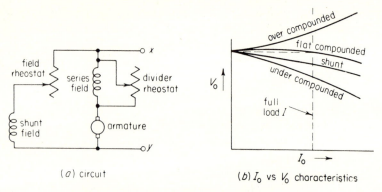

(a) circuit   (b) I_o vs V_o characteristics

Fig. 12-10   Compound generator: (a) circuit: (b) I_o vs. V_o characteristics.

The extent to which V_o decreases as a function of generator loading is adequately described by the term *voltage regulation*. Voltage regulation is stated in percent and is found from

$$\text{VR} = \frac{V_{NL} - V_{FL}}{V_{FL}} \times 100 \qquad \textbf{(12-6)}$$

where VR = voltage regulation, %
     V_{NL} = output voltage, no-load condition
     V_{FL} = output voltage, full-load condition

It is apparent that it is desirable to have a generator in which the output voltage V_o remains constant for all loading conditions (zero voltage regulation). The addition of a coil of a few turns to each magnetic pole helps to accomplish this desirable objective. The placement of this extra coil, called a *series field*, is shown in Fig. 12-10a. The series field develops a flux of its own and replaces the drop in voltage created by the $I_{\text{arm}}R_{\text{arm}}$-drop. This is called a *compound generator*. The I_o-vs.-V_o characteristic is shown in Fig. 12-10b. *Undercompounded* is the condition where the flux of the series field is in opposition to the flux of the main field. In this condition V_o substantially decreases with large I_o values. *Overcompounded* is the condition in which the series-field flux aids the flux of the main field and the output voltage increases with larger values of I_o. Since a steady value of V_o is desired, a diverter rheostat (see Fig. 12-10a) can be connected in parallel with the series field. This provides a means to control the amount of compounding, and the condition of *flat compounding*, which is the most desirable of all conditions, can be achieved.

12-4 THE DC MOTOR

In this section you will learn about dc motor operation, factors affecting the induced voltage and speed regulation, the compound motor, and the major voltage losses.

Recall that the passing of electron current through a conductor develops a magnetic field around that conductor. This magnetic field can be made to exert a force by allowing it to interact with a second magnetic field. This will be examined in greater detail with the aid of Fig. 12-11.

Consider conductors 1 and 2 as being mounted on an armature and simultaneously making contact with the brushes. Since contact is being made with the brushes, current will flow in both conductors. The direction of current flow is as shown in Fig. 12-11. The rotating armature is moving the two conductors through the flux of the magnet from left to right, as indicated by the arrows. The flux of conductor 2 nearest to the main field assists the main field and is thereby attracted toward it. At the same time, the flux of conductor 1 found nearest the main field opposes the main field and is thereby repelled by it. Therefore, these two conductors produce a force toward the right. Assume these two conductors are at the top of the armature and that there also are two conductors at the bottom of the armature which are at the same instant carrying current in the opposite direction. The two bottom conductors will develop a force in the same manner, but the direction of this force will be toward the left. These two factors are *coupled,* and the result is the production of a *turning torque* on the armature. Figure 12-12 illustrates the turning-torque action. It is seen, therefore, that the south

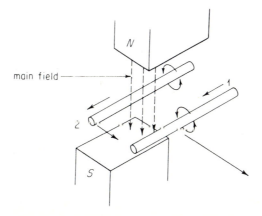

main field

Fig. 12-11   Interaction of two magnetic fields.

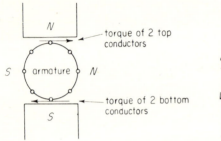

Fig. 12-12 Turning torque in an armature.

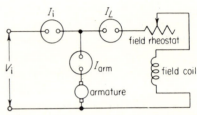

Fig. 12-13 Dc motor connections.

pole of the armature seeks to move toward the north pole of the main field. The flux field of the armature cannot rotate, of course, because of the commutation process, but the armature itself does rotate in a clockwise direction.

The manner in which a dc motor is connected is shown in Fig. 12-13.

It should be pointed out that there is very little difference in construction between the dc motor and the dc generator studied in the preceding section, the location of the brushes being one of the major differences.

Now examine the overall behavior of the dc motor when it is connected. Upon being connected, a large value of *starting torque* is produced by the heavy armature current. This starting torque permits the motor to gain speed. The rotation of the armature initiates a generator action in that an emf is developed within the windings of the armature. The armature emf V_{arm} increases with the speed of the armature. Recall that

$$V_i = V_{arm} + I_{arm} R_{arm}$$

From this relationship it is seen that the value of I_{arm} must decrease from its starting value.

As was pointed out at the beginning of this section, the motor torque is produced by the interaction of the two magnetic fields. Also, the torque is proportional to the product of the two fields:

$$T = K_1 \Phi I_{arm} \tag{12-7}$$

where K_1 = constant
Φ = main field flux
I_{arm} = armature current
T = torque of motor

When the motor speed increases, the armature current decreases, and the motor torque also decreases. The decrease in torque is permissible since the greatest amount of torque is needed at the start in order to overcome the inertia of rest.

The emf of the armature is found from the following relationship:

$$V_{arm} = K\Phi S \tag{12-8}$$

Although V_{arm} cannot be greater than V_o, the two will be very close in value since $I_{arm}R_{arm}$ is usually a relatively small quantity. The field rheostat in Fig. 12-13 is set so that the desired flux value Φ is obtained. The final speed of the motor is in fact determined by the magnitude of the armature voltage. The torque produced by the interaction of the two fields is not in any way a function of the motor speed. The speed of the motor will continue to build up until a dynamic equilibrium is achieved where the load and motor-loss requirements are met by the torque.

Theory of Operation

The operation of the dc motor will be examined briefly. Assume that V_{arm} is constant and the no-load motor conditions are satisfied by the relationships

$$I_o = I_{arm} + I_L$$
$$V_{arm} = K\Phi S$$

and

$$T = K_1\Phi I_{arm}$$

Now assume that a load has been placed on the output shaft of the motor. There is an immediate demand for additional torque to accommodate the additional loading. The armature current is increased. The input power of the motor V_oI_o is accordingly increased. When the load is removed, the motor-torque demand is reduced. This results in a corresponding decrease in both I_{arm} and I_o. It should be noted that the speed of the motor is relatively unaffected by the change in load. Hence, the dc shunt motor is a constant-speed motor for all practical purposes. There is only a slight change in the motor speed because of the small change in V_{arm} between full-load and no-load conditions.

Speed Regulation

The speed of the shunt motor can be varied by changing the value of the field current. Therefore, it is seen that in such cases the field rheostat is the speed controller. One drawback to this feature is the demand for more armature current to maintain the required torque when the main flux field is reduced. This tends to restrict the range over which the speed can be controlled.

It should be noted that the motor will speed up as the main flux is weakened. The speed of the motor would become very high if the field flux were reduced to zero, and the torque would be a very small value. If this residual torque is so small that it cannot meet the load requirements, the motor will stall and burn out if it is not protected by a circuit breaker. A further danger is that the residual torque might be able to overcome the small motor losses at no-load condition. This could result in such a rapid speed that the motor could be destroyed. The runaway condition just described can be avoided by providing an automatic means of opening the entire motor circuit whenever the field current decreases to zero.

The motor output is usually given in horsepower and can be found by use of the following equation:

$$M_o = 2\pi\, ST \div 3.3(10)^4 = 0.00019 TS \qquad \text{(12-9)}$$

where M_o = motor output, hp
S = speed, rpm
T = torque, ft-lb

Speed regulation describes the relationship between changes in motor speed and loading. In equation form,

$$SR = \frac{S_{NL} - S_{FL}}{S_{FL}} \times 100 \qquad \text{(12-10)}$$

where SR = speed regulation, percent
S_{NL} = no-load motor speed
S_{FL} = full-load motor speed

A *compound motor*, which has a series field plus the shunt field described earlier, can be designed. The compound motor has a number of practical drawbacks which limit its actual usefulness.

A *series motor*, which has its main field coil connected in series with the armature, is used in cases where (1) a high starting torque is required, and (2) the load can be permanently connected to the output shaft.

Motor Losses

The major motor losses are (1) armature losses, (2) friction and windage losses, (3) field-circuit losses, and (4) magnetic losses. The armature losses vary to some extent with the changes in armature current, since R_{arm} varies. The series-field losses are considered as part of the armature losses and all are treated as $(I_{arm})^2 R_{arm}$ W. The friction and windage losses consist of bearing friction, air resistance to the rotating action, and sliding-contact friction of the brushes. The magnetic-circuit losses are eddy-current losses and hysteresis within the core laminations. The field-circuit loss is found by $V_o I_L$. The term *stray power* has been used to mean the sum of the magnetic losses and the friction and windage losses.

12-5 MOTOR STARTING CONSIDERATIONS

In this section you will learn about starting a motor, ways to limit the motor starting current, and how starting boxes function.

When a motor is first started, the current in the armature is limited by the resistance of the armature. In equation form,

$$I_{start} = \frac{V_o}{R_{arm}}$$

This initial current is so large that it cannot be tolerated except in small motors. A device that is used to limit the initial current is called a *starting box.*

Next examine a simple manual starter, which is illustrated in Fig. 12-14. The starting resistance consists of three parts: R_1, R_2 and R_3. As the manual switch is closed, it makes successive contacts at points 1, 2, 3, and 4. Notice, in Fig. 12-14a, that the field coil is connected to the line before the switch is closed. In this way the flux required for the starting torque is available. Furthermore, this prevents the final motor speed from becoming too great.

The manual switch first makes contact with point 1. At that instant,

$$I_{arm} = \frac{V_o}{R_{arm} + R_1 + R_2 + R_3}$$

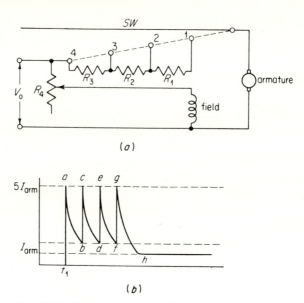

Fig. 12-14 Motor starter considerations: (*a*) the manual
starter; (*b*) current transient.

Assume that this is equal to five times the value of the full-load current, which is the value shown at point *a* in Fig. 12-14*b*. The required
starting torque is obtained from this current. The motor speed increases,
which causes the armature voltage to decrease. The reduction in armature voltage results in a decrease in armature current. The current
reduces to the value found at point *b* of Fig. 12-14*b*.

At the instant the armature current falls to the point *b* value, the
starter switch touches point 2. This action shorts out starter resistor
R_1. The armature current increases to its original value of five times the
normal load current, shown as point *c* of Fig. 12-14*b*. This increases the
motor speed again, V_{arm} increases, and I_{arm} decreases to the point *d*
value. At this instant, the switch touches point 3. R_2 as well as R_1 is now
shorted out of the circuit. The armature current again rises to its
maximum value, shown as point *e*, and then proceeds to decrease to
point *f* because of the increase in motor speed. When the current
assumes the value of point *f*, the switch makes contact with point 4, which
now shorts out R_3 as well as R_2 and R_1. The current increases to point *g*.
Now the motor speed increases to its normal running speed, and the
armature current falls to its normal operating level, which is point *h*
in Fig. 12-14*b*.

The *three-point starting box* shown in Fig. 12-15 is one of the common

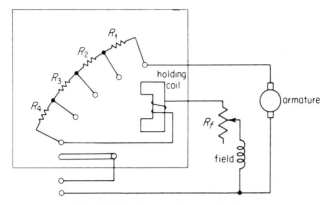

Fig. 12-15   Three-point starting box.

manual starters. R_1 to R_4 are used in the manner described for Fig. 12-14. This starter is provided with a coil spring with tension that maintains the starting lever in the open position. Upon completion of the starting process, the *holding coil* holds the starting lever. Since the holding coil obtains its energy from the field current, the starting lever is released, and the circuit is thereby opened when the field-coil current opens. The starting box will open if the line circuit breaker should open.

PROBLEMS

12-1   An armature coil has eight coil sides, each of which develops an induced emf of 2.5 V. Find the output voltage of the generator.

12-2   Refer to Fig. 12-9. The total resistance of the field circuit is 10 Ω, and the resistance of the field coil is 2 Ω. Find the resistance of the field rheostat.

12-3   Refer to Fig. 12-9. Assume the field-coil resistance is 6 Ω and the field rheostat is 3.5 Ω. Find the total resistance of the field circuit.

12-4   A dc generator has the following parameters: $V_{arm} = 20$ V; $I_{arm} = 2$ A; $R_{arm} = 0.5$ Ω. Find the output voltage V_o.

12-5   A dc generator has the following parameters: $V_o = 12$ V; $V_{arm} = 11.4$ V; $I_{arm} = 5$ A. Find R_{arm}.

12-6   A dc generator has the following output voltages: $V_{FL} = 14$ V; $V_{NL} = 15$ V. Find the voltage regulation.

12-7   A dc generator has the following parameters: voltage regulation $= 5$ percent; $V_{NL} = 25$ V. Find V_{FL}.

12-8   A dc motor has the following parameters: $V_i = 10$ V; $I_{arm} = 3$ A; $R_{arm} = 0.2$ Ω. Find V_{arm}.

12-9   A dc motor has the following parameters: $S = 500$ rpm; $T = 2$ ft-lb. Find the motor output in horsepower.

12-10 A dc motor has the following parameters: $S = 250$ rpm; hp $= 2$. Find the torque.

12-11 A 5-hp dc motor has a torque of 0.08 ft-lb. Find its rpm.

12-12 A dc motor has the following parameters: $S_{NL} = 300$ rpm; $SR = 4.7$ percent. Find S_{FL}.

QUESTIONS

12-1   What is the process of commutation?

12-2   Why is there a ripple component in the output waveform of the dc generator?

12-3   What is the armature in a dc generator?

12-4   What is the purpose of the field coil in a dc generator?

12-5   What is the purpose of the pole face illustrated in Fig. 12-6?

12-6   What is meant by the term *prime mover?*

12-7   In a dc generator, what is the relationship between the armature speed and the voltage generated between the brushes?

12-8   What is the purpose of the field rheostat in Fig. 12-9?

12-9   What is the chief difference between an externally excited and self-excited dc generator?

12-10 What is the purpose of flashing a generator?

12-11 What are three possible reasons for a generator's failing to build up to its normal operating-point potential?

12-12 What are the components of the armature resistance?

12-13 Why does the armature have a negative resistance characteristic?

12-14 What is meant by voltage regulation of a dc generator?

12-15 What is the purpose of the series field in Fig. 12-10a?

12-16 What is a compound generator?

12-17 What is the flat-compounding condition, and why is it most desirable?

12-18 What is meant by the turning torque of a dc motor?

12-19 What is meant by the starting torque of a dc motor?

12-20 What produces the motor torque in a dc motor?

12-21 What is the relationship between motor output and motor speed?

12-22 What does the term *speed regulation* mean?

12-23 What is a compound motor?

12-24 What is a series motor?

12-25 Why are starting boxes necessary?

sine-wave analysis
13

The sine wave is perhaps the most commonly treated bidirectional wave-form in electrical and electronic textbooks. Most public power companies furnish their customers with alternating voltage and current that is reasonably sinusoidal. For this reason, the sine wave is perhaps the most important bidirectional waveform in the power field. Although it is not the sole waveform to be considered in the various communication and industrial specialties, it is of great importance and merits separate consideration in this text.

13-1 CHARACTERISTICS OF A SINE WAVE

In this section you will learn how a sine wave is produced and how the instantaneous value of the induced voltage is determined.

One of the most common methods used in the development of the sine wave is the rotation of a conductor in a magnetic field, producing an induced voltage in the conductor. The magnitude of the induced voltage is a function of the angle at which the conductor cuts the flux field; the polarity is determined by the direction of the cutting.

Figure 13-1 represents a simplified version of a mechanical sine-wave generator. The conductor is in the form of a loop (*ABCD*), called the armature, which is to be rotated in a clockwise fashion at a constant speed. A fixed uniform magnetic field exists between the poles of the magnet.

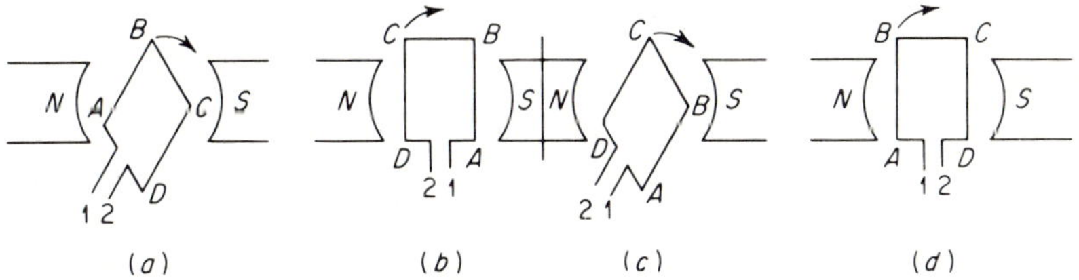

Fig. 13-1 Generation of a sine wave: (*a*) start; (*b*) quarter; (*c*) half; (*d*) three-quarters.

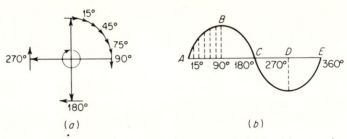

Fig. 13-2 **Analysis of a loop cutting a magnetic field:** (*a*) **loop cutting angle;** (*b*) **sine wave generated by cutting action.**

On the assumption that an emf will be induced, assign the notation $V_{in,\max}$ to the maximum value of this voltage. Assume that the loop is initially at the position shown in Figs. 13-1*a* and 13-2*a*. At this time, the top portion of the conductor is *AB*, and the bottom is *CD*. At the instant the loop moves from this position, it is moving parallel to the magnetic field; there is no cutting action, and the induced voltage is zero in the conductor. A short time later, with the loop rotating in the clockwise direction, *AB* cuts the flux field at some small angle (such as 15° in Fig. 13-2*a*). An induced voltage is developed in the conductor; it is determined by

$$v_{in} = V_{in,\max}\sin\theta \qquad\qquad \textbf{(13-1)}$$

Since $\sin\theta = \sin 15° = 0.259$,

$$v_{in} = 0.259\,V_{in,\max} \qquad \text{at } 15°$$

As *AB* continues to rotate, the induced voltage increases in accordance with the sine of the cutting angle. The maximum value is attained when the cutting angle is 90° (since the loop is cutting the flux lines in a perpendicular manner). This is the position illustrated by Fig. 13-1*b*, and it can be seen in Fig. 13-2*a*. The waveform for the first quarter-cycle of rotation (0 to 90°) is illustrated in Fig. 13-2*b* (points *A* to *B*). Since the direction of cutting is unchanged during this time, the polarity will be (arbitrarily) positive.

As *AB* continues its rotation from the 90° position, the cutting angle begins to decrease until it is again zero (parallel with the flux field) at the half-cycle (180°) position. This is position *C* of Fig. 13-1. Since the angle of cutting is zero, the induced voltage is also zero (point *C* of Fig. 13-2*b*).

For the first half cycle, *AB* was moving in an overall downward direction, resulting in the positive values of induced voltage shown in Fig.

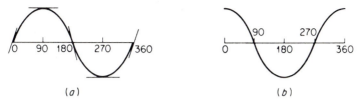

Fig. 13-3   Sine wave: (*a*) voltage; (*b*) roc *v*.

13-2*b*. The overall movement of *AB* is upward for the last half of the cycle, resulting in a negative induced voltage. The angles of cutting from 180 to 360° progress in the same manner as the cutting angle from 0 to 180°. Therefore the induced voltage developed in the second half of the cycle will be a replica of the first half, but inverted (see *C* to *E* of Fig. 13-2*b*). The complete revolution of the sine wave is frequently referred to as one cycle (or period) and is divided into 360°, or 6.28 rad.

The rate of change of the sine wave is of fundamental importance in analyzing a circuit containing inductance and/or capacitance whose input voltage is sinusoidal. The rate of change of a voltage (roc *v*) is the ratio of the change in voltage magnitude during a given unit of time.

$$\text{roc } v = \frac{\Delta v}{\Delta t} \tag{13-2}$$

Refer to Fig. 13-3 for the following discussion. Observation of Fig. 13-3*a* reveals that roc *v* is greatest at 0, 180, and 360°, since the slope is most vertical at those points. At 90 and 270°, the voltage has just increased to its maximum value and is on the verge of decreasing; roc *v* is zero at these times. Figure 13-3*b* shows that roc *v* is positive when the voltage is graphically rising and negative when it is moving graphically downward. Further examination leads to the conclusion that the roc *v* waveform varies with the cosine of the sine wave voltage angle.

13-2 CALCULATION OF INSTANTANEOUS VOLTAGE AND CURRENT

In this section you will learn how to use the sine function to determine instantaneous values of sinusoidal current and voltage.

The instantaneous value of a sine wave, as developed by the simple generator of constant speed, is determined by the sine of the angle of armature rotation. This fact applies to both voltage and current values.

$$v = V_{max} \sin \theta \qquad \text{(13-3)}$$
$$i = I_{max} \sin \theta \qquad \text{(13-4)}$$

where v = instantaneous voltage
V_{max} = maximum voltage
θ = angle of rotation
i = instantaneous current
I_{max} = maximum current

Example 1

$V_{max} = 150$ V. Find v at: (*a*) 30°; (*b*) 45°; (*c*) 160°.

Solution

(*a*) At 30°

$$v = 150 \sin 30° = 150 \times 0.500 = 75 \text{ V}$$

(*b*) At 45°

$$v = 150 \sin 45° = 150 \times 0.707 = 106 \text{ V}$$

(*c*) At 160°

$$v = 150 \sin 160° = 150 \times 0.342 = 51 \text{ V}$$

Example 2

$I_{max} = 5$ A. Find i at: (*a*) 40°; (*b*) 75°; (*c*) 240°.

Solution

(*a*) At 40°

$$i = 5 \sin 40° = 5 \times 0.643 = 3.22 \text{ A}$$

(*b*) At 75°

$$i = 5 \sin 75° = 5 \times 0.966 = 4.83 \text{ A}$$

(*c*) At 240°

$$i = 5 \sin 240° = 5 \times (-0.866) = -4.33 \text{ A}$$

Note The polarity of the sine function must be observed. Since all angles in the third and fourth quadrants possess negative sine function values, instantaneous current and voltage values for these quadrants are negative, as seen in the preceding and following examples.

Example 3

V_{max} = 200 V. Find v at 330°.

Solution

$$v = 200 \sin 330° = 200 \times (-0.500) = -100 \text{ V}$$

13-3 FREQUENCY

In this section you will learn the relationship between frequency and period.

The *cycle* (or *period*) of the sine wave encompasses the sequence of variations from 0 to 360°. The waveform development from 0 to 180° is repeated in an inverse fashion from 180 to 360°. Each half cycle is called an *alternation*. A cycle consists of one positive and one negative alternation.

Frequency may be generally defined as the number of completed cycles undergone by a waveform in a specified period of time. In most electrical and electronic applications it is defined thus:

Frequency is specifically defined as the number of completed cycles undergone by the waveform in one second.

In equation form,

$$f = \frac{1}{T} \qquad\qquad \textbf{(13-5)}$$

where f = frequency, Hz
  T = time duration of one period or cycle, s

$$T = \frac{1}{f} \qquad\qquad \textbf{(13-5a)}$$

13-4 AVERAGE, RMS, AND MAXIMUM VALUES

In this section you will learn about the equations used for conversion from one sinusoidal value to others.

Since the sine wave is a symmetrical bidirectional waveform, the negative and positive alternations are equal in area, and the average of the waveform for the entire period is zero. On the other hand, the average of any one alternation is equal to 0.636 of the maximum value.

The *rms current* is the heating effect of the current. It is a fixed current value which, when replacing the original bidirectional current, develops the same amount of heat within the circuit. Rms values are also called *effective values*. These are the sine wave values which are read on most ac voltmeters and ammeters. In dealing with sinusoidal waveforms, an unspecified voltage or current may be assumed to be an rms value. For example, 120 V (60 Hz), which is the common household power source in many parts of the United States, is an rms value. In considering the average power dissipated by a component, the rms value of voltage and/or current must be used in its computation. *The rms value of a sine wave is equal to 0.707 of the maximum voltage and/or current.*

The maximum (or peak) value of current or voltage occurs at 90° and again at 270° of the sine wave. Maximum values are considered the instantaneous values at 90 and 270°.

Following are several conversion relationships for a sine wave:

$$I_{avg} = 0.636I_{max}$$
$$I_{rms} = 0.707I_{max}$$
$$I_{max} = 1.414I_{rms} = 1.57I_{avg}$$

These relationships are true for voltage also.

Example 1

$V_{rms} = 120$ V. Find V_{max}.

Solution

$$V_{max} = 1.414 \times 120 = 170 \text{ V}$$

Example 2

$V_{rms} = 200$ V; $R = 100 \ \Omega$. Find: (a) I_{rms}; (b) V_{max}; (c) I_{max}.

Solution

(a) $I_{rms} = \dfrac{V_{rms}}{R} = \dfrac{200}{100} = 2$ A

(b) $V_{max} = I_{max}R = 1.414I_{rms} \times 100 = 1.414 \times 2 \times 100 = 282.8$ V

(c) $I_{max} = \dfrac{V_{max}}{R} = \dfrac{282.8}{100} = 2.828$ A

13-5 POWER IN A SINUSOIDAL RESISTIVE CIRCUIT

In this section you will learn how to determine several power values: instantaneous, peak or maximum, and average.

Inasmuch as a sine wave is continuously changing in magnitude in a periodic fashion, the values of voltage and current used in the computations will determine the power found. Two general types of power computations are frequently encountered:

1 Instantaneous power
   (a) for any angle of rotation between 0 and 360°
   (b) for peak or maximum power, which occurs at 90 and 270°
2 Average power (or effective power)

Instantaneous Power

Recall that power can be determined by the following relationships:

$$P = VI = I^2R = \frac{V^2}{R}$$

In those cases where the current and voltage are of constant magnitude, the equations as stated are sufficient for power computations. Here the problem is varying current and voltage, however. Because of this, the current and voltage values used must be carefully specified. For the calculation of instantaneous power, the (instantaneous) values of current and voltage which both exist at the specified time must be used, resulting in the preceding relationships changing to

$$p = vi = i^2R = \frac{v^2}{R} \qquad \textbf{(13-6)}$$

where p = instantaneous power, W
v = instantaneous voltage, V
i = instantaneous current, A
} all evaluated at the same instant

Example 1

$V_{max} = 400$ V; $R = 200$ Ω. Find the instantaneous power at: (a) 25°; (b) 80°; (c) 230°.

Solution

First determine I_{max}:

$$I_{max} = \frac{V_{max}}{R} = \frac{400}{200} = 2 \text{ A}$$

(a) p at 25°:

$$i \text{ at } 25° = I_{max} \sin 25°$$
$$i = 2 \times 0.423 = 0.846$$

Using the i^2R relationship,

$$p = (.846)^2 \times 200 = 143 \text{ W}$$

(b) p at 80°:

$$i \text{ at } 80° = I_{max} \sin 80°$$
$$i = 2 \times 0.985 = 1.97 \text{ A}$$

Using the i^2R relationship,

$$p = (1.97)^2 \times 200 = 776 \text{ W}$$

(c) p at 230°:

$$i \text{ at } 230° = I_{max} \sin 230°$$
$$i = 2 \times (-0.766) = -1.53 \text{ A}$$

Using the i^2R relationship,

$$p = (-1.53)^2 \times 200 = 468 \text{ W}$$

Peak or Maximum Power

A specific instantaneous-power value frequently used is the peak or maximum value:

$$P_{max} = V_{max} I_{max} = (I_{max})^2 R = \frac{(V_{max})^2}{R}$$

Example 2

$V_{max} = 500$ V; $R = 400$ Ω. Find the peak power.

Solution

Using the $(V_{max})^2/R$ relationship,

$$P_{max} = \frac{(500)^2}{400} = 625 \text{ W}$$

Example 3

$V = 150$ V; $R = 300$ Ω. Find the peak power.

Solution

Since the given voltage is not identified, it is the rms value and must be converted to the maximum value.

$$V_{max} = 1.414 V_{rms} = 1.414 \times 150 = 212 \text{ V}$$

Using the $(V_{max})^2/R$ relationship,

$$P_{max} = \frac{(212)^2}{300} = 150 \text{ W}$$

Average Power

Of the two types of power computations, average power is most commonly used. Calculation of average power incorporates the rms values of voltage and current, resulting in the following relationships:

$$P_{avg} = I_{rms} V_{rms} = (I_{rms})^2 R = \frac{(V_{rms})^2}{R} \tag{13-6a}$$

Example 4

$V = 120$ V; $R = 20$ Ω. Find the average power.

Solution

Since V_{rms} and R are given, use the $(V_{rms})^2/R$ relationship.

$$P_{avg} = \frac{(120)^2}{20} = 720 \text{ W}$$

Example 5

$I = 3.5$ A; $R = 500$ Ω. Find the average power.

Solution

Since I_{rms} and R are given, use the $(I_{rms})^2/R$ relationship.

$$P_{avg} = (3.5)^2 \times 500 = 6125 \text{ W}$$

13-6 THE DECIBEL

In this section you will learn about a special measure of power gain (or loss) commonly used in circuits that operate in the audio range.

In many communication circuits, the power gains or losses are frequently in terms of sound energy. Sound intensity, as heard by the human ear, responds in a logarithmic fashion. The decibel (dB), which varies logarithmically, is therefore a good unit for expressing power ratios in these circuits. One decibel is the difference between two sound intensities which is barely distinguishable to the human ear

$$dB = 10 \log \frac{P_2}{P_1} \qquad \text{(13-7)}$$

the fraction being the ratio of the two powers being considered.

The fact that the human ear responds to sound intensity in a logarithmic fashion is significant. In effect, it means that the ear is much more sensitive to changes in low-intensity sounds than in high-intensity sounds.

Example 1

A certain amplifier has an input of 20 mW and an output of 140 mW. Find the power gain in decibels.

Solution

$$dB = 10 \log \frac{P_2}{P_1}$$

Substituting values,

$$dB = 10 \log \tfrac{140}{20} = 10 \log 7 = 10 \times 0.845 = 8.45 \text{ dB}$$

Example 2

A certain network has an input of 50 mW and an output of 10 mW. Find the power loss in decibels.

Solution

$$dB = 10 \log \frac{P_2}{P_1}$$

Substituting values,

$$dB = 10 \log \tfrac{10}{50} = 10 \log 0.2 = 10(-0.699) = -6.99 \text{ dB}$$

Note   A loss in gain may be designated by a negative decibel value. A negative decibel value may also be stated as so many "decibels down."

Example 3

An amplifier has a power gain of 45 dB. Find the power ratio which corresponds to this gain.

Solution

$$dB = 10 \log \frac{P_2}{P_1}$$

Substituting values,

$$45 \text{ dB} = 10 \log \frac{P_2}{P_1}$$

Dividing by 10,

$$4.5 = \log \frac{P_2}{P_1}$$

$$\text{antilog } 4.5 = \text{antilog} \frac{P_2}{P_1} = 31,623$$

Therefore a 45-dB gain corresponds to a power ratio of 31,623:1.

Example 4

A network has a loss of 12 dB. Find the power ratio which corresponds to this loss.

Solution

$$dB = 10 \log\frac{P_2}{P_1}$$

Since the network has a loss, P_2 and P_1 can be inverted for computation purposes and

$$12 \text{ dB} = 10 \log\frac{P_1}{P_2}$$

Dividing by 10,

$$1.2 \text{ dB} = \log\frac{P_1}{P_2}$$

$$\text{antilog } 1.2 = \text{antilog}\frac{P_1}{P_2} = 15.85$$

Therefore the ratio of input power to output power is 15.85:1; and the ratio of output power to input power, which is the inverse of this ratio, is 1:15.85.

Voltage and current ratios may be incorporated for the decibel gain or loss of a circuit as long as the input and output resistances are taken into consideration. For voltage,

$$dB = 20 \log \frac{V_2(R_1)^{1/2}}{V_1(R_2)^{1/2}} \tag{13-7a}$$

where V_2 = output voltage
$\quad V_1$ = input voltage
$\quad R_1$ = input resistance
$\quad R_2$ = output resistance

For current,

$$dB = 20 \log\frac{I_2(R_2)^{1/2}}{I_1(R_1)^{1/2}} \tag{13-7b}$$

where I_1 = input current
$\quad I_2$ = output current
$\quad R_1$ = input resistance
$\quad R_2$ = output resistance

In those special cases where the input and output resistances are *equal*, the relationships are simplified to:

$$\text{Voltage: dB} = 20 \log \frac{V_2}{V_1} \qquad \textbf{(13-7c)}$$

$$\text{Current: dB} = 20 \log \frac{I_2}{I_1} \qquad \textbf{(13-7d)}$$

Example 5

Refer to Fig. 13-4. An amplifier has the following parameters: $R_1 = 400\ \Omega$; $R_o = 900\ \Omega$; $V_i = 0.3$ V; $V_o = 250$ V. Find the power gain in decibels.

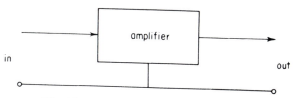

Fig. 13-4   Block diagram of an amplifier.

Solution

$$\text{dB} = 20 \log \frac{V_2(R_1)^{1/2}}{V_1(R_2)^{1/2}} = 20 \log \frac{250(400)^{1/2}}{0.3(900)^{1/2}}$$
$$= 54.9$$

Example 6

Refer to Fig. 13-4. An amplifier has the following parameters: $R_i = 50\ \Omega$; $R_o = 4000\ \Omega$; $I_i = 20\ \mu\text{A}$; $I_o = 4$ mA. Find the power gain in decibels.

Solution

$$\text{dB} = 20 \log \frac{I_2(R_2)^{1/2}}{I_1(R_1)^{1/2}} = 20 \log \frac{0.004(4000)^{1/2}}{(20)(10^{-6})(50)^{1/2}}$$
$$= 65.1$$

The preceding discussion points out that the power gain in decibels is a function of the logarithm of the power ratio. In order to utilize this method of expressing power gain, the power input must be specified. Simply stating that an amplifier or network has a gain or loss of so many decibels is meaningless without a specified input as a reference for the power output. There are a number of zero-decibel levels (or reference levels) in use: 6 mW, 12.5 mW, and 1 mW (volume unit).

PROBLEMS

13-1 State the angles when v is:
    a) maximum   b) minimum

13-2 At what angles is roc v of a sine-wave voltage maximum?

13-3 At what angles is roc v of a sine-wave voltage minimum?

13-4 A sine-wave input voltage has a maximum value of 225 V. Find v at the following points:
    a) 45°   b) 30°
    c) 70°   d) 100°
    e) 120°   f) 140°
    g) 195°   h) 260°
    i) 300°   j) 355°

13-5 In the circuit of Prob. 13-4, $R = 4500\ \Omega$. Find the instantaneous-current values for the angles given in Prob. 13-4.

13-6 A sine-wave input potential has a frequency of 200 Hz. Find the time of:
    a) one period.   b) one alternation

13-7 A sine-wave input generator has a period time of 0.0167 s. Find the generator frequency.

13-8 Repeat Prob. 13-7 for a period time of 0.00005 s.

13-9 Convert the following maximum current values into rms values:
    a) 5 A   b) 1.4 A
    c) 23 A   d) 73 mA
    e) 42 mA   f) 4.75 mA
    g) 37 μA   h) 139 mA
    i) 88 μA   j) 250 μA

13-10 Assume that the current values of Prob. 13-9 are rms values: convert them into maximum values.

13-11 Assume that the current values of Prob. 13-9 are maximum values: convert them into average values.

13-12 A resistive network has the following parameters: $R = 500\ \Omega$; $V_{max} = 200\ V$. Find the following:
    a) V_{rms} b) I_{rms}
    c) P_{avg} d) p at 30°
    e) p at 230°   f) p at 300°

13-13 Repeat Prob. 13-12 with the following parameters: $R = 2\ k\Omega$; $V_{max} = 160\ V$.

13-14 Find the maximum power of Prob. 13-12.

13-15   Find the maximum power of Prob. 13-13.

13-16   A series-resistive network has the following parameters: $R_1 = 40\ \Omega$; $R_2 = 65\ \Omega$; $V_{max} = 90$ V. Find the following:

a) V_{rms} b) I_{max}

c) I_{rms} d) $P_{R1,avg}$

e) $P_{R2,avg}$ f) P_{avg}

g) $P_{R1,max}$ h) $P_{R2,max}$

i) P_{max}

13-17   Repeat Prob. 13-16 with the following parameters: $R_1 = 180\ \Omega$; $R_2 = 50\ \Omega$; $V_{max} = 170$ V.

13-18   Find the common logarithms of the following:

a) 17   b) 142   c) 450

d) 732   e) 36,500

13-19   Find the common logarithms of the following:

a) 0.252   b) $1500(10)^{-12}$

c) $96(10)^{-6}$ d) $770(10)^{-6}$

e) $5.6(10)^{-6}$

13-20   Find the antilogarithms of the following logarithms:

a) 1.450   b) 2.334   c) 8.842

d) 7.672   e) 0.114

13-21   An amplifier has an input of 15 mW and an output of 2.4 W. Find the power gain in decibels.

13-22   An amplifier has an input of 25 mW and an output of 2 mW. Find the power loss in decibels.

13-23   Calculate the decibel gain of an amplifier having the following output powers (use 6 mW as a reference):

a) 50 mW   b) 125 mW   c) 2.48 W

d) 24 W   e) 14 W

13-24   A network has the following parameters: $V_i = 0.25$ V; $V_o = 300$ V; $R_i = 45\ \Omega$; $R_o = 4\ k\Omega$. Find the power gain in decibels.

13-25   A network has the following parameters: $I_i = 30\ \mu A$; $I_o = 0.250$ A; $R_i = 150\ \Omega$; $R_o = 4\ k\Omega$. Find the power gain in decibels.

13-26   A network with equal input and output resistances has $V_i = 3$ V and $V_o = 280$ V. Find the power gain in decibels.

13-27   A network with equal input and output resistances has $I_i = 0.15$ mA and $I_o = 80$ mA. Find the power gain in decibels.

QUESTIONS

13-1   Why does one cycle of a sine wave consist of two alternations?

13-2   What is the relationship between the cutting angle in Fig. 13-1 and the magnitude of the induced emf?

13-3   What effect does increasing the rotational speed of the loop in Fig. 13-1 have upon the induced voltage?

13-4   In the sine wave, what is the relationship between the maximum and rms values?

13-5   What is average power?

13-6   What is frequency?

13-7   What is the frequency of common household current?

13-8   What is instantaneous power?

13-9   What is peak power?

13-10   What is one decibel?

13-7 HARMONICS

In this section you will learn about sine waves with frequencies that are multiples of the fundamental sine wave and the effect of such combinations on the composite waveform.

A pure sine wave is rarely generated in actual practice. In many cases,

The pure sine wave, called the fundamental, is associated with other sine waves the frequencies of which are whole multiples of the fundamental, which are called harmonics.

The resultant waveform is the composite of the fundamental and the harmonics. Harmonics of frequencies an even number of times greater than the fundamental are called even-order harmonics; those with frequencies that are an odd number of times greater than the fundamental are called odd-order harmonics.

The fundamental sine wave generally is much greater in amplitude than the harmonics. The amount of distortion caused by the presence of harmonics upon the composite waveform varies with the magnitude and number of harmonics.

The instantaneous composite-wave value, consisting of a sine wave fundamental and n number of harmonics, is determined as follows:

$$y = y_1 + y_2 + \cdots + y_n \qquad (13\text{-}8)$$

where y = instantaneous composite-wave value

y_1 = instantaneous value of the fundamental wave

y_2 = instantaneous value of the second harmonic

y_n = instantaneous value of the nth harmonic

Refer to Fig. 13-5. Consider point A, which is the instant when the fundamental is at 90°. At the same instant, the second harmonic is at

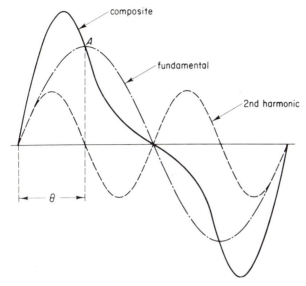

Fig. 13-5 **Relationships of the fundamental and second harmonic.**

180°, which is 2θ. Examination of Fig. 13-5 reveals that the instantaneous angle of the second harmonic is always equal to twice the instantaneous angle of the fundamental when the two waves begin together. Based on this observation, one can obtain the equations of the waveforms:

$$\text{Fundamental:} \quad v_1 = V_{1,\max} \sin \theta$$
$$\text{Second harmonic:} \quad v_2 = V_{2,\max} \sin 2\theta$$
$$\text{Composite:} \quad v = v_1 + v_2$$

Substituting values,

$$v = V_{1,\max} \sin \theta + V_{2,\max} \sin 2\theta \qquad \textbf{(13-8a)}$$

Refer to Fig. 13-6. When the fundamental is at point A, it is at angle θ, which is at 90° in the illustration. At that same instant, the second harmonic is at 180° (2θ), and the third harmonic is at 270° (3θ). Further examination of the waveforms reveals that these relationships are true throughout the illustration, as long as the waveforms begin together. Now there is a basis for determining the equations for each waveform:

$$\text{Fundamental:} \quad v_1 = V_{1,\max}$$
$$\text{Second harmonic:} \quad v_2 = V_{2,\max} \sin 2\theta$$

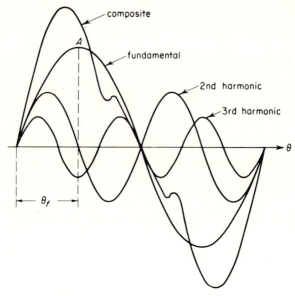

Fig. 13-6   Relationships of the fundamental and second and third harmonics.

$$\text{Third harmonic:} \quad v_3 = V_{3,\text{max}} \sin 3\theta$$
$$\text{Composite:} \quad v = v_1 + v_2 + v_3$$

Substituting values,

$$v = V_{1,\text{max}} \sin \theta + V_{2,\text{max}} \sin 2\theta + V_{3,\text{max}} \sin 3\theta \qquad \textbf{(13-8b)}$$

Figure 13-7 illustrates the fundamental, second to fifth harmonics, and composite waveforms. The preceding analysis revealed that the instantaneous angle of a harmonic is equal to $n\theta$, where n is the harmonic and θ is the angle of the fundamental at that instant. On this basis, the equation for the composite waveform of Fig. 13-7 is

$$v = V_{1,\text{max}} \sin \theta + V_{2,\text{max}} \sin 2\theta + V_{3,\text{max}} \sin 3\theta$$
$$+ V_{4,\text{max}} \sin 4\theta + V_{5,\text{max}} \sin 5\theta \qquad \textbf{(13-9)}$$

A sine wave fundamental plus a number of odd harmonics has only a composite wave which is distorted; but it is still symmetrical, and pulse 2 is a mirror image of pulse 1. (A pulse is the voltage or current waveform of one alternation.) On the other hand, a fundamental plus a number of even harmonics results in distortion and loss of the mirror-image

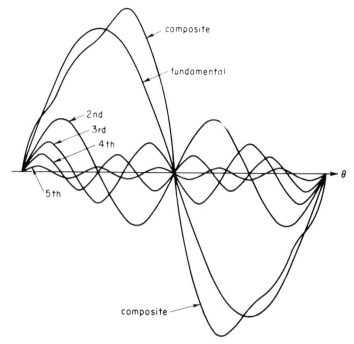

Fig. 13-7 **Fundamental, second, third, fourth, and fifth harmonics and composite.**

symmetry (which is the case where the second alternation is an inverted replica of the first alternation, and is known also as half-wave symmetry).

Figure 13-8 illustrates the effect of adding odd harmonics to the sine wave fundamental. The composite waveform approaches that of a square wave as more odd harmonics are added. A sine wave with an infinite number of odd harmonics will have a square-wave composite waveform if the relative phase and amplitude for each are correct. The equation of the square wave is

$$v = V_{max} \sin \theta + \tfrac{1}{3} V_{max} \sin 3\theta + \tfrac{1}{5} V_{max} \sin 5\theta$$
$$+ \cdots + \tfrac{1}{n} V_{max} \sin n\theta \quad \textbf{(13-10)}$$

where v = instantaneous voltage
V_{max} = maximum voltage of fundamental
θ = angle of the fundamental at the instant
n = nth odd-order harmonic

The alternating triangular wave can also be generated by a sine wave with harmonics. Since the alternating triangular wave is symmetrical

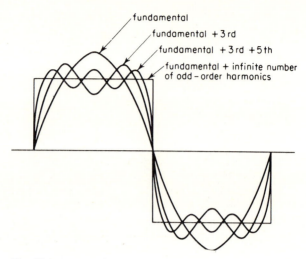

fundamental

fundamental + 3rd

fundamental + 3rd + 5th

fundamental + infinite number
of odd – order harmonics

Fig. 13-8   Generation of a square wave by odd-order harmonics.

and a mirror image of pulse 1 and 2 is present, it must incorporate only the odd harmonics. The harmonics are very small in magnitude, as shown in the following equation for the alternating triangular wave:

$$v = V_{max} \sin \theta - \tfrac{1}{9} V_{max} \sin 3\theta + \tfrac{1}{25} V_{max} \sin 5\theta \cdots \qquad \textbf{(13-11)}$$

Notice that the fraction preceding V_{max} for each odd harmonic is the reciprocal of the harmonic number squared.

The alternating sawtooth-wave equation is

$$v = V_{max} \sin \theta - \tfrac{1}{2} V_{max} \sin 2\theta + \tfrac{1}{3} V_{max} \sin 3\theta - \tfrac{1}{4} V_{max} \sin 4\theta \cdots$$
$$\textbf{(13-12)}$$

In Fig. 13-7, where the fundamental, second to fifth harmonics, and composite waveforms are considered, notice that the composite waveform is beginning to resemble the alternating sawtooth wave. The second pulse of the sawtooth wave is not a mirror image of the first pulse; therefore even-order harmonics are present in the composite.

13-8 PHASE RELATIONSHIP OF v, i, AND POWER IN A RESISTIVE CIRCUIT

In this section you will learn about the phase angle between i and v, leading and lagging phase angles, v and i phase angles in a pure resistive circuit, and power waveform in a pure resistive circuit.

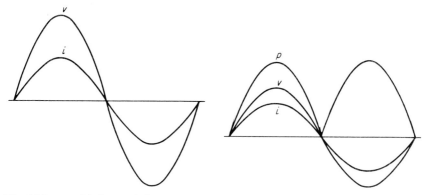

Fig. 13-9   *v* and *i* phase relationships in a pure resistive circuit.

Fig. 13-10   *v*, *i*, and *p* relationships in a pure resistive circuit.

There are many circuits in which *i* undergoes its sinusoidal variations before the voltage does; then *i* *leads* *v*. For example, if *v* is at 0° when *i* is at 90°, the condition is described as *i* leading *v* by 90°. Also, there are circuits where *i* *lags* *v*. The *phase angle* between *v* and *i* is the difference between their angles at any instant.

In a pure resistive circuit, there are no properties that impose a leading or lagging effect upon the current with respect to the voltage. The current and voltage undergo their amplitude and directional changes together, i.e., *the current and voltage are in step, or in phase.* For example, when the current is at 30°, the voltage is also at 30°. Therefore, in a pure resistive circuit, *v* and *i* are in phase, and the phase angle is zero. This point is graphically illustrated in Fig. 13-9.

Therefore, in a pure resistive circuit, power may be computed by any of the three relationships. Consider the use of *vi* for the calculation of power. In Fig. 13-10, *v* and *i*, and their product *p*, are graphically illustrated.

Of special interest is the fact that the instantaneous power in a resistive circuit is always positive. That is to say, in a purely resistive circuit, power always flows from the source to the load, never back. In the first alternation, *p* is determined by the product of a positive *v* and positive *i*, resulting in a positive power value. Since the sine wave is symmetrical, the instantaneous products during the second alternation are the same as those for the first alternation, resulting in the power curve's always being positive and sinusoidal and having one cycle for each sine wave alternation. The instantaneous-power curve of a resistive circuit has a repetition frequency twice that of the current and voltage.

It should be recalled that a resistor is a circuit component which converts electric energy into thermal energy (heat). Generally speaking, the thermal energy is lost to the surrounding atmosphere and is not returned to the circuit power source. In other words, a resistor creates a one-way energy conversion process. The amount of electric energy converted into heat by a fixed resistance varies directly as the product of v and i. This explains why the power curve of Fig. 13-10 is at its maximum value at 90 and 270°. Furthermore, the direction of current flow through the resistance has nothing to do with the amount of energy conversion. In the sine wave, 0 to 180° develops the same heat as 180 to 360°. Even though the current has reversed direction, the same amount of energy is being converted into heat. *A positive power curve indicates that electric energy is converted into heat. Therefore the entire power curve of a resistive circuit must be positive.*

It should be pointed out at this time that resistance is only one factor which opposes the flow of current in sinusoidal circuits. The total opposition to the current flow is termed impedance Z. In a pure resistive circuit, the impedance is composed solely of resistance ($Z = R$).

13-9 EFFECTIVE RESISTANCE OF A SINUSOIDAL CIRCUIT

In this section you will learn about four types of energy losses in sinusoidal circuits and their effect on overall circuit performance.

The preceding section pointed out that the presence of resistance in a circuit results in a conversion of electric energy into heat, as determined by one of the three power formulas. For the input generator, a resistor is a component which draws energy from the source and does not return it. Furthermore, *any circuit element that draws energy from the input and does not return the energy to the source possesses resistance for the source.* Heat is only one of the nonconvertible energy transformations which may occur in circuits where the magnitude of the current is made to vary. The following paragraphs describe the most significant losses of bidirectional-current circuits.

Magnetic-field Energy Losses

In a perfect inductor (containing 0 Ω of resistance), all the energy drawn from the source is converted into potential energy during current rise, and the same amount of potential is converted back into kinetic energy during the current-decay period. In a practical inductor, a portion of the energy drawn from the source and returned by the coil is converted into heat because of the ohmic value of the coil. In such cases, the source will see a perfect inductor in series with a resistor of a value at least equal to the resistance of the windings.

When the current is varying, particularly at frequencies of 20 kHz and greater, a number of the expanding flux lines may never return to the coil. Expanding and collapsing the flux field at even faster rates tends to increase the number of flux lines which never return to the inductor. In such cases, a portion of the electric energy which was converted into stored or potential energy in the electromagnetic field is never returned to the circuit. The source will see this loss, which is called *radiation loss*, as a resistance in addition to the ohmic value of the coil windings. Radiation losses are a direct function of frequency. It is of special interest that radiation losses are utilized in the space transmission of electromagnetic waves (radio, television, and radar signals are typical examples).

Another type of magnetic-field energy loss is developed in the iron core of an inductor in bidirectional-current circuits. An earlier section pointed out that an emf is induced in a conductor in accordance with the speed and angle of cutting between the flux lines and the conductor. When the flux lines undergo expansion and contraction, they cut across the iron core of the coil. This cutting action occurs four times per cycle (twice for the expansions and twice for the contractions). Therefore the frequency of the bidirectional current directly determines the number of times the flux lines cut across the core in 1 s. The induced voltage built up in the core may develop a core current, called the eddy current, which heats up the core. Some of the stored magnetic-field energy is converted into *core heat;* this portion of the potential energy of the flux field is not returned to the circuit. The input generator will see this as another resistance in series with those already described. The core loss is a direct function of frequency, and special design features (such as powdered iron and laminations in the core structure) must be incorporated in coils used in high-frequency circuits.

A third type of magnetic-field energy loss is the development of induced voltage by flux lines which do not follow the ideal prescribed paths and which cut across nearby components. This is called the *leakage-flux loss.* Here again, eddy currents may be developed, resulting in heat losses, thereby reducing the amount of energy returned to the circuit upon the complete collapse of the flux field. Leakage-flux losses, which are a direct function of frequency, are kept to a minimum by proper design of the inductor (magnetic poles which are kept close together).

A fourth type of magnetic-field energy loss is the effect of self-induced voltage upon a conductor. The flux originates in the center of the wire, and the greatest amount of cutting occurs in the immediate area surrounding the center of the conductor. At high frequencies, the rate of cutting is great, and the induced emf developed in the center of the conductor may be great enough to prevent electron drift from taking place in that area. This restricts the current flow to the surface area of the conductor; it is called the *skin effect*. This effectively reduces the cross-sectional area of the conductor, resulting in increased resistance. Skin effect is directly proportional to frequency. To reduce the skin effect in high-frequency circuits, a special type of wire (litz wire), may be used. Litz wire consists of many small insulated wires woven together. Distributing the circuit current in this manner reduces the skin effect. Hollow and flat-strip conductors, which have large surface areas, may also be used to reduce skin-effect losses. Litz wire is used most frequently for lower-current circuits, and the hollow conductor is utilized for higher-current applications.

In conclusion, magnetic-field energy losses may be classified into four main categories:

1 Radiation losses
2 Core losses
3 Leakage-flux losses
4 Skin-effect losses

Any of or all these factors may contribute to inductor losses in bidirectional circuits. They are all directly proportional to the frequency of the energizing current. In bidirectional-current applications, these factors must be considered along with the ohmic resistance of the windings in calculating the bidirectional or effective resistance of the inductor.

Capacitive Energy Losses

All capacitors display some value of resistance due to the ohmic resistance of the plates, leads, and plate connections. This resistance is relatively independent of frequency and, when not negligible, is equivalent to a small R in series with C. In addition, there are two types of capacitor energy losses which are a function of the frequency: (1) *leakage* (this is a function of frequency only indirectly) and (2) *dielectric*.

If a capacitor were perfect, it would remain charged for an indefinite period. In actual practice, a number of electrons from the negative plate flow through the dielectric to the positive plate. This action, called leakage, is due to the imperfections of the insulator used as the dielectric. The leakage loss is present to some extent even in the best capaci-

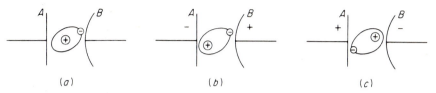

Fig. 13-11 **Effect of a charge upon an orbital electron in a dielectric:** (a) **neutral;** (b) **when plate** A **is charged;** (c) **when plate** B **is charged.**

tors, since there is no perfect insulator. Leakage losses are kept to low values by using very high-resistance dielectrics, such as ceramics and mica. The drifting of electrons through the dielectric converts a portion of the electric energy into heat, and this is not returned to the circuit when the capacitor reverses its action. The input generator will see this loss as a relatively high-value resistance in parallel with the capacitor.

When a capacitor is charged, the orbits of the electrons in the dielectric are known to be distorted, as shown in Fig. 13-11. Figure 13-11a depicts the normal orbit, which exists when the capacitor is not subjected to a charge. When plate A is charged negatively, the orbit distorts as shown in Fig. 13-11b; Fig. 13-11c illustrates the effect when plate B is charged. During the time current flows in a capacitive circuit, part of the current causes heat dissipation in the dielectric, as a result of this orbit distortion. At higher frequencies, the energy used to distort the electron orbits may become considerable and is called the *dielectric hysteresis loss.* The input generator will see the dielectric loss as a relatively low value of resistance in series with the capacitor. Capacitors designed to carry large values of *RF* currents usually have this current rating indicated, along with capacitor value and working voltage. The internal heat developed by the dielectric hysteresis loss because of *excessive* currents can permanently damage the unit.

These losses, which are associated with inductance and capacitance, are generally negligible at low frequencies, but they must be considered in high-frequency applications. The total of these losses plus the ohmic resistance may be called the bidirectional (or effective) resistance of the circuit and can be much greater than the ohmic (unidirectional) resistance in many cases.

13-10 WHAT IS A VECTOR?

Quantities are often stated as numbers, and no further specification is required. For example, the population of a city is 54,845. This is a complete statement. Such a quantity, which states the magnitude (or amount)

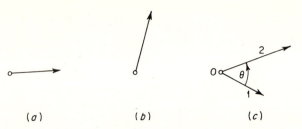

(a) (b) (c)

Fig. 13-12 Vectors of different quantities and directions.

only, is called a *scalar*. A line whose length represents the magnitude may be called a scalar. On the other hand, it is necessary in some cases to specify direction as well as magnitude. For example, to determine the effect of a force upon a body, the direction of the force and its magnitude should be known. Hence the quantity and its direction may be illustrated as shown in Fig. 13-12.

A *vector* is a line which represents quantity and direction.

The magnitude is represented by the length of the line and the direction by the arrowhead. The origin may be considered that end of the vector which does not have the arrowhead. Figure 13-12 illustrates two vectors which originate at the same point *O*. Judging from the line lengths, quantity 2 is greater than quantity 1, and the difference in their directions is shown by angle *θ*.

13-11 ROTATING VECTORS

An earlier section pointed out that the rotation of a conductor within a magnetic field develops an induced emf in the conductor which is a function of the angle of rotation (see Figs. 13-1 and 13-2). A simpler method for analyzing this action is to replace the rotating conductor with a rotating vector, which is called a *phasor*.

Refer to Fig. 13-13. The rotating phasor is kept at a constant length, which is to designate the maximum value of the induced voltage. The

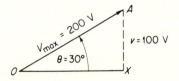

Fig. 13-13 Vector of an instantaneous voltage.

instantaneous-emf value is equal to the vertical component of the rotating phasor. In Fig. 13-13,

$$\sin \theta = \frac{AX}{OA} = \frac{AX}{V_{\max}}$$

Transposing yields

$$AX = V_{\max} \sin \theta = 200 \sin 30° = 200 \times 0.5 = 100 \text{ V}$$

This is recognized as the equation by which the instantaneous voltage may be determined, and AX is the magnitude of the instantaneous induced voltage at the particular angle of rotation. This technique enables you to determine readily the instantaneous voltage at any angle of rotation.

13-12 APPLICATIONS OF VECTORS TO MULTIPHASE CIRCUITS

In this section you will learn how vectors can be used to determine the instantaneous values of several sine waves of identical frequency but unlike phases.

The use of vectors simplifies the determination of the instantaneous value of several voltages which are of the same frequency but out of phase.

Example 1

Refer to Fig. 13-14a. $V_{1,\max} = 200$ V; $V_{2,\max} = 100$ V; v_1 leads v_2 by 60°. Find the instantaneous value of v_1, v_2, and v at time t, when v_1 is at 100°.

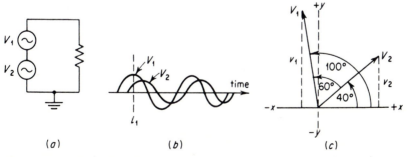

(a)   (b)   (c)

Fig. 13-14 Analysis of two out-of-phase voltages: (*a*) circuit; (*b*) waveforms; (*c*) vector representation.

Solution

Refer to Fig. 13-14b and c, which illustrate the waveforms and vector representation of this problem. The instantaneous values of v_1 and v_2 are determined by the vertical components of the two vectors.

$$v_1 = V_{1,\text{max}} \sin \theta = 200 \sin 100° = 197 \text{ V}$$
$$v_2 = V_{2,\text{max}} \sin (\theta - 60°) = V_{2,\text{max}} \sin (100° - 60°) = V_{2,\text{max}} \sin 40°$$
$$= 100 \times 0.643 = 64 \text{ V}$$
$$v = v_1 + v_2 = 197 + 64 = 261 \text{ V}$$

Example 2

Refer to Fig. 13-15 for the circuit and vector diagrams. v_1 lags v_2 by 120°, and v_1 lags v_3 by 240°. Find the instantaneous values of each

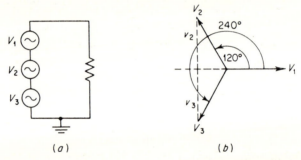

(a) (b)

Fig. 13-15 A three-phase circuit: (a) circuit; (b) vector representation.

voltage and the resultant when v_1 is at 0 and 70°. $V_{1,\text{max}} = V_{2,\text{max}} = V_{3,\text{max}} = 300$ V.

Solution

The instantaneous voltage equations for this condition are:

$$v_1 = V_{1,\text{max}} \sin \theta$$
$$v_2 = V_{2,\text{max}} \sin (\theta + 120°)$$
$$v_3 = V_{3,\text{max}} \sin (\theta + 240°)$$

where θ is the angle at which v_1 is considered. Substituting values when $\theta = 0°$,

$$v_1 = 300 \sin 0° = 0 \text{ V}$$
$$v_2 = 300 \sin 120° = 300 \sin 60° = 300 \times 0.866 = 260 \text{ V}$$
$$v_3 = 300 \sin 240° = 300 (-0.866) = -260 \text{ V}$$
$$v = v_1 + v_2 + v_3 = 0 + 260 - 260 = 0 \text{ V}$$

Substituting values when $\theta = 70°$,

$$v_1 = 300 \sin 70° = 300 \times 0.94 = 282 \text{ V}$$
$$v_2 = 300 \sin 190° = 300\,(-0.174) = -52 \text{ V}$$
$$v_3 = 300 \sin 310° = 300\,(-0.766) = -230 \text{ V}$$
$$v = v_1 + v_2 + v_3 = 282 - 52 - 230 = 0 \text{ V}$$

13-13 APPLICATIONS OF VECTORS TO MULTIPLE-FREQUENCY CIRCUITS

In this section you will learn how vectors can be used in finding composite voltage values of several sine waves of unlike frequencies.

The phase angle between two voltages of different frequencies continuously changes during the entire cycle. In the case of voltages which are harmonically related, the phase angle at the start of each fundamental cycle is the same (see Figs. 13-5 to 13-8). The phase angle between the harmonic and the fundamental at the beginning of the fundamental cycle is a common way of expressing the phase relation between two such waves. When the voltages are not harmonically related, a statement of the phase angle would have little meaning as such, since it is not the same at that point of each cycle. Therefore vectors can be used to illustrate only the phase relationships of harmonically related waves unless the relative phase angles of all components are known at some particular time; only at this time can they be compared. From the vector diagram, the instantaneous value of each voltage and the composite waveform can be determined.

Example

Refer to 13-16*a*. A fundamental and second and fourth harmonics are illustrated. $V_{1,\text{max}} = 100$ V; $V_{2,\text{max}} = 50$ V; $V_{4,\text{max}} = 10$ V. (*a*) What is

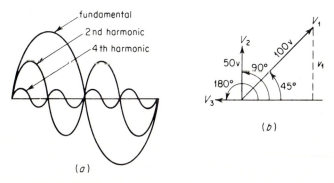

Fig. 13-16   (*a*) **Representation of the fundamental and second and fourth harmonics;** (*b*) **vector representation at 45°.**

the phase relation between the harmonics and the fundamental at the start of each fundamental cycle? (b) Find the instantaneous composite voltage when the fundamental is 45°.

Solution

(a) The waveforms of Fig. 13-16a show that the fundamental and second and fourth harmonics are all at 0° at the beginning of each fundamental cycle.

(b) The waveforms also show that the phase angle between the fundamental and each harmonic is according to the following relationships:

$$\text{Second harmonic angle} = 2\theta$$
$$\text{Fourth harmonic angle} = 4\theta$$

where θ is the angle of the fundamental. Using these relationships, when θ is 45°,

$$\text{Second harmonic angle} = 2\theta = 2 \times 45° = 90°$$
$$\text{Fourth harmonic angle} = 4\theta = 4 \times 45° = 180°$$

The vector relationship between these voltages when the fundamental is at 45° is illustrated in Fig. 13-16b. As pointed out in a preceding section, the vertical component of each is the instantaneous value, and the sum of the instantaneous values is the composite instantaneous value.

$$v_1 = V_{1,\text{max}} \sin \theta = 100 \sin 45° = 100 \times 0.707 = 71 \text{ V}$$
$$v_2 = V_{2,\text{max}} \sin 2\theta = 50 \sin 90° = 50 \times 1.00 = 50 \text{ V}$$
$$v_3 = V_{3,\text{max}} \sin 3\theta = 10 \sin 180° = 10 \times 0 = 0 \text{ V}$$
$$v = v_1 + v_2 + v_3 = 71 + 50 + 0 = 121 \text{ V}$$

PROBLEMS

13-28 A composite wave contains the fundamental and second harmonics, which begin at the same time (in phase). $V_{1,\text{max}} = 200$ V and $V_{2,\text{max}} = 80$ V. Find the following instantaneous values at 40, 150, 240, and 355°:
a) fundamental
b) second harmonic
c) composite

13-29 Repeat Prob. 13-28 with $V_{1,max} = 150$ V and $V_{2,max} = 25$ V.

13-30 In Prob. 13-29, assume the third harmonic has a maximum value of 20 V. Find the following at the times stated in Prob. 13-28:
a) third harmonic
b) composite of Prob. 13-29 and the third harmonic

13-31 Assume that the circuit considered in Prob. 13-30 has a fourth harmonic, with a maximum value of 15 V, and a fifth harmonic, with a maximum value of 7 V. Find the following values at the times stated in Prob. 13-28:
a) fourth harmonic
b) fifth harmonic
c) composite of Prob. 13-30 and the fourth and fifth harmonics

13-32 A composite waveform resembles the alternating square wave. What order of harmonics is present?

13-33 In Prob. 13-32, $V_{max} = 100$ V. Calculate the instantaneous value at 30° for the:
a) fundamental
b) third harmonic
c) fifth harmonic
d) seventh harmonic
e) ninth harmonic
f) composite

13-34 A composite waveform resembles the alternating square wave. $V_{max} = 250$ V. Calculate the instantaneous values of the following at 135°:
a) fundamental   b) third harmonic
c) fifth harmonic   d) seventh harmonic
e) ninth harmonic   f) composite

13-35 $V_{max} = 40$ V. Find the instantaneous values at 45° of an alternating triangular wave for:
a) fundamental   b) third harmonic
c) fifth harmonic   d) composite

13-36 Repeat Prob. 13-35 for a composite waveform which resembles an alternating sawtooth waveform up to and including the third harmonic.

13-37 Two voltages are of the same frequency. v_1 leads v_2 by 75°. $V_{1,max} = 150$ V; $V_{2,max} = 120$ V. When v_1 is 45°, find:
a) v_1 b) v_2 c) v

13-38 Two voltages are of the same frequency. v_1 lags v_2 by 24°. $V_{1,max} = 40$ V; $V_{2,max} = 60$ V. When v_1 is at 35°, find:
a) v_1 b) v_2 c) v

13-39 $V_{1,\text{max}} = 200$ V. Its second harmonic has a maximum value of 80 V. When the fundamental is at 130°, find:

a) v_1 b) v_2 c) composite

13-40 In Prob. 13-39, the third harmonic has a maximum value of 40 V; the fourth harmonic has a maximum value of 15 V. When the fundamental is at 75°, find:

a) v_1 b) v_2 c) v_3

d) v_4 e) composite

QUESTIONS

13-11 What are harmonics?

13-12 What are even-order harmonics?

13-13 What are odd-order harmonics?

13-14 What is the fundamental wave?

13-15 What is the composite wave?

13-16 What does the composite wave of the square wave consist of?

13-17 What does the composite wave of the alternating triangular wave consist of?

13-18 What does the composite wave of an alternating sawtooth wave consist of?

13-19 What does the term *in phase* mean regarding v and i?

13-20 What are the implications for power in a circuit when v and i are in phase?

13-21 Explain the phase relationships in a resistance circuit.

13-22 Why is the power curve always positive in a resistance circuit?

13-23 What are magnetic-field losses?

13-24 What are core losses?

13-25 What are leakage-flux losses?

13-26 What are skin-effect losses?

13-27 What is leakage loss in a capacitor?

13-28 What is dielectric loss in a capacitor?

13-29 What is the dielectric hysteresis loss of a capacitor?

13-30 What is a vector?

series circuits with a sine-wave input
14

In Chap. 13, the action of a resistive circuit with a sinusoidal input voltage was considered. This chapter deals with the behavior of series-RC and -RL combinations with a sine wave input.

It should be recalled that a capacitor stores and discharges electrostatic energy in relation to the *changes* in the input voltage. In the case of the sine wave, which has a continuously varying rate of change, the capacitor is always either storing or discharging electrostatic energy. When resistance is present in the circuit, a portion of the source energy, before it has a chance to be stored, is converted into thermal energy; another portion of the discharged electrostatic energy is likewise converted into heat. Therefore, with resistance present, part of the energy furnished by the source is not returned.

The inductor stores electromagnetic energy during current rises and discharges electromagnetic energy when the current decreases. With the presence of resistance in the circuit, a portion of the energy drawn from the source (when i increases) and meant to be returned to the source (when i decreases) is converted into heat. The amount of power actually used, like the capacitive circuit, hinges on the magnitude of the resistance.

14-1 BEHAVIOR OF A PURE CAPACITIVE CIRCUIT

In this section you will learn how a pure capacitor alternately stores energy and then returns it to the circuit.

In Chap. 11 it was shown that capacitors store electrostatic energy during voltage rises and discharge electrostatic energy during voltage decreases. In earlier chapters, it was pointed out that the voltage and current waveforms of the capacitor hinge on roc v_c. The following relationship was used to determine the instantaneous current:

$$i_c = C \text{ roc } v_c$$

315

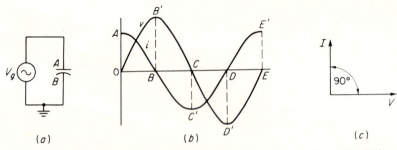

Fig. 14-1 Pure capacitive circuit: (*a*) circuit; (*b*) waveforms; (*c*) vector relationships.

Now apply these facts to the circuit of Fig. 14-1, a pure capacitor in series with a sinusoidal voltage.

Assuming that the circuit possesses no resistance, roc v_c is equal to roc v_g, since the capacitor tc (RC) is equal to 0 s. Since $i_c = C$ roc v_c,

$$i_c = C \text{ roc } v_g$$

Roc v_g is maximum at point 0 of Fig. 14-1*b*, and i_c is maximum at this same time (point A). Roc v_g is zero at B'; therefore i_c is zero at this same time (B). After reaching B', v_g reverses its direction of change (graphically, downward is negative); hence roc v_c reverses, and i_c begins to flow in the opposite (negative) direction. i_c is maximum at 180° (C'), since $-$roc v_g is maximum at this time (C). The current then begins to decrease, since $-$roc v_g decreases until it is zero at D'.

The outcome of this analysis reveals that *i leads v by 90° in a pure capacitive circuit*, as shown in Fig. 14-1*b*. The following equations allow the instantaneous values of current and voltage to be determined:

$$i_c = I_{max} \sin (\theta + 90°) \tag{14-1}$$
$$v_c = V_{max} \sin \theta \tag{14-2}$$

The vector representation of this relationship is shown in Fig. 14-1*c*. With zero resistance present in the circuit, the electrostatic energy stored is equal to that discharged, resulting in no dissipation of power.

Using the equation of $p = vi$, the instantaneous power for a number of points can be computed, resulting in the power waveform illustrated by the shaded area of Fig. 14-2. The positive areas of the power curve are associated with the positive changes in v_g, which is the time when the capacitor is storing electrostatic energy. When v_g is undergoing negative changes, the capacitor is discharging electrostatic energy. Since there

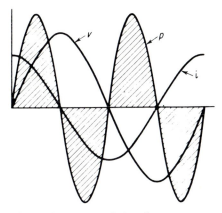

Fig. 14-2   Power relation in a pure capacitive circuit.

is no resistance present in the circuit, all the stored energy is returned to the source. *A pure capacitive circuit dissipates no power,* as shown by the fact that the average area of the power curve for an entire cycle is zero.

Notice that the capacitor alternately stores and discharges electrostatic energy every quarter-cycle, resulting in the power curve having twice the repetition frequency of v_g; the instantaneous-power relationship is

$$p = \frac{V_{max}I_{max}}{2} \sin 2\theta \qquad \text{(14-3)}$$

where θ is the angle of the generator voltage.

14-2   CAPACITIVE REACTANCE X_C

In this section you will learn about the definition of capacitive reactance, how its opposition to current flow dissipates no power, and the elements that make up capacitive reactance.

Earlier discussions have revealed that a capacitor offers an opposition to current flow in the form of cemf, which is related to roc v_g.

$$i_c = C \text{ roc } v_c$$

and roc v_c is related directly to roc v_g, making i_c greatest when roc v_g is at its maximum. For the sine wave, roc v_g varies from a maximum at 0 and 180° to zero at 90 and 270°. The maximum value of roc v_g at 0 and 180° is determined by the repetition frequency of the sine wave. That is, the maximum value of roc v_g is greater at higher frequencies, and the capacitor has less time to build up the cemf, which opposes the current flow. In determining i_c, the size of the capacitor is also an important factor in the magnitude of the cemf. Larger capacitor values result in a smaller cemf and less opposition to the flow of current. Summarizing, the capacitive opposition to current is proportional to $1/f$ and to $1/c$, or $1/(fc)$. To provide a working formula, the proper conversion constant must be provided, as follows.

Frequency is the number of cycles or periods per second, and there are 6.28 rad in one cycle or revolution. Roc v_g might be expressed in terms of either frequency (hertz) or angular velocity (radians per second). Frequency is converted into angular velocity in the following manner:

$$\omega = 2\pi f$$

where ω = angular velocity, rad/s
2π = number of radians in one revolution or cycle
f = number of revolutions per second

Reactance X is the opposition offered to current which dissipates no power. Capacitive reactance X_C is the opposition offered by a capacitor to current which dissipates no power.

Since reactance is an opposition, it is expressed in ohms. Capacitive reactance is determined by

$$X_C = \frac{1}{2\pi fc} = \frac{1}{\omega C} \qquad \text{(14-4)}$$

where X_C = reactance, Ω
2π = 6.28
f = frequency, Hz
C = capacitance, F
ω = angular velocity

In a pure capacitive circuit, the Ohm's law relationships are

$$I = \frac{V}{X_C} \qquad X_C = \frac{V}{I} \qquad V = IX_C$$

This indicates that X_C is an opposition. One of the important differences between resistance and X_C is that the latter does not dissipate any power.

Example 1

A series circuit has a sine wave input of 500-Hz frequency. $C = 4$ μF. Find X_C.

Solution

Substituting in the preceding equation,

$$X_C = \frac{1}{2\pi \times 500 \times 4(10)^{-6}} = 80 \ \Omega$$

Example 2

Find X_C of the capacitor in Example 1 for the following frequencies: (a) 100 Hz; (b) 10,000 Hz.

Solution

(a)   At 100 Hz:

$$X_C = \frac{1}{2\pi \times 100 \times 4(10)^{-6}} = 398 \ \Omega$$

(b)   At 10,000 Hz:

$$X_C = \frac{1}{2\pi \times 10(10)^3 \times 4(10)^{-6}} = 3.98 \ \Omega$$

Note the inverse relationship between frequency and X_C.

14-3   VECTOR RELATIONSHIPS IN A SERIES-*RC* CIRCUIT

In this section you will learn how to represent R and X_C with vectors, determine the circuit phase angle, determine the impedance (Z) of a series-RC circuit by use of vectors, and find the power factor of the circuit.

Figure 14-3 illustrates a series-*RC* circuit with a sine wave input and the vector relationships. Since the current is the same throughout any series circuit, the current is used as the reference vector. The voltage across the resistor is always in phase with the current through it, and its

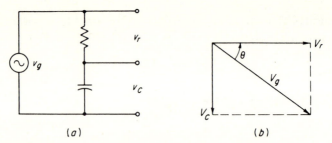

Fig. 14-3 Series-*RC* circuit: (*a*) circuit; (*b*) *V* and *i* vector diagram.

vector coincides with the current vector. The current leads the voltage across the capacitor by 90°, resulting in the V_c vector being drawn 90° behind the V_r vector. The total voltage is equal to the vector sum of V_r and V_c, as shown in Fig. 14-3*b*, and the instantaneous total voltage is equal to v_r and v_c at that same time.

Since the circuit is not purely resistive or capacitive, the phase angle between the source potential and the current is more than 0° but less than 90°. If the total opposition to current flow (impedance) consisted of pure resistance, the source potential and current would be completely in step and the phase angle θ would be 0°. On the other hand, if the total opposition consists of capacitive reactance, the source potential will lag behind the current by 90°. The phase angle θ between the source potential and current, called the *circuit phase angle*, is determined by the V_c/V_r ratio. Figure 14-3*b* shows that this ratio is the tangent function of the phase angle.

$$\tan \theta = \frac{V_c}{V_r} \qquad \textbf{(14-5)}$$

Figure 14-4 is an impedance vector diagram for the series-*RC* circuit. *R* is drawn as the reference vector, inasmuch as it is an opposition which does not, of itself, alter the phase relationship of the current and source voltage. X_C, on the other hand, offers an opposition that, of itself, would

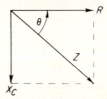

Fig. 14-4 *Z* vector diagram.

cause the current to lead the source voltage by 90°. The impedance is equal to the vector sum of X_C and R. The phase angle between Z and R is equal in magnitude to the circuit phase angle.

Example 1

In the circuit of Fig. 14-5, find: (a) θ; (b) Z; (c) I; (d) V_c; (e) V_r.

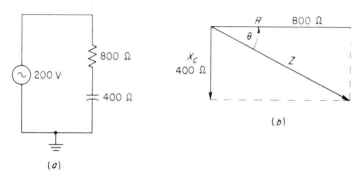

Fig. 14-5 Impedance relationships in a series-*RC* circuit: (*a*) circuit; (*b*) impedance diagram.

Solution

(a) Find θ. Since the Z phase angle is equal in magnitude to the current phase angle, determination of θ in Fig. 14-5*b* will give the circuit phase angle.

$$\tan \theta = \frac{X_C}{R} = \frac{400}{800} = 0.50$$

$$\theta = 26.6°$$

(b) Find Z:

$$\cos \theta = \frac{R}{Z} \quad \text{and} \quad Z = \frac{R}{\cos \theta}$$

$$Z = \frac{800}{\cos 26.6°} = \frac{800}{0.894} = 895 \ \Omega$$

(c) Find I:

$$I = \frac{V}{Z} = \frac{200}{895} = 0.223 \ \text{A}$$

(d) Find V_c:

$$V_c = IX_C = 0.223 \times 400 = 89.2 \text{ V}$$

(e) Find V_r:

$$V_r = IR = 0.223 \times 800 = 178.4 \text{ V}$$

The cosine of the phase angle is an important dimension of circuits which possess both reactance and resistance, because it indicates the extent to which the current is out of phase with the source voltage. This indicates the portion of source power dissipated by R. In the series-RC circuit, $\cos \theta = R/Z$; in a circuit containing no reactance, the cosine ratio is equal to unity, since $R = Z$, allowing power dissipation to be determined by the product of V and I. In a circuit where $R = 0$, but which has some reactance, $R/Z = 0$, and the circuit dissipates no power. Thus the power dissipation of the circuit is directly proportional to cosine θ, which is termed the *power factor* (PF) of the circuit. In any sinusoidal circuit,

$$P = \cos \theta \, EI \qquad\qquad \text{(14-6)}$$

where P = power, W
   $\cos \theta$ = PF as a value between 0 (for a pure reactive circuit) and 1 (for
      a pure resistive circuit)

Example 2

A 400-V 120-Hz source is connected to a series-RC circuit. $R = 20 \text{ k}\Omega$; $C = 0.05 \ \mu\text{F}$. Find: (a) the power factor; (b) power dissipation.

Solution

(a) Find the power factor. The phase angle must be determined first.

$$\tan \theta = \frac{X_C}{R}$$

Finding that $X_C = 1/(\omega C)$,

$$X_C = \frac{1}{2\pi \times 120 \times 5(10)^{-8}} = 26{,}526 \ \Omega$$

Substituting into the tangent relationship,

$$\tan \theta = \frac{26,526}{20(10)^3} = 1.33$$
$$\theta = 53.1°$$
$$\text{PF} = \cos \theta = \cos 53.1° = 0.6$$

(b)   Find the power dissipation. First find Z. Since $\cos \theta = R/Z$,

$$Z = \frac{R}{\cos \theta} = \frac{2(10)^4}{0.6} = 33,333 \ \Omega$$

and I is

$$I = \frac{V}{Z} = \frac{400}{33,333} = 0.012 \text{ A}$$

The power dissipation may now be found.

$$P = VI \cos \theta = 400 \times 0.012 \times 0.6 = 2.88 \text{ W}$$

It should be pointed out that the power factor may be determined in other ways. The method used depends upon the known circuit factors. Example 3 illustrates another technique.

Example 3

In a series-RC circuit, $V_c = 50$ V; $V_r = 35$ V; $Z = 400$ Ω. Find the power factor and power dissipation.

Solution

(a)   Find PF:

$$\tan \theta = \frac{V_c}{V_r} = \frac{50}{35} = 1.43$$
$$\theta = 55°$$
$$\text{PF} = \cos \theta = \cos 55° = 0.574$$

(b)   Find the power dissipation: the total power dissipation occurs in the resistor. The resistance value can be determined from

$$\cos \theta = \frac{R}{Z} \quad \text{and} \quad R = (\cos \theta)Z$$
$$R = 0.574 \times 400 = 230 \ \Omega$$

and

$$P = \frac{(V_r)^2}{R} = \frac{(35)^2}{230} = 5.33 \ \text{W}$$

14-4 WAVEFORM ANALYSIS FOR SEVERAL R/X_C RATIOS

In this section you will learn about the relationships between the ratio R/X_C and v_r and v_c, as well as the circuit phase angle.

Figure 14-6 illustrates the series-RC circuit and the waveforms for several R/X_C ratios. The waveforms do not indicate the phase relationships. Since the current is sinusoidal, all the waveforms are sinusoidal. Consider first the waveforms when the ratio of R/X_C is 1:10.

At this condition, V_r/V_c must be at the same ratio, as determined by Ohm's law.

$$V_r = IR \qquad V_c = IX_c$$

Since I is the same throughout,

$$\frac{V_r}{V_c} = \frac{R}{X_C}$$

The vectors of Fig. 14-7a apply. Here the magnitude of $v_{r,\text{max}}$ and $v_{c,\text{max}}$ may be computed in a simple manner. Since v_r and v_c are always 90° out

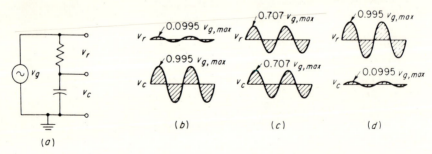

(a)   (b)   (c)   (d)

Fig. 14-6 Waveform relationships in a series-RC circuit: (a) circuit; (b) $R/X_C = 1{:}10$; (c) $R/X_C = 1{:}1$; (d) $R/X_C = 10{:}1$.

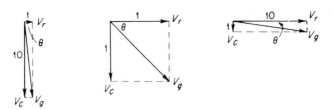

Fig. 14-7   Voltage relationships in a series-*RC* circuit.

of phase and v_g is equal to the hypotenuse of the right triangle formed by their vectors, the Pythagorean theorem may be utilized. This theorem states:

$$\text{Hypotenuse} = [(\text{side } x)^2 + (\text{side } y)^2]^{1/2} \qquad \textbf{(14-7)}$$

Substituting terms from the *RC*-circuit vector diagram.

$$V_g = [(V_r)^2 + (V_c)^2]^{1/2} \qquad \textbf{(14-7a)}$$

When $V_r/V_c = 1:10$,

$$V_g = (1^2 + 10^2)^{1/2} = (101)^{1/2} = 10.05 \text{ V}$$

Expressing V_r and V_c as percentages of V_g,

$$V_r = \frac{V_r}{V_g} \times 100 = \frac{1}{10.05} \times 100 = 9.95\% \text{ of } V_g$$
$$V_c = \frac{V_c}{V_g} \times 100 = \frac{10}{10.05} \times 100 = 99.5\% \text{ of } V_g$$

Note In the preceding equations, 9.95 and 99.5 percent total to 100 percent, since they represent vector rather than scalar quantities.

$$\tan \theta = \frac{V_c}{V_r} = \frac{10}{1} = 10$$
$$\theta = 84.3°$$

When the V_r/V_c ratio is 1:10 or smaller and θ is 84.3° or larger, the circuit is considered capacitive in many practical applications, with the greater portion of the voltage appearing across *C*.

When $V_r/V_c = 1:10$; substituting into the preceding relationship yields

$$V_g = (1^2 + 1^2)^{1/2} = (2)^{1/2} = 1.414$$

Expressing V_r and V_c as percentages of V_g,

$$V_r = \frac{V_r}{V_g} \times 100 = \frac{1}{1.414} \times 100 = 70.7\% \text{ of } V_g$$

$$V_c = \frac{V_c}{V_r} \times 100 = \frac{1}{1.414} \times 100 = 70.7\% \text{ of } V_g$$

$$\tan \theta = \frac{V_c}{V_r} = \frac{1}{1} = 1$$

$$\theta = 45°$$

When the ratio of V_r/V_c is 1:1 and θ is 45°, the circuit is equally resistive and capacitive, with equal voltages appearing across R and C. This ratio may be considered the demarcation point between a circuit which is primarily capacitive or resistive. Section 14-7 reveals other characteristics associated with this important condition.

When $V_r/V_c = 10:1$, substituting into the previous relationship gives

$$V_g = (10^2 + 1^2)^{1/2} = (101)^{1/2} = 10.05 \text{ V}$$

Expressing V_r and V_c as percentages of V_g,

$$V_r = \frac{V_r}{V_g} \times 100 = \frac{10}{10.05} \times 100 = 99.5\% \text{ of } V_g$$

$$V_c = \frac{V_c}{V_g} \times 100 = \frac{1}{10.05} \times 100 = 9.95\% \text{ of } V_g$$

$$\tan \theta = \frac{V_c}{V_r} = \frac{1}{10} = 0.10$$

$$\theta = 5.7°$$

When the ratio of V_r/V_c is 10:1 or greater and θ is 5.7° or less, the circuit may be considered resistive in many practical cases, with the greater portion of the voltage appearing across R.

PROBLEMS

14-1   A source generator has a frequency of 200 Hz. The capacitance varies from 2 to 10 μF in step of 2 μF. Find X_C for each capacitance value.

14-2   The circuit frequency can be varied from 200 to 1000 Hz in steps of 200 Hz. $C = 0.5$ μF. Find X_C for each frequency.

14-3   In a series-RC circuit, $R = 500$ Ω; $C = 3$ μF; $V_g = 240$ V; $f = 120$ Hz. Find the following:

    a) X_C b) θ c) Z
    d) I e) PF   f) power dissipated

14-4 Repeat Prob. 14-3 for $C = 0.4$ μF.

14-5 In a series-RC circuit, $R = 20$ kΩ; $C = 0.0005$ μF; $f = 5000$ Hz; $V_g = 50$ V. Find the following:
a) X_C b) θ c) Z
d) I e) PF f) power dissipated

14-6 In a series-RC circuit, $R = 4$ kΩ; $f = 300$ Hz; PF $= 0.707$. Find:
a) X_C b) C

14-7 In Prob. 14-6, what is the value of θ?

14-8 In Prob. 14-6, what C value must be used to have a PF of 0.4?

14-9 In a series-RC circuit, $V_g = 80$ V, $C = 0.004$ μF, and $f = 700$ Hz. Find the resistance required to obtain the following phase angles:
a) $60°$ b) $25°$ c) $45°$

14-10 In a series-RC circuit, $X_C = 2$ kΩ, $f = 120$ Hz, $V_r = 40$ V, and $\theta = 30°$. Find the following:
a) C b) V_c c) V_g
d) R e) PF f) power dissipation

14-11 In a series-RC circuit, $V_r = 0.9V_g$; $f = 1500$ Hz; $C = 0.005$ μF. Find the following:
a) X_C b) θ
c) R d) PF

14-12 In a series-RC circuit, $R = 4700$ Ω; $f = 10,000$ Hz; $\theta = 6°$. Find the following:
a) X_C b) C c) PF

QUESTIONS

14-1 State the relationship which exists between the capacitance value and X_C.

14-2 State the relationship between frequency and X_C.

14-3 Why does the current lead the generator voltage in a series-RC circuit?

14-4 What effect does the series resistance have on the phase angle between the current and voltage?

14-5 What effect does the series resistance have on the power dissipation in a series-RC circuit?

14-6 What is capacitive reactance?

14-7 Why is it that the presence of capacitive reactance does not increase the power dissipation of a series-RC circuit?

14-8 What is the relationship between angular velocity and frequency?

14-9 What is impedance?

14-10 What factors make up the impedance of a series-RC circuit?

14-11   When θ is less than 45°, what is the relationship between R and X_C?

14-12   When θ is 45°, what is the relationship between R and X_C?

14-13   When θ is greater than 45°, what is the relationship between R and X_C?

14-14   With a fixed R, but a reduction in frequency, how does θ change?

14-15   With a fixed R, but an increase in frequency, how does θ change?

14-5   THE SERIES-*RC* RELATIONSHIP OF FREQUENCY AND POWER DISSIPATION

In this section you will learn how the power factor and power dissipation of a circuit are affected by changes in the value of R or C or both in that circuit.

In an earlier section it was shown that X_C is inversely related to frequency, since, with an increase in the repetition frequency, X_C of a fixed capacitor becomes less, while the resistance essentially remains fixed. The circuit impedance decreases accordingly and approaches the value of the resistance, which plays a more important part as R/Z approaches unity.

The power factor, which is equal to cos θ, also becomes closer to unity, and the power *dissipation* increases. Furthermore, the current increases with frequency up to a point because of the reduced Z, resulting in more heat being developed by the resistor.

Example

Refer to the circuit of Fig. 14-8. Find the power dissipation for the stated frequencies.

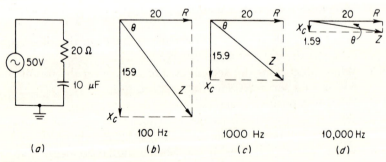

Fig. 14-8 R, X_C, and Z relationships in a series-*RC* circuit: (*a*) circuit; (*b*) 100 Hz; (*c*) 1000 Hz; (*d*) 10,000 Hz.

Solution

(a)   Power dissipation when $f = 100$ Hz:

$$X_C = \frac{1}{2\pi \times 100 \times 10(10)^{-6}} = 159\ \Omega$$

(See Fig. 14-8*b* for the vector illustration.)

$$\tan \theta = \frac{X_C}{R} = \frac{159}{20} = 7.95$$
$$\theta = 82.8°$$
$$\sin \theta = \frac{X_C}{Z} \quad \text{and} \quad Z = \frac{X_C}{\sin \theta}$$
$$Z = \frac{159}{\sin 82.8°} = \frac{159}{0.99} = 160\ \Omega$$
$$I = \frac{V}{Z} = \frac{50}{160} = 0.313\ \text{A}$$
$$P = \cos \theta V I = \cos 82.8° \times 50 \times .313 = 1.961\ \text{W}$$

(b)   Power dissipation when $f = 1000$ Hz:

$$X_C = \frac{1}{2\pi \times 1000 \times 10(10)^{-6}} = 15.9\ \Omega$$

(See Fig. 14-8*c* for the vector illustration.)

$$\tan \theta = \frac{X_C}{R} = \frac{15.9}{20} = 0.795$$
$$\theta = 38.5°$$
$$Z = \frac{15.9}{\sin 38.5°} = \frac{15.9}{0.623} = 25.5\ \Omega$$
$$I = \frac{V}{Z} = \frac{50}{25.5} = 1.961\ \text{A}$$
$$P = \cos \theta V I = \cos 38.5 \times 50 \times 1.961 - 76.7\ \text{W}$$

(c)   Power dissipation when $f = 10$ kHz:

$$X_C = \frac{1}{2\pi \times 10(10)^3 \times 10(10)^{-6}} = 1.59 \ \Omega$$

$$\tan \theta = \frac{X_C}{R} = \frac{1.59}{20} = 0.0795$$

$$\theta = 4.55°$$

$$Z = \frac{X_C}{\sin 4.55°} = \frac{1.59}{0.0793} = 20.1 \ \Omega$$

$$I = \frac{V}{Z} = \frac{50}{20.1} = 2.488 \ \text{A}$$

$$P = \cos 4.55° \times 50 \times 2.488$$
$$= 124.03 \ \text{W}$$

Figure 14-9a depicts the exponential decrease of X_C from a value of infinite Ω at 0 Hz to near 0 Ω at the higher end of the frequency band. Since X_C is a part of the circuit impedance, Z decreases exponentially in the same manner, except that it tapers off to the value of the circuit resistance (see Fig. 14-9b). In accord with Ohm's law, the current increases in an exponential manner from zero at 0 Hz to a maximum value which flows when $Z = R$. This is at the high end of the frequency band when X_C is close enough to zero to be neglected in computations. In part (c) of Example 6, $X_C = 1.59 \ \Omega$. With a frequency of 100,000 Hz, $X_C = 0.159 \ \Omega$. This is less than 10 percent of R and may be omitted from the Z computations in practical cases, since it is too small to affect the magnitude of the impedance to any marked degree. Therefore the impedance is the same at 100,000 Hz as it was at 10,000 Hz. Since V_g is still 50 V, the current and power values are the same as those at 10,000 Hz. Figure 14-9c illustrates this leveling off of the series-RC power dissipation.

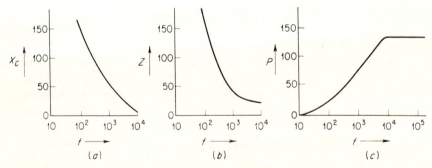

Fig. 14-9 The effect of C on a series-RC circuit with a variable frequency: (a) f versus X_C; (b) f versus Z; (c) f versus p.

14-6   THE EFFECT OF *R* AND *C* ON A SERIES-*RC* CIRCUIT

In this section you will learn about the effect of R on I, Z, and θ; C on I, Z, and θ.

The current magnitude and voltage distribution of a series-*RC* circuit are affected by changes in *R* or *C*.

The Effect of a Variable Resistance with Fixed *f* and *C*

See Fig. 14-10. Let $X_C = 100\ \Omega$; R varies from 1 to $1000\ \Omega$; $V_g = 100$ V. Find θ, Z, I, and PF when R is: (*a*) $1\ \Omega$; (*b*) $50\ \Omega$; (*c*) $100\ \Omega$; (*d*) $500\ \Omega$; (*e*) $1\ k\Omega$.

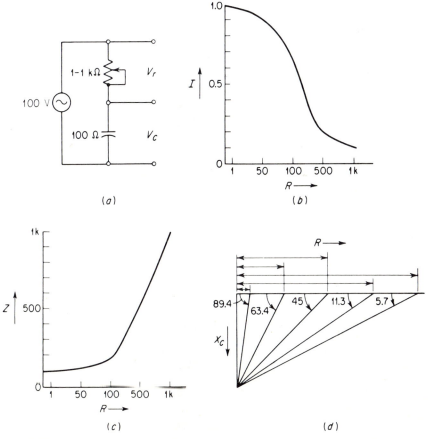

Fig. 14-10   The effect of a variable *R* on *I*, *Z*, and *θ* in a series-*RC* circuit: (*a*) circuit; (*b*) *R* versus *I*; (*c*) *R* versus *Z*; (*d*) *θ* versus *R*.

When $R = 1\ \Omega$,

$$\tan\theta = \frac{X_C}{R} = \frac{100}{1} = 100$$
$$\theta = 89.4°$$
$$Z = \frac{X_C}{\sin 89.4°} = \frac{100}{1.000} = 100\ \Omega$$
$$I = \frac{V}{Z} = \frac{100}{100} = 1.000\ A$$
$$PF = \cos 89.4° = 0.010$$

When $R = 50\ \Omega$,

$$\tan\theta = \frac{X_C}{R} = \frac{100}{50} = 2$$
$$\theta = 63.4°$$
$$Z = \frac{X_C}{\sin\theta} = \frac{100}{0.894} = 112\ \Omega$$
$$I = \frac{V}{Z} = \frac{100}{112} = 0.893\ A$$
$$PF = \cos 63.4° = 0.448$$

When $R = 100\ \Omega$,

$$\tan\theta = \frac{X_C}{R} = \frac{100}{100} = 1$$
$$\theta = 45°$$
$$Z = \frac{X_C}{\sin\theta} = \frac{100}{0.707} = 141\ \Omega$$
$$I = \frac{V}{Z} = \frac{100}{141} = 0.709\ A$$
$$PF = \cos 45° = 0.707$$

When $R = 500\ \Omega$,

$$\tan\theta = \frac{X_C}{R} = \frac{100}{500} = 0.2$$
$$\theta = 11.3°$$
$$Z = \frac{X_C}{\sin\theta} = \frac{100}{0.196} = 510\ \Omega$$
$$I = \frac{V}{Z} = \frac{100}{510} = 0.196\ A$$
$$PF = \cos 11.3° = 0.981$$

When $R = 1000\ \Omega$,

$$\tan \theta = \frac{X_C}{R} = \frac{100}{1000} = 0.1$$
$$\theta = 5.7°$$
$$Z = \frac{X_C}{\sin \theta} = \frac{100}{0.099} = 1010\ \Omega$$
$$I = \frac{V}{Z} = \frac{100}{1010} = 0.099\ \text{A}$$
$$\text{PF} = \cos 5.7° = 0.995$$

Figure 14-10b depicts the R-vs.-I characteristic for the series-RC circuit of Fig. 14-10a and X_C is fixed at 100 Ω. This points out that the current decreases in a nonlinear fashion with increases of resistance. Figure 14-10c illustrates the R-vs.-Z characteristic. With zero resistance, the impedance is equal to X_C. With increases in resistance, the total impedance increases accordingly. The effect of an increasing resistance on θ is shown in Fig. 14-10d.

The magnitudes of V_c and V_r are altered by the change in resistance value. Referring to the circuit of Fig. 14-10a again, calculate the values of V_c and V_r. The following relationships will be utilized for determining V_r and V_c for each resistor value:

$$V_r = \cos \theta\ V_g \tag{14-8}$$

and

$$V_c = \sin \theta\ V_g \tag{14-9}$$

When $R = 1\ \Omega$ and $\theta = 89.4°$ (as computed earlier),

$$V_r = \cos 89.4° \times 100 = 1\ \text{V}$$
$$V_c = \sin 89.4° \times 100 = 100.0\ \text{V}$$

When $R = 50\ \Omega$ and $\theta = 63.4°$,

$$V_r = \cos 63.4° \times 100 = 44.8\ \text{V}$$
$$V_c = \sin 63.4° \times 100 = 89.4\ \text{V}$$

When $R = 100\ \Omega$ and $\theta = 45°$,

$$V_r = \cos 45° \times 100 = 70.7\ \text{V}$$
$$V_c = \sin 45° \times 100 = 70.7\ \text{V}$$

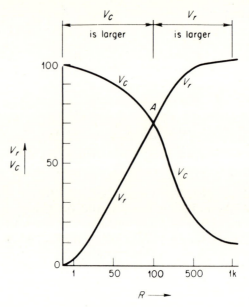

Fig. 14-11   R versus V_r.

When $R = 500\ \Omega$ and $\theta = 11.3°$,

$$V_r = \cos 11.3° \times 100 = 98.1\ \text{V}$$
$$V_c = \sin 11.3° \times 100 = 19.6\ \text{V}$$

When $R = 1\ \text{k}\Omega$ and $\theta = 5.7°$,

$$V_r = \cos 5.7° \times 100 = 99.5\ \text{V}$$
$$V_c = 10\ \text{V} \sin 5.7° \times 100 = 9.9\ \text{V}$$

The computed values of V_r and V_c, and their relationship to the resistance values, are illustrated in Fig. 14-11.

Point A of Fig. 14-11 is the condition where $X_C = R$ and $\theta = 45°$. From the lowest value of R to the condition where $R = X_C$, V_c is greater than V_r. From $R = X_C$ to the largest value of R, V_r is greater than V_c. Figure 14-11 illustrates the effect of a changing resistance upon the voltage distribution of a series-RC circuit.

The Effect of a Variable Capacitance

Consider the circuit of Fig. 14-12. Calculate θ, Z, I, and PF for the following X_C values: (a) 1 Ω; (b) 50 Ω; (c) 100 Ω; (d) 500 Ω; (e) 1 kΩ.

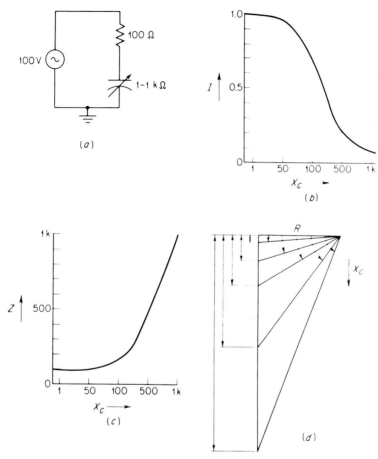

Fig. 14-12   The effect of X_C on I, Z, and θ: (a) circuit; (b) X_C versus I; (c) X_C versus Z; (d) θ versus X_C.

When $X_C = 1\ \Omega$,

$$\tan \theta = \frac{X_C}{R} = \frac{1}{100} = 0.01$$
$$\theta = 0.57°$$
$$Z = \frac{X_C}{\sin \theta} = \frac{1}{0.01} = 100\ \Omega$$
$$I = \frac{V}{Z} = \frac{100}{100} = 1\ A$$
$$PF = \cos \theta = 1.000$$

Using similar computations:
When $X_C = 50\ \Omega$,

$$\theta = 26.6°$$
$$Z = 112\ \Omega$$
$$I = 0.893\ A$$
$$PF = 0.894$$

When $X_C = 100\ \Omega$,

$$\theta = 45°$$
$$Z = 141\ \Omega$$
$$I = 0.709\ A$$
$$PF = 0.707$$

When $X_C = 500\ \Omega$,

$$\theta = 78.7°$$
$$Z = 510\ \Omega$$
$$I = 0.196\ A$$
$$PF = 0.196$$

When $X_C = 1\ k\Omega$,

$$\theta = 84.3°$$
$$Z = 1005\ \Omega$$
$$I = 0.100\ A$$
$$PF = 0.100$$

Figure 14-12b depicts the manner in which an increasing X_C decreases the magnitude of the current. This is due to the effect of X_C upon Z, which is illustrated in Fig. 14-12c. Figure 14-12d illustrates the relationship of θ and an increasing X_C.

As in the case where the resistance was varied, the changing X_C alters the distribution of the circuit voltage. Using Eq. (14-8) for V_r and Eq. (14-9) for V_c, their respective values, with $V_g = 100$ V, are as follows.

When $X_C = 1\ \Omega$ and $\theta = 0.57°$,

$$V_r = 100\ V$$
$$V_c = 1\ V$$

When $X_C = 50\ \Omega$ and $\theta = 26.6°$,

$$V_r = 89.4 \text{ V}$$
$$V_c = 44.8 \text{ V}$$

When $X_C = 100 \ \Omega$ and $\theta = 45°$,

$$V_r = 70.7 \text{ V}$$
$$V_c = 70.7 \text{ V}$$

When $X_C = 500 \ \Omega$ and $\theta = 78.7°$,

$$V_r = 19.6 \text{ V}$$
$$V_c = 98.1 \text{ V}$$

When $X_C = 1 \text{ k}\Omega$ and $\theta = 84.3°$,

$$V_r = 9.9 \text{ V}$$
$$V_c = 99.5 \text{ V}$$

Figure 14-13 illustrates the characteristics of X_C versus V_r and X_C versus V_c. Again note that V_r is greater when R exceeds X_C and V_c is greater when R is smaller than X_C.

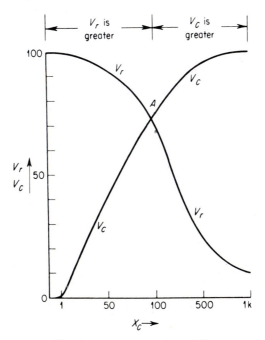

Fig. 14-13 X_C versus V_r and V_c.

14-7 FREQUENCY-DISCRIMINATION CHARACTERISTICS OF A SERIES-*RC* CIRCUIT

In this section you will learn about the relationships between frequency, V_r, and V_c, and the use of series-RC frequency discriminator circuits.

In an earlier discussion on voltage dividers, the following relationship was found to be useful in determining the voltage across one of the series resistors:

$$V_{r_1} = V_o = \frac{R_1}{R} V_i$$

Refer to Fig. 12-14*a*. V_o is some value less than V_i as long as R_2 is greater than 0 Ω. A resistive voltage divider is an attenuator in which the distribution of the voltage hinges on the R_1/R ratio. Since the resistors are not altered in their values by frequency changes, this circuit (Fig. 14-14*a*) may be called a fixed attenuator for the entire range of frequency. It does not "discriminate" against any portion of the frequency range.

Figure 14-14*b* illustrates the series-*RC* circuit with V_o taken off the resistor. At lower frequencies, X_C is greater than the ohmic value of R, resulting in a relatively small V_o. With increases in frequency, X_C decreases and V_o becomes larger. For this reason, this circuit may be called a low-frequency discriminator or high-pass circuit. In many practical cases, the minimum useful V_o is that value which is equal to 0.707 V. At this condition, $\theta = 45°$, $R = X_C$, $V_r = V_c$, and the power dissipated by R is 50 percent of the power delivered by the source (the half-power point). This condition is one method of defining the *frequency cutoff point* f_{co} of the circuit. That is, at frequencies below this value, V_o is less than 0.707

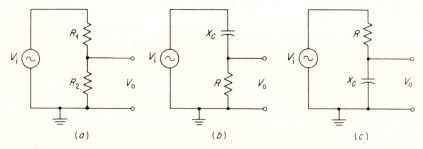

Fig. 14-14 Series-*RC* frequency-discriminator circuit: (*a*) voltage divider or attenuator; (*b*) low-frequency discriminator (high-pass); (*c*) high-frequency discriminator (low-pass).

V_i in the low-frequency discriminator circuit. In considering the high-frequency discriminator (low-pass) circuit, as illustrated in Fig. 14-14c, the f_{co} point is the highest frequency that can be considered and still have $V_o = 0.707\ V$, or greater.

Example 1

In the circuit of Fig. 14-14b, let $R = 50\ k\Omega$; $C = 0.005\ \mu F$; $V_g = 400\ V$. Find: (a) f_{co}; (b) power dissipated at f_{co}; (c) ratio of power dissipated at f_{co} to the power delivered by the source at f when $X_c = 0$; (d) attenuation in decibels at f_{co}.

Solution

(a)   Find f_{co}. Since $X_C = R = 50\ k\Omega$,

$$f = \frac{1}{2\pi C X_C} = \frac{1}{2\pi \times 5(10)^{-9} \times 50(10)^3} = 637\ Hz$$

(b)   Power dissipation at f_{co}:

$$\theta = 45°$$
$$I = \frac{V_r}{R} = \frac{0.707 \times 400}{50(10)^3} = 0.0057\ A$$
$$P = (\cos \theta)(IV_g) = 0.707 \times 400 \times 0.0057 = 1.6\ W$$

(c)   Power ratio of (b) to the power delivered by the source is V_g^2/R.

$$\text{Power delivered} = \frac{(400)^2}{15,000} = 3.2\ W$$
$$\text{Power ratio} = \frac{P\ \text{dissipated}}{P\ \text{delivered}} = \frac{P_o}{P_i} = \frac{1.6}{3.2} = 0.5$$

Therefore this is the half-power condition.

(d)   Attenuation in decibels: from Sec. 13-6, recall that a ratio which is less than unity may be inverted before its logarithm is determined. The addition of a minus sign to the result will indicate that attenuation has occurred.

$$P = 10 \log \frac{P_o}{P_i}$$

Inverting,

$$P = -10 \log \frac{P_i}{P_o} = -10 \log \frac{3.22}{1.61} = -10 \log 2 = -10 \times 0.301$$
$$= -3.01 \text{ dB}$$

At the half-power point, the power output is 3 dB *down from the delivered power value.*

Note Small discrepancies are due to rounding.

Figure 14-15 illustrates the frequency characteristics of the series-*RC* circuit. f_{co} is the demarcation point between the high-frequency end of

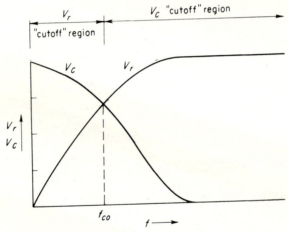

Fig. 14-15 V_r **and** V_c **versus** f **in a series-***RC*** circuit.**

the high-pass circuit (see Fig. 14-14*b*) and the low-frequency end of the low-pass circuit (see Fig. 14-14*c*). The following equations may be utilized in the design and evaluation of an *RC*-discriminator circuit:

$$V_r = V_i \frac{R}{Z} \qquad (14\text{-}10)$$

$$V_c = V_i \frac{X_C}{Z} \qquad (14\text{-}11)$$

$$\tan \theta = \frac{X_C}{R}$$

f_{co} occurs when $\tan \theta = 1$ (where $X_C = R$).

Example 2

A high-pass *RC* circuit is to be designed with $C = 10 \ \mu$F, such that $f_{co} = 100$ Hz. Find the required resistance.

Solution

$$X_C = \frac{1}{2\pi \times 100 \times 10(10)^{-6}} = 159 \ \Omega$$

Since $X_C = R$ at f_{co},

$$X_C = R = 159 \ \Omega$$

is required for f_{co} to be 100 Hz.

Example 3

A low-pass *RC* circuit is to be designed such that f_{co} at the lower end is 500 Hz. $R = 150$ kΩ. Find the required capacitance.

Solution

Since $X_C = R$ at f_{co},

$$X_C = R = 150 \text{ k}\Omega \qquad \text{at 500 Hz}$$
$$C = \frac{1}{2\pi \times 500 \times 150(10)^3} = 0.00212 \ \mu\text{F}$$

14-8   *RC* AS A COUPLING TECHNIQUE

In this section you will learn how a series-RC circuit can be used to couple a signal of sinusoidal variations from one unit to another while blocking the dc component of the first unit from entering the second unit.

The series-*RC* circuit is frequently used to deliver a bidirectional signal from one unit (such as an amplifier) to another. This is called *coupling*. Figure 14-16 illustrates the manner in which this can be done in some cases. Notice that the input voltage for unit 2 is taken off *R*, which is actually the low-frequency discriminator (high-pass) attenuator

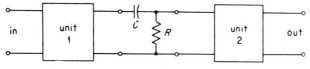

Fig. 14-16   *RC* coupling (block diagram).

discussed in Sec. 14-7. X_C is inversely related to the signal frequency being coupled. Therefore it is important that the R and C values be selected to ensure an f_{co} not greater than the lowest frequency to be coupled. This is one of the disadvantages associated with the RC coupling technique. Another drawback is that V_o varies directly with frequency increases up to that frequency which reduces X_C to less than 10 percent of the R value (see Fig. 14-15). The phase shift of V_r and V_i may or may not be desirable, depending upon the application.

These disadvantages may be minimized in a great many cases by careful design. In those instances where the RC technique cannot be used to advantage, an attenuator pad or another type of coupling may be incorporated. Consider several typical RC coupling problems and determine the manner in which they may be solved.

Example 1

Two units are to be coupled by the RC technique. For impedance-matching reasons, R must be 2 kΩ. The signal-frequency range is 50 to 10,000 Hz. Find the required capacitance.

Solution

Since the RC coupling functions as a low-frequency discriminator, attention should be focused on the low end of the signal-frequency range. Assuming that a loss of up to 3 dB and a phase-shift characteristic no greater than 45° are permissible, let $f_{co} = 50$ Hz. When $f_{co} = 50$ Hz, $X_c = R = 2$ kΩ at 50 Hz. Solving for C gives

$$C = \frac{1}{2\pi \times 50 \times 2000} = 1.59 \ \mu\text{F}$$

Example 2

Two units are to be coupled by the RC technique. R must be 75 kΩ. The signal-frequency range is 40 Hz to 50 MHz. There is to be less than 5° phase shift between V_o and V_i. Find the required capacitance.

Solution

In order to maintain a phase shift of 5° or less between V_o and V_i, the value of R must be more than 10 times larger than the largest value of X_C. When $\theta = 5°$, $\tan \theta = 0.087$. Since $\tan \theta = X_C/R$,

$$\frac{X_C}{R} = 0.087$$

Substituting and transposing,
$$X_C = 0.087 \times 75(10)^3 = 6525 \ \Omega$$

at its *maximum* value, which occurs at the *lowest* frequency (40 Hz). Solving for C yields

$$C = \frac{1}{2\pi \times 6525 \times 40} = 0.61 \ \mu\text{F}$$

Note The use of a smaller resistance value would have made it possible to use a larger capacitor and vice versa.

Example 3

Two units are to be coupled by the RC technique. R must be 25 kΩ. The signal-frequency range is 100 kHz to 1 MHz. The phase shift is to be at least 85° for all signal conditions. Find the required capacitance.

Solution

In order to maintain such a large phase shift, X_C must be more than 10 times the value of R at all frequencies. When $\theta = 85°$, $\tan \theta = 11.43$.

$$X_C = (\tan \theta) \ R$$

Substituting values,

$$X_C = 11.43 \times 25(10)^3 = 285.8 \ \text{k}\Omega$$

as a *minimum*, which occurs at the highest frequency. Hence,

$$X_C = 285.8 \ \text{k}\Omega$$

when $f = 1$ MHz. Solving for C,

$$C = \frac{1}{2\pi \times 1(10)^6 \times 285.8(10^3)} = 0.557 \ \text{pF}$$

Note The use of a smaller resistor would permit the use of a larger capacitor and vice versa.

Now examine a circuit condition where the impedance-matching considerations enter directly into the selection of R and C.

Example 4

Unit 1 $Z_o = 50$ kΩ. Unit 2 $Z_i = 100$ kΩ. The signal-frequency range is from 60 to 5000 Hz. RC coupling is to be used. Z_i of unit 2, as seen by unit 1, should be no greater than 60 kΩ. Find: (a) required resistance to meet the impedance-matching requirements; (b) required capacitance so that $f_{co} = 60$ Hz.

Solution

(a)   Find R. Since the capacitor to be selected will be so large that its reactance is small for the signal-frequency range, unit 1 will not see its X_C for all practical purposes. The equivalent circuit, as seen from the output terminals of unit 1, is as illustrated in Fig. 14-17a.

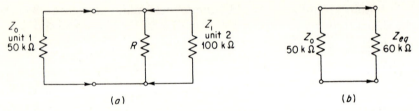

(a)   (b)

Fig. 14-17   RC coupling (equivalent circuits): (a) equivalent of RC coupling as seen by the input unit; (b) impedance seen by the input unit.

The output terminals of unit 1 will see the equivalent impedance consisting of R and the input impedance of unit 2 in parallel as shown in Fig. 14-17b. Therefore R must be selected so that Z is 60 kΩ. Since

$$Z = \frac{RZ_o}{R + Z_o}$$

then

$$R = \frac{Z_o Z}{Z_o - Z}$$

Substituting values,

$$R = \frac{1(10)^5 \times 60(10)^3}{100(10)^3 - 60(10)^3} = 150 \text{ k}\Omega$$

(b)   Find C so that $f_{co} = 60$ Hz. At 60 Hz, $X_c = Z = 60$ kΩ. Solving for C,

$$C = \frac{1}{2\pi \times 60 \times 60(10)^3} = 0.044 \ \mu F$$

The preceding examples show that the RC coupling technique can be utilized in the coupling of very low- and high-frequency signals in many cases and that impedance matching can be achieved to some extent. It should be pointed out, however, that when the input and output impedances are substantially dissimilar, RC coupling may not serve the purpose. In such cases, other types of coupling are utilized. This type of coupling also can satisfactorily handle f_{co} and phase-shift considerations in many instances, as illustrated in the examples.

PROBLEMS

14-13 The following are parameters of a series-RC circuit:
$V_g = 120$ V; $R = 800 \ \Omega$; $C = 2 \ \mu F$. Find Z at:
a) 10 Hz   b) 50 Hz   c) 2500 Hz

14-14 Repeat Prob. 14-13 if $R = 30$ kΩ; $C = 0.04 \ \mu F$, and $V_g = 150$ V.

14-15 In Prob. 14-13, find I for the stated frequencies.

14-16 In Prob. 14-13, find the power dissipation for the stated frequencies.

14-17 Find I for the conditions of Prob. 14-14 at the stated frequencies.

14-18 Find the power dissipation for the conditions of Prob. 14-14.

14-19 In a series-RC circuit, $X_C = 500 \ \Omega$; $V_g = 250$ V. Find θ, Z, and I for the following values of R:
a) 50 Ω b) 500 Ω c) 5 kΩ

14-20 Refer to Prob. 14-19. Find V_r and V_c for each R value.

14-21 Refer to Prob. 14-19. Find C for $f = 60$ Hz.

14-22 In a series-RC circuit, $R = 2400 \ \Omega$; $V_g = 90$ V. Find θ, Z, and I for the following X_C values:
a) 240Ω b) 2400Ω c) 24,000Ω

14-23 Refer to Prob. 14-22. Find V_r and V_c for each value of X_C.

14-24 Refer to Prob. 14-22. $F = 100$ Hz. Find C for each X_C value.

14-25 The parameters of an RC circuit are $R = 100$ kΩ and $V_g = 200$ V. Find the required C for the attenuation to be 3 dB at 100 Hz.

14-26 $C = 0.05 \ \mu F$; $f_{co} = 50$ Hz. What is the required R if this is to be a low-frequency discriminator?

14-27 In a low-frequency discriminator circuit, $R = 15$ kΩ; $X_C = 50$ kΩ at 20 Hz; $V_g = 90$ V. Find:
a) f_{co}
b) I at f_{co}
c) P dissipation at f_{co}
d) P delivered at the frequency $f > 10 f_{co}$; $X_C < R/10$.

14-28   Two amplifiers are RC-coupled: $C = 0.02$ μF; signal-frequency range is 60 to 5000 Hz. Find the resistance.

14-29   In Prob. 14-28, find the required R if the low end of the frequency range is:
a)   20 Hz   b)   100 Hz

14-30   Two units are RC-coupled. The signal-frequency range is 550 Hz to 1500 kHz. $R = 25$ kΩ. Find C.

14-31   Two units are RC-coupled. Signal-frequency range is 550 Hz to 1500 kHz; $C = 0.5$ μF. Find R.

14-32   Two units are RC-coupled. $R = 250$ kΩ; signal-frequency range is 50 Hz to 100 kHz; the phase shift is to be at least 85° for all signal conditions. Find C.

14-33   Two units are RC-coupled. $R = 180$ kΩ; signal-frequency range is 450 Hz to 460 kHz; the phase shift is to be less than 5° for all signal conditions. Find C.

14-34   Two units are RC-coupled. Unit 1 $Z_o = 20$ kΩ; unit 2 $Z_i = 32$ kΩ; frequency range is 20 to 15,000 Hz. Find the following:
a)   resistance so that unit 1 sees 22 kΩ
b) C so that $f_{co} = 20$ Hz

14-35   Two units are RC-coupled. Unit 1 $Z_o = 4$ kΩ; unit 2 $Z_i = 12$ kΩ; frequency range is 550 to 1550 kHz. Find:
a)   resistance so that unit 1 sees 6 kΩ
b)   capacitance so that $f_{co} = 550$ kHz

QUESTIONS

Note   All questions below pertain to series-RC circuits.

14-16   Under what condition does the power factor approach unity?

14-17   What is the relationship between the power factor and power dissipation?

14-18   What is the relationship between the phase angle and power dissipation of the circuit?

14-19   What is the relationship between X_C and frequency?

14-20   What is the relationship between frequency and impedance?

14-21   What is the relationship between frequency and power dissipation?

14-22   What is the relationship between R and the power factor?

14-23   What is the relationship between C and the power factor?

14-24   What is the relationship between circuit phase angle and frequency?

14-25   What is the relationship between R and current?

14-26   What is the relationship between C and current?

14-27   What is the relationship between R and Z?

14-28   What is the relationship between C and Z?

14-29   What is the relationship between R and circuit phase angle?

14-30   What is the relationship between C and circuit phase angle?

14-31   How does R affect the power factor?

14-32   How does C affect the power factor?

14-33   In a low-frequency discriminator, what is frequency cutoff?

14-34   How does V_r vary with frequency?

14-35   How does V_c vary with frequency?

14-36   When is V_r equal to -3 dB?

14-37   Why is a series-RC circuit a frequency-discriminator circuit?

14-38   How can a series-RC circuit be used as a coupling device between two circuits?

14-39   Where does V_o have to be taken in a series-RC circuit for it to be a low-frequency discriminator?

14-40   Where does V_o have to be taken for it to be a high-frequency discriminator?

14-41   If V_o is V_r, what provisions must be made to make the phase shift of the circuit phase angle less than 5° for all signal conditions?

14-42   If V_o is V_r, what provisions must be made to ensure that the phase shift of the circuit phase angle is at least 85° for all signal conditions?

14-43   What is the relationship between R and X_C at the condition of -3 dB when V_r is V_o?

14-44   When V_r is V_o, is this a high-pass or a low-pass circuit?

14-9   BEHAVIOR OF A PURE INDUCTIVE CIRCUIT

In this section you will learn how a pure inductance reacts to the continuous changes of a sinusoidal voltage.

An inductor alternately stores electromagnetic energy during the time the current rises and discharges electromagnetic energy when the current decreases. This results in the power waveform completing a half-cycle for each quarter-cycle of the current. With negligible resistance present in the circuit, there will be virtually no heat dissipation. In such a circuit, all the electromagnetic energy stored during the current-rise time is returned to the source during the following current quarter-cycle, when it is decreasing. The power waveform is included in Fig. 14-18b.

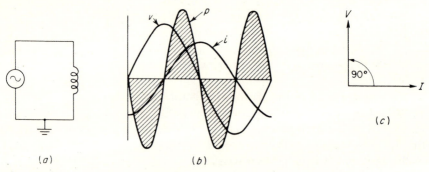

Fig. 14-18   Pure inductive circuit considerations: (a) circuit; (b) waveforms; (c) vector relationships.

In Chap. 10, in an analysis of inductance when subjected to a constant unidirectional source voltage, the following relationship was discussed:

$$V = iR + L\frac{di}{dt}$$

If the circuit resistance is negligible and the generator voltage is sinusoidal, this relationship becomes

$$v = V_{max} \sin \theta = L\frac{di}{dt} \tag{14-12}$$

The instantaneous current in such a circuit may be found by the following equation:

$$i = \frac{V_{max}}{2\pi f L} \sin(\theta - 90°) \tag{14-13}$$

The induced voltage, it will be recalled, is the reaction of the inductor against *changes* in current (roc i). Since $R = 0\ \Omega$, the tc $= L/R =$ infinitely long, so the induced voltage is always present. The voltage is maximum at 90 and 270°. Roc i is maximum at 0 and 180°; i.e., when the voltage is at 90°, the current is at 0°, and when v is at 270°, i is at 180°. This analysis brings out the fact that the *current lags behind the voltage by 90° in a pure inductive circuit with a sinusoidal waveform.*

The v, i, and p waveforms are illustrated in Fig. 14-18b. Notice that the power repetition frequency is twice that of the input voltage and that all waveforms are sinusoidal. The vector relationship between v and i is illustrated in Fig. 14-18c.

14-10 INDUCTIVE REACTANCE

In this section you will learn about the nature of inductive reactance and how it is computed.

The inductor offers opposition to the *changes* in current. With a sinusoidal input, the current is continuously changing in a nonlinear manner for the entire cycle. Roc v_g is directly proportional to the repetition frequency of the voltage. Since $2\pi f = \omega$, roc v_g is determined by the angular velocity of the generator potential. Also, as was pointed out in Chap. 10, larger values of inductors produce greater induced voltages for a given roc v_g. These facts lead to the following important statement:

The reactance of an inductor, called inductive reactance X_L, is directly proportional to the angular velocity and the inductance.

In a pure inductive circuit,

$$I_{max} = \frac{V_{max}}{2\pi f L} = \frac{V_{max}}{\omega L}$$

and

$$\omega L = \frac{V_{max}}{I_{max}} \quad \Omega$$

This results in the inductive-reactance equation

$$X_L = 2\pi f L = \omega L \qquad \text{(14-14)}$$

where X_L = inductive reactance, Ω
f = frequency, Hz
ω = angular velocity, rad/s
L = inductance, H

Example

A 0.4-H inductor is connected across a 220-V 60-Hz source. Find: (*a*) inductive reactance; (*b*) current.

Solution

(*a*) Find the inductive reactance:

$$X_L = 2\pi f L = 2\pi \times 60 \times 0.4 = 151 \ \Omega$$

(*b*)   Find the current:

$$I = \frac{V}{X_L} = \frac{220}{151} = 1.457 \text{ A}$$

14-11   VECTOR RELATIONSHIPS IN A SERIES-*RL* CIRCUIT

In this section you will learn about the phase relationship between V$_r$, V$_l$, and V$_g$ and the power factor.

With a sinusoidal input voltage, all voltages and the current will be sinusoidal. The following analysis rests on the assumption that the inductor itself has negligible resistance and may be considered pure. As it is a series arrangement, the current is the same throughout the circuit. The current and voltage-drop of the resistor are in phase. The inductive voltage is 90° ahead of the current, as established in Sec. 14-9. The vector sum of the inductive and resistive voltages is equal to the source voltage. The phase angle θ taken by the source voltage with respect to the current hinges on the ratio of V_L/V_R. These facts are illustrated in Fig. 14-19*b*.

The inductive reactance opposes the current in such a way that it causes the current to lag the source voltage; therefore its vector is drawn 90° ahead of the resistance vector. The magnitude of the impedance hinges on the *ratio* of X_L to R, as shown in Fig. 14-19*c*. In terms of basic circuit laws, X_L/R actually determines V_L/V_R, and these ratios are equal. The circuit phase angle must be less than 90° (pure inductive circuit) and more than 0° (pure resistive circuit).

As in the series-*RC* circuit, the cosine of the phase angle indicates how

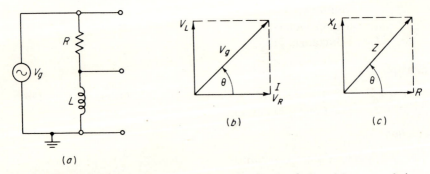

(*a*)

(*b*)

(*c*)

Fig. 14-19   Series-*RL* circuit considerations: (*a*) circuit; (*b*) *V* and *I* vector relationships; (*c*) impedance relationships.

far apart the current and source voltage are in terms of phase and also what portion of the impedance consists of resistance (cos $\theta = R/Z$), which develops the power dissipation of the circuit. Therefore the power factor is also utilized in determining the power dissipation of a series-RL circuit.

$$P = (\cos \theta)(VI)$$

Example

A series-RL circuit has the following parameters: $R = 5$ kΩ; $L = 0.25$ H; $f = 10,000$ Hz; $V_g = 80$ V. Find: (a) X_L; (b) θ; (c) Z; (d) I; (e) PF; (f) power dissipation.

Solution

(a)   Find X_L:

$$X_L = 2\pi \times 10(10)^3 \times 0.25 = 15.7 \text{ k}\Omega$$

(b)   Find θ:

$$\tan \theta = \frac{X_L}{R} = \frac{15.7(10)^3}{5(10)^3} = 3.14$$
$$\theta = 72.3°$$

(c)   Find Z:

$$Z = \frac{X_L}{\sin 72.3°} = \frac{15.7(10)^3}{0.953} = 16.47 \text{ k}\Omega$$

(d)   Find I:

$$I = \frac{V}{Z} = \frac{80}{16.47(10)^3} = 4.86 \text{ mA}$$

(e)   Find PF:

$$\text{PF} = \cos 72.3° = 0.304$$

(f)   Find the power dissipation:

$$P = (\cos \theta)(VI) = 0.304 \times 80 \times 4.86(10)^{-3} = 118 \text{ mW}$$

14-12 IMPERFECT COILS: COIL Q

In this section you will learn about: the figure of merit of a coil, the effect of a coil's resistance on the phase relationships in the circuit, and how to determine the inductance of an imperfect coil.

Up to this point in the analysis of inductors in this chapter, only perfect coils were considered. In actual practice, however, the resistance of the inductor windings may have to be taken into consideration. This is especially true in cases where the coil is used in low-frequency circuits. One criterion for determining the quality of a coil is the ratio of its reactance to its resistance, which is called the *figure of merit*, or Q, of the inductor. In equation form,

$$Q = \frac{X_L}{R} = \text{figure of merit} = \frac{\text{energy stored}}{\text{energy dissipated}} \qquad \textbf{(14-15)}$$

where R represents all dissipative losses within the coil.

An imperfect coil may be illustrated as a perfect inductor in series with a resistance equal to that of its winding; all other dissipation losses are within the coil, which is a series-RL circuit. In using this approach, the techniques for analyzing the imperfect coil across a source voltage are the same as those for the series-RL circuit. Notice that the coil Q is equal to the tangent of the phase angle. Larger Q values indicate that the reactance of the coil is large compared with its resistance. In many practical circuits, an inductor with a Q of 20 or greater is considered a perfect coil, since the resistance is small enough to be considered negligible. Notice that the angle (between V_t and I) of a coil with a Q of 20 is slightly greater than 87.1°. For all practical purposes, this may be considered 90° with no substantial error in circuit calculations. The Q of a given coil varies directly with the repetition frequency, since X_L varies in such a manner. (Practically, losses also increase with frequency but not at the same rate as X_L for most frequencies.)

Example 1

An 0.08-H coil has a resistance of 20 Ω. Find its Q at the following frequencies: (*a*) 60 Hz; (*b*) 300 Hz; (*c*) 800 Hz.

Solution

(*a*)   At 60 Hz:

$$Q = \frac{2\pi fL}{R} = \frac{2\pi \times 60 \times 0.08}{20} = 1.51$$

(*b*)   At 200 Hz:

$$Q = \frac{2\pi \times 200 \times 0.08}{20} = 5.03$$

(*c*)   At 800 Hz:

$$Q = \frac{2\pi \times 800 \times 0.08}{20} = 20.1$$

Note For frequencies greater than 800 Hz, the 0.08-H inductor is considered perfect in many practical applications.

A series-*RL* circuit may consist of an imperfect coil in series with a resistance. The following example describes a method which may be used in analyzing such a problem.

Example 2

Refer to Fig. 14-20. $L = 0.06$ H; $R = 30\ \Omega$; $R_L = 10\ \Omega$; $V_g = 120$ V (60 Hz). Find: (*a*) X_L; (*b*) α; (*c*) Z_L; (*d*) Z; (*e*) θ; (*f*) I.

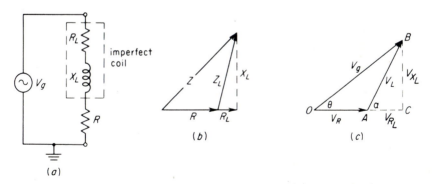

Fig. 14–20   The effect of an imperfect coil: (*a*) circuit; (*b*) impedance diagram; (*c*) voltage diagram.

Solution

(*a*)   Find X_L:

$$X_L = 2\pi \times 60 \times 0.06 = 22.6\ \Omega$$

(b)   Find α, the phase angle of Z_L in the problem.

$$\tan \alpha = \frac{X_L}{R_L} = \frac{22.6}{10} = 2.26$$
$$\alpha = 66.1°$$

(c)   Find Z_L:

$$Z_L = \frac{X_L}{\sin 66.13°} = \frac{22.6}{0.914} = 24.7 \ \Omega$$

(d)   Find Z (refer to Fig. 14-20b). Z is equal to the vector sum (resultant) of R and Z_L. Z can be determined by the law of cosines, which is as follows for this application:

$$Z^2 = (Z_L)^2 + R^2 + 2RZ_L \cos \alpha$$

Substituting values,

$$Z^2 = 24.7^2 + 30^2 + (2 \times 30 \times 24.7 \times \cos 66.1°) = 2110$$

and

$$Z = (2110)^{1/2} = 46 \ \Omega$$

(e)   Find θ (refer to Fig. 14-20b): θ may be found by the law of sines, which for this application is:

$$\frac{\sin \theta}{Z_L} = \frac{\sin (180° - \alpha)}{Z}$$

and

$$\sin \theta = \frac{Z_L \sin (180° - 66.1°)}{Z} = \frac{24.7 \times 0.914}{46}$$

and

$$\sin \theta = 0.491$$
$$\theta = 29.4°$$

(*f*) Find *I*:

$$I = \frac{V}{Z} = \frac{120}{46} = 2.609 \text{ A}$$

The inductance of an imperfect coil is determined in Example 3.

Example 3

The voltage across an imperfect coil is 150 V, and across the series resistor is 100 V; $V_g = 222$ V (60 Hz); $R_L = 50 \ \Omega$. Find the inductance of the coil.

Solution

Using the law of cosines, find angle α:

$$\cos \alpha = \frac{(V_g)^2 - (V_L)^2 - (V_R)^2}{(2)(V_L)(V_R)}$$

Substituting values,

$$\cos \alpha = \frac{(222)^2 - (150)^2 - (100)^2}{(2)(150)(100)} = 0.559$$
$$\alpha = 56°$$

Now find V_{X_L} and V_{R_L} (see triangle *ABC* of Fig. 14-20c):

$$V_{X_L} = (\sin \alpha)(V_L) = 0.829 \times 150 = 124 \text{ V}$$
$$V_{R_L} = (\cos \alpha)(V_L) = 0.559 \times 150 = 84 \text{ V}$$

Since the ratio of these two voltages is equal to the ratio of X_L/R, now it is easy to solve for X_L.

$$\frac{V_{X_L}}{V_{R_L}} = \frac{X_L}{R_L} \quad \text{and} \quad X_L = \frac{V_{X_L} R_L}{V_{R_L}}$$

$$X_L = \frac{124 \times 50}{84} = 73.8 \ \Omega$$

Solving for *L*,

$$L = \frac{X_L}{2\pi f} = \frac{73.8}{2\pi \times 60} = 196 \text{ mH}$$

It should be noticed that the use of vectors made it possible to arrive at solutions in Examples 2 and 3. In Example 2, the impedance of the coil was determined by using the $y(X_L)$ and $x(R_L)$ components of the coil impedance. The coil impedance was then vectorially added to the series resistance, and the total impedance was found by the law of cosines and the circuit phase angle by the law of sines.

Example 3 is a practical problem, in that the inductance of a coil under a particular circuit condition is to be determined. The phase angle of the coil impedance may be found by the law of cosines. Since this phase angle α is known, the $y(X_L)$ voltage component and $x(R_L)$ voltage component can be determined. Equating the ratio of these two voltages to X_L/R makes it possible to find X_L. Since the source voltage frequency and X_L are known, the inductance is readily determined.

14-13 WAVEFORM ANALYSIS FOR SEVERAL R/X_L RATIOS

In this section you will learn about the effect of the R/X_L ratio upon both the magnitude of v_r and v_l, and the impedance characteristic of the series-RL circuit.

The circuit and waveforms for several R/X_L ratios are illustrated in Fig. 14-21. Notice the similarity between these waveforms and those of Fig. 14-18. All waveforms are sinusoidal, since the current is sinusoidal. The determination of the correct R/X_L ratio ensures an output voltage (whether it is v_r or v_l) of the desired magnitude.

The following general statements apply to the circuit of Fig. 14-21a in most practical cases:

1   When $R/X_L = 1{:}10$, $\theta = 84.3°$, and the circuit may be considered inductive.

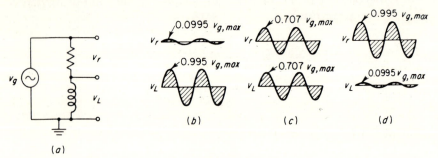

Fig. 14-21   **The effect of the R/X_L ratio on waveforms: (*a*) circuit; (*b*) $R/X_L = 1{:}10$; (*c*) $R/X_L = 1/1$; (*d*) $R/X_L = 10{:}1$.**

2   When $R/X_L = 1:1$, $\theta = 45°$, and the circuit is equally resistive and inductive.

3   When $R/X_L = 10:1$, $\theta = 5.7°$, and the circuit may be considered resistive.

PROBLEMS

14-36   A pure inductance of 10 H is across a 220-V (60-Hz) source. Find the instantaneous current at:
a)   10°   b)   25°   c)   60°
d)   130°   e)   200°

14-37   An inductor of 0.42 H is across a 50-V, variable-frequency source. Find X_L at the following frequencies:
a)   50 Hz   b)   100 Hz   c)   500 Hz
d)   1 kHz   e)   5 kHz

14-38   In Prob. 14-37, find I_{max} for each frequency.

14-39   A series-RL circuit has the following values: $R = 2500 \ \Omega$; $L = 0.10$ H; $V_g = 60$ V (8000 Hz). Find:
a) X_L b) θ c)   Z
d) I e)   PF   f)   power dissipation

14-40   Repeat Prob. 14-39 for a frequency of 500 Hz.

14-41   Assume that the inductor of 0.42 H possesses 180 Ω of resistance. Find:

a) Q values for 50 Hz, 500 Hz, 5 kHz
b)   lowest frequency at which the coil may be considered perfect

14-42   A 3-H inductor has $R_L = 150 \ \Omega$ and $f = 60$ Hz. Find X_L and Q.

14-43   Refer to Fig. 14-20. $L = 0.03$ H; $R = 25 \ \Omega$; $R_L = 12 \ \Omega$; $V_g = 120$ V (60 Hz). Find:
a) X_L b) α c) Z_L
d) Z e) θ f) I

14-44   Refer to Fig. 14-20. $V_L = 50$ V; V_R (series resistor) $= 33$ V; $V_g = 74$ V (120 Hz); $R_L = 20 \ \Omega$. Find the inductance of the coil.

14-14   RELATIONSHIP OF FREQUENCY AND POWER DISSIPATION IN A SERIES-RL CIRCUIT

In this section you will learn that while inductive reactance and impedance increase with frequency, current and power dissipation decrease with frequency increases.

The circuit Z is linear when $Z \geq 10R/(2\pi L)$ and when $f \leq R/(2\pi L \times 10)$. Z is not linear at other times. From this one can deduce that I decreases with increases in f in a nonlinear manner when f exceeds $R(2\pi L \times 10)$ until f exceeds $10R/2\pi L$). Since power is directly related to I, it also decreases in a nonlinear manner with increases in f.

14-15 EFFECT OF VARIABLES R AND L IN A SERIES-*RL* CIRCUIT

In this section you will learn about the changes in V_r and V_l that result from varying R or L.

Variable *R*, Fixed *L*, and Constant Frequency

With a fixed inductor, frequency, and source voltage, the effect of a variable resistance upon the circuit current is as follows: the circuit Z is linear with R when $R \geq 10X_L$, and Z is about constant when $R \leq 0.1X_L$. In the interval $0.1X_L \leq R \leq 10X_L$, Z is not linear with R. Circuit I is also not linear in that interval. V_r and V_l are not linear during that interval.

Variable *L*, Fixed *R*, and Constant Frequency

From Fig 14-19, $Z = \sqrt{R^2 + (2\pi fL)^2}$. When L is varied, keeping R and f fixed, Z is linear for $L \geq 10R/(2\pi f)$ $(X_L \geq 10R)$ and is approximately a constant when $L \leq 0.1R/(2\pi f)$ $(X_L \leq R/10)$. In the interval

$$\frac{0.1R}{2\pi f} \leq L \leq \frac{10R}{2\pi f} \quad \left(\frac{R}{10} \leq X_L \leq 10R\right)$$

Z is not linear with changes in L.

14-16 FREQUENCY-DISCRIMINATION CHARACTERISTICS OF A SERIES-*RL* CIRCUIT

In this section you will learn that the series-RL circuit can be utilized as a low-frequency discriminator by taking the output off of L, or a high-frequency discriminator by taking the output off of R.

Refer to Fig. 14-22. The following equations are useful in the design and evaluation of *RL* frequency-discriminator circuits:

$$V_r = V_i \frac{R}{Z} \qquad \text{(14-16)}$$

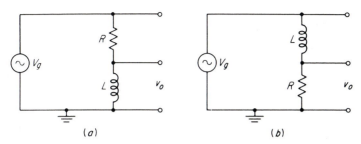

Fig. 14-22 Series-*RL* frequency-discriminator circuit: (*a*) low-frequency discriminator (high-pass); (*b*) high-frequency discriminator (low-pass).

$$V_l = V_i \frac{X_L}{Z}$$ (14-17)

$$\tan \theta = \frac{X_L}{R}$$

Since X_L increases with frequency, V_{X_L} is lowest at the low frequency and approaches V_g at the frequencies where X_L is at least 10 times greater than R. Here f_{co}, as in the RC discriminator, is defined as that frequency where $V_r = V_l$.

In a series-*RL* frequency-discriminator circuit, the low-frequency discriminator utilizes V_l as V_o, and V_r is V_o for the high-frequency discriminator.

The selection of parameters in the design of a particular frequency-discriminator circuit is somewhat similar to the procedures used in the RC discriminator.

Example

A series-*RL* low-frequency discriminator is to be used. $R = 5$ kΩ; the signal frequency varies from 50 to 5000 Hz. Find the inductance in order to have $f_{co} = 50$ Hz.

Solution

$$X_L = R = 5 \text{ k}\Omega \qquad \text{at } f_{co} \text{ (50 Hz)}$$

Solving for L,

$$L = \frac{X_L}{2\pi f_{co}} = \frac{5000}{6.28 \times 50} = 15.9 \text{ H}$$

PROBLEMS

14-45   The parameters of a series-RL circuit are $R = 270 \ \Omega$; $L = 0.2$
       H; $V_g = 60$ V; $f = 100$ Hz. Find:
       a) X_L b) θ c) Z
       d) I e) power dissipation

14-46   Find V_r and V_l of Prob. 14-45.

14-47   A series-RL circuit is to be used as a high-frequency discrimi-
       nator. $f_{co} = 800$ Hz; $R = 720 \ \Omega$. Find the required L.

14-48   A series-RL circuit is to be used as a high-frequency discrimi-
       nator. $f_{co} = 2000$ Hz; $L = 2$ H. Find the required R.

14-49   A series-RL circuit is to be used as a low-frequency discrimi-
       nator. $f_{co} = 20$ Hz; $L = 10$ H. Find R.

14-50   A series-RL circuit is to be used as a low-frequency discrimi-
       nator. $f_{co} = 150$ Hz; $R = 2400 \ \Omega$. Find the required L.

QUESTIONS

Note   The following questions relate to inductive and series-RL circuits.

14-45   Why does current lag the voltage in an inductive circuit?
14-46   Under what condition does I lead V by 90°?
14-47   When would I and V be in phase?
14-48   What is the relationship of L to frequency?
14-49   What is the relationship of L to θ?
14-50   What is the relationship of X_L to frequency?
14-51   What is the relationship of X_L to θ?
14-52   What effect does R have on θ?
14-53   What effect does R have on Z?
14-54   Why is the power curve twice the frequency of V and I?
14-55   What effect does X_L have on the PF?
14-56   What effect does R have on the PF?
14-57   What is Q of a coil?
14-58   What is the relationship of energy stored to the coil Q?
14-59   At what R/X_L value is $\theta = 45°$?

vector algebra
15

The major purpose of this chapter is to introduce the student to those basic concepts of vector algebra considered necessary for the analysis of certain sinusoidal circuits. These basic concepts are presented in a practical manner. The development of each topic is followed by completely worked out examples of how that concept is used. There is no attempt here to delve into the mathematical development of these concepts. The last two sections of the chapter are devoted to showing how vector algebra is used in series- and parallel-circuit calculations.

15-1 EXPRESSING SERIES-CIRCUIT Z IN RECTANGULAR AND POLAR NOTATION

In this section you will learn how to express impedance in a series circuit in polar and rectangular notation, convert from polar to rectangular notation, and convert from rectangular to polar notation.

Recall that the impedance diagram was analyzed in conjunction with the series-RC and series-RL circuits in Chap. 14. Now these impedance diagrams can be analyzed in another manner. Refer to Fig. 15-1. The vector representing the total impedance of the circuit can be described in terms of its *magnitude* and the *phase angle* θ that the magnitude has with the reference (x) axis. When an impedance is described in this manner, its *polar coordinates* are being stated. Therefore, the impedance

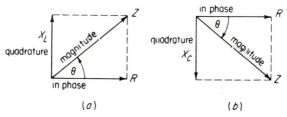

(a)   (b)

Fig. 15-1   Impedance diagrams: (a) series-RL; (b) series-RC.

of a circuit is expressed in *polar notation* when it is described by its magnitude and phase angle.

The polar notation for the series-*RL* circuit is

$$Z = \text{magnitude } \underline{/\theta} \qquad \text{(15-1)}$$

and the polar notation for the series-*RC* circuit is

$$Z = \text{magnitude } \underline{/-\theta} \qquad \text{(15-2)}$$

Notice that θ is negative in the series-*RC* circuit because the impedance diagram lies in the fourth quadrant.

The impedance can also be expressed in terms of the resistive and reactive components, and this is called *rectangular notation*. When an impedance is expressed in rectangular notation, the resistive (in-phase) component is expressed first and is followed by the reactive (quadrature) component. The reactive component is called the quadrature component because it is represented as a vector in the $+90°$ or $-90°$ regions of the coordinate graph. The term $+j$ is used to designate the $+90°$ position while $-j$ represents the $-90°$ position on the coordinates. The j factor is called the j *operator*. A j operator is used to designate whether the diagram is in the first or fourth quadrant.

The rectangular notation for the series-*RL* circuit is

$$Z = R + jX_L \qquad \text{(15-3)}$$

where $+j$ is used since the impedance diagram is in the first quadrant.

The rectangular notation for the series-*RC* circuit is

$$Z = R - jX_C \qquad \text{(15-4)}$$

where $-j$ is used since the impedance diagram is in the fourth quadrant.

Converting from Polar to Rectangular Notation

As will be seen in the sections that follow, it is often desirable to convert the impedance from polar notation to its equivalent rectangular notation. This relationship between polar and rectangular notation is shown by the following equation:

$$Z\underline{/\theta} = Z \cos \theta \pm jZ \sin \theta = Z (\cos \theta \pm j \sin \theta) \qquad \text{(15-5)}$$

where θ = phase angle formed between magnitude and in-phase component

      j = positive for first-quadrant diagrams and negative for fourth-quadrant diagrams

Converting from Rectangular to Polar Notation

It is also necessary at times to convert a value expressed in rectangular notation to its equivalent polar notation. The following procedure may be used in such cases:

1   Find θ:

$$\theta = \tan^{-1} \frac{\text{quadrature component}}{\text{in-phase component}} = \tan^{-1} \frac{X}{R} \qquad \textbf{(15-6)}$$

Note $\tan^{-1}$ means "an angle whose tangent is . . . ."

2   Find the magnitude:

$$\text{Magnitude} = \frac{\text{in-phase component}}{\cos \theta} \qquad \textbf{(15-7)}$$

or

$$\text{Magnitude} = \frac{\text{quadrature component}}{\sin \theta} \qquad \textbf{(15-7a)}$$

or

$$\text{Magnitude} = [(\text{in-phase component})^2 \qquad \textbf{(15-7b)}$$
$$+ (\pm \text{ quadrature component})^2]^{1/2}$$

Therefore, to convert from rectangular to polar form:

$$Z = \frac{\text{in-phase component}}{\cos \theta} \Big/ \tan^{-1} \frac{\text{quadrature}}{\text{in phase}} \qquad \textbf{(15-8)}$$

or

$$Z = \frac{\text{quadrature component}}{\sin \theta} \Big/ \tan^{-1} \frac{\text{quadrature}}{\text{in phase}} \qquad \textbf{(15-8a)}$$

The use of these relationships will be shown by several examples.

Example 1

A series-*RL* circuit has the following parameters. $R = 100 \ \Omega$; $X_L = 200 \ \Omega$. Express the impedance of this circuit in rectangular notation.

Solution

1 First draw the impedance diagram, putting in the given values. See Fig. 15-2.

200

100

Fig. 15-2   Example 1.

2 Following the format of $Z = R \pm jX$, where j is positive, as seen in Fig. 15-2, one obtains

$$A = 100 + j200$$

Example 2

Convert the impedance of Example 1 into polar notation.

Solution

The following relationship will be useful:

$$Z = \frac{\text{quadrature component}}{\sin \theta} \Big/ \ \tan^{-1} \frac{\text{quadrature}}{\text{in phase}}$$

1 Find

$$\tan^{-1} \frac{\text{quadrature}}{\text{in phase}}$$

where quadrature $= 200 \ \Omega$
        in phase $= 100 \ \Omega$

Hence,

$$\theta = \tan^{-1} \tfrac{200}{100} = \tan^{-1} 2$$

and

$$\theta = 63.4°$$

2 Find the magnitude:

$$\text{Magnitude} = \frac{\text{quadrature component}}{\sin \theta} = \frac{200}{0.894} = 224 \ \Omega$$

3 Now, expressing the circuit impedance in polar notation,

$$Z = 224\underline{/63.4°} \ \Omega$$

Example 3

A series-RC circuit has an impedance of $500\underline{/-40°} \ \Omega$. Express this impedance in rectangular form.

Solution

1 Draw the impedance diagram with the given parameters, as shown in Fig. 15-3.

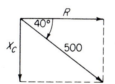

Fig. 15-3   Example 3.

2 Using the conversion formula,

$$Z\underline{/\theta} = Z \cos \theta \pm jZ \sin \theta$$

where $-\theta = 40°$
  $j = $ negative, as seen in Fig. 15-3
  $Z = 500 \ \Omega$

Substitute this value and you obtain

$$Z/\theta = 500 \cos 40° - j500 \sin 40°$$
$$Z\underline{/\theta} = 500 \times 0.766 - j500 \times 0.643$$

and

$$Z\underline{/\theta} = 383 - j322 \ \Omega$$

Example 4

A series-*RC* circuit has $R = 800$ Ω and $X_C = 400$ Ω. Express the impedance of this circuit in rectangular form.

Solution

1   Draw the impedance diagram and substitute the given values, as shown in Fig. 15-4.

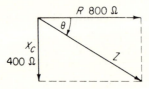

Fig. 15-4   Example 4.

2   Expressing the above in rectangular form,

$$Z = 800 - j400 \ \Omega$$

Example 5

Convert the impedance of the series-*RC* circuit of Example 4 into polar notation.

Solution

$$Z = \frac{\text{quadrature component}}{\sin \theta} \Big/ \tan^{-1} \frac{\text{quadrature}}{\text{in phase}}$$

1   Find θ. From the above, quadrature = 400 Ω; in phase = 800 Ω; hence,

$$\theta = \tan^{-1} \tfrac{400}{800} = \tan^{-1} 0.5$$
$$= 26.6°$$

2   Find the magnitude:

$$\text{Magnitude} = \frac{\text{quadrature component}}{\sin \theta} = \frac{400}{0.448} = 895$$

3   Now expressing the circuit impedance in polar notation,

$$Z = 893\underline{/-26.6°} \ \Omega$$

15-2 EXPRESSING SERIES-CIRCUIT VOLTAGES IN POLAR AND RECTANGULAR NOTATION

In this section you will learn how to express voltage in a series circuit in polar and rectangular notation, convert from polar to rectangular notation, and convert from rectangular to polar notation.

Recall that the voltage diagrams were studied in conjunction with the series-*RC* and series-*RL* circuits in Chap. 14. By use of these diagrams and the techniques described in Sec. 15-1, the voltage of a series circuit can be expressed in polar and rectangular form.

Refer to Fig. 15-5, which illustrates the components for both rectangular and polar notation of the voltage in series-*RL* (diagram *a*) and series-*RC* (diagram *b*). V_R, V_L, V_t are rotating vectors, rotating at an angular frequency. This vector diagram represents the voltages and their phase angles at a particular instant of time when the instantaneous value of V_R is zero. Here are the equations for converting from one form to the other for each type of circuit:

To Convert from Polar to Rectangular:

$$V \underline{/\theta} = \cos \theta \, V \pm j \sin \theta \, V \tag{15-9}$$

where *j* is minus for the series-*RC* and plus for the series-*RL*.

To Convert from Rectangular to Polar:

$$V = \frac{\text{in-phase component}}{\cos \theta} \underline{/ \tan^{-1} \frac{\text{quadrature}}{\text{in phase}}} \tag{15-10}$$

or

$$V = \frac{\text{quadrature component}}{\sin \theta} \underline{/ \tan^{-1} \frac{\text{quadrature}}{\text{in phase}}} \tag{15-10a}$$

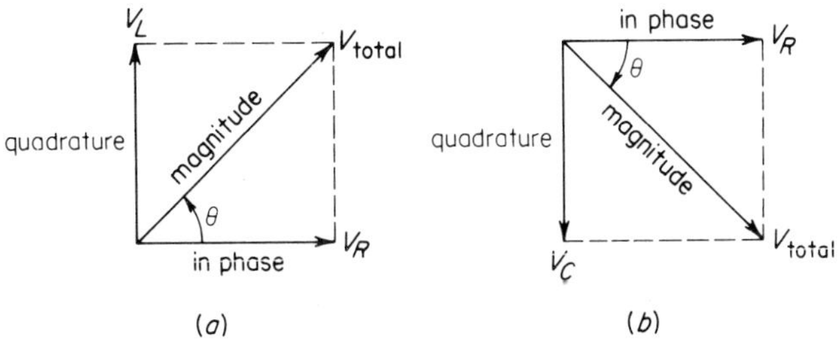

Fig. 15-5 Voltage diagrams: (*a*) series-*RL*; (*b*) series-*RC*.

Example 1

A series-*RC* circuit has the following parameters: $V_R = 10$ V and $V_C = 15$ V, as shown in Fig. 15-6. The total voltage in rectangular notation is $V = 10 - j15$ V.

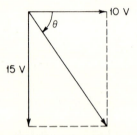

Fig. 15-6   Example 1.

Example 2

Express the V value of Example 1 in polar notation.

Solution

Use the preceding equation and the voltage diagram of Fig. 15-6.

1   Find θ:

$$\theta = \tan^{-1} \frac{\text{quadrature}}{\text{in phase}}$$

Substituting values and solving yield

$$\theta = \tan^{-1} \frac{-15}{10} = \tan^{-1}(-1.5) = -56.3°$$

2   Find the magnitude:

$$\text{Magnitude} = \frac{\text{quadrature component}}{\sin \theta} = \frac{15}{0.832} = 18$$

3   Expressing in polar form:

$$V = 18\underline{/-56.3°} \text{ V}$$

Example 3

A series-RL circuit voltage is $20\underline{/+25°}$ V. Express the circuit voltage in rectangular notation.

Solution

Use the following conversion equation:

$$V\underline{/\theta} = \cos\theta\,V \pm j\sin\theta\,V$$

where $V = 20$ V
     $\theta = 25°$
     $j = $ plus for the series-RL voltage diagram, as seen in Fig. 15-7

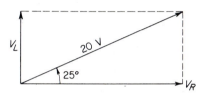

Fig. 15-7   Example 3.

1   Find $\cos\theta$ and $\sin\theta$:

$$\cos\theta = \cos 25° = 0.906$$

and

$$\sin\theta = \sin 25° = 0.423$$

2   Substituting into the conversion equation and solving,

$$V\underline{/\theta} = 0.906 \times 20 + j0.423 \times 20$$

and

$$V\underline{/\theta} = 18.1 + j8.5 \text{ V}$$

15-3   ADDITION AND SUBTRACTION BY VECTOR ALGEBRA

In this section you will learn how to add and subtract in rectangular notation.

First examine the rules for *adding in vector algebra:*

1 Express the quantities to be added in rectangular form. Before quantities in the polar form can be added, they must be converted into rectangular form.
2 Find the algebraic sum of the in-phase components and the algebraic sum of the quadrature components. These are the sums of the in-phase and quadrature components.

Example 1

Find the sum of $400\underline{/30°}$ Ω and $500\underline{/45°}$ Ω.

Solution

First convert each polar quantity into its equivalent rectangular notation value.

1 Using the relationship $Z\underline{/\theta} = Z \cos \theta \pm jZ \sin \theta$,

$$400\underline{/30°} = 400 \cos 30° + j400 \sin 30°$$

and

$$400\underline{/30°} = 400 \times 0.866 + j400 \times 0.500 = 346 + j200 \ \Omega$$

Repeating the conversion for the second quantity,

$$500\underline{/45°} = 500 \cos 45° + j500 \sin 45°$$
$$= 500 \times 0.707 + j500 \times 0.707$$
$$= 354 + j354 \ \Omega$$

2 Now find the algebraic sums of the in-phase and quadrature components:

$$\begin{array}{r} 346 + j200 \\ 354 + j354 \\ \hline 700 + j554 \ \Omega \end{array}$$

The *rules for subtraction* in vector algebra are as follows:

1 Express the quantities to be subtracted in rectangular form.
2 Algebraically subtract the quadrature components and then algebraically subtract the in-phase components.

Example 2

Subtract $20 + j30$ from $30 - j40$ Ω.

Solution

$$\begin{array}{r} 30 - j40 \\ \underline{-20 - j30} \\ 10 - j70 \text{ Ω} \end{array}$$

15-4 MULTIPLICATION AND DIVISION BY VECTOR ALGEBRA

In this section you will learn how to multiply and divide in polar notation.

Multiplication and division can be performed with the quantities expressed in rectangular notation or in polar notation. However, these processes are simplest when performed with the quantities expressed in polar form.

The *rules for multiplication* are:

1 Express all quantities in polar form.
2 Multiply the magnitudes.
3 Algebraically add the phase angles.

Example 1

Find the product of $20\underline{/-40°}$ Ω and $5\underline{/30°}$ Ω.

Solution

$$20\underline{/-40°} \times 5\underline{/30°} = 100\underline{/-10°} \text{ Ω}$$

The *rules for division* are:

1 Express all quantities in polar form.
2 Divide the magnitudes.
3 Algebraically subtract the phase angles.

Example 2

Find the quotient of $500\underline{/60°}$ Ω and $200\underline{/20°}$ Ω.

Solution

$$\frac{500\underline{/60°}}{200\underline{/20°}} = 2.5\underline{/40°} \text{ Ω}$$

15-5   SERIES-CIRCUIT COMPUTATIONS

In this section you will learn how series-circuit computations can be performed by vector algebra.

It will be recalled that the fundamental series-circuit laws for resistive circuits were developed and analyzed in Chap. 5. *The same laws are applicable to series impedance circuits, but all calculations must be performed by vector algebra.* Therefore, the total impedance of a series circuit can be determined in the following manner:

$$Z = Z_1 + Z_2 + \cdots + Z_n$$

where all Z's are expressed in rectangular notation so that they can be added, i.e.,

$$Z = (R_1 \pm jX_1) + (R_2 \pm jX_2) + \cdots + (R_n \pm jX_n) \qquad \textbf{(15-11)}$$

Example

Find the total impedance of the series circuit shown in Fig. 15-8.

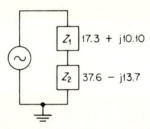

Fig. 15-8   Series-circuit computations.

Adding the two impedances,

$$\begin{array}{r} 17.3 + j10.0 \\ 37.6 - j13.7 \\ \hline 54.9 - j\ 3.7\ \Omega \end{array}$$

And expressing Z in rectangular form,

$$Z = 54.9 - j3.7\ \Omega$$

The total impedance may now be converted into polar form:

$$\theta = \tan^{-1}\frac{X}{R} = \tan^{-1}\frac{-3.7}{54.9} = \tan^{-1} 0.067 = -3.8°$$

$$\text{Magnitude} = \frac{3.7}{0.066} = 55 \qquad \frac{\text{quadrature}}{\sin\theta} = \frac{3.7}{0.068} = 56$$

And now expressing Z in polar form,

$$Z = 56\underline{/-3.8°}\ \Omega$$

15-6 PARALLEL-CIRCUIT COMPUTATIONS

In this section you will learn how parallel-circuit computations can be performed by vector algebra.

The parallel-resistive-circuit laws were also developed and analyzed in Chap. 5. *The same laws are applicable to parallel impedance circuits, but all calculations must be performed by vector algebra.*

Example

Find the total impedance of the parallel circuit shown in Fig. 15-9.

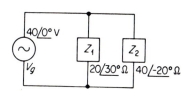

Fig. 15-9   Parallel-circuit computations.

Solution

1 Find the branch currents.

$$I_a = \frac{V_g}{Z_1} = \frac{40\underline{/0°}}{20\underline{/30°}} = 2\underline{/-30°}\ \text{A}$$

$$I_b = \frac{V_g}{Z_2} = \frac{40\underline{/0°}}{40\underline{/-20°}} = 1\underline{/20°}\ \text{A}$$

Since the value of the branch currents has been determined, it is suggested that the current diagram be drawn, as shown in Fig. 15-10.

2 Now express the branch currents in rectangular notation and determine the total current.

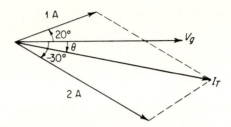

Fig. 15-10   Current diagram of Fig. 15-9.

$$I_a = 2\underline{/-30°} = 2 \cos 30° - j2 \sin 30°$$
$$= 2 \times 0.866 - j2 \times 0.500 = 1.732 - j1.0 \text{ A}$$
$$I_b = 1\underline{/20} = 1 \cos 20° + j1 \sin 20°$$
$$= 0.940 + j0.342 \text{ A}$$

Now adding,

$$\begin{array}{r} 1.732 - j1.000 \\ 0.940 + j0.342 \\ \hline 2.672 - j0.658 \text{ A} = I \end{array}$$

and expressing the total current in polar form,

$$\theta = \tan^{-1} \frac{\text{quadrature}}{\text{in phase}} = \tan^{-1} \frac{-0.658}{2.672} = \tan^{-1} - 0.246 = -13.8°$$

and the magnitude is

$$\text{Magnitude} = \frac{\text{quadrature}}{\sin \theta} = \frac{0.658}{\sin 13.8} = \frac{0.658}{0.239} = 2.75$$

and

$$I = 2.75\underline{/-13.8°} \text{ A}$$

3   Now the total impedance can be found:

$$Z\underline{/\theta} = \frac{V_g\underline{/\theta}}{I\underline{/\theta}} = \frac{40\underline{/0°}}{2.75\underline{/-13.8°}} = 14.5\underline{/13.8°} \text{ } \Omega$$

PROBLEMS

15-1   A series-RC circuit has the following parameters: $R = 300$ Ω; $X_C = 500$ Ω. Express Z in rectangular form.

15-2 Refer to Prob. 15-1. Express Z in polar form.
15-3 A series-RL circuit has the following parameters: $R = 60\ \Omega$; $X_L = 45\ \Omega$. Express Z in rectangular form.
15-4 Refer to Prob. 15-3. Express Z in polar form.
15-5 A series-RC circuit has the following parameters: $V_R = 5$ V; $V_C = 10$ V. Express V in rectangular form.
15-6 Refer to Prob. 15-5. Express V in polar form.
15-7 A series-RL circuit has the following parameters: $V_R = 12$ V; $V_L = 9$ V. Express V in rectangular form.
15-8 Refer to Prob. 15-7. Express V in polar form.
15-9 A series-RL circuit has $V = 20/\underline{50°}$ V. Express this in rectangular form.
15-10 A series-RC circuit has $V = 15/\underline{35°}$ V. Express this in rectangular form.
15-11 Find the sum of $25 - j30$ and $34 + j18$.
15-12 Subtract $9 - j9$ from $12 - j11$.
15-13 Find the product of $500/\underline{-24°}$ and $650/\underline{45°}$.
15-14 Divide $24/\underline{34°}$ into $12/\underline{60°}$.
15-15 A series circuit has the following impedances: $200/\underline{45°}\ \Omega$ and $300/\underline{-30°}\ \Omega$. Find the total impedance.

QUESTIONS

15-1 On what axis is the in-phase component always located?
15-2 On what axis is the quadrature component always located?
15-3 What is the polarity of the j operator for the impedance in rectangular notation for the series-RL circuit?
15-4 What is the polarity of the j operator for the voltage in rectangular notation for the series-RL circuit?
15-5 What is the polarity of the j operator for the impedance in rectangular notation for the series-RC circuit?
15-6 What is the polarity of the j operator for the voltage in rectangular notation for the series-RC circuit?
15-7 Why is the impedance diagram of the series-RC circuit opposite to that of the series-RL circuit?
15-8 Why is the voltage diagram of the series-RC opposite to the impedance diagram of the series-RC circuit?
15-9 For what arithmetic processes is it suggested that the quantities be expressed in polar form?
15-10 For what arithmetic processes is it required that the quantities be expressed in rectangular form?

parallel circuits with a sine-wave input
16

In this chapter are considered parallel-*RC* and -*RL* circuits with a sinusoidal input voltage. The characteristics and behavior of parallel-*RC* and -*RL* combinations merit separate analysis because of their many uses in electronics. Vector algebra techniques are utilized in the treatment of these circuits. In all circuits, *assume that Z_g is negligible.*

16-1 CHARACTERISTICS OF A PARALLEL-*RC* CIRCUIT

In this section you will learn how to compute the phase angle, current, and impedance of a parallel-RC circuit.

Figure 16-1 illustrates the parallel-*RC* combination. Since R and C are in parallel, V_c and V_r are equal, and the total current is equal to the

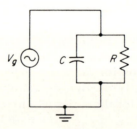

Fig. 16-1   Parallel-*RC* circuit.

vector sum of I_c and I_r. I_c leads I_r by 90°, and I leads I_r by some angle between 0 and 90°, as determined by the ratio of R/X_C. The impedance is smaller than either branch impedance. The current and impedance relationships can be verified with a typical problem.

Example 1

Refer to the circuit of Fig. 16-1. $V_g = 50$ V; $R = 100\ \Omega$; $X_C = 75\ \Omega$. Find: (a) $I_c\underline{/\theta}$; (b) $I_r\underline{/\theta}$; (c) $I\underline{/\theta}$; (d) $Z\underline{/\theta}$.

Solution

(a)   Find $I_c/\underline{\theta}$:

$$I_c\underline{/\theta} = \frac{V_g\underline{/\theta}}{X_c\underline{/\theta}} = \frac{50\underline{/0°}}{75\underline{/-90°}} = 0.667\underline{/90°} \text{ A}$$

(b)   Find $I_r/\underline{\theta}$:

$$I_r\underline{/\theta} = \frac{V_g\underline{/\theta}}{R\underline{/\theta}} = \frac{50\underline{/0°}}{100\underline{/0°}} = 0.5\underline{/0°} \text{ A}$$

(c)   Find $I\underline{/\theta}$: in a parallel circuit, the total current is equal to the vector sum of the branch currents. I_c and I_r should be converted to rectangular form prior to adding them. I_c is a pure reactive current and I_r a pure resistive current; the conversion results in

$$I_c = 0 + j\,0.667 \text{ A} \qquad \text{and} \qquad I_r = 0.500 + j\,0$$

Adding,

$$\begin{array}{r} 0 \;+ j\,0.667 \\ 0.500 + j\,0 \\ \hline I = 0.500 + j\,0.667 \text{ A} \end{array}$$

Converting I back to polar form,

$$\theta = \tan^{-1}\frac{\text{quadrature}}{\text{in phase}} = \tan^{-1}\frac{0.667}{0.500} = \tan^{-1} 1.334 = 53.1°$$

$$\text{Magnitude} = \frac{\text{quadrature}}{\sin\theta} = \frac{0.667}{0.800} = 0.834 \text{ A}$$

$$I = 0.834\underline{/53.1°} \text{ A}$$

(d)   Find $Z\underline{/\theta}$:

$$Z\underline{/\theta} = \frac{V\underline{/\theta}}{I\underline{/\theta}} = \frac{50\underline{/0°}}{0.834\underline{/53.1°}} = 60\underline{/-53.1°} \text{ } \Omega$$

Note that the source voltage is taken as a reference, since it is common to both branches. Also note that *the phase angle associated with the im-*

pedance is the same value but opposite in polarity to the current phase angle. The current phase angle is always positive, and the impedance phase angle is always negative in a parallel-*RC* circuit when the source voltage is the reference.

Further analysis of the parallel-*RC* circuit reveals that the entire power dissipation occurs in the resistive branch (assuming that C is pure and perfect). Since this is the case, the power dissipation can be obtained with or without using the power factor.

$$P = (I_r)^2 R = (\cos \theta)(VI)$$

The method selected depends on which circuit parameters are known at the time.

Example 2

Find the power dissipation of the circuit in Example 1.

Solution

$$P = (I_r)^2 R = (0.5)^2 \times 100 = 25 \text{ W}$$

Checking, by the power-factor relationship, gives

$$P = (\cos \theta)(EI) = 0.6 \times 50 \times 0.834 = 25 \text{ W}$$

16-2 THE EFFECT OF A VARYING RESISTANCE IN A PARALLEL-*RC* COMBINATION

In this section you will learn that reducing the ohmic value of the resistive branch of a parallel-RC circuit increases the circuit phase angle and current while reducing the circuit impedance.

Figure 16-2 illustrates a parallel-*RC* combination in which the resistance is variable. Assign values to the capacitive reactance and resistance, in order to determine the effect upon Z, θ, and I.

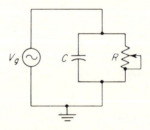

Fig. 16-2 Parallel-*RC* circuit with a variable *R*.

Example

Refer to the circuit of Fig. 16-2. $X_C = 30\ \Omega$; R may be varied from 1 to 300 Ω; $V_g = 100$ V. Find Z, θ, and I when R is at the following values: (a) 1 Ω; (b) 30 Ω; (c) 300 Ω.

Solution

(a) When $R = 1\ \Omega$,

$$Z = \frac{Z_C Z_R}{Z_C + Z_R}$$

(Note that it is normal practice to have X_C and R as real numbers and Z_L and Z_R as representing complex numbers.) Since we shall multiply in the numerator, Z_C and Z_R will be expressed in polar form. And Z_C and Z_R are expressed in rectangular form in the denominator since they are to be added:

$$Z = \frac{30\underline{/-90^\circ} \times 1\underline{/0^\circ}}{(0 - j30) + (1 + j0)} = \frac{30\underline{/-90^\circ}}{1 - j30}$$

Converting the denominator into polar form,

$$1 - j30 = 30\underline{/-88.1^\circ}$$

now substituting back,

$$Z\underline{/\theta} = \frac{30\underline{/-90^\circ}}{30\underline{/-88.1^\circ}} = 1\underline{/-1.9^\circ}\ \Omega$$

and finding I,

$$I\underline{/\theta} = \frac{V_g\underline{/\theta}}{Z\underline{/\theta}} = \frac{100\underline{/0^\circ}}{1\underline{/-1.9^\circ}} = 100\underline{/1.9^\circ}\ \text{A}$$

(b) When $R = 30\ \Omega$,

$$Z\underline{/\theta} = \frac{30\underline{/-90^\circ} \times 30\underline{/0^\circ}}{(0 - j30) + (30 + j0)} = \frac{900\underline{/-90^\circ}}{30 - j30}$$

Converting the denominator into polar form,

$$30 - j30 = 42\underline{/-45^\circ}$$

now substituting back,

$$Z/\theta = \frac{900/-90°}{42/-45°} = 21.4/-45° \ \Omega$$

and finding I,

$$I/\theta = \frac{V_g/\theta}{Z/\theta} = \frac{100/0°}{21.4/-45°} = 4.67/45° \ A$$

(c)   When $R = 300 \ \Omega$,

$$Z = \frac{30/-90° \times 300/0°}{(0 - j\,30) + (300 + j\,0)} = \frac{9000/-90°}{300 - j\,30}$$

Converting the denominator into polar form,

$$300 - j\,30 = 303/-5.7°$$

now substituting back,

$$Z/\theta = \frac{9000/-90°}{303/-5.7°} = 29.7/-84.3° \ \Omega$$

and finding I,

$$I/\theta = \frac{V_g/\theta}{Z/\theta} = \frac{100/0°}{29.7/-84.3°} = 3.37/84.3° \ A$$

These results point out a number of important relationships.
    In a parallel-RC circuit:

1   The circuit impedance is always smaller than the lowest branch im-
    pedance.
2   The circuit phase angle is less than 45° when R is smaller than X_C,
    $\theta = 45°$ when $R = X_C$, and θ is greater than 45° when R is larger than
    X_C.
3   When X_C is fixed and R is varied, θ increases as R is made larger, and
    the total circuit current becomes smaller in magnitude.

With a comparatively low-resistance branch, the larger portion of the current passes through that leg, resulting in the source seeing a predominately resistive circuit. Consequently the current phase angle is small. When R and X_C are equal, the in-phase and quadrature components of the current are also equal in magnitude, resulting in the source seeing a load which is equally resistive and capacitive. When the resistance is many times greater than X_C, the greatest portion of the current is taken by the capacitive branch, and the source sees a predominantly capacitive load; therefore the current phase angle is large (greater than $45°$). Note that in all three cases I_g leads V_g.

16-3 THE EFFECT OF A VARYING CAPACITANCE IN A PARALLEL-*RC* COMBINATION

In this section you will learn that reducing the capacitance in a parallel-RC circuit increases the circuit impedance and results in a reduction in circuit phase angle and current.

A parallel-*RC* circuit with a variable capacitance is illustrated in Fig. 16-3. It should be recalled that X_C varies inversely as the capacitance. Since increasing the capacitance reduces X_C, this results in an increase in current through the capacitive branch. When the capacitive current is greater than the resistive current and when X_C is smaller than R, the circuit current takes a phase angle greater than $45°$ and the source sees a predominantly capacitive load. When X_C and R are equal, the branch currents are equal, the circuit-current phase angle is $45°$, and the source sees a load which is equally resistive and capacitive. The capacitive current is less than the resistive current when X_C is greater than R. With this condition, the circuit-current phase angle is less than $45°$, and the source sees a predominantly resistive load.

In conclusion, consider the following statements (with V_g, frequency, and R fixed):

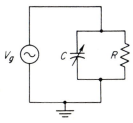

Fig. 16-3 Parallel-*RC* circuit with a variable *C*.

1   An increase in C results in a reduction of X_C and Z, causing an increase in the magnitude of the total current and its phase angle.
2   When X_C is 10 times greater (or more) than R, the source sees a predominantly resistive circuit.
3   When X_C is 10 percent or less of R, the source sees a predominantly capacitive circuit.
4   A change in capacitance does not affect the power dissipation of a parallel-RC circuit (this is so since the change has no effect on V_r and I_r). (The generator Z is assumed to be negligible.)

16-4   THE EFFECT OF A VARYING FREQUENCY IN A PARALLEL-RC COMBINATION

In this section you will learn that increasing the frequency of a parallel-RC circuit has the same effect upon circuit impedance, current, and phase angle as increasing C.

The effect of a varying frequency is somewhat similar to the effect produced by a varying capacitance, since X_C varies inversely with the repetition frequency. An increase in the repetition frequency results in a reduction in X_C, and X_C is increased by a frequency decrease. The capacitive reactance can be varied by a frequency change or a variation in capacitance, whichever is more practical or convenient.

At high frequencies, where X_C is comparatively small with respect to R, the source sees a predominantly capacitive load. When the input repetition frequency is low and X_C is comparatively high, the source sees a predominantly resistive load.

Of special interest, because of its common use, is the behavior of the parallel-RC combination with an input which is a composite of a constant unidirectional potential and a sine wave (See Fig. 16–4). That is, the in-

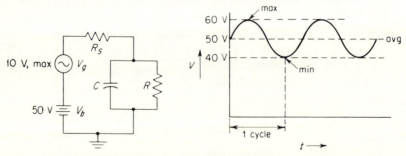

Fig. 16-4 Varying unidirectional-input voltage.

Fig. 16-5 Input waveform of Fig. 16-4.

put voltage consists of a unidirectional potential varying in a sinusoidal fashion, as illustrated in Fig. 16-5. Note the addition of R_S to the parallel-*RC* network.

In many cases, the purpose of the capacitor in parallel with R may be to eliminate effectively the current variations through R. In order to do this, the capacitor must offer a low-impedance path for these variations. A general rule of thumb is to select a capacitor value such that its reactance at the frequency of the variations is 10 percent or less of the ohmic value of R. When serving such a function, C is often called a *bypass capacitor,* since it bypasses the variations away from R. It should be noted that the bypassing arrangement reduces the sinusoidal variations across the entire parallel arrangement (since $V_c = V_r$) because of the low-impedance path offered to this current by the capacitor. What happens to these variations? They appear across R_S. Assuming that the capacitor has very low leakage, the unidirectional current will be restricted in its flow to passing through R_S and R.

Example 1

Refer to the circuit of Fig. 16-4 and waveform of Fig. 16-5. $R = 20 \text{ k}\Omega$. The sinusoidal variations are at a frequency of 5000 Hz. Find the capacitance required to bypass these variations from R.

Solution

Using the preceding rule of thumb, $X_C = 0.10R = 2 \text{ k}\Omega$ at 5 kHz. Solving for C,

$$C = \frac{1}{2\pi \times 5000 \times 2000} = 0.0159 \ \mu F$$

Another common application of this arrangement, as shown in Fig. 16-4, is in conjunction with a circuit where the sinusoidal component contains frequencies over a relatively wide range. A portion of the higher end of the range may be deemed undesirable for the particular application. The purpose of the capacitor in such a case is to serve as a bypass only at the undesirable, higher portion of the frequency range. One method by which the problem may be handled is to see that X_C is 10 percent of R at the lower end of the undesirable frequency range. This, in effect, will shunt all frequencies above this value from R.

Example 2

Refer to the circuit of Fig. 16-4. All frequencies above 10 kHz are to be shunted away from R. $R = 4 \text{ k}\Omega$. Find the required capacitance.

Solution

X_C at 10 kHz $= 0.10R = 400$ Ω. Solving for C,

$$C = \frac{1}{2\pi \times 10(10)^3 \times 400} = 0.0398 \ \mu\text{F}$$

16-5 EQUIVALENT SERIES AND/OR PARALLEL CIRCUITS

In analyzing many circuits, the concept of determining what the source sees is an invaluable tool. No matter how complex the circuit may seem, it appears either as a relatively simple series circuit, called the equivalent series circuit, to the source, or as an equivalent parallel circuit.

Example 1

Consider the circuit of Fig. 16-1 and the parameters given in Example 1. Find the equivalent series circuit seen by the source.

Solution

The use of Fig. 16-6 will clarify the following analysis. The source potential is 50 V. The current leads the source voltage by 53.2°. The source sees a capacitive element between its terminals because the current leads the potential. Also seen is a resistance in series with the capacitance, since the current leads by a phase angle which is less than 90°, and only a portion of the energy delivered is returned to the source. The total opposition offered to the current flow, 60 Ω, is readily apparent from Ohm's law. Projecting the magnitude and phase angle of this impedance upon a right triangle will determine the value of X_C and R (see Fig. 16-6*b*). Solving for X_C and R,

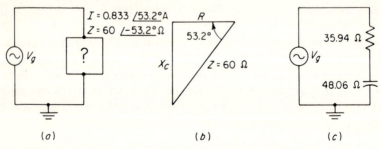

(*a*)   (*b*)   (*c*)

Fig. 16-6 Equivalent-circuit analysis: (*a*) circuit; (*b*) vector diagram as seen by the source; (*c*) equivalent series circuit.

$$X_C = (\sin\ \theta)(Z) = \sin 53.2° \times 60 = 0.801 \times 60 = 48.06\ \Omega$$

and

$$R = (\cos\ \theta)(Z) = \cos 53.2° \times 60 = 0.599 \times 60 = 35.94\ \Omega$$

Hence the source sees a series circuit consisting of 35.94 Ω of resistance and 48.06 Ω of capacitive reactance. If these two components were connected in place of the unknown network (Fig. 16-6a), *neither the magnitude of the current nor the phase angle would be changed.*

Example 2

Refer to Fig. 16-6. $R = 100\ \Omega$; $X_C = 100\ \Omega$; $V_g = 200$ V. Assume this is a parallel-RC circuit. Find the equivalent series circuit seen by the source.

Solution

$Z\underline{/\theta}$ and $I\underline{/\theta}$ must be determined first. Solve for $I\underline{/\theta}$.

$$I = I_r + I_c \qquad \text{(vectorially)}$$

$$I_r\underline{/\theta} = \frac{V_r\underline{/\theta}}{R\underline{/\theta}} = \frac{200\underline{/0°}}{100\underline{/\theta°}} = 2\underline{/0°}\ \text{A}$$

$$I_c\underline{/\theta} = \frac{V_c\underline{/\theta}}{X_C\underline{/\theta}} = \frac{200\underline{/0°}}{100\underline{/-90°}} = 2\underline{/90°}\ \text{A}$$

Converting each into rectangular form and adding,

$$I = (2 + j0) + (0 + j2) = 2 + j2\ \text{A}$$

Expressing in polar form,

$$\theta = \tan^{-1}\tfrac{2}{2} = \tan^{-1} 1 = 45°$$

$$\text{Magnitude} = \frac{\text{quadrature}}{\sin\ \theta} = \frac{2}{0.707} = 2.829\ \text{A}$$

$$I\underline{/\theta} = 2.829\underline{/45°}\ \text{A}$$

$$Z\underline{/\theta} = \frac{V_g\underline{/\theta}}{I\underline{/\theta}} = \frac{200\underline{/0°}}{2.829\underline{/45°}} = 70.7\underline{/-45°}\ \Omega$$

The source sees a load which is equally capacitive and resistive, since the current takes a leading phase angle of 45°. The equivalent series circuit must have X_C and R values which are equal. The quadrature and in-phase values can now be determined:

$$X_C = (\sin\ \theta)(Z) = \sin 45° \times 70.7 = 50\ \Omega$$
$$R = (\cos\ \theta)(Z) = \cos 45° \times 70.7 = 50\ \Omega$$

It should be noted that this technique may be utilized in the analysis of any parallel combination and is frequently helpful in understanding the behavior of many circuits.

PROBLEMS

16-1 Refer to the circuit of Fig. 16-1. $V_g = 150$ V; $R = 240\ \Omega$; $X_c = 325\ \Omega$. Find the following:
 a) $I_c\underline{/\theta}$ b) $I_r\underline{/\theta}$
 c) $I\underline{/\theta}$ d) $Z\underline{/\theta}$
16-2 In Prob. 16-1, find:
 a) PF b) power dissipation
16-3 Assume $X_c = 500\ \Omega$. Find the R values such that θ is the following:
 a) 10° b) 45° c) 81°
16-4 Refer to Fig. 16-3. $R = 500\ \Omega$; $V_g = 80$ V. Find the following when X_c is 50 Ω, 500 Ω, and 5 kΩ:
 a) $I_c\underline{/\theta°}$ b) $I_r\underline{/\theta°}$
 c) $I\underline{/\theta°}$ d) $Z\underline{/\theta°}$
16-5 Refer to Fig. 16-1. $R = 4700\ \Omega$; θ is 30° when the frequency is 1400 Hz. Find:
 a) X_c b) C
16-6 Refer to Prob. 16.5. Find the frequency necessary to produce the following phase angles:
 a) 6° b) 45° c) 85°
16-7 Refer to Fig. 16-4. The frequency of the sinusoidal variations is equal to 3000 Hz, and they are to be bypassed by C. $R = 2200\ \Omega$. Find C.
16-8 Refer to Fig. 16-5. The frequency range of the sinusoidal variations is 20 to 20,000 Hz. $R = 500\ \Omega$. Find the C required to by-pass all frequencies above 15 kHz.
16-9 Find the equivalent series circuit of Prob. 16-1.

QUESTIONS

16-1 In a parallel-*RC* circuit, why does the total current lead I_r?

16-2 Why does the ratio $X_C R$ determine the phase angle in a parallel-*RC* combination?

16-3 Why are the impedance and current phase angles equal in value but opposite in polarity?

16-4 In a parallel-*RC* combination, explain what happens to the circuit phase angle and the current as *R* is increased.

16-5 In a parallel-*RC* combination, explain what happens to the circuit phase angle and the current as *C* is increased.

16-6 In a parallel-*RC* combination, explain what happens to the circuit phase angle and the current as *f* is increased.

16-7 What is the relationship between a parallel-*RC* combination and its equivalent series circuit?

16-8 Why does every series-*RC* circuit have an equivalent parallel-*RC* circuit?

16-9 How is the value of a bypass capacitor determined?

16-10 What is the relationship between a bypass capacitor and the resistor with which it is in parallel?

16-6 CHARACTERISTICS OF A PARALLEL-*RL* COMBINATION

In this section you will learn when a coil may be considered perfect and how to calculate the phase angle, current, and impedance in a parallel-RL circuit.

Figure 16-7 illustrates a parallel combination. The characteristics of this circuit depend partially on the coil *Q*. As a general rule of thumb, *the inductor may be considered perfect if it has a Q of 20 or greater.* Consider such a circuit first, since it is the simpler of the two possibilities.

In those cases where *Q* is 20 or greater, the circuit is represented by a perfect inductor in parallel with a resistance. $V_l = V_r = V_g$ since voltages

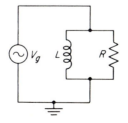

Fig. 16-7   Parallel-*RL* circuit.

of parallel branches are equal. I_l lags V_l by 90°, I_r is in phase with V_r, and I lags V_g by some phase angle between 0° and 90°. The circuit impedance is less than that of any individual branch. The magnitude of the line current phase angle varies with the ratio of X_L to R. When X_L is larger than R, the circuit current is predominantly resistive, and θ is less than 45°. θ is greater than 45° when the circuit current is predominantly inductive, which occurs when X_L is smaller than R. When $X_L = R$, the circuit-current phase angle is 45°, and the source sees a load which is equally resistive and inductive.

Example 1

Refer to the circuit of Fig. 16-7. $X_L = 500\ \Omega$; $Q = 25$; $R = 200\ \Omega$; $V_g = 100$ V. Find: (a) I_l/θ; (b) I_r/θ; (c) I/θ; (d) Z/θ.

Solution

Since Q is greater than 20, the inductor may be considered perfect.
(a) Find I_l/θ:

$$I_l/\theta = \frac{V_g/\theta}{X_L/\theta} = \frac{100/0°}{500/90°} = 0.2/-90°\ \text{A}$$

(b) Find I_r/θ:

$$I_r/\theta = \frac{V_g/\theta}{R/\theta} = \frac{100/0°}{200/0°} = 0.5/0°\ \text{A}$$

(c) Find I/θ. Addition can be performed in rectangular form only; hence I_l and I_r must be converted so that the total current can be determined. Since I_l is a pure quadrature component and I_r is a pure in-phase component, the conversion is simply

$$I_l = 0 - j0.2\ \text{A}$$

and

$$I_r = 0.5 + j0\ \text{A}$$
$$I = (0 - j0.2) + (0.5 + j0) = 0.5 - j0.2\ \text{A}$$

Converting I into polar form,

$$\theta = \tan^{-1}\frac{\text{quadrature}}{\text{in phase}} = \tan^{-1}\frac{-0.2}{0.5}$$

$$= \tan^{-1} -0.40 = -21.8°$$

$$\text{Magnitude} = \frac{\text{quadrature}}{\sin\theta} = \frac{0.2}{0.371} = 0.539 \text{ A}$$

$$I/\underline{\theta} = 0.539/\underline{-21.8°} \text{ A}$$

(d)   Find $Z/\underline{\theta}$:

$$Z/\underline{\theta} = \frac{V_g/\underline{\theta}}{I/\underline{\theta}} = \frac{100/\underline{0°}}{0.539/\underline{-21.8°}} = 185.5/\underline{21.8°} \text{ }\Omega$$

In order to achieve a reasonable degree of accuracy in circuit computations, the resistance of an inductor of Q less than 20 should be considered. As stated in prior discussions, the resistance of the coil is treated as a resistance in series with a perfect inductor. The use of an imperfect coil in parallel with a resistor increases the complexity of the circuit computations to some extent, but utilization of the vector algebra technique simplifies the calculations.

Example 2

Following are the parameters of a parallel-RL circuit: $X_L = 400$ Ω; $Q_L = 5$ of the coil alone; $R = 800$ Ω; $V_g = 200$ V. Find: (a) $Z/\underline{\theta}$; (b) $I/\underline{\theta}$.

Solution

The circuit is illustrated in Fig. 16-8. The effective resistance of the coil must be determined first.

$$R_L = \frac{X_L}{Q} = \frac{400}{5} = 80 \text{ }\Omega$$

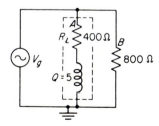

Fig. 16-8   Imperfect coil in parallel with R.

(a)   Find Z_l/θ:

$$Z_l = \frac{Z_l Z_R}{Z_l + Z_R}$$

$$= 80 + j400 \ \Omega$$

Converting to polar form,

$$\theta = \tan^{-1}\frac{\text{quadrature}}{\text{in phase}} = \frac{400}{80} = 5 = 78.7°$$

$$\text{Magnitude} = \frac{\text{quadrature}}{\sin \theta} = \frac{400}{0.981} = 408 \ \Omega$$

$$Z_l/\theta = 408/78.7° \ \Omega$$

$$Z_R = 800 + j0 = 800/0° \ \Omega$$

Now that Z_l and Z_R are expressed in both types of notation, one can substitute into the preceding impedance equation.

$$Z = \frac{408/78.7° \times 800/0°}{(80 + j400) + (800 + j0)} = \frac{326{,}400/78.7°}{880 + j400}$$

Converting the denominator into polar form,

$$\theta = \tan^{-1} \tfrac{400}{880} = \tan^{-1} 0.455 = 24.5°$$

$$\text{Magnitude} = \frac{\text{quadrature}}{\sin \theta} = \frac{400}{0.415} = 964 \ \Omega$$

Substituting back into the denominator of the Z equation and solving,

$$Z = \frac{326{,}400/78.7°}{964/24.5°} = 339/54.2° \ \Omega$$

(b)   Find I/θ:

$$I/\theta = \frac{V_g/\theta}{Z/\theta} = \frac{200/0°}{339/54.2°} = 0.590/{-54.2°} \ \text{A}$$

The circuit of Example 2 merits further discussion in order to clarify its behavior. Branch A has an impedance of $408\underline{/78.7°}$ Ω. Branch B has an impedance of $800\underline{/0°}$ Ω. Therefore the greater portion of the circuit current will flow through branch A, which means that the line current will lag by more than 45°. The total impedance of the circuit is smaller than that of either branch. It should be noted that the resistance of the coil reduced the effect of the inductor upon the current, since it decreased the branch A phase angle from 90° with a perfect coil to 78.7° with the given condition. This in turn reduced the lagging phase angle of the total circuit current.

Also note the frequent conversion from polar to rectangular notation and vice versa. In some cases, such as where addition is to be performed, a conversion must be made from polar to rectangular. In other instances, the rectangular notation is converted into polar to perform the multiplication and division processes. Maintaining a systematic and neat development of computations is strongly recommended, since it facilitates the solution of circuit problems.

16-7 THE EFFECT OF A VARYING RESISTANCE, INDUCTANCE, AND FREQUENCY IN A PARALLEL-*RL* CIRCUIT

In this section you will learn about the changes in phase angle, current, and impedance that result from changing the frequency, resistance, or inductance.

The inductor of Fig. 16-9 is considered to possess a Q value greater than 20 in this analysis. As in the case of the parallel-*RC* combination, the load seen by the source varies with the ratio of the resistance to the reactance. When R or X_L is varied, the following characteristics may be observed:

1 When $R/X_L = 0.1$ or less, the load may be considered resistive in many practical cases.

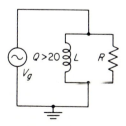

Fig. 16-9   High-*Q* coil in parallel with *R*.

2   When $R/X_L = 1$, the load seen by the source is equally resistive and inductive.

3   When $R/X_L = 10$ or more, the source sees a load which is predominantly inductive.

It should be noted that the ratio of R/X_L may be altered by changes in R, L, or frequency. At low frequencies, X_L is smallest for a fixed L, and the R/X_L ratio is largest. As the frequency is increased, R/X_L becomes smaller and the load takes on a more resistive appearance to the source, since the inductive current becomes a smaller fraction of the circuit current and the phase angle is reduced. Recall that the phase angle of a pure inductive load is $-90°$, and a pure resistive-load phase angle is $0°$. Therefore the characteristics of the parallel-RL combination may be altered by the variations of resistance, inductance, and/or frequency.

16-8   COIL Q AND ITS EFFECT ON THE PARALLEL-RL CIRCUIT

In this section you will learn about the way an imperfect coil in a parallel-RL circuit increases the total current and decreases the total impedance and circuit phase angle.

Section 16-6 stated a general criterion for deciding when the resistance of the inductor windings may be conveniently ignored in circuit calculations. The coil Q is also the tangent of the phase angle between the ◗ductance branch current and the potential across that branch.

$$Q = \frac{X_L}{R} = \tan \theta$$

Therefore, an inductor of $Q = 20$ is passing a current which lags its voltage by an angle equal to the tangent of 20, which is about 87.1°. Arbitrarily assuming a current with such a phase angle as purely inductive (90°) does not materially affect the circuit computations to a great extent in most cases.

Consider two parallel-RL circuits, one in which Q is 20 or greater and the second in which Q is less than 20. Using the same parameters of each circuit (other than Q) and comparing $Z/\underline{\theta}$ and $I/\underline{\theta}$ of each will reveal the effect of Q upon the parallel-RL circuit.

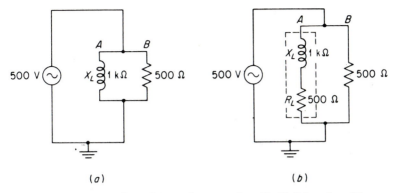

Fig. 16-10   The effect of Q: (a) Q greater than 20; (b) Q less than 20.

Example

Refer to the circuits of Fig. 16-10 for parameters. Find $I\underline{/\theta}$ and $Z\underline{/\theta}$ for: (a) circuit a; (b) circuit b.

Solution

(a)   Circuit a: first find $I\underline{/\theta}$ of circuit a.

$$I_l\underline{/\theta} = \frac{V_g\underline{/\theta}}{X_L\underline{/\theta}} = \frac{500\underline{/0°}}{1000\underline{/90°}} = 0.5\underline{/-90°} \text{ A}$$

Converting into rectangular form,

$$I_l = 0 - j0.5 \text{ A}$$
$$I_r\underline{/\theta} = \frac{V_g\underline{/\theta}}{R\underline{/\theta}} = \frac{500\underline{/0°}}{500\underline{/0°}} = 1\underline{/0°} \text{ A}$$

Converting into rectangular form,

$$I_r = 1 + j0 \text{ A}$$

Adding to find I,

$$I = (0 - j0.5) + (1 + j0) = 1 - j0.5 \text{ A}$$

Converting to polar form,

$$\theta = \tan^{-1}\frac{\text{quadrature}}{\text{in phase}} = \tan^{-1}\frac{-0.5}{1} = \tan^{-1} -0.5 = -26.6°$$

$$\text{Magnitude} = \frac{\text{quadrature}}{\sin \theta} = \frac{0.5}{0.448} = 1.116 \text{ A}$$

$$I\underline{/\theta} = 1.116\underline{/-26.6°} \text{ A}$$

$$Z\underline{/\theta} = \frac{V_g\underline{/\theta}}{I\underline{/\theta}} = \frac{500\underline{/0°}}{1.116\underline{/-26.6°}} = 448\underline{/26.6°} \text{ }\Omega$$

(b)   Circuit *b:* find $Z_a\underline{/\theta}$.

$$Z_a = 500 + j1000 \text{ }\Omega$$

Converting to polar form,

$$\theta_a = \tan^{-1}\frac{\text{quadrature}}{\text{in phase}} = \tan^{-1}\frac{1000}{500} = \tan^{-1} 2 = 63.4°$$

$$\text{Magnitude} = \frac{\text{quadrature}}{\sin \theta_a} = \frac{1000}{0.894} = 1119 \text{ }\Omega$$

$$Z_a = 1119\underline{/63.4°} \text{ }\Omega$$

Now determine $I_a\underline{/\theta}$.

$$I_a\underline{/\theta} = \frac{V_g\underline{/\theta}}{Z_a\underline{/\theta}} = \frac{500\underline{/0°}}{1119\underline{/63.4°}} = 0.447\underline{/-63.4°}$$

Let us convert $I_a\underline{/\theta}$ into rectangular form for future use.

$$\text{In phase} = \cos \theta \times \text{magnitude} = 0.448 \times 0.447 = 0.2 \text{ A}$$
$$\text{Quadrature} = \sin \theta \times \text{magnitude} = 0.894 \times 0.447 = 0.4 \text{ A}$$
$$I_a = 0.2 - j0.4 \text{ A}$$

Next determine I_b.

$$I_b\underline{/\theta} = \frac{V_g\underline{/\theta}}{Z_b\underline{/\theta}} = \frac{500\underline{/0°}}{500\underline{/0°}} = 1\underline{/0°} \text{ A}$$

Converting to rectangular form,

$$I_b = 1 + j0 \text{ A}$$

The addition of I_a and I_b in rectangular form will lead to I:

$$I = (0.2 - j0.4) + (1 + j0) = 1.2 - j0.4 \text{ A}$$

Converting to polar form,

$$\theta = \tan^{-1}\frac{\text{quadrature}}{\text{in phase}} = \tan^{-1}\frac{-0.4}{1.2} = -0.333 = -18.4°$$

$$\text{Magnitude} = \frac{\text{quadrature}}{\sin\theta} = \frac{0.4}{0.316} = 1.266 \text{ A}$$

$$I\underline{/\theta} = 1.266\underline{/-18.4°} \text{ A}$$

$$Z\underline{/\theta} = \frac{V_g\underline{/\theta}}{I\underline{/\theta}} = \frac{500\underline{/0°}}{1.266\underline{/-18.4°}} = 395\underline{/18.4°} \text{ }\Omega$$

Summarizing, in circuit a, where the coil Q is greater than 20, $I\underline{/\theta} =$ 1.116$\underline{/-26.6°}$ A and $Z\underline{/\theta} = 448\underline{/26.6°}$ Ω. In circuit b, where the coil Q is 2, $I\underline{/\theta} = 1.266\underline{/-18.4°}$ A and $Z\underline{/\theta} = 395\underline{/18.5°}$ Ω.

Notice that the impedance of circuit b is smaller than that of circuit a, although its inductive branch was higher in impedance. The addition of a resistance in the inductive branch reduced the difference in phase angles of the two branch currents. In circuit a, $I_a = 0.5\underline{/-90°}$ A; $I_b = 1\underline{/0°}$ A. In circuit b, $I_a = 0.447\underline{/-63.4°}$ A; $I_b = 1\underline{/0°}$ A.

Although the branch B current of circuit b was reduced because of the low-Q coil, its phase angle was reduced to such an extent that the total current was greater than that of the high-Q coil circuit. The reduced difference in the phase angles of the branch currents results in a total circuit current of greater magnitude but smaller phase angle. A larger magnitude of circuit current indicates that the circuit impedance was reduced by use of a lower-Q coil. In conclusion, the introduction of a lower-Q coil results in a reduced circuit impedance.

16-9 EQUIVALENT SERIES CIRCUIT OF THE PARALLEL-*RL* COMBINATION

In this section you will learn how to determine the equivalent series circuit of a parallel-RL circuit.

As in the case of the parallel-*RC* circuit, the source will see an equivalent series circuit connected across its terminals. Since the circuit current takes a lagging phase angle, an equivalent series-*RL* combination will be seen by the source. Determine the equivalent series circuit of the two parallel-*RL* combinations considered in Example 10.

Example 1

Refer to circuit *a* of Fig. 16-10. $I\underline{/\theta} = 1.116\underline{/-26.6°}$ A; $Z\underline{/\theta°} = 448\underline{/26.6°}$ Ω. Find the equivalent series circuit.

Solution

Find the in-phase and quadrature components of Z.

$$\text{In phase} = \cos\theta \times \text{magnitude} = 0.894 \times 448 = 400.5 \text{ Ω}$$
$$\text{Quadrature} = \sin\theta \times \text{magnitude} = 0.448 \times 448 = 200.7 \text{ Ω}$$
$$Z = 400.5 + j200.7 \text{ Ω}$$

Drawing the equivalent circuit, the source sees 400.5 Ω of resistance in series with 200.7 Ω of X_L (see Fig. 16-11).

Example 2

Refer to circuit *b* of Fig. 16-10. $I\underline{/\theta} = 1.266\underline{/-18.4°}$ A; $Z\underline{/\theta} = 395\underline{/18.4°}$ Ω. Find the equivalent series circuit.

Solution

Find the in-phase and quadrature components of Z.

$$\text{In phase} = \cos\theta \times \text{magnitude} = 0.949 \times 395 = 375 \text{ Ω}$$
$$\text{Quadrature} = \sin\theta \times \text{magnitude} = 0.316 \times 395 = 125 \text{ Ω}$$
$$Z = 375 + j125 \text{ Ω}$$

Drawing the equivalent circuit, the source sees 375 Ω of resistance in series with 125 Ω of X_L (see Fig. 16-12).

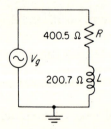

Fig. 16-11 Equivalent series circuit of Fig. 16-10*a*.

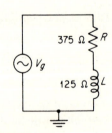

Fig. 16-12 Equivalent series circuit of Fig. 16-10*b*.

PROBLEMS

16-10 The inductive branch of a parallel-*RL* combination has a coil
 Q of 3.5. Find the phase angle of the inductive branch current.

16-11 Refer to Fig. 16-7. $X_L = 1000\ \Omega$; $R = 1500\ \Omega$; $V_g = 250$ V. Find:
 a) $I_l/\underline{\theta}$ b) $I_r/\underline{\theta}$
 c) $I/\underline{\theta}$ d) $Z/\underline{\theta}$

16-12 In Prob. 16-11, find:
 a) equivalent series circuit
 b) power dissipation

16-13 In a parallel-*RL* combination, $Q = 8$; $f = 400$ Hz; inductor
 resistance $= 40\ \Omega$; $V_g = 120$ V. Find:
 a) X_L
 b) inductance
 c) $Z/\underline{\theta}$ of inductive branch
 d) $I/\underline{\theta}$ of inductive branch

16-14 Refer to Fig. 16-7. $X_L = 50\ \Omega$; θ of circuit $I = -60°$. Find the
 resistance in parallel with the coil.

16-15 Refer to Prob. 16-14. $V_g = 70$ V; $f = 800$ Hz. Find:
 a) L b) $Z/\underline{\theta}$

16-16 Find the equivalent series circuit of Prob. 16-15.

QUESTIONS

16-11 In a parallel-*RL* circuit: why does the magnitude of the line
 current vary with the ratio of X_L to R?

16-12 Why is the load equally resistive and inductive when the circuit
 phase angle is 45°?

16-13 For all practical purposes, at what phase angle will the circuit
 appear "inductive"?

16-14 For all practical purposes, at what phase angle will the circuit
 appear "resistive"?

16-15 What relationship exists between coil *Q* and its effect upon the
 inductance?

16-16 When the coil *Q* is 20 or greater, the inductor may be considered
 perfect. Explain the effect this assumption has on circuit current
 and impedance computations.

16-17 What is the relationship between power dissipation of a parallel-
 RL circuit and its equivalent series circuit?

16-18 Explain why every series-*RL* circuit has an equivalent parallel-
 RL circuit and vice versa.

16-19 What effect does an increase in frequency have on a parallel-*RL*
 circuit?

16-20 What effect does an increase in *R* have on a parallel-*RL* circuit?

resonance

17

This chapter is primarily concerned with the behavior of series- and parallel-RLC circuits.

The series-RLC is considered in the first part of this chapter. The series-RLC circuit is different from the series-RC and -RL in that it is capable of responding to a certain band of frequencies while rejecting all frequencies above and below this band. It will be recalled that the series-RC and -RL circuits are able to reject those frequencies above f_{co} in one case, or below f_{co} in another case, depending upon where the output is taken (from R or from the reactive component).

In the many applications where an amplifier or device is to respond to a relatively wide range of frequencies, the possibilities of the series-RC and -RL circuits are worthy of consideration. However, there are applications where the device is to respond to a relatively small portion of the frequency range to which it is exposed. In such cases, the device is to reject all those frequencies below some value and all those above some slightly higher frequency, while accepting only those frequencies between the two values. The series-RLC circuit is one of the combinations which is capable of such a response. The same criterion is used for considering the low f_{co} and high f_{co}: the frequency where the circuit response is down to the half-power point (3 dB down) compared with maximum response.

In this chapter the principles of resonance, the determination of the resonant frequency, and many of the characteristics associated with resonance will be considered. The concepts of selectivity and bandwidth, and several methods by which they may be controlled, are also considered. The second portion of the chapter studies parallel-RLC circuits.

There are striking similarities and differences between the characteristics of series and parallel circuits. This chapter brings out the major aspects of these characteristics. While at series resonance, the circuit current is at its maximum value, the converse is true of a parallel-resonant circuit; i.e., the line current is minimum at the resonant frequency. In the series-resonant combination, impedance was at the value of the effective resistive component of the circuit. Although the im-

pedance is also resistive at the resonant frequency of the parallel combination, it is at a very high value. In fact, if a perfect inductor and
capacitor could be used with no losses in the circuit, the impedance
at resonance would be infinite and assumed resistive. The shape of
certain frequency-response curves is similar in both types of combinations. Also of interest is that, within limits, the resonant frequency
of a parallel-tuned circuit can be varied by resistance, which was not
true in the series arrangement. Vector algebra techniques are used
for circuit analysis.

17-1 SERIES-TUNED CIRCUIT: RESONANCE

*In this section you will learn the characteristics of resonance and how
to determine the resonant frequency of the RLC circuit.*

The term *tuned circuit* is another name for those circuits which contain both inductance and capacitance. Therefore we may refer to the
series-*RLC* circuit as a series-tuned circuit. The frequency at which the
circuit response is greatest (allowing I_{max}) is the frequency to which the
circuit is tuned. This is determined by the value of capacitance and
inductance possessed by the circuit. The tuned frequency is often called
the *resonant frequency* and is that frequency where $X_L = X_C$.
An equation for determining the resonant frequency of an *LC* combination can be derived. Since $X_L = X_C$,

$$2\pi fL = \frac{1}{2\pi fC}$$
$$f^2 = \frac{1}{4\pi^2 LC}$$

Taking the square root of each side,

$$f_o = \frac{1}{2\pi (LC)^{1/2}} \tag{17-1}$$

where f_o = resonant frequency
 L = inductance, H
 C = capacitance, F

Notice that the circuit resistance has no effect upon the determination
of the resonant frequency. The effect of the resistance is considered in
the following section.

Example 1

Calculate the resonant frequency of a series-tuned circuit having the following parameters: $L = 30$ mH; $C = 0.06$ μF.

Solution

$$f_0 = \frac{1}{2\pi \times [0.030 \times 0.06(10)^{-6}]^{1/2}} = 3751 \text{ Hz}$$

17-2 CHARACTERISTICS OF SERIES RESONANCE

In this section you will see how X_C and X_L vary with frequency in such a manner that they are equal in value only at the resonant frequency.

It was revealed earlier that X_C decreased and X_L increased with frequency increases. At some frequency, and only one frequency, the two

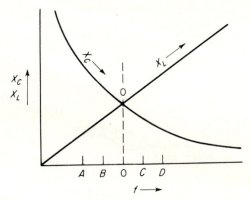

Fig. 17-1 X_C and X_L versus f.

reactances will be equal, and their effects are canceled. The frequency at which this occurs is called the *resonant frequency*. Figure 17-1 illustrates the changes in the two reactances as a function of frequency. Point 0 is the resonant frequency for the particular L and C combination.

Examination of Fig. 17-1 shows that X_C is the larger reactance at frequencies below resonance, while X_L is the larger at those frequencies above resonance.

17-3 VECTOR RELATIONSHIPS IN A SERIES-TUNED CIRCUIT

In this section you will see how the circuit phase angle, impedance, and current of a series-RLC circuit vary with frequency.

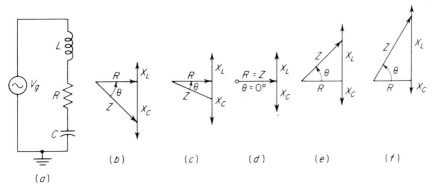

Fig. 17-2 f versus Z and θ: (a) circuit; (b) $f = A$; (c) $f = B$; (d) $f = 0$; (e) $f = C$; (f) $f = D$.

Figure 17-2 illustrates a series-tuned circuit and the vector relationships of R, X_L, X_C, θ, and Z as a function of frequency. The frequencies (A, B, 0, C, and D) are relative to each other. A is the lowest frequency, 0 is resonance, and D is the highest frequency, as shown in Fig. 17-1. At frequency A, X_C is greater than X_L. Notice that the two reactances are $180°$ out of phase. This seems logical when you stop to examine their effects upon the circuit, which has a single current path: X_C is an opposition such that it tends to produce a *voltage lagging I*. X_L tends to cause a *voltage leading I*. In a series-tuned circuit, where both reactances are present, X_C offsets the effect of X_L (or vice versa) to an extent which is determined by the magnitude of each.

In Fig. 17-2b, where the frequency is below resonance, X_L is smaller than X_C, so a portion of X_C equal to the value of X_L is canceled. The total reactance presented to the source is equal to the difference of X_C and X_L. Therefore the impedance is equal to the vector resultant of $X_C - X_L$ and R. Since this is a right triangle, Z and θ can be determined by the following relationships:

$$Z = [R^2 + (X_L - X_C)^2]^{1/2} = R + j(X_L - X_C)$$
$$\theta = \tan^{-1} \frac{(X_L - X_C)}{R}$$

At a higher frequency B, but still below resonance, X_C decreases and X_L increases. The difference between the two reactances is smaller, resulting in a lower value of Z; θ is closer to 0. At frequency 0, which is resonance, the reactances are equal, and the circuit appears resistive only.

$$Z = R + j(X_L - X_C)$$

Since $X_L = X_C$,

$$Z = R + j0 \quad \text{and} \quad \theta = 0°$$

At frequencies above resonance, X_L becomes greater than X_C, and the reactance seen by the source is inductive. The circuit phase angle becomes positive (whereas it was negative at frequencies below resonance).

The voltages (V_l and V_c) vary in the same manner as the reactances and may be determined from the following relationships:

$$V_l = jX_L I \qquad V_c = jX_C I$$

since V_L and V_C are 180° out of phase, V_L leads I by 90° and V_C lags I by 90°.

Example

Let $L = 30$ mH; $C = 0.06\ \mu$F. Find V_l and V_c at 3.5 kHz. $I = 0.045$ A.

Solution

(a)   Find V_l at 3.5 kHz:

$$X_L = 2\pi \times 3500 \times 0.03 = 660\ \Omega$$
$$V_l = j(660 \times 0.045) = +j29.70\ \text{V}$$

(b)   Find V_c at 3.5 kHz:

$$X_C = \frac{1}{2\pi \times 3500 \times 0.06(10)^{-6}} = 758\ \Omega$$
$$V_c = -j(758)(0.045) = -j34.11\ \text{V}$$

Notice that V_c exceeds V_l, since the frequency under consideration is below resonance.

17-4 EQUIVALENT CIRCUITS BELOW, AT, AND ABOVE RESONANCE

In this section you will learn why the series-RLC circuit appears as a series-RC network below resonance, a pure resistive network at resonance, and a series-RL network above resonance.

As the frequency is increased from the minimum, Z decreases to its lowest value, which occurs at resonance. At frequencies below reso-

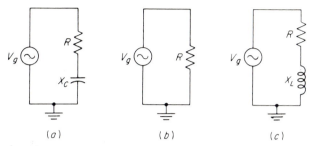

Fig. 17-3 Equivalent circuits: (a) below resonance; (b) at resonance; (c) above resonance.

nance, the source sees a series-RC circuit (Fig. 17-3a). At resonance, where the canceling effect of X_L and X_C is complete, the source sees a pure resistive circuit (Fig. 17-3b). When the frequency is above resonance, X_L predominates over X_C in the canceling effect, and the source sees a series-RL circuit (Fig. 17-3c).

Example

A series-tuned circuit has the following parameters: $L = 25$ mH; $C = 0.04$ μF; $R = 200$ Ω. Find: (a) f_o; (b) equivalent circuit at resonance; (c) equivalent circuit at $f_{co,\min}$; (d) equivalent circuit at $f_{co,\max}$.

Solution

(a) Find f_o:

$$f_o = \frac{1}{2\pi (0.025 \times 0.04 \times 10^{-6})^{1/2}} = 5033 \text{ Hz}$$

(b) Equivalent circuit at resonance: since $X_L - X_C = 0$, then

$$Z = R + j0 = 200 + j0$$

(c) Equivalent circuit at $f_{co,\min}$ (also referred to as lower half-power point): at this frequency X_C is greater than X_L by a value equal to that of R, which is 200 Ω.

$$Z = 200 - j200 \text{ } \Omega$$

(d) Equivalent circuit at $f_{co,\max}$ (also referred to as upper half-power point): at this frequency X_L is greater than X_C by a value equal to that of R, which is 200 Ω. Hence,

$$Z = 200 + j200 \text{ } \Omega$$

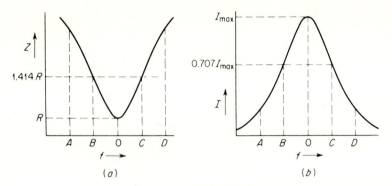

Fig. 17-4 *f* versus *Z* and *I*.

17-5 RELATIONSHIP OF *Z*, *I*, AND FREQUENCY

*In this section you will learn that, in a series-*RLC *circuit at resonance, the impedance is minimum and equal to the circuit* R *and current is at its maximum.*

At all frequencies other than resonance, the impedance consists of some reactive quality and hence is greater than the value of *R* alone. This relationship is illustrated in Fig. 17-4*a*. Assuming that the magnitude of the source potential is constant, the circuit current will vary inversely with the impedance, as dictated by Ohm's law (as shown in Fig. 17-4*b*).

Figure 17-4 shows that maximum current flows at resonance because the impedance is minimum and equal to *R*. In terms of current, the frequency response, or *bandpass*, of the series-tuned circuit is between frequencies *B* and *C*, where the current is down to 70.7 percent of the resonant-frequency current. The series-tuned circuit effectively rejects all frequencies below *B* and above *C* in Fig. 17-4*b*. The impedance at frequencies *B* and *C* is equal to 1.414 times more than the resonant-frequency impedance (which is the resistance alone), as proved by the following relationship.

At resonance,

$$I = \frac{V}{Z} = \frac{V}{R}$$

Let *V* = 100 V and *R* = 100 Ω.

$$I = \tfrac{100}{100} = 1A \qquad I = \frac{100\underline{/0°}}{100\underline{/0°}} = 1\underline{/0°}$$

At frequency B of Fig. 17-4a,

$$I = \frac{V}{Z} = \frac{100\underline{/0°}}{141.4\underline{/-45°}} = 0.707\underline{/45°} \text{ A}$$

At frequency C of Fig. 17-4a,

$$I = \frac{V}{Z} = \frac{100\underline{/0°}}{141.4\underline{/45°}} = 0.707\underline{/-45°} \text{ A}$$

In a series-tuned circuit, the *low-* and *high-frequency cutoff values* are those frequencies at which the impedance is equal to 1.414R and the current is 0.707 of the resonant-frequency current. These are the half-power points of the circuit at which the magnitude of the phase angle is 45°.

17-6 BANDPASS AND SELECTIVITY

In this section you will learn: that the frequency spread between the lower and upper cutoff values is called the bandpass; how to determine the upper and lower cutoff frequency values and bandpass; the meaning of selectivity and that it is directly related to the L/C ratio; and the effect of circuit resistance upon bandpass and selectivity.

The *bandpass* is the frequency spread between $f_{co,min}$ and $f_{co,max}$. Larger values of circuit resistance result in a reduced resonant-frequency current and a broader bandwidth. Worthy of mention at this point is the concept of circuit Q, which is the ratio of the coil reactance to the circuit resistance.

$$\text{Circuit } Q = \frac{X_L}{\text{circuit } R} \qquad \text{(17-2)}$$

where R is the equivalent R of all circuit losses. The circuit Q and coil Q are nearly identical in many tuned circuits, since the major portion of the loss is found in the inductor. By correlating the concept of circuit Q and its relationship to the characteristics of a series-tuned circuit, the following statements can be made:

1 A decrease in circuit Q results in an increased bandwidth, which is a reduction in the selectivity.

2   An increase in the selectivity and a narrower bandpass is brought about by an increase in circuit Q.

Selectivity, as used here, may be defined as the ability of the tuned circuit to select a particular band of frequencies and to discriminate against all other frequencies above and below that band. High-Q coils are used for high-selectivity tuned circuits and vice versa. A general guide for the determination of $f_{co,min}$, $f_{co,max}$, and the bandwidth is as follows:

$$f_{co,max} = f_o + \frac{R}{4\pi L} \tag{17-3}$$

$$f_{co,min} = f_o - \frac{R}{4\pi L} \tag{17-4}$$

$$\text{Bandwidth} = f_{co,max} - f_{co,min} = \frac{R}{2\pi L} \tag{17-5}$$

Note   Bandpass is sometimes measured at other operating points, such as 6 dB down from reference. Unless otherwise specified, the bandpass is considered to be those frequencies between the two half-power points.

The preceding relationships point out that the selectivity is determined by the R/L, ratio with the selectivity increasing as the ratio decreases. The bandwidth can also be computed by the following relationship:

$$\text{Bandwidth} = \frac{f_o}{Q} \tag{17-6}$$

The Q of a series-tuned circuit is obtainable (from the following relationship) when the values of capacitance, inductance, and resistance are known.

$$Q = \frac{1}{R}\left(\frac{L}{C}\right)^{1/2} \tag{17-7}$$

This shows that the selectivity of the circuit is directly proportional to the square root of the L/C ratio.

Consider now a series-tuned circuit with several values of resistance, each representing a variation of circuit Q. Of primary interest is the effect of resistance upon the resonant-frequency current and the bandpass.

Example 1

A series-tuned circuit resonates at 2 kHz. $L = 80$ mH. Find $f_{co,min}$, $f_{co,max}$, and bandpass when the resistance of the tuned circuit is: (a) 100 Ω; (b) 200 Ω; (c) 300 Ω.

Solution

(a)   When $R = 100$ Ω,

$$f_{co,min} = f_0 - \frac{R}{4\pi L} = 2000 - \frac{100}{4\pi \times 0.080}$$

$$= 2000 - 99.5 = 1900.5 \text{ Hz}$$

$$f_{co,max} = f_0 + \frac{R}{4\pi L} = 2000 + 99.5 = 2099.5 \text{ Hz}$$

$$\text{Bandpass} = f_{co,max} - f_{co,min} = 2099.5 - 1900.5 = 199 \text{ Hz}$$

(b)   When $R = 200$ Ω,

$$f_{co,min} = 2000 - \frac{200}{4\pi \times 0.080} = 2000 - 199 = 1801 \text{ Hz}$$

$$f_{co,max} = 2000 + 199 = 2199 \text{ Hz}$$

$$\text{Bandpass} = 2199 - 1801 = 398 \text{ Hz}$$

(c)   When $R = 300$ Ω,

$$f_{co,min} = 2000 - \frac{300}{4\pi \times 0.080} = 2000 - 299 = 1701 \text{ Hz}$$

$$f_{co,max} = 2000 + 299 = 2299 \text{ Hz}$$

$$\text{Bandpass} = 2299 - 1701 = 598 \text{ Hz}$$

Example 2

Find the current at resonance for each value of circuit resistance stated in Example 3. $V_o = 200$ V.

Solution

(a)   When $R = 100$ Ω,

$$I = \frac{200\underline{/0°}}{100\underline{/0°}} = 2\underline{/0°} \text{ A}$$

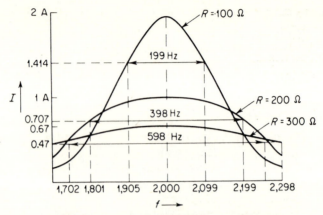

Fig. 17-5 f versus I with different resistances.

(*b*) When $R = 200\ \Omega$,

$$I = \frac{200\underline{/0^\circ}}{200\underline{/0^\circ}} = 1\underline{/0^\circ}\ \text{A}$$

(*c*) When $R = 300\ \Omega$,

$$I = \frac{200\underline{/0^\circ}}{300\underline{/0^\circ}} = 0.67\underline{/0^\circ}\ \text{A}$$

The effect of the circuit resistance upon the resonant-frequency current and the bandpass is plotted in Fig. 17-5. These curves of Fig. 17-5 prove that the selectivity becomes broader with an increase in circuit resistance. With 300 Ω, for example, the bandpass is comparatively large (598 Hz), and the circuit has lost many of its discriminatory characteristics.

The magnitude of V_c and V_l at resonance is greater than V_g by the amount of Q; this is called the *resonant rise in voltage.* Either of these voltages, V_c or V_l, may be used separately but cannot be combined, since their vector sum is zero.

PROBLEMS

17-1 The parameters of a series-tuned circuit are $L = 5$ mH; $C = 1.5$ μF. Find:
    a) f_o b) X_L and X_C

17-2 In the circuit of Prob. 17-1, $R = 6\ \Omega$ and $V_g = 140$ V. Find the
      following:
      a) coil Q b) $f_{co,min}$ c) $f_{co,max}$
      d) bandwidth   e) I at resonance
17-3 Find the resonant frequency for each of the following tuned
      circuits:
      a) $L = 10$ H; $C = 5\ \mu$F
      b) $L = 0.05$ H; $C = 0.9\ \mu$F
      c) $L = .0.6$ H; $C = 30\ \mu$F
17-4 For the circuit of Prob. 17-2, find the circuit Q.
17-5 In the circuit of Prob. 17-2, find the circuit R required to obtain
      a bandwidth of:
      a) 100 Hz   b) 500 Hz   c) 1000 Hz
17-6 A series-tuned circuit has the following parameters: $L = 4$ mH;
      $f_o = 353.3$ kHz. Find C.
17-7 $C = 250$ pF; $f_o = 150$ kHz. Find L.
17-8 In Prob. 17-2, find I at $f_{co,min}$ and $f_{co,max}$.

QUESTIONS

17-1 Explain how a series-RLC circuit is able to reject all frequencies
      above and below a certain band of frequencies.
17-2 What condition exists between X_C and X_L at resonance?
17-3 What does the circuit see as impedance at resonance?
17-4 Explain how X_C varies from low to high frequencies.
17-5 Explain how X_L varies from low to high frequencies.
17-6 Explain how the circuit phase angle varies from below to above
      resonance.
17-7 What is the equivalent circuit of a series-RLC circuit below
      resonance?
17-8 What is the equivalent circuit of a series-RLC circuit above
      resonance?
17-9 What is circuit selectivity?
17-10 What is the relationship between bandwidth and circuit R?

17-7 CHARACTERISTICS OF A PARALLEL-TUNED CIRCUIT

*In this section you will learn that the parallel-RLC circuit has three
resonant conditions and that three conditions of resonance occur at
the same frequency only in high-Q parallel-RLC circuits.*

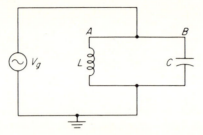

Fig. 17-6   Parallel-tuned circuit.

Figure 17-6 illustrates a parallel-tuned combination, also called a *tank circuit* if its Q is reasonably high. The resonant frequency of the tank circuit may be determined by any one of three possible conditions:

1   When $X_L = X_C$
2   When I is minimum
3   When Z is pure resistance (phase angle is zero, and PF $= 1$)

The three conditions occur at approximately the same frequency only when a very high-Q coil is utilized and there is no appreciable loss associated with the tank circuit. $X_L = X_C$ at a frequency determined by the same dimensions of the series-resonant circuit analysis, namely,

$$f_{o1} = \frac{1}{2\pi(LC)^{1/2}}$$

For simplicity, the initial analysis is confined to the condition where the coil Q is greater than 20 and the circuit losses are negligible. *At the resonant frequency, $X_L = X_C$.* Examination of Fig. 17-6 reveals that this results in I_l and I_c being of the same magnitude. Furthermore, since I_l lags by very nearly 90° and I_c leads by the same angle, these reactive currents are for practical purposes 180° out of phase, and their sum (vectorially) is zero. The total line or generator current would be zero if no losses were present in the circuit. The presence of even negligible effective resistance enables some line current to flow. The reason for this is discussed in Sec. 17-9.

Because the two reactive branch currents cancel out, *the source sees a resistive load.* Since the current is minimum and resistive, the circuit impedance at the resonant condition is resistive and maximum. As stated in a previous paragraph, these three characteristics occur at approximately the same frequency only when $Q = 20$ or greater. Consider a typical example.

Example

Refer to the circuit of Fig. 17-6, assuming no losses. $L = 50$ mH; $C = 800$ pF; $V_g = 150$ V; $f_o = 25.165$ kHz. Find $Z\underline{/\theta}$ and $I\underline{/\theta}$ at: (a) 300 Hz; (b) 25.165 Hz; (c) 50 kHz.

Solution

(a) Find $Z\underline{/\theta}$ and $I\underline{/\theta}$ at 300 Hz. First find the reactances.

$$X_L = 2\pi \times 0.05 \times 300 = 94.2 \ \Omega$$

$$X_C = \frac{1}{2\pi \times 8(10)^{-10} \times 300} = 663{,}146 \ \Omega$$

Expressing each reactance in appropriate forms in the impedance equation,

$$Z\underline{/\theta} = \frac{94.2\underline{/90°} \times 663{,}146\underline{/-90°}}{(0 + j94.2) + (0 - j663{,}146)}$$
$$= \frac{62{,}468{,}353\underline{/0°}}{663{,}052\underline{/-90°}} = 94.2\underline{/90°} \ \Omega$$

and

$$I\underline{/\theta} = \frac{V_g\underline{/0}}{Z\underline{/\theta}} = \frac{150\underline{/0°}}{94.2\underline{/90°}} = 1.592\underline{/-90°} \ A$$

(b) Find $Z\underline{/\theta}$ and $I\underline{/\theta}$ at resonance (25.165 kHz):

$$X_L = 2\pi \times 25{,}165 \times 0.05 = 7906 \ \Omega$$

$$X_C = \frac{1}{2\pi \times 25{,}165 \times 8(10)^{-10}} = 7906 \ \Omega$$

Expressing each reactance in the appropriate form in the impedance equation,

$$Z\underline{/\theta} = \frac{7906\underline{/90°} \times 7906\underline{/-90°}}{(0 + j7906) + (0 - j7906)}$$
$$= \frac{(7906)^2\underline{/0°}}{0\underline{/0°}} = \infty\underline{/0°} \ \Omega$$

and

$$I\underline{/\theta} = \frac{V_g\underline{/\theta}}{Z\underline{/\theta}} = \frac{150\underline{/0°}}{\infty\underline{/0°}} = 0\underline{/0°} \ A$$

(c)   Find $Z\underline{/\theta}$ and $I\underline{/\theta}$ at 50 kHz.

$$X_L = 2\pi \times 50(10)^3 \times 0.05 = 15{,}708 \ \Omega$$

$$X_C = \frac{1}{2\pi \times 50(10)^3 \times 8(10)^{-10}} = 3979 \ \Omega$$

Expressing each reactance in the appropriate forms in the impedance equation and solving,

$$Z\underline{/\theta} = \frac{15{,}708\underline{/90°} \times 3979\underline{/-90°}}{(0 + j15{,}708) + (0 - j3979)}$$

$$= \frac{62{,}502{,}132\underline{/0°}}{11{,}729\underline{/90°}} = 5329\underline{/-90°} \ \Omega$$

and

$$I\underline{/\theta} = \frac{V_g\underline{/\theta}}{Z\underline{/\theta}} = \frac{150\underline{/0°}}{5329\underline{/-90°}} = 0.0281\underline{/90°} \ A$$

The preceding example points out the current, impedance, and phase-angle characteristics of the low-resistance tank circuit at conditions below, at, and above resonance. Obviously, this loss-free circuit cannot readily be achieved in practice. Once it is "excited," currents could be assumed to continue flowing through L and C, even after the generator is disconnected, since the line current is zero. Recall the phase characteristics of X_L and X_C: electron displacement would be downward in one branch and upward in the other at the same instant; with these currents equal in magnitude, Kirchhoff's law would dictate zero-line current. The current flow from one branch to the other, which represents an exchange of stored energy (from L to C, then from C to L), is referred to as the *tank circulating current*, or *mesh current*. In the theoretical case with no losses, this circulating current would approach infinite value, since the series Z through which it flows, recalling that $Z = (R^2 + X^2)^{1/2}$, is 0 Ω.

17-8 GRAPHIC RELATIONSHIP OF X_L, X_C, AND Z TO FREQUENCY

In this section you will graphically see that at resonance the reactances are equal and impedance is maximum while current and circuit phase angle are minimum.

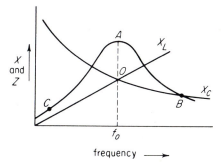

Fig. 17-7 X_C, X_L, and Z versus f.

Figure 17-7 illustrates the relationship of the reactances and impedance of a parallel-tank circuit as a function of frequency. Assume a tank circuit which has small but negligible loss. At some low frequency (point C), determined by the values of L and C, X_L will be so low compared with X_C that the inductor effectively shunts the capacitive branch for all practical purposes, and the circuit impedance is equal to X_L. This is the condition where X_L is less than 10 percent of X_C in ohmic value. At point C, the source sees an inductive load.

As the frequency is increased, the inductive current decreases (since X_L increases) and the capacitor current increases (since X_C decreases). The line current becomes smaller as the two reactive currents approach each other in magnitude, since they are 180° out of phase. The impedance increases in the same manner in which the circuit current decreases.

At resonance, the reactive currents are equal, and the canceling effect is complete, resulting in minimum current. The source sees a resistive load, the ohmic value of which is at its highest point for the entire frequency range. (With zero losses, point A on the Z curve would approach infinity.)

As the frequency is increased above resonance, the inductive current decreases (since X_L is increasing) while the capacitive current increases (since X_C is decreasing). As the two reactive currents differ in magnitude, the circuit current increases; since the capacitive current is larger, the source sees a capacitive load. At some high frequency, where X_C is less than 10 percent of X_L, the capacitance effectively shunts the inductance for all practical purposes, and the circuit impedance is equal to X_C (point B).

Note the reversed relationship between series and parallel circuits below resonance, at resonance, and above resonance: the parallel circuit appears inductive below resonance, resistive at resonance, and capacitive above resonance. Note that the impedance at resonance, although resistive in both cases, is minimum in the series combination and maximum for the parallel-tuned circuit.

17-9   THE EFFECT OF COIL Q AND RESISTANCE

In this section you will learn that the three resonant frequencies of the parallel-RLC are nearly equal when coil Q is 20 or greater and in a low-Q circuit the resonant frequency at which the circuit phase angle is zero is the one most commonly considered most desirable of the three frequencies to utilize.

One of the most common tank circuits containing significant loss is one in which a low-Q coil is used. Such a circuit is illustrated in Fig. 17-8.

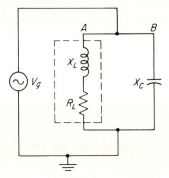

Fig. 17-8   Tank circuit with a low-Q coil.

The three conditions stated in Sec. 17-7 do not occur at the same frequency.

Condition I: $X_L = X_C$

The vector diagrams of Fig. 17-9 illustrate the effect of a low-Q coil in a tank circuit at the condition where $X_L = X_C$, which is one possible way of defining parallel resonance. The impedance of branch A (Z_a) is greater than that of branch B, even though $X_L = X_C$ (see Fig. 17-9a), because of the resistive component in leg A. I_a is smaller than I_b, since Z_a is greater than Z_b. In illustrating the current vectors, the quadrants are interchanged (see Fig. 17-9b), since the current phase angle is the same but opposite in sign to the impedance phase angle. *In condition I, where $X_L = X_C$, the line-current phase angle is not zero, and it is not at its minimum value.*

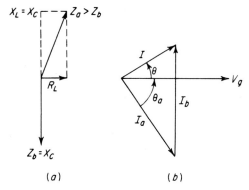

Fig. 17-9 Low-Q tank-circuit analysis: condition I. (a) Z of each branch; (b) circuit relationship when $X_L = X_C$ in a low-Q tank circuit.

This behavior occurs at the frequency where the reactances are equal, which is determined by the previously stated equation

$$f_{o1} = \frac{1}{2\pi(LC)^{1/2}}$$

where f_{o1} = resonant frequency, Hz
$\quad L$ = inductance, H
$\quad C$ = capacitance, F

Condition II: I Line Is Minimum

Figure 17-10 illustrates the vector relationships of the currents for condition II, when I is minimum; this is the second method of defining

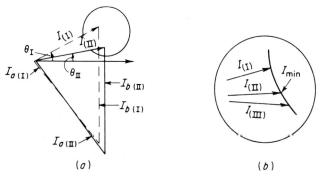

Fig. 17-10   Low-Q tank-circuit analysis: condition II. (a) current relationships of condition II; (b) locus of I magnified for conditions I, II, and III.

parallel resonance. If the frequency is reduced below that of condition I, Z_a and θ_a decrease, and Z_b (which is X_C) becomes greater (the dotted-line vectors illustrate condition I). Z_a became less because X_L goes down in value as the frequency is reduced, resulting in a still lower Q value (tan θ_a). Hence θ_a is reduced. Although I_b maintains its 90° leading phase angle, it is reduced in magnitude because of an increase in X_C which came about because of the frequency reduction. The result of the increased I_a, reduced θ_a, and decreased I_b is a smaller magnitude of I. This trend continues until I minimum is achieved at a frequency determined by the following relationship:

$$f_{o2} = \frac{1}{2\pi (LC)^{1/2}} \left(1 - \frac{1}{4Q^2} \right)^{1/2} \tag{17-8}$$

Note Q has the same value as in condition I in the equation.

Condition III: θ Is Zero

Refer to the vector diagram of Fig. 17-11 for the following analysis of condition III (circuit current is pure resistive). The dotted lines illustrate the vectors of condition II (where I was minimum). As the frequency is further reduced from the value of f_{o2}, X_C increases, resulting in a further reduction in I_b. At the same time, X_L decreases and I_a becomes greater. There will be some frequency where the quadrature component of I_a is equal to I_b (which is a pure quadrature component in the circuit under consideration). When this condition is achieved, the quadrature currents completely cancel, allowing the circuit current to be equal to the in-phase (resistive) component of I_a. The tank circuit appears resistive at this frequency, which is determined from the following relationship when Q is determined at f_{o3}:

$$f_{o3} = \frac{1}{2\pi (LC)^{1/2}} \left(1 - \frac{CR_1^2}{L} \right)^{1/2} \tag{17-9}$$

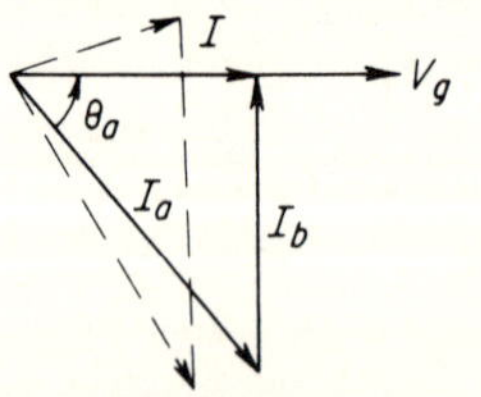

Fig. 17-11   Current relationships when I is resistive in a low-Q tank circuit.

or

$$f_{o3} = \frac{1}{2\pi(LC)^{1/2}} \left(\frac{Q^2}{Q^2+1}\right)^{1/2}$$

(17-9a)

If the f_{o1} Q is used, then

$$f_{o3} = \frac{1}{2\pi(LC)^{1/2}} \left(1 - \frac{1.}{QL^2}\right)$$

(17-9b)

Examination of the three equations for determining the frequency at which each condition is achieved reveals that f_{o2} and f_{o3} are very nearly equal to f_{o1} when the coil Q is 20 or greater.

The definition in condition III (where the tank circuit appears resistive) is commonly used as the resonant-frequency condition when the tank circuit contains significant resistance. Here the expression *adjusted for unity PF* will be encountered.

17-10   TANK CIRCUITS CONTAINING RESISTANCE IN BOTH LEGS

In this section you will learn that the resonant frequency of a parallel-RLC in which the circuit phase angle is to be zero can be varied within limits by introducing resistance in each branch. You will also learn how to calculate the resistance values used for obtaining a given resonant frequency.

Some low-Q tank circuits, for special applications, contain resistance in both branches. As previously stated, resonance in such cases is considered to occur at the frequency where the circuit-current phase angle is zero (quadrature components of each branch current are equal). The resonant frequency may be varied to some extent by changes in R_L and R_C, because they partially control the magnitudes of the two branch quadrature-current components. The resistance required for each branch to obtain resonance at a given frequency may be determined from the following relationships:

$$R_L = \left[\frac{X_L}{X_C}(R_C)^2 + X_L X_C - X_L^2\right]^{1/2}$$

(17-10)

and

$$R_C = \left[\frac{X_C}{X_L}(R_L)^2 + X_L X_C - X_C^2\right]^{1/2}$$

(17-11)

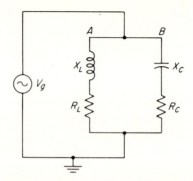

Fig. 17-12   Tank circuit with resistance in both branches.

Example

Refer to Fig. 17-12. $X_L = 58\ \Omega$; $Q = 2$; $X_C = 60\ \Omega$. Find the R_C value at which the circuit will resonate.

Solution

Find R_C: first determine R_L.

$$R_L = \frac{X_L}{Q} = \frac{58}{2} = 29\ \Omega$$

$$R_C = [(\tfrac{60}{58} \times 841 + (58 \times 60) - 60^2)]^{1/2} = 27.4\ \Omega$$

When $R_L = R_C$, the tank-circuit resonance condition is determined by the f_{01} equation, with stated L and C values. The reason for this exists in the effect of each resistance upon the phase angle of its branch current. Refer to Fig. 17-12. R_L reduces θ of I_a from $-90°$ to a smaller value, as shown in the vector diagram of Fig. 17-13, while I_b is reduced from a $+90°$ phase angle to a smaller value because of R_C.

There will be a condition where I_a and I_b are of such magnitudes that their quadrature components cancel and the circuit current is resistive. This condition occurs when $R_C = R_L$, and the resonant frequency can then be computed from the f_{01} equation. Figure 17-13 vectorially describes this condition.

An additional feature of interest pertaining to the effect of the resistance in a tank circuit is that it may be made resonant for all frequencies when $R_C = R_L$ if each resistance is equal to $(L/C)^{1/2}$.

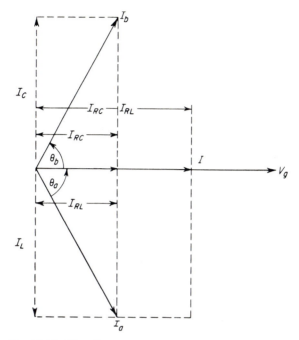

Fig. 17-13   The effect of R_L and R_C on the circuit current.

PROBLEMS

17-9   Refer to Fig. 17-6. $L = 0.5$ H; $C = 5$ μF; $Q = 25$; $V_g = 150$ V.
Note: assume the coil is perfect. Find the following:
a) f_o b) $I_l\underline{/\theta}$ c) $I_c\underline{/\theta}$
d) $I\underline{/\theta}$ e) $Z\underline{/\theta}$

17-10   In Prob. 17-9, assume L is variable from 0.1 to 1 H. Find f_o at
the:
a)   minimum L setting
b)   maximum L setting

17-11   In the circuit of Prob. 17-9, find the following at $f_o - 10$ Hz:
a) $Z\underline{/\theta}$ b) $I\underline{/\theta}$

17-12   In the circuit of Prob. 17-9, find the following at $f_o + 10$ Hz:
a) $Z\underline{/\theta}$ b) $I\underline{/\theta}$

17-13   Indicate the type of load the source sees for the conditions of
Probs.:
a)   17-9   b)   17-11   c)   17-12

QUESTIONS

17-11   What is a tank circuit?

17-12   What are the three possible conditions of a tank circuit at resonance?

17-13   When does a tank circuit see a resistive load?

17-14   When does a tank circuit see a capacitive load?

17-15   When does a tank circuit see an inductive load?

17-16   What are the comparative values of X_L and X_C below resonance?

17-17   What are the comparative values of X_L and X_C above resonance?

17-18   How does Z vary with frequency in a tank circuit?

17-19   How does the circuit phase angle vary with frequency in a tank circuit?

17-20   What effect does a low-Q coil have on the circuit phase angle and magnitude at resonance?

17-11   VOLTAGE- AND IMPEDANCE-VERSUS-FREQUENCY-RESPONSE CURVES

In this section you will learn about the effect of frequency upon the impedance of and voltage across the parallel-RLC.

Figure 17-14a illustrates the tank circuit in series with a resistor R_S (which may be that of the source) necessary in this circuit to enable the voltage across the tank to vary with its impedance. Without R_S, the voltage across the tank circuit would always be that of V_g, even though its

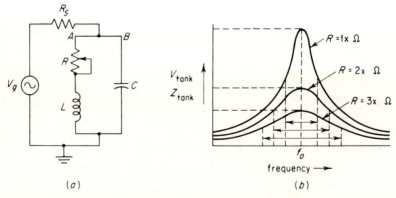

(a)   (b)

Fig. 17-14   *V*- and *Z*-versus-frequency-response curves of a tank circuit: (*a*) circuit; (*b*) curves.

impedance varied with frequency changes. Figure 17-14a illustrates the relationship of tank impedance versus frequency and tank voltage versus frequency. The impedance and voltage are plotted on the y axis, and frequency is on the x axis, since it is the controlling variable. Assume that the tank-circuit Q is reasonably high.

Notice that the impedance of the tank circuit is at its maximum value at the resonant frequency. At frequencies below resonance, the impedance decreases as the departure from resonance becomes greater. At frequencies above resonance, the impedance also decreases as the departure from resonance becomes greater. Also notice the effect of tank resistance upon the response curves. The tank circuit containing the least resistance displays the greatest impedance at resonance and possesses the narrowest bandwidth (highest *selectivity*). It has been pointed out that the inductive and capacitive currents are exactly 180° out of phase at resonance; if the tank circuit contained no losses, the impedance would be infinite in value and resistive in nature. With some losses in the tank, the branch currents do not cancel out completely, resulting in a total current of some small magnitude. If this resistance is a small value ($X_L/R = 20$ or more if it is in the inductance branch, or $X_C/R = 20$ or more if it is in the capacitive branch), the small resultant circuit current will have a phase angle of only several degrees. For all practical purposes, such a circuit may be considered resistive at resonance. Doubling the resistance value in the tank (5 to 10 Ω in Fig. 17-14b) reduces the impedance at resonance to 50 percent of the original resonant value. In other words, a reduction in tank-circuit Q results in a reduction in the resonant-frequency impedance.

In an earlier section, low- and high-frequency cutoffs ($f_{co,\text{min}}$ and $f_{co,\text{max}}$) were defined as those frequencies where the tuned-circuit response is down to the half-power point. At these points the magnitude of the tank I is 0.707 times the maximum value which occurs at resonance. The basis for determining bandwidth of a parallel-tuned circuit is the same as the series-tuned circuit: the bandwidth is the frequency spread from the frequency below resonance where the V and Z response is 0.707 of the maximum response at resonance to the frequency above resonance where the V and Z response is 0.707 of the response at resonance.

Examination of the V- and Z-response curves of Fig. 17-14b shows that the *tank-circuit selectivity is highest with the minimum tank resistance.* The mathematical relationship is

$$\text{Bandwidth} = f_{co,\text{max}} - f_{co,\text{min}} = \frac{f_o}{Q}$$

where $f_{co,max}$ = frequency above resonance where V and Z are 0.707 of resonant value

$f_{co,min}$ = frequency below resonance where V and Z are 0.707 of resonant value

Q = circuit $Q = X_L/($circuit $R)$

f_o = resonant frequency

Example 1

Refer to the circuit of Fig. 17-14a. $X_C = X_L = 150$ Ω; $f_o = 8$ kHz; $Q = 15$. Find: (a) $Z_{tank}\underline{/\theta}$; (b) bandwidth; (c) $f_{co,min}$; (d) $f_{co,max}$.

Solution

(a) Find $Z_{tank}\underline{/\theta}$: find the impedance of each branch in both rectangular and polar forms. In branch A,

$$R = \frac{X_L}{Q} = \frac{150}{15} = 10 \text{ Ω}$$
$$Z_a = 10 + j150 \text{ Ω} = 150\underline{/86.2°} \text{ Ω}$$

In branch B,

$$Z_b = 0 - j150 = 150\underline{/-90°} \text{ Ω}$$

Substituting into the impedance equation,

$$Z\underline{/\theta} = \frac{150\underline{/86.2°} \times 150\underline{/-90°}}{(10 + j150) + (0 - j150)} = \frac{22,500\underline{/-3.8°}}{10\underline{/0°}} = 2250\underline{/-3.8°} \text{ Ω}$$

(b) Find the bandwidth:

$$\text{Bandwidth} = \frac{f_o}{Q} = \frac{8000}{15} = 533.3 \text{ Hz}$$

(c) Find $f_{co,min}$. Since the Q is high, the bandwidth extends equally on both sides of the resonant frequency; hence

$$f_{co,min} = \frac{533}{2} \text{below } f_o = 8000 - 266.5 = 7733.3 \text{ Hz}$$

(d) Find $f_{co,max}$:

$$f_{co,max} = 8000 + 266.5 = 8266.5 \text{ Hz}$$

Example 2

Refer to the parameters of Example 1. Assume that the tank potential at f_o is 200 V. Find the tank potential at $f_{co,\text{max}}$ and $f_{co,\text{min}}$.

Solution

Based on the definition of bandwidth, the tank-circuit potential at $f_{co,\text{max}}$ and $f_{co,\text{min}}$ is 0.707 of its potential at resonance. Hence V_{tank} at $f_{co,\text{max}}$ and $f_{co,\text{min}} = 0.707 \times 200 = 141.4$ V.

Example 3

Refer to the parameters of Example 1. Find the circuit Q and resistance value required to increase the selectivity such that the bandwidth is reduced to 200 Hz.

Solution

(a)   Find the circuit Q:

$$Q = \frac{f_o}{\text{bandwidth}} = \frac{8000}{200} = 40$$

(b)   Find the resistance:

$$R = \frac{X_L}{Q} = \frac{150}{40} = 3.75 \ \Omega$$

The Effect of Q on Frequency-Response Symmetry

It should be noted that the response curve above and below resonance is symmetrical only for high-Q circuits unless special provisions are made. Refer to Fig. 17-15 for the following discussion of the fre-

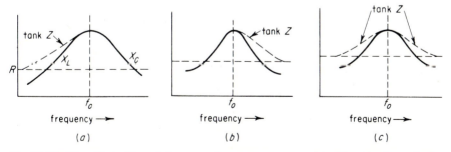

Fig. 17-15   The effect of branch losses on the response curves: (a) with major losses in the L branch; (b) with major losses in the C branch; (c) with losses equally balanced in the L and C branches.

quency response of low-Q tank circuits. When the major losses are present in the inductive branch, the response curve takes the shape illustrated by Fig. 17-15a. Although X_L decreases with frequency reductions below resonance, the tank Z response is less abrupt than the high-frequency portion of the curve and reduces only down to the value of R. Hence the $f_{co,min}$-to-f_o frequency span is greater than that from $f_{co,max}$ to f_o. The inverse relationship occurs if the major losses occur in the capacitive branch (see Fig. 17-15b). The lack of symmetry generally is considered undesirable. Introducing equal losses in both branches alters the response curve in the same fashion above and below f_o, resulting in a fairly symmetrical response (see Fig. 17-15c). This is commonly the case in low-Q tank circuits, where a resistance is deliberately inserted in the capacitive branch to equalize the response on both sides of f_o. Since the three resonant conditions occur at the same frequency, in such a case, the circuit can be adjusted for unity PF merely by adjusting for minimum line current.

17-12 CURRENT-VERSUS-FREQUENCY-RESPONSE CURVES

In this section you will learn about the effect of frequency upon parallel-RLC circuit current with several values of resistance.

Figure 17-16 illustrates the current-vs.-frequency-response curves of a tank circuit with several values of tank resistance. In Sec. 17-11, it was pointed out that the maximum impedance and minimum current would result in a minimum tank resistance. The reduction in resonant current is most abrupt with the smaller tank-resistance values. The preceding analysis of the relationship of V, I, and Z versus frequency points out

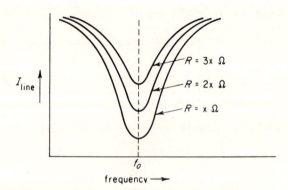

Fig. 17-16 *I*-versus-frequency-responses curves of a tank circuit.

that the parallel-resonant circuit is used in those applications where a large impedance and/or voltage is desired for a specific frequency band.

The Effect of Loading

In many practical cases, a resistive load is connected across the tank circuit. The resistive load may be treated as a shunt resistance of the tank capacitor, and its equivalent series effect is determined by the following relationship:

$$R_{o,\text{eq}} = \frac{1}{R_o(2\pi fC)^2} = \frac{(X_C)^2}{R_o} \qquad (17\text{-}12)$$

This equivalent circuit is shown in Fig. 17-12 for the circuit of Fig. 17-17a, which illustrates a tank circuit with a shunt load (resistive).

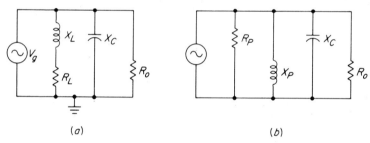

(a)   (b)

Fig. 17-17   The effect of shunt loading: (a) tank circuit with resistive load R_o; (b) equivalent parallel coil components R_p and X_p.

Another equivalent circuit is shown in Fig. 17-17b. The series X_L and coil R_L are converted to their equivalent parallel components X_P and R_P, which results in the equivalent circuit of Fig. 17-17b, where R_P is parallel with R_0. In Fig. 17-17b:

$$R_P = R_L + QX_L = \frac{R_L{}^2 + X_L{}^2}{R_L}$$

$$X_P = X_L + \frac{R_L}{Q} = \frac{R^2 + X_L{}^2}{X_L}$$

17-13   EQUIVALENT SERIES CIRCUIT AT RESONANCE

In this section you will learn about the equivalent series circuit of a parallel-RLC at resonance.

The equivalent series circuit at resonance varies with the circuit Q. When the circuit Q is 20 or greater, the source sees a resistive load of relatively high ohmic value. When the circuit Q is less than 20, the resonant frequency is usually taken as that frequency at which the load appears resistive to the source; this is determined by the condition III equation (f_{o3}).

17-14   EQUIVALENT SERIES CIRCUIT BELOW RESONANCE

In this section you will learn that the equivalent series circuit of a parallel-RLC below its resonant frequency is inductive.

Refer to Fig. 17-18. Assume that the coil Q is greater than 20, and so its resistance may be neglected. At frequencies below resonance, X_C is greater than X_L, resulting in I_a being greater than I_b. Since I_a and I_b are

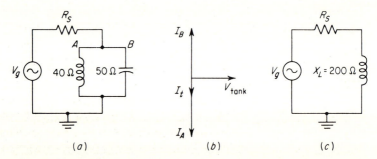

Fig. 17-18   Equivalent series circuit below f_o: (a) circuit; (b) vector diagram; (c) equivalent series circuit.

180° out of phase, the resultant current is equal to their arithmetic difference, as shown by the current-vector relationships in Fig. 17-18b. The total current is a lagging current, and the source will see the tank circuit as an inductor.

Example

Determine the X_C value seen by the source for the parameters of Fig. 17-18.

Solution

Assume a tank voltage, such as 50 V. Find I_a and I_b.

$$I_a \underline{/\theta} = \frac{50\underline{/0°}}{40\underline{/90°}} = 1.25\underline{/-90°} \text{ A}$$

$$I_b \underline{/\theta} = \frac{50\underline{/0°}}{50\underline{/-90°}} = 1\underline{/90°} \text{ A}$$

Expressing each current in rectangular form and finding the total,

$$I\underline{/\theta} = (0 - j1.25) + (0 + j1.00) = 0 - j0.25$$

Converting to polar form,

$$I\underline{/\theta} = 0.25\underline{/-90°} \text{ A}$$

and

$$Z_{\text{tank}}\underline{/\theta} = \frac{50\underline{/0°}}{0.25\underline{/-90°}} = 200\underline{/90°} \text{ }\Omega$$

Hence the source sees the tank circuit as a coil of 200-Ω inductive reactance.

17-15   EQUIVALENT SERIES CIRCUIT ABOVE RESONANCE

In this section you will learn that the equivalent series circuit of a parallel-RLC above its resonant frequency is capacitive.

Refer to Fig. 17-19. At frequencies above resonance, I_b is greater than I_a, resulting in the total tank current being a portion of I_b (again assum-

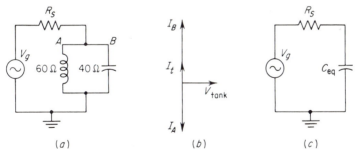

(a)   (b)   (c)

Fig. 17-19   Equivalent series circuit above f_o: (a) circuit; (b) vector diagram; (c) equivalent series circuit.

ing a circuit Q of 20 or greater). The source will see the tank circuit as a capacitor at frequencies above resonance.

Example

Find the capacitive reactance seen by the source in Fig. 17-19. Assume that the tank potential is 50 V.

Solution

Find the branch currents:

$$I_a\underline{/\theta} = \frac{50\underline{/0°}}{60\underline{/90°}} = 0.833\underline{/-90°} = 0 - j0.833 \text{ A}$$

$$I_b\underline{/\theta} = \frac{50\underline{/0°}}{40\underline{/-90°}} = 1.25\underline{/90°} = 0 + j1.25 \text{ A}$$

$$I = (0 - j0.833) + (0 + j1.25) = 0 + j0.417 = 0.417\underline{/90°} \text{ A}$$

and

$$Z_{\text{tank}}\underline{/\theta} = \frac{50\underline{/0°}}{0.417\underline{/90°}} = 120\underline{/-90°} \text{ } \Omega$$

Hence the source sees the tank as a capacitive reactance of 120 Ω.

PROBLEMS

17-14 Refer to Fig. 17-14a. $X_C = X_L = 3000 \text{ } \Omega; f_o = 5 \text{ kHz}; Q = 25$. Find:
    a) L b) C c) R_L

17-15 For the circuit with parameters as in Prob. 17-14, find the following (assume the coil is perfect):
    a) $Z_{\text{tank}}\underline{/\theta}$ b) bandwidth
    c) $f_{co,min}$ d) $f_{co,max}$

17-16 Refer to Fig. 17-14a. $X_C = X_L = 400 \text{ } \Omega; f_o = 455 \text{ kHz}; Q = 20 \text{ V}$. Find the following (assume the coil is perfect):
    a) $Z_{\text{tank}}\underline{/\theta}$ b) bandwidth
    c) $f_{co,min}$ d) $f_{co,max}$

17-17 Find the inductance and capacitance of Prob. 17-16.

17-18 The coil of Prob. 17-16 is a permeability-tuned type. It can be varied to the extent that the tank circuit can resonate at frequencies from 425 to 485 kHz. Find minimum and maximum L.

17-19 In Prob. 17-17, assume L is fixed but C is the trimmer type. It may be varied such that f_o can range from 445 to 465 kHz. Find the minimum and maximum values of C.

17-20 A tank circuit resonates at 1500 kHz and has a bandwidth of 10 kHz. Find the circuit Q.

QUESTIONS

17-21 In Fig. 17-14a, what is the purpose of the resistor R_S?

17-22 At what frequency is the tank-circuit impedance at a maximum value?

17-23 What is the relationship between resistance in a tank circuit and its resonant-frequency impedance?

17-24 What is the relationship between resistance in a tank circuit and its bandwidth?

17-25 What is the relationship between resistance in a tank circuit and voltage across the tank circuit at resonance?

17-26 Why is the bandwidth less for a higher circuit Q?

17-27 What portion of the tank circuit Z at resonance exists at $f_{co,min}$ and $f_{co,max}$?

17-28 Why is the response curve symmetrical only for high-Q tank circuits?

17-29 What relationship exists between line I at resonance and tank-circuit resistance?

17-30 What effect does shunt loading have on the tank circuit?

the transformer
18

The transformer is a device frequently utilized in electric and electronic circuits. One of the chief characteristics of this device is that it transfers electric energy from a source to a load by means of mutual induction. The source and load, which are not electrically connected, are joined by the linkage of the magnetic flux. The use of properly designed transformers can result in good impedance matching and a high degree of efficiency. The voltages and currents associated with the device can be altered to a considerable extent by design, resulting in the possibility of matching a load impedance of quite different value than the impedance of the source. The transformer has found wide use in the power field and in audio and high-frequency circuits of many types. The particular application of the device largely determines its design.

18-1 FUNDAMENTAL TRANSFORMER ACTION (NO LOAD)

In this section you will learn about how an unloaded transformer works, the nature of the magnetization current, and the voltage, turns, and current ratios.

Figure 18-1 illustrates an iron-core transformer. The simplest transformer consists of two coils which are electrically isolated from each other. The core may or may not be a magnetic material, depending upon the intended application. Consider the transformer with an iron core, since this is used most commonly. The coil associated with the source is called the *primary*, and the coil which is eventually connected to the load is called the *secondary*.

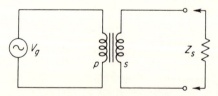

Fig. 18-1   Iron-core transformer

The source voltage drives a current through the primary and, being sinusoidal, undergoes continuous changes in magnitude and direction. During the positive pulse, the core is magnetized in one direction; during the negative pulse, it is magnetized in the opposite direction. An induced emf, which is counter to the source voltage, is developed in the primary and secondary coils. The primary induced voltage is slightly less than the source voltage, and they are opposite in polarity to each other. The small difference between the source voltage and primary induced voltage is just great enough to permit the flow of a small primary current, called the *magnetization,* or *excitation, current,* when the secondary is not connected to a load. The magnitude of the magnetization current is small, being only sufficient to magnetize the core of the transformer. Since this current is bidirectional in nature, it alternately magnetizes the core in one direction and in the opposite direction.

The magnetization current develops a flux field which encompasses the core and two coils. Because the flux field is continuously in motion, a cutting action across the primary and secondary coils is always present, resulting in the development of induced voltage in both coils.

If the primary and secondary coils are placed about the core in such a manner that unity coupling is achieved, the magnitude of the induced voltages per turn of each coil must be equal, and their polarity must be the same. In other words, the induced voltages per turn of the primary and secondary are identical if no flux leakage exists in the circuit.

The concept of flux leakage warrants further consideration at this point. With the development of current through the primary, flux lines expand out of the primary (and vice versa when the current decreases). Most of the expanding flux lines in a well-designed iron-core transformer will also cut the secondary coil, and the two coils are magnetically linked. Some of the flux lines from the primary do not succeed in cutting the secondary, and they are called *leakage flux.* The extent to which leakage flux exists is directly related to the coefficient of coupling.

If an ideal transformer could be designed, the following characteristics would be achieved:

1   Zero magnetic leakage
2   Zero thermal losses

All transformers, in addition to possessing some magnetic leakage, have thermal losses due to several factors. The coil windings display some resistance, resulting in an I^2R loss in each winding under loaded conditions. Thermal losses also occur in the core because of the hysteresis effect and eddy currents. Hysteresis is the magnetic-lag property of the core, requiring energy from the source to realign the flux field continuously in the core material, which develops heat. Eddy currents are currents developed by the induced voltage in the core, which also develop core heat. Well-designed iron-core transformers generally utilize low-retentivity iron, thereby reducing hysteresis losses. Core construction in the form of laminations, separated by a high-resistance material, greatly increases the resistance to the flow of eddy currents.

Assume that the secondary coil is placed in such a position that no magnetic leakage exists. In such a case, the induced voltages per turn of each coil will be equal. If there is no primary resistance and the core losses are zero, the voltage across the primary is equal to the source voltage. The induced voltage across each primary turn is equal to the source voltage divided by the number of turns possessed by the primary; i.e., in a lossless transformer,

$$V_p = V_g$$

and

$$V_{np} = \frac{V_g}{N_p}$$

where V_p = voltage across primary coil
V_g = source voltage
V_{np} = voltage across each primary turn
N_p = number of primary-coil turns

The same relationship would apply for the secondary coil of a lossless transformer.

$$V_{ns} = \frac{V_s}{N_s}$$

where V_{ns} = voltage across each secondary turn
V_s = voltage across secondary coil
N_s = number of secondary-coil turns

The primary and secondary voltages are equal if the two coils possess the same number of turns. Since the primary voltage is equal to the source voltage, the secondary potential can be greater or less than this value, in accordance with the number of secondary-coil turns compared with the number of primary-coil turns. This must be true since the voltages per turn are equal in both primary and secondary coils. When the secondary has a greater number of windings, the secondary voltage is greater than the primary voltage and is called a *step-up transformer.* A *step-down* transformer is one in which the secondary voltage is less than the primary voltage.

The primary and secondary voltages are directly proportional to the number of primary- and secondary-coil turns. In equation form;

$$\frac{V_p}{V_s} = \frac{N_p}{N_s}$$

where V_p = primary induced voltage
   V_s = secondary induced voltage
   N_p = primary turns
   N_s = secondary turns
N_p/N_s = turns ratio
V_p/V_s = voltage ratio

The magnetization current is also called the *no-load current*, since it flows with no secondary load connected. This current lags the primary voltage by 90° and is a wattless current, since it draws no energy from the source in the ideal transformer. The magnitude of the no-load current can be reduced by increasing the number of primary turns. Now examine the reason for this. Increasing the number of primary turns results in an increase in the induced primary voltage. Therefore the difference between the source voltage and the primary induced voltage is smaller, resulting in a reduced voltage being available to drive the excitation, or magnetization, current. The magnitude of this current is one of the basic considerations of the designer in determining the turns ratio and cross-sectional area of the transformer circuit.

Example 1

A transformer is to have the following parameters: $V_p = 120$ V; $V_s = 20,000$ V. Find the required turns ratio.

Solution

Find the turns ratio: the turns ratio is equal to the voltage ratio; hence

$$\frac{N_p}{N_s} = \frac{120}{20,000} = \frac{0.006}{1}$$

The actual number of turns in the primary is in great part determined by the desired magnitude of the no-load current.

Example 2

A transformer has the following parameters: $N_p = 4000$; $N_s = 400$; $V_p = 500$ V. Find: (a) volts per turn; (b) secondary voltage.

Solution

(a)   Find the volts per turn:

$$V_{np} = V_{ns} = \frac{V_p}{N_p}$$
$$V_{np} = \tfrac{500}{4000} = 0.125 \text{ V/turn}$$

(b)   Find the secondary voltage: the secondary voltage is readily determined by the product of the volts-per-turn value and the number of turns possessed by the secondary.

$$V_s = V_{ns}N_s = 0.125 \times 400 = 50 \text{ V}$$

18-2   TRANSFORMER ACTION WITH A RESISTIVE LOAD

In this section you will learn how power is used in a transformer with a resistive load and how transformer efficiency is determined.

Figure 18-2 illustrates a transformer connected to a resistive load. Notice that the load is connected across the secondary coil, thereby permitting a secondary-coil current to flow. The secondary current is driven by the induced voltage of the secondary coil. In many cases, the secondary induced voltage may be viewed as a voltage source in series with the secondary winding, as shown in Fig. 18-2.

The magnitude of the secondary current I_s varies with the power required by the load; in the ideal transformer,

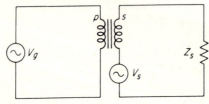

Fig. 18-2 Transformer with resistive load.

$$I_s = \frac{V_s}{Z_s}$$

where Z_s is the secondary load impedance.

Recall that the secondary current is continuously changing in magnitude and direction in a sinusoidal fashion. The secondary current develops a magnetic field which is counter to the field established by the magnetization current of the primary. The result is a tendency to reduce the primary and secondary induced voltages. A reduction in the primary induced voltage increases the difference between the source voltage and the primary induced voltage, thereby permitting a larger primary current to flow. The increase in primary current develops an increase in magnetizing force equal and opposite to the magnetizing force developed by the secondary current. Therefore the flux in the core remains at the no-load-condition value and is unaffected by the load.

The original no-load current is customarily a small value of the primary current under loaded conditions. No-load current values varying from 1 to 10 percent of the loaded primary current are considered usual. In many practical cases, the excitation current is considered negligible and is omitted in circuit calculations. Ignoring this current, and its magnetic effects, leads to the conclusion that the primary and secondary magnetic forces are equal under loaded conditions. Since the magnetomotive force is a direct function of the ampere-turns, the ampere-turns of the primary and secondary must be equal (since the core is common to both coils). In equation form,

$$I_p N_p = I_s N_s$$

Transposing,

$$\frac{I_p}{I_s} = \frac{N_s}{N_p}$$

where I_p = loaded primary current (no-load current is usually ignored)
$\quad\quad I_s$ = secondary load current
$\quad I_p/I_s$ = current ratio

The preceding relationship points out that the current ratio is equal to the inverse of the turns ratio. Since the turns ratio and voltage ratio are equal,

In an ideal transformer, the power of the primary circuit is equal to the power of the secondary circuit, as dictated by the conservation-of-energy law:

$$V_p I_p = V_s I_s$$

The *no-load current,* in an actual transformer, draws power because of the primary I^2R loss and the core losses. The core losses are relatively constant for all load conditions, with a fixed source voltage. The I^2R loss of the primary winding varies with the magnitude of the primary current and the primary winding resistance. Leakage flux can reduce the primary and secondary load currents, as described in Sec. 18-3.

Example 1

A transformer has the following parameters. At no-load conditions, because of the core losses, 25 W of energy is drawn from the source, and the I^2R losses of the primary are negligible. Under a secondary load of 20 A, the primary and secondary coils each have an I^2R loss of 20 W. V_s (with load) = 220 V. Find: (*a*) power taken from the source under the given load conditions; (*b*) transformer efficiency.

Solution

(*a*)   Find the power taken from the source: the total power taken from the source is equal to the sum of all losses plus that taken by the load.

$$P = P_{R_p} + P_{R_s} + P_c + P_{Z_s}$$

where $P_{R_p} = I^2R$ loss of primary
$P_{R_s} = I^2R$ loss of secondary
P_c = core losses
P_{Z_s} = power drawn by load

First find the power drawn by the load.

$$P_{Z_s} = I_s V_s = 20 \times 220 = 4.4 \text{ kW}$$

Substituting into the original relationship,

$$P = 20 + 20 + 25 + 4400 = 4.465 \text{ kW}$$

(b) Find the transformer efficiency: *the efficiency of a transformer is determined by the ratio of the power drawn by the load to the total power drawn from the source.* Multiplying this ratio by 100 expresses the efficiency in percent. In equation form,

$$\text{Eff} = \frac{P_{Z_s}}{P} \times 100$$

where Eff = efficiency, percent
P_{Z_s} = power drawn by load Z_s
P = total power drawn from source

Substitute into the preceding relationship and now solve for the efficiency of the transformer in this problem.

$$\text{Eff} = \frac{4400}{4465} \times 100 = 98.5 \text{ percent}$$

The efficiency of iron-core transformers is generally much higher than that of those which utilize a core entirely or partially composed of nonmagnetic materials (such as an air-core transformer).

The rms induced secondary voltage due to the mutual inductance, with a sinusoidal source potential, may be determined from the following relationship:

$$V_p = 2\pi f M I_p$$

The same relationship may be used to determine the induced primary voltage due to the mutual inductance.

$$V_s = 2\pi f M I_p$$

Example 2

A transformer has 80 mH of mutual inductance; $I_p = 2$ A; $I_s = 4$ A; frequency = 100 Hz. Find the induced voltage due to the mutual inductance of the primary and secondary.

Solution

(a) Find V_p due to the mutual inductance:

$$V_p = 2\pi \times 100 \times 0.08 \times 4 = 201.06 \text{ V}$$

(*b*) Find V_s due to mutual inductance:

$$V_s = 2 \pi \times 100 \times 0.08 \times 2 = 100.53 \text{ V}$$

18-3 EQUIVALENT TRANSFORMER CIRCUIT ANALYSIS

In this section you will learn about the various elements in the general equivalent transformer network, the equivalent T network, and how the transformer is seen by the source.

General Equivalent Transformer Network

Reference is made to Fig. 18-3, which illustrates the general equivalent transformer circuit. The effect of the various components can be discussed with the preceding circuit as a basis. The internal resistance R_{int} of the input generator deprives the remaining circuit of some portion of its voltage. The remainder of the input is still not available for useful transformer action because of the primary winding resistance R_p and the leakage flux associated with the primary X_p. The voltage-drop attributed to R_p reduces the effective primary voltage by that amount. The self-induced voltage associated with those flux lines that originate in the primary and do not succeed in cutting the secondary behaves as if it originated from an inductor in series with the primary, resulting in a reduction in the effective primary-induced voltage. Large values of leakage reactance and winding resistance can result in a primary voltage

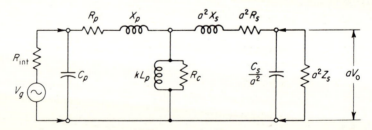

Fig. 18-3   Equivalent transformer circuit.

V_g = rms input-generator voltage
V_o = rms output voltage
a = turns ratio N_p/N_s
R_i = input-generator impedance
R_p = primary-coil resistance
R_s = secondary-coil resistance
R_c = equivalent shunt resistance due to core losses
L_p = inductance of primary

X_p = leakage reactance of primary
X_s = leakage reactance of secondary
C_p = equivalent shunt capacitance of primary
C_s = equivalent shunt capacitance of secondary
Z_s = load impedance
k = coefficient of coupling

which is considerably lower than the input-generator potential, although this problem is greatly reduced in well-designed transformers.

The core losses R_c act as a constant draw upon the input generator in terms of energy. The amount of inductance seen by the load is determined by the product of the primary inductance and coefficient of coupling kL_p. Both the secondary leakage reactance and the winding resistance appear to have values equal to their actual values times the turns ratio squared ($a^2 X_s$ and $a^2 R_s$). The load impedance seen by the source is equal to the product of the turns ratio squared times the load impedance ($a^2 Z_s$). This fact is frequently utilized in the principle of impedance matching.

Equivalent T Network

The second equivalent transformer network to be considered is the equivalent T network. Figure 18-4 illustrates a simplified transformer

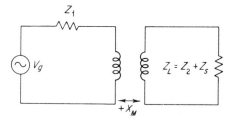

Fig. 18-4 **Simplified transformer circuit.**

circuit where $Z_1 =$ total primary impedance; $Z_2 =$ total secondary impedance minus the load impedance; $Z_s =$ load impedance; $Z_L =$ total secondary impedance including the load impedance; $X_M =$ mutual reactance $= 2\pi fM$. In order to form an equivalent T network, the source must see the same impedances in both cases.

The equivalent T network of the transformer is shown in Fig. 18-5. The formulas for determining the values of the T-network arms are

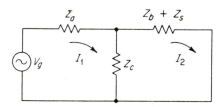

Fig. 18-5 **Equivalent T network of a transformer.**

$$Z_a = Z_1 + X_M$$
$$Z_b = Z_2 + X_M$$
$$Z_c = -X_M$$
$$Z_b + Z_s = Z_s + Z_2 + X_M = Z_L + X_M$$

where Z_1, Z_2, X_M, Z_L, and Z_s are as defined in the preceding paragraph.

Example 1

A transformer has the following parameters: $Z_1 = 5 + j12; Z_2 = 4 + j18;$ $Z_s = 20 + j0; X_M = 7\underline{/90°}$. Find the arm values for the equivalent T network.

Solution

$$Z_a = Z_1 + X_M = (5 + j12) + (0 + j7) = 5 + j19 \ \Omega$$
$$Z_b = Z_2 + Z_M = 4 + j18 + 0 + j7 = 4 + j25$$
$$Z_b + Z_s = 4 + j25 + 20 + j0 = 24 + j25$$
$$Z_c = -X_M = -(0 + j7) = 0 - j7 \ \Omega$$

Transformer as Seen by the Source

The third equivalent circuit of the transformer to be considered is that circuit seen by the source generator, called Z_{eq}. This Z_{eq}, as seen by the input potential, is the impedance which determines the magnitude of the primary current. In equation form,

$$Z_{eq} = Z_1 - \frac{(X_M)^2}{Z_2 + Z_s}$$

where Z_{eq} = impedance seen by source
  Z_1 = total primary impedance
  X_M = mutual reactance = $2\pi fM$
  Z_2 = total secondary impedance minus load impedance
  Z_s = total secondary impedance including load impedance

Example 2

Using the parameters of Example 1, find the impedance seen by the source.

Solution

$$Z_{eq} = Z_1 - \frac{(X_M)^2}{Z_2 + Z_s}$$

Note Z_s is equivalent to the vector sum of Z_2 and Z_s.

$$Z_{eq} = (5 + j12) - \frac{(7\underline{/90°})^2}{(4 + j18) + (20 + j0)}$$
$$= (5 + j12) = \frac{49\underline{/180°}}{24 + j18}$$

Note Since $(X_M)^2$ has an angle of 180°, a reversal of polarity is indicated; hence the minus sign is changed to plus in the following expression:

$$Z_{eq} = (5 + j12) + \frac{49\underline{/0°}}{30\underline{/36.9°}}$$
$$= (5 + j12) + 1.075\underline{/-52.1°} = (5 + j12) + 1.306 - j0.981$$
$$= 6.306 + j11.019 = 12.7\underline{/60.2°}\ \Omega$$

18-4 THE AUTOTRANSFORMER

In this section you will learn about the operation of the step-down and step-up autotransformer and the differences in power output and turns ratio between the conventional transformer and the autotransformer.

Up to this point in the discussion, the transformer was considered with two windings which are electrically insulated from each other. The autotransformer, which is illustrated in Figs. 18-6 and 18-7, differs from this basic connection in that a single winding is used for both the

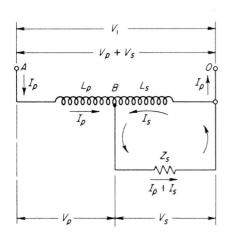

Fig. 18-6 The step-down autotransformer.

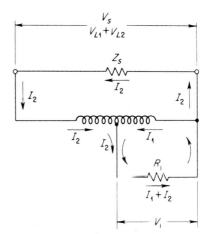

Fig. 18-7 The step-up autotransformer.

primary and the secondary coils. In the step-down type, the input voltage is applied across terminals A and O (see Fig. 18-6) so that a cemf is developed across the entire winding equal in magnitude to V_i. This cemf may be considered in two parts: (1) that which is developed across AB of the winding and (2) that which exists across BO.

The current through the secondary coil L_s is driven by the induced voltage across BO. The current through Z_s is the sum of the primary and secondary currents, as indicated by the arrows in Fig. 18-6. Therefore the secondary load power is obtained in two ways:

1   It is directly conducted from the primary to the secondary ($I_p V_s$).
2   It is transformed ($I_s V_s$).

The primary and secondary coils possess equal volt-amperes, as is the case in the conventional two-coil transformer. If a two-coil transformer is connected as an autotransformer, its power output is greater than when it is used as a two-coil transformer, because a portion of the load is directly conducted; the ratio of transformation (voltage and turns ratio) is greater for the same reason.

Example 1

A conventional two-coil transformer has the following parameters: $V_p = 200$ V; $V_s = 10$ V; $I_p = 3$ A; $I_s = 60$ A; the load is resistive. Find the power output and ratio of transformation when connected as: (a) conventional two-coil transformer; (b) autotransformer.

Solution

(a)   When connected as a conventional two-coil transformer:

$$P_{oc} = V_s I_s = 10 \times 60 = 600 \text{ W}$$
$$\text{Ratio of transformation} = \frac{V_p}{V_s} = \frac{200}{10} = 20$$

(b)   When connected as an autotransformer:

$$P_{oa} = V_s I_s + V_s I_p = V_s(I_s + I_p)$$
$$= 10 \times 63 = 630 \text{ W}$$
$$\text{Ratio of transformation} = \frac{V_p + V_s}{V_s} = \frac{200 + 10}{10} = \frac{210}{10} = 21$$

Comparing the power output of the transformer in Example 1, which has the step-down configuration, shows that the power output and ratio of transformation of the autotransformer are 5 percent greater than that of the conventional connection.

The differences in power output and ratio of transformation between the two connections are greatest when the turns ratio of the conventional transformer is lower with greater initial turns ratios.

Example 2

A conventional two-coil transformer has the following parameters: $V_p = 200$ V; $V_s = 100$ V; $I_p = 2$ A; $I_s = 4$ A. Find the power output and ratio of transformation for the conventional and autotransformer connections.

Solution

(*a*) For the conventional connection:

$$P_{oc} = V_s I_s = 100 \times 4 = 400 \text{ W}$$
$$\text{Ratio of transformation} = \frac{V_p}{V_s} = \frac{200}{100} = 2$$

(*b*) For the autotransformer connection:

$$P_{oa} = V_s(I_p + I_s) = 100(2 + 4) = 100 \times 6$$
$$= 600 \text{ W}$$
$$\text{Ratio of transformation} = \frac{V_p + V_s}{V_s} = \frac{200 + 100}{100} = \frac{300}{100} = 3$$

In the preceding example, where the conventional transformation ratio is 2, the power output and ratio of transformation in the autotransformer connection are 50 percent greater.

Figure 18-7 illustrates the autotransformer connected in a step-up arrangement. L_1 serves as the primary; $L_1 + L_2$ serves as the secondary. The secondary voltage is therefore the sum of the conventional connection V_p and V_s. The secondary current, as indicated by the arrows in Fig. 18-7, is I_2, and the primary current is composed of $I_1 + I_2$, which is the sum of I_p and I_s in the conventional connection. The primary current is greater than the secondary current, as is the normal case for a step-up transformer. Again, as in the step-down connection, a portion of the secondary load is transformed, and the remaining portion of the secondary load is directly conducted. The conducted portion of the load is the difference between the power output in the conventional connection and the power output of the autotransformer connection. The power output of the step-up autotransformer can be determined from the following relationship:

$$P_{oa} = V_{L_1}I_s + V_{L_2}I_s = I_s(V_{L_1} + V_{L_2})$$

where P_{oa} = power output of autotransformer
$V_{L_1} = V_p$ of conventional transformer
$V_{L_2} = V_s$ of conventional transformer

Example 3

A conventional transformer has the following parameters: $V_p = 10$ V; $V_s = 200$ V; $I_p = 60$ A; $I_s = 3$ A. Find the ratio of transformation and power output when connected as: (a) conventional transformer; (b) step-up autotransformer.

Solution

(a)   As a conventional transformer:

$$\text{Transformation ratio} = \frac{V_p}{V_s} = \frac{10}{200} = 0.05 \text{ or } \tfrac{1}{20}$$
$$\text{Power output} = V_s I_s = 200 \times 3 = 600 \text{ W}$$

(b)   In the step-up autotransformer, the output voltage is taken across the entire winding $(L_1 + L_2)$, which means that the output voltage is equal to $V_p + V_s$ of the conventional two-winding connection, and the input voltage is applied across L_1 (see Fig. 18-7).

$$\text{Transformation ratio} = \frac{V \text{ across input portion of winding}}{V \text{ across output portion of winding}}$$

$$= \frac{V_{L_1}}{V_{L_1} + V_{L_2}} = \frac{V_p}{V_p + V_s}$$
$$= \frac{10}{10 + 200} = \frac{10}{210} = 0.0476 \text{ or } \tfrac{1}{21}$$

Power output:

$$P_{oa} = I_s(V_{L_1} + V_{L_2}) = 3 \times 210 = 630 \text{ W}$$

Notice that the transformation ratio and power output were increased by 5 percent in the preceding example. A comparison of the results of

Examples 1 and 2 shows that the power output and transformation ratios are greater (autotransformer versus conventional transformer) when the conventional transformer has a lower transformation ratio.

The autotransformer transformation ratio can also be determined by the following relationship:

$$T_a = \frac{N_p}{N_s} \pm A\frac{N_p}{N_s} = \frac{N_p}{N_s}(1 \pm A)$$

where T_a = transformation ratio of autotransformer
N_p, N_s = primary and secondary turns of separate coils
A = ratio of low-voltage coil turns to high-voltage coil turns

Note A is positive for the step-down and negative for the step-up auto-transformer.

The power output of the autotransformer can be determined from the following equation when the power output in the conventional connection is known:

$$P_{oa} = P_{oc} + AP_{oc} = P_{oc}(1 + A)$$

where P_{oa} = power output of autotransformer
P_{oc} = power output when connected as a conventional two-coil transformer
A = ratio of low-voltage coil turns to high-voltage coil turns

These equations are used in the following example.

Example 4

A conventional transformer has the following parameters: $P_{oc} = 400$ W; $N_p/N_s = 5$. Find the transformation ratio and power output when the transformer is connected as a step-down autotransformer.

Solution

(a) Transformation ratio:

$$T_a = 5(1 + \tfrac{1}{5}) = 5 \times 1.2 = 6$$

(b) Power output:

$$P_{oa} = 400(1 + \tfrac{1}{5}) = 400 \times 1.2 = 480 \text{ W}$$

The autotransformer can be used to advantage as either a step-down or a step-up device. One of its chief advantages is that it can be constructed to handle as large a power output as a conventional transformer, which is physically larger (and therefore requires more copper and iron in its construction). The reduction in size of the transformer, for a given power requirement, is most apparent with the smaller transformation ratios. Therefore the autotransformer is put to its best power-efficiency advantage in those applications where the *step-down or step-up voltage ratio is relatively low*.

Several of the preceding examples illustrated the effect of the turns ratio. In Example 2, where the conventional-connection turns ratio was 2, the use of the autotransformer connection resulted in a 50 percent increase in the output power. In Example 1, with a transformation ratio of 20 for the conventional transformer, use of the autotransformer connection resulted in only a 5 percent increase in the output power. This major advantage of the autotransformer is minimized where the ratio of transformation is very high.

PROBLEMS

18-1   A transformer has the following parameters: $N_p = 200$; $N_s = 10$; $V_p = 40$ V. Find:
   a)   volts per turn
   b) V_s

18-2   A transformer has the following parameters: $V_p = 150$ V; $V_s = 5$ V; $N_s = 50$. Find:
   a)   volts per turn
   b) N_p

18-3   A transformer has the following parameters at no-load conditions: 5 W of energy is drawn from the source because of core losses, and I^2R losses of the primary winding are negligible. With a secondary load of 12 A, the primary and secondary coils each have an I^2R loss of 4 W. V_s (with load) is 50 V. Find:
   a)   power taken from the source
   b)   transformer efficiency under load conditions

18-4   A transformer has the following parameters: $Z_1 = 7 + j18$ Ω; $Z_2 = 8 + j25$ Ω; $Z_s = 75 + j0$ Ω; $X_M = 15\underline{/90°}$ Ω. Find the arm values of the equivalent T network.

18-5   In Prob. 18-4, find the Z seen by the source.

18-6   A conventional two-coil transformer has the following parameters: $V_p = 100$ V; $V_s = 5$ V; $I_p = 6$ A; $I_s = 120$ A. Find the power output and transformation ratio when connected as:

a) conventional two-coil transformer
b) autotransformer

QUESTIONS

18-1   How does a transformer transfer energy from a source to a load?

18-2   What is the function of the transformer's primary coil?

18-3   What is the function of the transformer's secondary coil?

18-4   How is the magnetization current developed?

18-5   What is leakage flux in a transformer?

18-6   What is the relationship between leakage flux and the coefficient of coupling?

18-7   What are the kinds of thermal losses that take place in the core of the transformer?

18-8   What is a step-up transformer?

18-9   What is a step-down transformer?

18-10   What is the no-load current of a transformer?

18-11   What drives the secondary current in a transformer?

18-12   What effect does the magnetic field developed by the secondary coil have on transformer operation?

18-13   Why does the no-load current actually draw power?

18-14   What is transformer efficiency?

18-15   Why is there a difference in the turns ratio when a conventional transformer is used as an autotransformer?

18-5 VECTOR ANALYSIS OF A UNITY-COUPLED TRANSFORMER WITH A RESISTIVE LOAD

In this section you will learn about the operation of the step-down and step-up autotransformer and the differences in power output and turns ratio between the conventional transformer and autotransformer.

Refer to Fig. 18-8 for the following discussion.

For simplicity, the vector diagram of Fig. 18-8 is that of a transformer which displays the following properties: the secondary load impedance is considered resistive because the secondary coil has an inductance value which may be considered negligible by comparison. Also, it is assumed that the resistance of the secondary windings is of

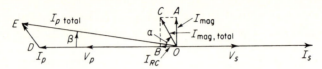

Fig. 18-8 Vector diagram of a loaded transformer which has unity coupling and no leakage reactance.

I_p = additional primary current due to connecting secondary load into circuit

I_s = secondary load

I_{mag} = magnetizing (excitation) current

I_{R_c} = portion of the primary current due to core losses

$I_{mag, total}$ = vector sum of I_{R_c} and I_{mag}

$I_{p, total}$ = vector sum of I_p and $I_{mag, total}$

negligible value. The transformer has unity coupling, which means that there is no leakage reactance present in the two coils. One can proceed into the theory of operation by means of the vector diagram, with and without the secondary load connected.

No Load

With no load connected to the secondary terminals, there is no secondary current. If the core displayed zero losses, the total primary current would consist of I_{mag} (*OA*). The phase angle between the primary current and voltage is 90°. With a power factor equal to cos 90° = 0, this is a wattless current. On the other hand, since the core does have losses, a small current flows because of these losses (*OB*). The resultant magnetizing current is then the vector sum of the wattless magnetizing current and the core-loss current. The core-loss current, as shown in the vector diagram, is an in-phase current (resistive). The phase angle of the resultant magnetizing current (*OC*) and V_p, which is α in the diagram, is less than 90°, and the total magnetizing current is no longer a wattless current. The tangent of this phase angle is determined by the ratio of the quadrature component I_{mag} to the in-phase component I_{R_c}. In effect, a transformer displaying larger core losses would have a smaller magnitude of angle α, which would result in a larger power factor.

With Load (Resistive)

Consider a 1:1 transformation ratio for simplicity. Also assume that the load resistance is large enough to make the secondary inductance effect negligible. The introduction of a secondary load resistance results in the flow of I_s. The secondary current establishes a flux which is counter to the flux originally set up by the magnetizing current. The primary current immediately increases in magnitude from $OC\underline{/\alpha}$ to the greater value required to establish a flux field to offset that flux set up by the secondary current. The increased primary current due to the secondary load current I_p is an in-phase current, since the secondary current is resistive. The value of ED in the vector diagram is that of CO, with the same angle, so as to make it possible to find the vector sum OE. The phase angle between $I_{p,\text{total}}$ and V_p — angle β — is considerably lower than its value without the secondary load, thereby increasing the power factor by a substantial amount, bringing it closer to unity.

In a well-designed transformer, where the magnetizing current is only 1 to 10 percent of the total primary current, β is very small and the power factor approaches unity.

18-6 VECTOR ANALYSIS OF A UNITY-COUPLED TRANSFORMER WITH AN INDUCTIVE LOAD

In this section you will learn by use of vectors how an inductive loaded transformer works.

Figure 18-9 illustrates the vector diagram of a transformer which has a high inductive load. In this illustration, the load inductance is so high that the load current I_s lags the secondary voltage by a phase angle very near 90° (α).

As in the previous illustration, OC is the vector representation of $I_{\text{mag,total}}$, which is the vector resultant of the magnetizing current and the current due to the core losses. Upon connecting the secondary terminals to the inductive load, a secondary current is developed by the

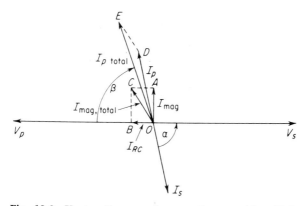

Fig. 18-9 Vector diagram of a transformer with a high inductive load.

secondary induced voltage. This lagging current sets up a flux field which is counter to the original magnetizing field. At the same time, an additional current I_p flows in the primary, whose magnitude is just sufficient to offset the flux developed by I_s, thereby maintaining the original magnetic field established by the flow of $I_{\text{mag,total}}$. The total primary current $I_{p,\text{total}}$ is the vector sum of $I_{\text{mag,total}}$ and I_p.

Notice the power factor of the primary and secondary circuits. Cos β is the power factor of the primary circuit. Angle β is much closer to 90° than was the case with a resistive load. Recall that I_p is to establish a flux field opposite to that produced by I_s. Since I_s has a large lagging phase angle, I_p must have a corresponding phase angle in order to establish the opposite flux field. Therefore the characteristics of I_p are determined by the properties of I_s. Note also that the magnetizing current contributes a greater effect upon $I_{p,\text{total}}$, since $I_{\text{mag,total}}$ and I_p are closer in phase with a secondary load which is predominantly inductive. The power factor of both primary and secondary circuits is relatively small, since angles β and α are close to 90°. In the illustration, the power factor of the primary circuit is greater than that of the secondary circuit. This is due to the fact that the core losses are seen as primary losses, resulting in $/\beta$ being smaller than $/\alpha$ by an extent determined by the magnitude of the core losses.

18-7 VECTOR ANALYSIS OF A UNITY-COUPLED TRANSFORMER WITH A RESISTIVE-INDUCTIVE LOAD

In this section you will learn by use of vectors how a resistive-inductive loaded transformer operates.

Figure 18-10 illustrates a unity-coupled transformer with a secondary load which is resistive and inductive. Notice that the angle of lag between

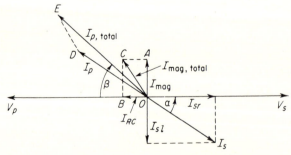

Fig. 18-10 Vector diagram of a transformer with an inductive-resistance load which has unity coupling.

I_s and V_s (α) is less than 90° but more than 0° The exact magnitude of this angle varies with the ratio of the secondary-current quadrature component I_{sl} to the in-phase component I_{sr}. Vector OC represents $I_{mag,total}$, as in the previous vector diagrams, and I_p is the additional primary current which flows when the secondary load is connected.

As in the previous load conditions, the magnitude of I_p must be such that its flux field is equal and opposite to the flux field established by I_s, thereby enabling the original flux field to remain constant.

Again assuming a 1:1 transformation ratio, the magnitude and phase angles of I_s and I_p are the same. Since the phase angles of I_s and $I_{p,total}$ are primarily dependent on the core losses and the secondary resistive properties, these elements also determine the power factor of the primary and secondary circuits. The primary power factor is larger by some extent than the power factor of the secondary circuit because of the core losses when $\angle\alpha$ is greater than $\angle I_{mag,total}$.

18-8   VECTOR ANALYSIS OF A PRACTICAL TRANSFORMER

In this section the operation of a practical transformer is examined by use of vectors.

Figure 18-11 is a vector diagram of a transformer which takes the leakage reactances and winding resistances into account. R_p and R_s are the winding resistances; X_p and X_s are the leakage reactances. The remaining symbols are those used in the previous vector illustrations. $V_{p,total}$ is the vector representation of the total primary voltage, which is the resultant of V_{R_p}, V_{X_p}, and V_p. The useful portion of this voltage, in terms of transformer action, is V_p. Notice that V_{R_p} is in phase with $I_{p,total}$ and V_{X_p} is 90° out of phase. The various components of the total primary current are as follows:

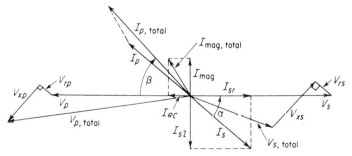

Fig. 18-11   Vector diagram of a practical transformer displaying RL secondary-load characteristics (both coils wound in the same direction)

1   Quadrature components: I_{X_p}; I_{mag}
2   In-phase components: I_{R_c}; I_{R_p}

$I_{\text{mag,total}}$ is the resultant of I_{R_c} and I_{mag}, as in previous cases, and I_p is the current required to offset the magnetic field established by I_s. Assuming a 1:1 transformation ratio, I_p and I_s must be of the same magnitude and phase angle in order for this reaction to be complete. The resultant primary current is the vector sum of $I_{\text{mag,total}}$ and I_p.

The entire voltage induced in the secondary V_s is equal in amount to, and 180° out of phase with, the useful portion of the primary voltage V_p. The remainder of the primary voltage is not available for transformation purposes. V_{X_p} represents the induced voltage developed by those flux lines which failed to cut across the secondary and therefore did not induce a secondary voltage. V_{R_p} is the voltage-drop across the resistance of the primary windings. The actual voltage induced in the secondary V_s in turn cannot be fully utilized in developing a counterflux to the magnetizing current because of its own resistance R_s and leakage reactance X_s. V_{R_s} is in phase with I_s, and V_{X_s} is 90° out of phase. The actual secondary voltage available for driving I_s, which is $V_{s,\text{total}}$, shifted in phase, is shown by the angle between V_s and $V_{s,\text{total}}$.

Because of the effect produced by the leakage reactances and winding resistances, the primary and secondary voltages do not have the same ratio as would have been the case in the ideal transformer. This effect is constant for a given frequency, and the load current is determined by the load impedance.

The variations in the transformation ratio of the transformer may or may not have to be taken into consideration. In some cases, where the transformer efficiency is high, the effects of core losses, winding resistance, and leakage reactance are often considered negligible and need not be considered for practical purposes. In other cases, where the efficiency is lower or a greater degree of computation accuracy is required, these effects must be incorporated in the circuit computations.

In some transformer circuits, the secondary load may be resistive-capacitive or highly capacitive. In the case of the resistive-capacitive load, its effect upon the secondary current varies with the magnitude of the resistive, capacitive, and leakage reactance components. In those cases where the capacitive property is greater than the inductance, the secondary current takes a leading phase angle with respect to its voltage. I_p, the primary current developed, the magnetic field of which is to counteract the flux associated with I , must take a corresponding phase angle with respect to V_p.

18-9 PRINCIPLES OF IMPEDANCE MATCHING AND REFLECTED LOAD

In this section you will learn about reflected impedance and impedance matching with a transformer.

First consider an ideal transformer with a resistive load which has a 10:1 transformation ratio (V_p is 10 times greater than V_s). In such a case, the primary has 10 times more turns than the secondary. Since the voltage per turn is equal in both coils, the primary voltage is 10 times greater than the secondary. The current flowing in the secondary is determined by V_s and the load resistance. This current sets up a flux field counter to that of the original excitation current. The flux field of the secondary current has 10 times as much effect upon the primary as it has upon the secondary, since the primary has 10 times more turns. Therefore the additional primary current must be one-tenth as great as the secondary load current in order to establish a magnetic field equal and opposite to that established by the secondary current. By assuming that the primary has no resistance and negligible core losses, the excitation current may be neglected. The primary current, in accord with Ohm's law, is determined by V_p and some value of resistance. But the primary has no physical resistance in our case! The primary will see, in series with itself, a resistance value (called the *reflected primary resistance*) equal to the product of the secondary resistance and the turns ratio squared. In equation form,

$$Z_p = \left(\frac{N_p}{N_s}\right)^2 Z_s$$

where Z_p = reflected impedance seen in series with primary
N_p/N_s = transformation (turns) ratio
Z_s = secondary load impedance

In analyzing the behavior of the transformer in terms of impedance matching, the reflected impedance Z_p may be shown as in Fig. 18-12.

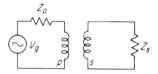

Fig. 18-12 The reflected primary impedance.

Z_p is the impedance seen by the primary, and it results from the magnitude of Z_s and the turns ratio. The energy used by the secondary is that energy represented by I_p flowing through the resistance of Z_p. Consider several examples.

Example 1

The transformer of Fig. 18-12 has the following parameters: $V_p = 100$ V; $N_p/N_s = 10{:}1$; $Z_s = 50$ Ω; assume an ideal iron-core transformer. Find: (a) V_s; (b) I_s; (c) I_p; (d) Z_p.

Solution

(a) Find V_s:

$$\frac{V_p}{V_s} = \frac{N_p}{N_s} = \frac{10}{1}$$

and

$$V_s = \tfrac{1}{10}V_p = 0.1 \times 100 = 10 \text{ V}$$

(b) Find I_s: since an ideal transformer is being considered, there is no leakage reactance or winding resistance; hence

$$I_s = \frac{V_s}{Z_s} = \frac{10}{50} = 0.2 \text{ A}$$

(c) Find I_p: the current ratio is the inverse of the voltage ratio; therefore,

$$I_p = 0.1 I_s = 0.1 \times 0.2 = 0.02 \text{ A}$$

(d) Find Z_p: First find the reflected impedance by Ohm's law.

$$Z_p = \frac{V_p}{I_p} = \frac{100}{0.02} = 5 \text{ k}\Omega$$

As a check, find Z_p by the preceding equation.

$$Z_p = \left(\frac{N_p}{N_s}\right)^2 Z_s = 100 \times 50 = 5 \text{ k}\Omega$$

Example 2

A transformer is to be used to match the following impedances: $R_i = Z_p = 300 \ \Omega$; $R_o = Z_s = 3 \ \Omega$. Find the required turns ratio (again assume an ideal iron-core transformer).

Solution

$$Z_p = \left(\frac{N_p}{N_s}\right)^2 Z_s \quad \text{and} \quad \frac{N_p}{N_s} = \left(\frac{Z_p}{Z_s}\right)^{1/2}$$

Substituting values,

$$\frac{N_p}{N_s} = \left(\frac{300}{3}\right)^{1/2} = \frac{10}{1}$$

Example 3

A transformer is to be used to match the following impedances: $R_i = Z_p = 4 \ k\Omega$; $R_o = 500 \ k\Omega$. Find the required turns ratio.

Solution

$$\frac{N_p}{N_s} = \left[\frac{4000}{500(10)^3}\right]^{1/2} = (0.0008)^{1/2} = \frac{0.089}{1} = \frac{1}{11.2}$$

Notice that a step-down transformer is used for matching a large Z_p to a small Z_s; a step-up transformer is required for matching a small Z_p to a large Z_s. The transformer is one of the most efficient means of coupling the output of one circuit or device to the input of a second circuit or device.

Example 4

A transformer has the following parameters: $X_p = 0 + j50 \ \Omega$; $X_s = 0 + j30 \ \Omega$; $R_p = 150 + j0 \ \Omega$; $R_s = 8 + j0 \ \Omega$; $Z_s = 75 + j0 \ \Omega$; $N_p/N_s = 20{:}1$. Find: (a) Z_p; (b) total Z seen by the primary.

Solution

(a) Find Z_p: the total secondary load impedance is equal to the vector sum of Z_s, R_s, and X_s.

$$
\begin{aligned}
Z_s &= 75 + j0 \\
R_s &= \ \ 8 + j0 \\
X_s &= \ \ 0 + j30 \\
\hline
Z_{s,\text{total}} &= 83 + j30 \ \Omega
\end{aligned}
$$

The impedance $Z_{s,\text{total}}$ is the limiting factor imposed upon I_s, which has a lagging phase angle the tangent of which is determined by $j30/83$, resulting in a phase angle of $-19.9°$. Therefore, the additional primary current possesses the same phase angle. Hence,

$$Z_p = -\left(\frac{N_p}{N_s}\right)^2 Z_{s,\text{total}} = 20^2(80 + j\,30) = 400(80 + j\,30)$$
$$= 33{,}200 - j\,12{,}000 \ \Omega$$

Or, in polar form,

$$Z_p = 35{,}300\underline{/-19.9°} \ \Omega$$

(*b*) Find the total impedance seen by the primary: the total impedance seen by the primary circuit is equal to the vector sum of R_p, X_p, and Z_p.

$$\begin{aligned}
Z_p &= 33{,}200 + j\,12{,}000 \\
\underline{R_p + jX_p = \quad 150 + j50} \\
Z_{p,\text{total}} &= 33{,}350 + j\,12{,}050 \ \Omega = 35{,}460\underline{/19.87°}
\end{aligned}$$

Notice that R_p and X_p had very little effect on $Z_{p,\text{total}}$.

18-10   FREQUENCY RESPONSE OF PRACTICAL TRANSFORMERS

In this section you will learn how the output voltage of a transformer varies with frequency.

Transformers, in actual practice, can be designed to have good frequency responses within many ranges. The general frequency-response curve of a transformer is illustrated in Fig. 18-13. The fre-

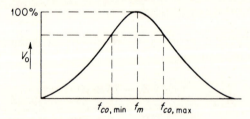

Fig. 18-13 *f*-versus-V_o response of a transformer

quency-cutoff points ($f_{co,min}$ and $f_{co,max}$) are defined as those frequencies where V_o is 0.707 of V_o at the mid-frequency (f_{max}) point of the transformer.

PROBLEMS

18-7   A transformer has the following parameters: $V_p = 200$ V; $N_p N_s = 20{:}1$; $Z_s = 7\ \Omega$. Find the following:
    a) V_s b) I_s
    c) I_p d) Z_p

18-8   A transformer is to be used for matching the following impedances: $R_i = 4\ \text{k}\Omega$ and $R_o = 15\ \Omega$. Find the required transformation ratio.

18-9   A transformer is to be used for matching the following impedances: $R_i = 600\ \Omega$; $R_o = 150\ \text{k}\Omega$. Find the required transformation ratio.

Note   The circuit of Fig. 18-14 may be useful as a reference for Prob. 18-10. X_p and X_s are leakage reactances.

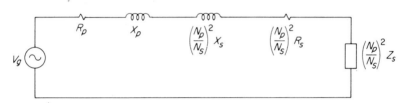

Fig. 18-14   Circuit for Prob. 8-11.

18-10   A transformer has the following parameters: $X_p = 50\ \Omega$; $X_s = 20\ \Omega$; $R_p = 70\ \Omega$; $R_s = 25\ \Omega$; $Z_s = 100\ \Omega$ (resistive); $N_p/N_s = 12{:}1$. Find:
    a) $Z_{s,total}$ b) Z_p c) $Z_{p,total}$

QUESTIONS

18-16   In Fig. 18-8, what is the relationship between $I_{mag,total}$, I_{mag}, and I_{RC}?

18-17   In Fig. 18-8, explain the phase angle beta between $I_{p,total}$ and I_p.

18-18   In Fig. 18-8, what effect does a high inductive load have on $I_{mag,total}$?

18-19   In Fig. 18-9, what effect does a high inductive load have on I_p and I_s phase angles with respect to their voltages?

18-20   With a resistive load, why are I_p and I_s 180° out of phase?

18-21   In the practical transformer, what are the quadrature components of the total primary current?

18-22   In the practical transformer, what are the in-phase components of the total primary current?

18-23   Why is the primary-to-secondary voltage ratio in a practical transformer different from what it would be in the ideal case?

18-24   Under what circumstances must the difference in the transformation ratio between the practical and ideal transformers be considered?

18-25   What is the reflected primary impedance?

18-11 UNTUNED-PRIMARY, TUNED-SECONDARY TRANSFORMER

In this section you will learn how the principles of resonance are incorporated in the untuned-primary and tuned-secondary transformer.

In previous sections, it was found that a well-designed nonresonant transformer could have a relatively wide frequency response, which is very important in certain applications. On the other hand, there are many cases in electronics where the desired frequency response needs to be more carefully controlled because of the nature of the signals being considered. The principles of resonance can be incorporated into the transformer in a more deliberate fashion than merely that which results from the interaction of the shunt capacitances and inductance of the coils. The primary and/or secondary circuits can be made into tuned circuits which resonate at a desired frequency. In this section one of these possibilities will be examined.

Figure 18-15 illustrates a transformer which has an untuned primary and a tuned secondary. As in previous cases, R_p and R_s represent the losses of the primary and secondary coils, respectively, and M is the mutual inductance of the transformer. Note that the secondary circuit possesses both types of reactances and resistance and that it appears

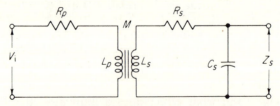

Fig. 18-15 Untuned-primary, tuned-secondary transformer.

as a series-tuned circuit. Therefore the current and voltage relationships developed in the secondary circuit will follow the series-tuned circuit laws. V_{L_s} and V_{C_s} are always 180° out of phase with each other, assuming perfect components. V_s, the induced emf, appears as a voltage in series with L_s, and the vector sum of V_s, V_{L_s}, V_{C_s}, and V_{R_s} is zero at all times. But X_{L_s} and X_{C_s} have a canceling effect on each other, resulting in series secondary-circuit impedance determined by

$$Z_{s,\text{total}} = R_s + j\left(2\pi f L_s - \frac{1}{2\pi f C_s}\right) \qquad \text{as seen by } V_s$$

At resonance, $Z_{s,\text{total}} = R_s$, and the secondary circuit appears resistive. Below resonant frequencies, X_{C_s} is greater than X_{L_s}, and the circuit appears as a series-RC network; it looks like a series-RL network at frequencies above resonance.

18-12 TUNED-PRIMARY, TUNED-SECONDARY TRANSFORMER

In this section you will learn how the principles of resonance are incorporated in several forms of the tuned-primary, tuned-secondary transformer.

Since there are many factors which can affect transformer behavior, begin by considering a tuned transformer with the following properties:

1 Primary and secondary circuits resonate at the same frequency.
2 Primary and secondary Q's are equal.
3 Primary and secondary Q's are high.

The Characteristics of a Tuned Transformer as a Function of k

Notice that the input voltage of Fig. 18-16 is in series with the primary-tuned circuit, and the secondary load impedance is in the shunt connection discussed in the previous section.

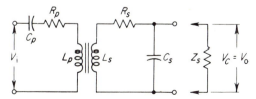

Fig. 18-16 One form of double-tuned transformer.

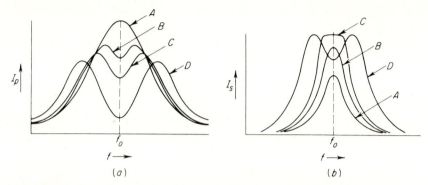

Fig. 18-17   (a) I_p versus f for various k values; (b) I_s versus f for various k values.

Recall that $Z_p = (2\pi f M)^2/Z_{s,\text{total}}$ (which is the reflected impedance). Assuming that the primary- and secondary-circuit Q's are equal and high, the effect of R_p and R_s may be neglected except at the resonant frequency. Also assume that the coefficient of coupling is some low value, such as 0.02. At resonance, the secondary circuit appears resistive and reflects a resistance back to the primary (Z_p is resistive), as determined by the preceding relationship. The response of the primary current for frequencies above and below resonance is nearly identical to what it would be if it were considered as a separate circuit. Owing to the low coefficient of coupling, the primary is relatively unaffected by the secondary. The secondary current, although comparatively small, is more peaked than it would be if it were not coupled to the primary. The response curves of these two currents are shown as curve A in Fig. 18-17a and b.

Now increase the coefficient of coupling. I_p develops the double-hump characteristic depicted in curve B of Fig. 18-17a. At resonance, Z_p is resistive and thereby acts to reduce I_p. Above resonance, the secondary is inductive, resulting in Z_p being capacitive-reactive. The primary impedance, exclusive of Z_p, is inductive-reactive at frequencies greater than resonance. The reflected capacitive reactance cancels a portion of the primary inductive reactance, resulting in $Z_{p,\text{total}}$ being inductive-reactive but at a reduced magnitude. Therefore $Z_{p,\text{total}}$ is reduced, and I_p is greater than its resonant value. Below resonance, the secondary impedance is capacitive reactance and is reflected back to the primary as inductive reactance. The total primary impedance is again reduced, since the primary is capacitive reactance without the reflected impedance; I_p again reaches a magnitude greater than its resonant-frequency current. There is a frequency on each side of resonance where the reflected reactance is exactly equal to the primary reactance; at these frequencies the primary current reaches its maximum values, resulting in the two humps.

The secondary current does not develop the double hump at as low a k value as the primary because of the isolation effect afforded by lower k values. The induced secondary voltage and its impedance determine the magnitude of I_s. The amplitude of I_s is higher with higher coefficients of coupling.

As the coefficient of coupling is increased, there will be a k value where Z_p at resonance is equal to R_p; I_s will achieve its greatest magnitude; this condition is called *critical coupling*. I_p, at resonance, is lower than was the case with smaller k values, and the humps are further apart. Curve C illustrates I_p and I_s versus frequency at critical coupling. At k values beyond those required for critical coupling, the secondary current develops the double humps also, but to a lesser extent than I_p. With higher coefficients of coupling, the secondary is not as effectively isolated from the primary, in that I_p increases affect V_s in a direct fashion to a greater extent with reduced flux leakage. Reducing the flux leakage (increasing k) makes the I_s response curve more similar to I_p. In the case of unity coupling, these two characteristics would be most similar. Curve D of Fig. 18-17 illustrates the primary and secondary response curves for a k value which exceeds critical coupling.

Applying V_i in Shunt

A second form of double-tuned transformer is illustrated in Fig. 18-18. This form differs from the one illustrated in Fig. 18-16 only in that the input voltage is applied in shunt with the primary capacitance and inductance. The secondary has a shunt load, as in the previous case. It should be noted that this form of a double-tuned transformer is in common use.

The equivalent primary and secondary circuits are shown in Fig. 18-19. The effect of R in the primary is to add resistance to that circuit, the value of which is determined by

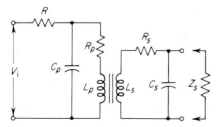

Fig. 18-18   A second form of double-tuned transformer.

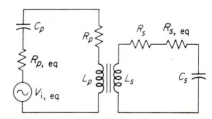

Fig. 18-19   Equivalent primary and secondary circuits of Fig. 18-18.

$$R_{eq} = \frac{(X_{C_p})^2}{R}$$

where R_{eq} = equivalent series resistance of R
 $\quad X_{C_p}$ = reactance of primary capacitance
 $\quad R$ = actual resistance in series with primary tuned circuit

The addition of R_{eq} to the primary circuit results in a reduction in effective Q_p. Since R is customarily very large compared with X_{C_p}, its equivalent effect is generally not too great. For this reason, the response curves of both forms of double-tuned transformers are essentially the same.

18-13 THE EFFECT OF A REACTIVE LOAD

In this section you will learn how a reactive load affects a tuned transformer.

There are occasions when the secondary load possesses a reactive quality (capacitive or inductive) to some extent. In such cases, the impedance reflected back to the primary is the conjugate of that present in the secondary (when Z_s is RL, the Z_p is RC; when Z_s is RC, then Z_p is RL). Since the reflected impedance is not pure resistance, the power factor is correspondingly reduced. The behavior of the transformer with such a secondary load may be similar to the description of the double-tuned transformer circuit above and below resonance, as given in the preceding section.

18-14 COUPLING

In this section you will learn how the tuned transformer is used as a coupling device.

Transformers are ideally suited for coupling the output of one device to the input of a second device in many cases. One situation where the use of a tuned transformer is of great value is the selection of one band of frequencies from a host of frequencies. The parallel-tuned circuit of the primary develops maximum voltage at the desired band, thereby setting up the greatest V_s at that condition. Frequencies above this band would be shunted by C_p, and frequencies below the band would be shunted by L_p. *The tuned transformer discriminates against all frequencies above and below the band at which it resonates and can be considered a bandpass circuit.*
 Also, as was pointed out in the preceding section, the unidirectional

content associated with the output of device 1 can be effectively kept out of the input of device 2 by use of a transformer. Both these features contribute to the popularity of tuned transformers.

The tuned-primary, tuned-secondary transformer is widely used in commercial radio and television receivers for (1) resonating to any frequency within the broadcast range and (2) resonating to one frequency only, called the intermediate frequency.

The required bandwidth of the transformer is determined in great part by its intended use. In commercial AM broadcast receivers, 5 kHz above and below the resonant frequency is generally sufficient. The maximum required bandwidth for commercial FM receivers is ±75 kHz, and the audio portion of most commercial television receivers requires a maximum bandspread of ±25 kHz.

Tuned transformers used for resonating at all frequencies within the commercial AM broadcast range (535 to 1605 kHz) incorporate capacitor or coil tuning. In capacitor tuning, the variable capacitor has air as the dielectric. When the plates are in full mesh, maximum capacity is obtained (this type of capacitor is described in Chap. 11). Permeability or coil tuning is frequently utilized, especially in those AM receivers subject to mechanical vibrations (such as automobile radios). Moving the powdered-iron core further into the coil form increases the inductance and vice versa. Both tuning techniques are used in FM broadcast receivers (broadcast range is 88 to 108 MHz), but the permeability type is most popular. The permeability type is also most commonly used in commercial television receivers. Because of the relatively broad frequency range of commercial television, several coils are frequently used. Coil 1 is variable over a portion of the broadcast range, coil 2 is tunable over another portion of it, and so on. In such cases, a switch is used to disconnect one coil and connect the second inductor.

The second type of tuned transformer used in commercial radio and television receivers is that which resonates to one frequency only. A trimmer type of capacitor or permeability tuning may be used to adjust the transformer to the exact frequency. These adjustments are considered semivariable, since, once they are properly made, they are to be left alone. In the popular types of radio and television receivers, any signal frequency is converted to one special frequency, called the receiver intermediate frequency. This is the frequency to which the semivariable type of transformer is tuned. The most common intermediate frequency used in each type of broadcast is as follows:

AM	455 kHz
FM	10.7 MHz
TV	4.5 MHz

This type of tuned transformer is often referred to as an intermediate frequency (IF) transformer. The maximum bandwidth is ±5 kHz for AM, ±75 kHz for FM, and ±25 kHz for television sound.

At first glance it would appear that the FM- and television-tuned transformers have a wider bandspread than the AM type. Comparison of the bandwidth of each with its resonant frequency shows that this is not true.

$$\text{In AM:} \qquad \frac{10 \text{ kHz}}{455 \text{ kHz}} \cong 2.2 \text{ percent}$$

$$\text{In FM:} \qquad \frac{150 \text{ kHz}}{10.7 \text{ MHz}} \cong 1.4 \text{ percent}$$

$$\text{In TV:} \qquad \frac{50 \text{ kHz}}{4.5 \text{ MHz}} \cong 1.1 \text{ percent}$$

A bandwidth equal to 1 or 2 percent of the resonant frequency is not considered a difficult response to obtain with tuned transformers.

QUESTIONS

18-26   Why does an untuned primary-tuned secondary transformer respond to a relatively narrow band of frequencies?

18-27   In Fig. 18-15, why does $Z_{s,\text{ total}} = R_s$ at resonance?

18-28   What does the transformer of Fig. 18-15 look like below resonance?

18-29   What does the transformer of Fig. 18-15 look like above resonance?

18-30   What is the difference in the way the input voltage is applied in Figs. 18-16 and 18-18?

18-31   Explain the double-hump I-vs.-F response for various k values in Fig. 18-17.

18-32   Why is the double-hump response in Fig. 18-17b much less pronounced for I_s than was found for I_p?

18-33   What is the effect of a capacitive load upon the reflected primary impedance?

18-34   What is the effect of an inductive load upon the reflected primary impedance?

18-35   Explain why the tuned transformer can be considered a band-pass circuit.

appendix

TABLE OF EXPONENTIAL FUNCTIONS

x	e^x	e^{-x}	x	e^x	e^{-x}
0.00	1.0000	1.000000	0.74	2.0959	.477114
0.02	1.0202	.980199	0.76	2.1383	.467666
0.04	1.0408	.960789	0.78	2.1815	.458406
0.06	1.0618	.941765	0.80	2.2255	0.449329
0.08	1.0833	.923116	0.82	2.2705	.440432
0.10	1.1052	0.904837	0.84	2.3164	.431711
0.12	1.1275	.886920	0.86	2.3632	.423162
0.14	1.1503	.869358	0.88	2.4109	.414783
0.16	1.1735	.852144	0.90	2.4596	0.406570
0.18	1.1972	.835270	0.92	2.5093	.398519
0.20	1.2214	0.818731	0.94	2.5600	.390628
0.22	1.2461	.802519	0.96	2.6117	.382893
0.24	1.2712	.786628	0.98	2.6645	.375311
0.26	1.2969	.771052	1.00	2.7183	0.367879
0.28	1.3231	.755784	1.05	2.8577	.349938
0.30	1.3499	0.740818	1.10	3.0042	.332871
0.32	1.3771	.726149	1.15	3.1582	.316637
0.34	1.4049	.711770	1.20	3.3201	.301194
0.36	1.4333	.697676	1.25	3.4903	0.286505
0.38	1.4623	.683861	1.30	3.6693	.272532
0.40	1.4918	0.670320	1.35	3.8574	.259240
0.42	1.5220	.657047	1.40	4.0552	.246597
0.44	1.5527	.644036	1.45	4.2631	.234570
0.46	1.5841	.631284	1.50	4.4817	0.223130
0.48	1.6161	.618783	1.55	4.7115	.212248
0.50	1.6487	0.606531	1.60	4.9530	.201897
0.52	1.6820	.594521	1.65	5.2070	.192050
0.54	1.7160	.582748	1.70	5.4739	.182684
0.56	1.7507	.571209	1.75	5.7546	0.173774
0.58	1.7860	.559898	1.80	6.0496	.165299
0.60	1.8221	0.548812	1.85	6.3598	.157237
0.62	1.8589	.537944	1.90	6.6859	.149569
0.64	1.8965	.527292	1.95	7.0287	.142274
0.66	1.9348	.516851	2.00	7.3891	0.135335
0.68	1.9739	.506617	2.05	7.7679	.128735
0.70	2.0138	0.496585	2.10	8.1662	.122456
0.72	2.0544	.486752	2.15	8.5849	.116484

TABLE OF EXPONENTIAL FUNCTIONS (continued)

x	e^x	e^{-x}	x	e^x	e^{-x}
2.20	9.0250	.110803	**5.00**	148.41	0.006738
			5.05	156.02	.006409
2.25	9.4877	0.105399	5.10	164.02	.006097
2.30	9.9742	.100259	5.15	172.43	.005799
2.35	10.486	.095369	5.20	181.27	.005517
2.40	11.023	.090718			
2.45	11.588	.086294	**5.25**	190.57	0.005248
			5.30	200.34	.004992
2.50	12.182	0.082085	5.35	210.61	.004748
2.55	12.807	.078082	5.40	221.41	.004517
2.60	13.464	.074274	5.45	232.76	.004296
2.65	14.154	.070651			
2.70	14.880	.067206	**5.50**	244.69	0.0040868
			5.55	257.24	.0038875
2.75	15.643	0.063928	5.60	270.43	.0036979
2.80	16.445	.060810	5.65	284.29	.0035175
2.85	17.288	.057844	5.70	298.87	.0033460
2.90	18.174	.055023			
2.95	19.106	.052340	**5.75**	314.19	0.0031828
			5.80	330.30	.0030276
3.00	20.086	0.049787	5.85	347.23	.0028799
3.05	21.115	.047359	5.90	365.04	.0027394
3.10	22.198	.045049	5.95	383.75	.0026058
3.15	23.336	.042852			
3.20	24.533	.040762	**6.00**	403.43	0.0024788
			6.05	424.11	.0023579
3.25	25.790	0.038774	6.10	445.86	.0022429
3.30	27.113	.036883	6.15	468.72	.0021335
3.35	28.503	.035084	6.20	492.75	.0020294
3.40	29.964	.033373			
3.45	31.500	.031746	**6.25**	518.01	0.0019305
			6.30	544.57	.0018363
3.50	33.115	0.030197	6.35	572.49	.0017467
3.55	34.813	.028725	6.40	601.85	.0016616
3.60	36.598	.027324	6.45	632.70	.0015805
3.65	38.475	.025991			
3.70	40.447	.024724	**6.50**	665.14	0.0015034
			6.55	699.24	.0014301
3.75	42.521	0.023518	6.60	735.10	.0013604
3.80	44.701	.022371	6.65	772.78	.0012940
3.85	46.993	.021280	6.70	812.41	.0012309
3.90	49.402	.020242			
3.95	51.935	.019255	**6.75**	854.06	0.0011709
			6.80	897.85	.0011138
4.00	54.598	0.018316	6.85	943.88	.0010595
4.05	57.397	.017422	6.90	992.27	.0010078
4.10	60.340	.016573	6.95	1043.1	.0009586
4.15	63.434	.015764			
4.20	66.686	.014996	**7.00**	1096.6	0.0009119
			7.05	1152.9	.0008674
4.25	70.105	0.014264	7.10	1212.0	.0008251
4.30	73.700	.013569	7.15	1274.1	.0007849
4.35	77.478	.012907	7.20	1339.4	.0007466
4.40	81.451	.012277			
4.45	85.627	.011679	**7.25**	1408.1	0.0007102
			7.30	1480.3	.0006755
4.50	90.017	0.011109	7.35	1556.2	.0006426
4.55	94.632	.010567	7.40	1636.0	.0006113
4.60	99.484	.010052	7.45	1719.9	.0005814
4.65	104.58	.009562			
4.70	109.95	.009095	**7.50**	1808.0	0.0005531
			7.55	1900.7	.0005261
4.75	115.58	0.008652	7.60	1998.2	.0005005
4.80	121.51	.008230	7.65	2100.6	.0004760
4.85	127.74	.007828	7.70	2208.3	.0004528
4.90	134.29	.007447			
4.95	141.17	.007083	**7.75**	2321.6	0.0004307

TABLE OF EXPONENTIAL FUNCTIONS (continued)

x	e^x	e^{-x}	x	e^x	e^{-x}
7.80	2440.6	.0004097	8.95	7707.9	.0001297
7.85	2565.7	.0003898			
7.90	2697.3	.0003707	**9.00**	8103.1	0.0001234
7.95	2835.6	.0003527	9.05	8518.5	.0001174
			9.10	8955.3	.0001117
8.00	2981.0	0.0003355	9.15	9414.4	.0001062
8.05	3133.8	.0003191	9.20	9897.1	.0001010
8.10	3294.5	.0003035			
8.15	3463.4	.0002887	**9.25**	10405	0.0000961
8.20	3641.0	.0002747	9.30	10938	.0000914
			9.35	11499	.0000870
8.25	3827.6	0.0002613	9.40	12088	.0000827
8.30	4023.9	.0002485	9.45	12708	.0000787
8.35	4230.2	.0002364			
8.40	4447.1	.0002249	**9.50**	13360	0.0000749
8.45	4675.1	.0002139	9.55	14045	.0000712
			9.60	14765	.0000677
8.50	4914.8	0.0002035	9.65	15522	.0000644
8.55	5166.8	.0001935	9.70	16318	.0000613
8.60	5431.7	.0001841			
8.65	5710.1	.0001751	**9.75**	17154	0.0000583
8.70	6002.9	.0001666	9.80	18034	.0000555
			9.85	18958	.0000527
8.75	6310.7	0.0001585	9.90	19930	.0000502
8.80	6634.2	.0001507	9.95	20952	.0000477
8.85	6974.4	.0001434			
8.90	7332.0	.0001364	**10.00**	22026	0.0000454

answers to odd-numbered problems

Chapter 1

1-1 (a) $3(10^2)$ (b) $8(10^5)$
      (c) $9(10^{-4})$ (d) $6.30(10^5)$
      (e) $5.5(10^{-11})$ (f) $2.0(10^{10})$
1-3 (a) $253.9(10)^4$
      (b) $8.23(10)^{-3}$
      (c) $52.77(10)^{-6}$
      (d) $90.05(10)^{-4}$
1-5 (a) $32(10)^9$ (b) $25.5(10)^{-10}$
      (c) $11(10)^{-6}$ (d) $51.25(10)^{11}$
1-7 (a) 800 kΩ (b) 0.8 MΩ
1-9 (a) 1.2 kΩ (b) 680 kΩ
      (c) 4300 kΩ (d) 2200 kΩ

Chapter 2

2-1 40 mA; 40,000 μA
2-3 0.000075 A; 0.075 mA
2-5 0.05 A; 50 mA; 50,000 μA
2-7 0.125 s
2-9 4 V
2-11 40 V
2-13 4 A
2-15 0.15 C
2-17 (a) 0.0002 C   (b) 0.0025 C
2-19 $19.968(10)^{18}$ electrons for (a), (b), and (c)
2-21 12 V
2-23 (a) 240 J   (b) 60 J
2-25 (a) 0.12 J   (b) 3.6 J
2-27 15 A

Chapter 3

3-1 200 Ω
3-3 80 V
3-5 0.1 A
3-7 20 Ω
3-9 8.1 V
3-11 2.2 A
3-13 600 Ω
3-15 0.5 V
3-17 5 μA
3-19 4 kΩ
3-21 0.0045 V
3-23 10 V
3-25 $4.05(10)^{-2}$ Ω

3-27 0.005 Ω
3-29 $4.78(10)^{-1}$ Ω
3-31 6.97 ft
3-33 (a) 24.69 mhos
      (b) 7.75 mhos
      (c) 200 mhos
      (d) 25.64 mhos
3-35 0.89 Ω
3-37 83.2 Ω
3-39 0.1006 Ω
3-41 0.6641 Ω
3-43 47 kΩ ($\pm 5\%$)
3-45 150 kΩ ($\pm 20\%$)
3-47 0.0247 Ω
3-49 5.28 Ω
3-51 5.04 Ω
3-53 8.16 Ω
3-55 45°C
3-57 (a) 3 Ω (b) 8 Ω
3-59 $+15$ Ω

Chapter 4

4-1 $1.5(10)^7$ ergs
4-3 600 W
4-5 1.25 A
4-7 0.006 W
4-9 $\frac{1}{2}$ W
4-11 0.36 J
4-13 18.8 W
4-15 0.0225 W
4-17 0.00027 W
4-19 5000 W
4-21 30,000 J
4-23 0.707 A
4-25 3.536 A
4-27 10 V
4-29 15 V
4-31 11 Ω
4-33 0.04 A

Chapter 5

5-1 125 Ω
5-3 200 Ω
5-5 0.2 A
      $V_{R_1} = 15$ V
      $V_{R_2} = 10$ V

5-7 $P_{R_1} = 300$ W
  $P_{R_2} = 200$ W
  $P = 500$ W

5-9 0.4 A
  $V_{R_1} = 16$ V
  $V_{R_2} = 24$ V
  $V_{R_3} = 10$ V
  $V_{R_4} = 30$ V

5-11 $I = 0.25$ A
  $V_{R_1} = 10$ V
  $V_{R_2} = 15$ V
  $V_{R_3} = 6.25$ V
  $V_{R_4} = 18.75$ V

5-13 $I = 0.001$ A
  $V_{R_1} = 4.7$ V
  $V_{R_2} = 3.3$ V
  $V_{R_3} = 1.0$ V

5-15 (a) 1 A   (b) 80 Ω
  (c) 400 V   (d) 80 V

5-17 (a) 2.75 V   (b) 217.25 V
  (c) 43.45 Ω (d) 44 Ω

5-19 (a) $R_2 = 6500$ Ω
  (b) $R_3 = 2500$ Ω
  (c) $V_{R_1} = 22$ V
  (d) $V_{R_2} = 143$ V

5-21 (a) $R_1 = 1250$ Ω
    $R_2 = 2500$ Ω
    $R_3 = 1250$
  (b) $V_{R_1} = 25$ V
    $V_{R_2} = 50$ V
    $V_{R_3} = 25$ V

5-23 $I = 0.632$ A
  $R_s = 140$ Ω

5-25 (a) 10 V   (b) 8.33 mA
  (c) 83.3 mW

5-27 Reading clockwise from point A:
  $0 - 50$ V $- 25$ V $- 150$ V $- 75$ V
  $+ 0 + 300$ V $= 0$

5-29 (a) $I_{R_1} = 0.25$ A
    $I_{R2} = 0.125$ A
  (b) $V_{R_1} = V_{R_2} = 100$ V
  (c) $R = 267$ Ω
  (d) $I = 0.375$ A

5-31 (a) $I_{R_1} = 0.3$ A
    $I_{R_2} = 0.3$ A
    $I_{R_3} = 0.4$ A
    $I_{R_4} = 0.24$ A
  (b) $I = 1.24$ A
  (c) $R = 96.8$ Ω

5-33 (a) $R_2 = 150$ Ω
  (b) $I_{R_1} = 0.125$ A
    $I_{R_2} = 0.500$ A
  (c) $R = 120$ Ω
  (d) $I = 0.625$ A

5-35 (a) $R = 8.88$ Ω
  (b) $V_b = 0.31$ V
  (c) $I_{R_1} = 9$ mA
    $I_{R_2} = 22$ mA
    $I_{R_3} = 4$ mA

5-37 (a) $V_b = 20$ V
  (b) $R_1 = 1400$ Ω
    $R_2 = 700$ Ω
    $R_3 = 2800$ Ω
  (c) $I_1 = 14$ mA
    $I_2 = 29$ mA
    $I_3 = 7$ mA

5-39 (a) $R_1 = R_2 = R_3 = 147$ Ω
  (b) $P_{R_1} = P_{R_2} = P_{R_3} = 330$ W
  (c) $P_1 = 330$ W
  (d) Power with three loads added $= 1980$ W
  (e) total I drain $= 9$ A, fuse would open

5-41 Loads 2 and 3 are 3.3 A each

5-43 (a) load $2 = 475$ mA
  (b) $R_1 = 867$ Ω
    $R_2 = 137$ Ω
  (c) $R = 118$ Ω
  (d) $P_{R_1} = 4.9$ W
    $P_{R_2} = 30.9$ W
  (e) $P = 35.8$ W

5-45 0.45 W

5-47 (a) $I = 1.92$ A
  (b) $P = 211$ W

Chapter 6

Note Some descrepancies in answers will be noted because of rounding.

6-1 (a) $I_{R_3} = 200$ mA
  (b) $R_1 = 30$ Ω
    $R_2 = 33.3$ Ω
    $R_3 = 50$ Ω
  (c) $P_{R_1} = 7.5$ W
    $P_{R2} = 3$ W
    $P_{R3} = 2$ W
  (d) 12.5 W

6-3 (a) $R_d = 39.2\ \Omega$
        (b) $P_{Rd} = 9.8\ \text{W}$
        (c) $R_s = 144\ \Omega$
        (d) $P_{Rs} = 17.64\ \text{W}$
6-5 (a) $I_{R_1} = I_{R_2} = 4.4\ \text{A}$
             $I_{R_3} = I_{R_4} = 2.0\ \text{A}$
        (b) $6.4\ \text{A}$
        (c) $V_{R_1} = 176\ \text{V}$
             $V_{R_2} = 44\ \text{V}$
             $V_{R_3} = 150\ \text{V}$
             $V_{R_4} = 70\ \text{V}$
        (d) $R = 34.38\ \Omega$
        (e) $P_{R_1} = 774.4\ \text{W}$
             $P_{R_2} = 193.6\ \text{W}$
             $P_{R_3} = 300\ \text{W}$
             $P_{R_4} = 140\ \text{W}$
        (f) $P = 1408\ \text{W}$
6-7 (a) $I_{R_1} = 2\ \text{A}$
             $I_{R_5} = 1.5\ \text{A}$
             $I_{R_6} = 2\ \text{A}$
        (b) $I = 2\ \text{A}$
        (c) $V_{R_2} = 20\ \text{V}$
             $V_{R_3} = 15\ \text{V}$
             $V_{R_5} = 35\ \text{V}$
             $V_{R_6} = 10\ \text{V}$
        (d) $V_b = 65\ \text{V}$
        (e) $R_5 = 23.3\ \Omega$
             $R_6 = 5\ \Omega$
        (f) $P_{R1} = 40\ \text{W}$
             $P_{R2} = 10\ \text{W}$
             $P_{R3} = 3.75\ \text{W}$
             $P_{R4} = 3.75\ \text{W}$
             $P_{R5} = 52.4\ \text{W}$
             $P_{R6} = 20\ \text{W}$
        (g) $P = 130\ \text{W}$
6-9 (a) $I_{R_1} = 2.4\ \text{A}$
             $I_{R_2} = I_{R_3} = 0.706\ \text{A}$
             $I_{R_4} = I_{R_5} = I_{R_6} = 0.12\ \text{A}$
        (b) $P_{R_1} = 28.8\ \text{W}$
             $P_{R_2} = 7.47\ \text{W}$
             $P_{R_3} = 0.997\ \text{W}$
             $P_{R_4} = 0.432\ \text{W}$
             $P_{R_5} = 0.288\ \text{W}$
             $P_{R_6} = 0.72\ \text{W}$
        (c) $P = 38.7\ \text{W}$
6-11 $I_{R_1} = I_{R_2} = 0.1264\ \text{A}$
         $V_{R_1} = 25.28\ \text{V}$
         $V_{R_2} = 37.92\ \text{V}$
         $I_{R_3} = 0.092\ \text{A}$
         $V_{R_3} = 36.8\ \text{V}$

$I_{R_4} = 0.0344\ \text{A}$
$V_{R_4} = 3.44\ \text{V}$
$V_{R_5} = 20.64\ \text{V}$
$I_{R_6} = 0.02544\ \text{A}$
$V_{R_6} = 12.72\ \text{V}$
$I_{R_7} = I_{R_8} = I_{R_9} = 0.0091\ \text{A}$
$V_{R_7} = 3.64\ \text{V}$
$V_{R_8} = 0.91\ \text{V}$
$V_{R_9} = 8.19\ \text{V}$
6-13 (a) $25.2 + 36.8 + 37.8 - 100$
               $= 0$
         (b) $25.2 + 3.4 + 12.5 + 20.4$
               $+ 37.8 - 100 = 0$
         (c) $25.2 + 3.4 + 3.6 + 8.1$
               $+ 0.9 + 20.4 + 37.8 - 100$
               $= 0$
6-15 $I_{R_1} = I_{R_2} = 0.0632\ \text{A}$
         $V_{R_1} = 12.64\ \text{V}$
         $V_{R_2} = 18.96\ \text{V}$
         $I_{R_3} = 0.046\ \text{A}$
         $V_{R_3} = 18.4\ \text{V}$
         $I_{R_4} = 0.0172\ \text{A}$
         $V_{R_4} = 1.72\ \text{V}$
         $V_{R_5} = 10.32\ \text{V}$
         $I_{R_6} = 0.0127\ \text{A}$
         $V_{R_6} = 6.36\ \text{V}$
         $I_{R_7} = 0.0045\ \text{A}$
         $V_{R_7} = 1.8\ \text{V}$
         $V_{R_8} = 0.45\ \text{V}$
         $V_{R_9} = 4.05\ \text{V}$
6-17 (a) $12.64 + 18.4 + 18.96$
               $- 50 = 0$
         (b) $12.64 + 1.72 + 6.36$
               $+ 10.32 + 18.96 - 50 = 0$
         (c) $12.64 + 1.72 + 1.8$
               $+ 4.05 + 0.045 + 10.32$
               $+ 18.96 - 50 = 0$
6-19 $I_{R_1} = I_{R_2} = 0.311\ \text{A}$
         $V_{R_1} = 31.1\ \text{V}$
         $V_{R_2} = 93.3\ \text{V}$
         $I_{R_3} = 0.151\ \text{A}$
         $V_{R_3} = V_{R_4} = 75.6\ \text{V}$
         $I_{R_4} = 0.095\ \text{A}$
         $I_{R_5} = 0.060\ \text{A}$
         $V_{R_5} = 54\ \text{V}$
         $I_{R_6} = 0.060\ \text{A}$
         $V_{R_6} = 12\ \text{V}$
         $I_{R_7} = 0.032\ \text{A}$
         $V_{R_7} = V_{R_8} = 9.6\ \text{V}$
         $I_{R_8} = 0.24\ \text{A}$

$I_{R_9} = I_{R_{10}} = 0.008$ A
$V_{R_9} = 3.2$ V
$V_{R_{10}} = 5.6$ V
$I_{R_{11}} = 0.002$ A
$V_{R_{11}} = V_{R_{12}} = 1.2$ V
$I_{R_{12}} = 0.006$ A

6-21 (a) $-30.91 - 76.36 - 92.73$
$+ 200 = 0$
(b) $-30.91 - 76.36 - 92.73$
$+ 200 = 0$
(c) $-30.91 - 54.81 - 9.37$
$- 12.18 - 92.73 + 200 = 0$
(d) $-30.91 - 54.81 - 9.37$
$- 12.18 - 92.73 + 200 = 0$

6-27 (a) $R_1 = 10,000$ Ω
$R_2 = 26,667$ Ω
$R_3 = 5000$ Ω
(b) $P_{R_1} = 1.44$ W
$P_{R_2} = 3.84$ W
$P_{R_3} = 0.72$ W
(c) $P = 6.0$ W

6-29 (a) $R_{L_1} = 6000$ Ω
$R_{L_2} = 5882$ Ω
$R_{L_3} = 5143$ Ω
(b) $P_{R_{L_1}} = 0.6$ W
$P_{R_{L_2}} = 6.8$ W
$P_{R_{L_3}} = 25.2$ W
(c) $P = 32.6$ W

6-31 (a) $R_{L_1} = 750$ Ω
$R_{L_2} = 1286$ Ω
$R_{L_3} = 7000$ Ω
(b) $P_{R_{L_1}} = 0.012$ W
$P_{R_{L_2}} = 0.063$ W
$P_{R_{L_3}} = 0.063$ W
(c) $P = 0.138$ W

6-33 (a) 3 mA
(b) $R_1 = 1000$ Ω
$R_2 = 667$ Ω
$R_3 = 231$ Ω
$R_4 = 91$ Ω
(c) $P_{R_1} = 0.009$ W
$P_{R_2} = 0.054$ W
$P_{R_3} = 0.039$ W
$P_{R_4} = 0.099$ W
$P = 0.201$ W

6-35 (a) $R_1 = 1500$ Ω
$R_2 = 300$ Ω
$R_3 = 222$ Ω
$R_4 = 91$ Ω
(b) $P_{R_1} = 0.006$ W

$P_{R_2} = 0.030$ W
$P_{R_3} = 0.072$ W
$P_{R_4} = 0.044$ W
(c) $P = 0.152$ W

6-37 $R_1 = 3000$ Ω
$R_2 = 500$ Ω

6-39 (a) $R_1 = 1500$ Ω
$R_2 = 833$ Ω
$R_3 = 154$ Ω
$R_4 = 111$ Ω
(b) $P_{R_1} = 0.006$ W
$P_{R_2} = 0.030$ W
$P_{R_3} = 0.026$ W
$P_{R_4} = 0.036$ W
(c) $P = 0.098$ W

Chapter 7

7-1 $V_{R_i} = 10$ V
$I = 0.0025$ A
$R_L = 16$ kΩ

7-3 $V_{R_i} = 40$ V
$I = 0.010$ A
$R_L = 1000$ Ω

7-5 $P_{R_L} = 0.156$ W
n = 50 percent

7-7 (a) $V_{R_i} = 25$ V
(b) $I = 0.0025$ A
(c) $R_L = 30$ kΩ

7-9 (a) $R_L = R_i = 10$ kΩ
(b) $P_{R_L} = 0.250$ W

7-11 (a) $R_i = 100$ Ω
(b) $I = 0.2$ A
(c) $P_{R_L} = 16$ W
(d) n = 80 percent

7-13 (a) $R_L = 67$ Ω
(b) $R_i = 67$ Ω
(c) $P_{R_L} = 0.136$ W
(d) $V_g = 6$ V

7-15 $R_L = 455$ Ω

7-17 28.5 kΩ

7-19 950 Ω

7-21 (a) $V_{R_1} = 1.7$ V
(b) $V_{R_2} = 0.9$ V
(c) $V_{R_3} = 5.1$ V
(d) $V_{R_4} = 4.3$ V

7-23 1.4 V

7-25 1067 Ω

7-27 (a) $I_1 = 0.0042$ A
          (b) $I_2 = 0.0108$ A
7-29 $R_1 = 236\ \Omega$
7-31 $I_{R_L} = 0.000273$ A
7-33 $I_{R_L} = 3.52$ mA
7-35 $I_{R_L} = 0.005227$A
7-37 (a) $R_{1_D} = 5600\ \Omega$
          (b) $R_{2_D} = 4667\ \Omega$
          (c) $R_{3_D} = 2800\ \Omega$
7-39 (a) $R_{1_W} = 50\ \Omega$
          (b) $R_{2_W} = 100\ \Omega$
          (c) $R_{3_W} = 33\ \Omega$

Chapter 8

8-1 12.5 μA/mm
8-3 0.333 μA/mm
8-5 (a) 1 μA/mm
         (b) 40 μV/mm
8-7 (a) Parallel-shunt
              $R_{S_1} = 0.3030\ \Omega$
              $R_{S_2} = 0.0752\ \Omega$
              $R_{S_3} = 0.0150\ \Omega$
              $R_{S_4} = 0.0015\ \Omega$
         (b) Series-shunt
              $R_{S_1} = 0.0015\ \Omega$
              $R_{S_2} = 0.0135\ \Omega$
              $R_{S_3} = 0.0602\ \Omega$
              $R_{S_4} = 0.2278\ \Omega$
8-9 (a) Parallel-shunt
              $R_{S_1} = 0.18072\ \Omega$
              $R_{S_2} = 0.04505\ \Omega$
              $R_{S_3} = 0.00900\ \Omega$
              $R_{S_4} = 0.00090\ \Omega$
         (b) Series-shunt
              $R_{S_1} = 0.00090\ \Omega$
              $R_{S_2} = 0.0081\ \Omega$
              $R_{S_3} = 0.03605\ \Omega$
              $R_{S_4} = 0.13567\ \Omega$
8-11 $R_{\text{ammeter}} = 9.09\ \Omega$
          8.3 percent disturbance
8-13 $R_{M_1} = 3000\ \Omega$
          $R_{M_2} = 7000\ \Omega$
          $R_{M_3} = 90\ \text{k}\Omega$
          $R_{M_4} = 200\ \text{k}\Omega$
8-15 6667 Ω/V
8-17 $R_{M_1} = 20\ \text{k}\Omega$
          $R_{M_2} = 46.667\ \text{k}\Omega$
          $R_{M_3} = 133.333\ \text{k}\Omega$

$R_{M_4} = 466.667\ \text{k}\Omega$
$R_{M_5} = 1333.333\ \text{k}\Omega$
8-19 $R_{M_1} = 300\ \Omega$
          $R_{M_2} = 700\ \Omega$
          $R_{M_3} = 2000\ \Omega$
          $R_{M_4} = 7000\ \Omega$
          $R_{M_5} = 20\ \text{k}\Omega$
8-21 $R_{M_1} = 6000\ \Omega$
          $R_{M_2} = 14\ \text{k}\Omega$
          $R_{M_3} = 40\ \text{k}\Omega$
          $R_{M_4} = 140\ \text{k}\Omega$
          $R_{M_5} = 400\ \text{k}\Omega$
8-23 (a) 2970 Ω (b) 42,857 Ω
          (c) 260,870
8-25 (a) 2996 Ω (b) 48,780 Ω
          (c) 1 MΩ
8-27 (a) $R_i = 3000\ \Omega$
          (b) $I = 0.001$ A
          (c) $I_{R_X} = 0.00095$ A
          (d) $R_X = 1.32\ \Omega$
          (e) $R_B = 2999\ \Omega$
8-29 (a) $R_i = 2\ \text{k}\Omega$
          (b) $I = 0.003$ A
          (c) $I_{R_X} = 0.002$ A
          (d) $R_X = 15\ \Omega$
          (e) $R_B = 1990\ \Omega$
8-31 (a) $I = 0.00285$ A
          (b) $I_{R_X} = 0.00185$ A
          (c) $R_X = 16.2\ \Omega$
8-33 (a) R_i on range $X_1 = 10,000\ \Omega$
          (b) $I = 0.0003$ A
          (c) $I_{R_X} = 0.00025$ A
          (d) $R_X = 4.8\ \Omega$
          (e) $R_B = 9996\ \Omega$
          (f) $R_1 = 1111\ \Omega$
          (g) $R_2 = 111\ \Omega$
8-35 (a) R_i at range $X_1 = 5000\ \Omega$
          (b) $I = 0.0012$ A
          (c) $I_{R_X} = 0.001$ A
          (d) $R_X = 5.4\ \Omega$
          (e) $R_B = 4996\ \Omega$
          (f) $R_1 = 556\ \Omega$
          (g) $R_2 = 56\ \Omega$

Chapter 10

10-1 0.2 H
10-3 200 V
10-5 0.5 H

10-7   423

10-9   (a)   0 V   (b)   39.3 V
           (c)   63.2 V   (d)   77.7 V
           (e)   86.5 V   (f)   95.0 V
           (g)   98.2 V   (h)   99.3 V

10-11 (a)   0.75 s; 0.375 s; 0.25 s;
                 0.188 s; 0.15 s
           (b)   37.5 A; 18.75 A; 12.5 A;
                 9.38 A; 7.5 A
           (c)   3.75 s; 1.875 s; 1.25 s;
                 0.94 s; 0.75 s
           (d)   32.4 A; 18.4 A; 12.48 A;
                 9.38 A; 7.5 A

10-13 0.25 Ω

10-15 0.0075 A

10-17 0.0124 A

10-19 (a) $L_a = 4.14$ H
           (b) $L_o = 0.06$ H

10-21 (a) $L_a = 11.12$ H
           (b) $L_o = 2.9$ H

10-23 (a) $M = 0.06$ H
           (b) $L_a = 0.42$ H
           (c) $L_o = 0.18$ H

Chapter 11

11-1   (a) $C = 1.55\ \mu$F
           (b) $V_{C_1} = 62$ V
                 $V_{C_2} = 103$ V
                 $V_{C_3} = 34$ V
           (c) $Q = 0.00031$ C

11-3   (a)   22.5 μF   (b)   13.3 μF
           (c)   16.7 μF

11-5 $C_2 = 2.5\ \mu$F $C_3 = 5\ \mu$F

11-7 $Q_{C_1} = 0.07(10)^{-6}$ C
           $Q_{C_2} = 0.28(10)^{-6}$ C
           $Q_{C_3} = 0.42(10)^{-6}$ C
           $Q_{C_4} = 0.7(10)^{-6}$ C
           $Q = 1.47(10)^{-6}$ C

11-9   (a) $Q_{C_1} = 0.00144$ C
                 $Q_{C_2} = 0.00036$ C
           (b) $Q = 0.0018$ C

Note   Discrepancies appear in some
           answers because of rounding.

11-11 (a)   2 A   (b)   0.184 A
           (c)   0.068 A   (d)   0.025 A

           (e)   0.009 A
           (f) 1.348×10^{-2} A

11-13 (a) $V_R = 500$ V; $V_C = 0$ V
           (b)   184 V; 316 V
           (c)   68 V; 432 V
           (d)   25 V; 475 V
           (e)   9 V; 492 V
           (f)   3 V; 497 V

11-15 (a) $V_R = 250$ V; $V_C = 0$ V
           (b)   152 V; 98 V
           (c)   92 V; 158 V
           (d)   34 V; 216 V
           (e)   13 V; 237 V
           (f)   8 V; 242 V
           (g)   5 V; 245 V
           (h)   2 V; 248 V

11-17 (a) $V_R = 250$ V; $V_C = 0$ V
           (b)   178 V; 72 V
           (c)   127 V; 123 V
           (d)   65 V; 185 V
           (e)   34 V; 216 V
           (f)   24 V; 226 V
           (g)   18 V; 232 V
           (h)   9 V; 241 V

11-19 (a) $I_1 = 0.184$ A
                 $I_2 = 0.068$ A
                 $I_3 = 0.025$ A
                 $I_4 = 0.009$ A
                 $I_5 = 0.003$ A
           (b) $I_1 = 0.046$ A
                 $I_2 = 0.017$ A
                 $I_3 = 0.006$ A
                 $I_4 = 0.002$ A
                 $I_5 = 0.0008$ A
           (c) $I_1 = 0.018$ A
                 $I_2 = 0.0068$ A
                 $I_3 = 0.0025$ A
                 $I_4 = 0.0009$ A
                 $I_5 = 0.0003$ A

11-21 (a)   0.0033 s   (b)   0.0165 s
           (c)   2 A   (d)   0.333 A

11-23 (a)   0.0016 s   (b)   0.008 s
           (c)   2.5 A
           (d) $1.684(10^{-2})$ A

Chapter 12

12-1   20 V

12-3   9.5 Ω

12-5   0.12 Ω

12-7 23.81 V
12-9 0.19 hp
12-11 329(10)³ rpm

Chapter 13

13-1 (a) 90°   (b) 270°
13-3 90°, 270°
13-5 (a) 0.035 A   (b) 0.025 A
        (c) 0.047 A   (d) 0.049 A
        (e) 0.043 A   (f) 0.032 A
        (g) −0.013 A
        (h) −0.049 A
        (i) −0.043 A
        (j) −0.004 A
13-7 60 Hz
13-9 (a) 3.535 A   (b) 0.990 A
        (c) 16.261 A
        (d) 51.6 mA
        (e) 29.7 mA
        (f) 3.36 mA
        (g) 26.2 μA
        (h) 98.3 mA
        (i) 62.2 μA
        (j) 176.8 μA
13-11 (a) 3.18 A   (b) 0.89 A
        (c) 14.63 A   (d) 46.4 mA
        (e) 26.7 mA   (f) 3.02 mA
        (g) 23.5 μA   (h) 88.4 mA
        (i) 56 μA   (j) 159 μA
13-13 (a) 113 V   (b) 0.057 A
        (c) 6.5 W   (d) 3.20 W
        (e) 7.51 W   (f) 9.60 W
13-15 12.8 W
13-17 (a) 120 V   (b) 0.739 A
        (c) 0.522 A   (d) 49.0 W
        (e) 13.6 W   (f) 62.7 W
        (g) 98.3 W   (h) 27.3 W
        (i) 125.6 W
13-19 (a) −0.599   (b) −8.824
        (c) −4.018   (d) −3.114
        (e) −5.252
13-21 22.04 dB
13-23 (a) 9.2 dB   (b) 13.2 dB
        (c) 26.2 dB   (d) 36.0 dB
        (e) 33.0 dB
13-25 92.7 dB

13-27 54.5 dB
13-29 (a) 96 V   (b) 25 V
             75 V   −22 V
             −130 V   22 V
             −13 V   −4 V
        (c) 121 V
             53 V
             −108 V
             −17 V
13-31 (a) 5 V   (b) −2 V
             −13 V   3 V
             −13 V   6 V
             −5 V   −3 V
        (c) 141 V
             63 V
             −115 V
             −30 V
13-33 (a) 50 V   (b) 33 V
        (c) 10 V   (d) −7 V
        (e) −11 V   (f) 75 V
13-35 (a) 28 V   (b) 3 V
        (c) −1 V   (d) 24 V
13-37 (a) $v_1 = 106$ V
        (b) $v_2 = -60$ V
        (c) $v = 46$ V
13-39 (a) $v_1 = 153$ V
        (b) $v_2 = -79$ V
        (c) $v = 74$ V

Chapter 14

14-1 (a) 398 Ω (b) 199 Ω
        (c) 133 Ω (d) 99 Ω
        (e) 80 Ω
14-3 (a) 442 Ω (b) 41.5°
        (c) 667 Ω (d) 0.360 A
        (e) 0.749   (f) 64.8 W
14-5 (a) 63,662 Ω (b) 72.6°
        (c) 66,730 Ω (d) 749 μA
        (e) 0.299   (f) 11 mW
14-7 45°
14-9 (a) 32,856 Ω
        (b) 121,976 Ω
        (c) 56,841 Ω
14-11 (a) 21,221 Ω (b) 25.8°
        (c) 43,926 Ω (d) 0.900
14-13 (a) 7998 Ω (b) 1783 Ω
        (c) 800 Ω

14-15 (a) 0.015 A (b) 0.067 A
(c) 0.150 A
14-17 (a) 376 μA (b) 1.76 mA
(c) 4.9 mA
14-19 (a) 84.30°; 503 Ω; 0.497 A
(b) 45°; 707 Ω; 0.354 A
(c) 5.71°; 5051 Ω; 0.049 A
14-21 5.31 μF
14-23 (a) $V_r = 89.6$ V; $V_c = 9.0$ V
(b) $V_r = 63.7$ V; $V_c = 63.7$ V
(c) $V_r = 8.9$ V; $V_c = 89.6$ V
14-25 0.016 μF
14-27 (a) 67 Hz (b) 4.2 mA
(c) 265 mW (d) 540 mW
14-29 (a) 397.887 kΩ
(b) 79.577 kΩ
14-31 579 Ω
14-33 0.023 μF
14-35 (a) 12 kΩ (b) 48 pF
14-37 (a) 132 Ω (b) 264 Ω
(c) 1319 Ω (d) 2639 Ω
(e) 13,195 Ω
14-39 (a) 5027 Ω (b) 63.6°
(c) 5610 Ω (d) 11 mA
(e) 0.445 (f) 302 mW
14-41 (a) 0.7; 7.3; 73.3
(b) 1385 Hz
14-43 (a) 11.3 Ω (b) 43.3°
(c) 16.5 Ω (d) 38.7 Ω
(e) 17° (f) 3.101 A
14-45 (a) 126 Ω (b) 25°
(c) 298 Ω (d) 0.201 A
(e) 10.9 W
14-47 143 mH
14-49 1257 Ω

Chapter 15

15-1 $Z = 300 - j500$ Ω
15-3 $Z = 60 + j45$ Ω
15-5 $V = 5 - j10$ V
15-7 $V = 12 + j9$ V
15-9 $V = 12.86 + j15.32$ V
15-11 $59 - j12$
15-13 $325,000/21°$
15-15 $401 - j9$ Ω

Chapter 16

Note Some discrepancies may be
found due to rounding.
16-1 (a) $0.462/90°$ A
(b) $0.625/0°$ A
(c) $0.776/36.5°$ A
(d) $193/-36.5°$ Ω
16-3 (a) 2841 Ω (b) 500 Ω
(c) 79 Ω
16-5 (a) 2712 Ω (b) 0.042 μF
16-7 0.024 μF
16-9 $R = 155$ Ω
$X_c = 115$ Ω
16-11 (a) $\cdot 0.25/-90°$ A
(b) $0.167/0°$ A
(c) $0.300/-56.3°$ A
(d) $833/56.3°$
16-13 (a) 320 Ω
(b) 0.127 H
(c) $323/82.9°$ Ω
(d) $0.372/-82.9$ A
16-15 (a) .010 H
(b) $43.29/60$ Ω

Chapter 17

17-1 (a) 1838 Hz (b) 58 Ω
17-3 (a) 3183 Hz
(b) 3.536777 MHz
(c) 38 Hz
17-5 (a) 3.2 Ω (b) 15.8 Ω
(c) 31.5 Ω
17-7 4.5 mH
Note Discrepancies in some answers
are due to rounding.
17-9 (a) 101 Hz
(b) $0.473/-90°$ Ω
(c) $0.473/90°$ Ω
(d) $0/0°$ A
(e) $\infty/0°$ Ω
17-11 (a) $1560/90°$
(b) $0.096/-90°$ A
17-13 (a) resistive
(b) inductive
(c) capacitive
17-15 (a) $\infty/0°$ (b) 200 Hz
(c) 4900 Hz (d) 5100 Hz

17-17 $L = 140\ \mu\text{H}$
$\qquad C = 874\ \text{pF}$

17-19   837 pF
$\qquad$ 915 pF

Chapter 18

$\quad$**18-1**   (a)   0.2 V/turn
$\qquad$ (b)   2 V

18-3   (a)   613 W
$\qquad$ (b)   97.9 percent

18-5 $19.687\underline{/61.2°}$

18-7   (a)   10 V
$\qquad$ (b)   1.429 A
$\qquad$ (c)   0.071 A
$\qquad$ (d)   2800 Ω

18-9   1:15.8

index